The

FALL

of the

HOUSE *of*

WALWORTH

The
FALL
of the
HOUSE *of*
WALWORTH

A Tale of
Madness and Murder
in Gilded Age America

Geoffrey O'Brien

A John Macrae Book
Henry Holt and Company
New York

Henry Holt and Company, LLC
Publishers since 1866
175 Fifth Avenue
New York, New York 10010
www.henryholt.com

Henry Holt® and ® are registered trademarks of Henry Holt and Company, LLC.

Distributed in Canada by H. B. Fenn and Company Ltd.

Library of Congress Cataloging-in-Publication Data

O'Brien, Geoffrey, 1948–
  The fall of the house of Walworth : a tale of madness and murder in gilded age
America / Geoffrey O'Brien.—1st ed.
      p. cm.
  "A John Macrae book."
  Includes bibliographical references.
  ISBN 978-0-8050-8115-2
  1. Walworth, Mansfield Tracy, 1830–1873.   2. Walworth, Mansfield Tracy,
1830–1873—Family.   3. Walworth, Frank H. (Francis Hardin), 1853–1886.
4. Walworth, Clara Grant, b. 1886.   5. Families—New York (State)—Saratoga
Springs—Biography.   6. Mental illness—New York (State)—Saratoga Springs—
History—19th century.   7. Parricide—New York (State)—New York—History—
19th century.   8. Saratoga Springs (N.Y.)—Biography.   9. Saratoga Springs
(N.Y.)—Social life and customs.   10. Social change—New York (State)—Saratoga
Springs—History.   I. Title.
  F129.S3O24 2010
  974.7'48041092—dc22
  [B]   2010000394

Henry Holt books are available for special promotions and premiums.
For details contact: Director, Special Markets.

First Edition 2010

Designed by Meryl Sussman Levavi
Printed in the United States of America
1 3 5 7 9 10 8 6 4 2

This book is for

Flaminia Ocampo

They were angry voices, too; and then a low curse succeeded, as if muttered savagely, between closed teeth. Then an agonized cry, such a cry as once heard, never fails to haunt the memory: "Murder! murder! Oh! God! don't kill me! Murder!"

MANSFIELD TRACY WALWORTH
Hotspur, A Tale of the Old Dutch Manor (1864)

"This is dreadful news. What an unfortunate family!—are you sure he was murdered?—were there marks of violence?"

MANSFIELD TRACY WALWORTH
Stormcliff, A Tale of the Highlands (1864)

At this instant a cry reached her ears which made her blood curdle. "Murder! murder!" . . . The sound was immediately followed by a heavy fall, and then all was still again.

MANSFIELD TRACY WALWORTH
Warwick, or The Lost Nationalities of America (1869)

In less than ten minutes the whole household were startled by the cry of *"help, help—murder."*

MANSFIELD TRACY WALWORTH
Beverly, or The White Mask (1872)

He was alone, and the blood was flowing rapidly from him. He tried to call succor to him. His voice reached no human ear. He saw that he was to go upon the last journey without a friend to clasp his hand and receive his dying commissions. He could not summon his relatives. He must bleed and die alone.

MANSFIELD TRACY WALWORTH
Married in Mask (1873)

Contents

The

FALL

of the

HOUSE *of*

WALWORTH

1

~~~~~~~~

A Haunted House

THERE was a woman who lived alone in a house with fifty-five rooms. It was dark in the house. She kept the curtains drawn by day, and most of the rooms she never entered after nightfall.

The house stood at the north end of Broadway, the celebrated main thoroughfare of the city of Saratoga Springs, New York. It was built in 1815 and acquired the name Pine Grove from the stand of pines that loomed over it. Back then its site was an outlying corner of a village just beginning to grow into a national showcase. The house grew larger along with the village. By the time Clara Grant Walworth was born in 1886, it had expanded extravagantly beyond its original dimensions and went by the name of the Walworth Mansion.

In 1952, as Clara contemplated the end of her days, the house was very much in the center, but of what? Saratoga Springs was a place she now found hard to recognize. The house was different too from what it had been in the time of her ancestor Chancellor Walworth. The protective pines were long gone, most of them cut down before her birth, the surrounding grounds sold off, and the original compact Walworth home obscured (as it changed from residence to courthouse to boarding school to hotel, reverting finally to residential seclusion) within the annexes and additional stories built around and on top of it.

The original one-and-a-half-story dwelling had been buried within the creaking hulk of a Victorian warren of tiny bedrooms and airless corridors. Within that warren Clara had spent her first months, her summers, and her holidays. Since turning fifty she had hardly left the place.

Outside, in the Saratoga Springs of the early 1950s, the old hotels—those still standing—were falling into decay. The decline had been steady for as long as Clara could remember. The symptoms were by now unmistakable. The splendors of Saratoga Springs were reduced to parking lots and orange-juice stands and neon-lit taverns, thronged with a new generation of tourists who knew nothing of the history that had taken shape here. At night cheap gamblers padded in bathrobes through the dark and narrow hallways of the once luxurious Grand Union Hotel.

The corruption of Saratoga was nowadays a national scandal. Local politicians and racket bosses submitted to federal investigation. The hearings were on television, so the whole world could see how thoroughly the town had been bought up, decades ago, by the likes of Arnold Rothstein and Joe Adonis and Meyer Lansky, gangsters in whose gaudy "lake houses" anything could happen. The townspeople had been happy to take the money and look the other way.

One way or another, this had been going on for years. You might say it had been going on ever since John Morrissey, a low-life Irish boxer from the back streets of Troy, had started up his gambling business during the Civil War. But the ruffians and vulgarians of Clara's parents' and grandparents' time began in retrospect to assume an air of respectability—even dignity—compared with the rot that had set in since. Morrissey, after all, had at least kept the locals out of his establishment, and shut down the gambling tables on Sundays.

She had lived to witness the final degradation of what had been not just beautiful but noble. The Saratoga Springs of racetracks and gambling dens was not the town Clara thought of as hers. Her Saratoga was an older, more rarefied place steeped in the memory of Revolutionary War heroes, inspired religious teachers, and women who had dedicated themselves for generations to preserving an America that seemed always on the verge of disappearing into some brutal caricature of itself. Her great-grandmother had been part of the effort to preserve

George Washington's home at Mount Vernon; her grandmother had seen to it that the battlefield of Saratoga, where the tide of war had turned against the British, would endure as a historical monument; her mother had renovated this very house.

Why hadn't anyone stopped America from becoming a nation run by crooks? Not that there were not plenty of crooks in the old days, but forces also existed that were capable of holding them in check, forces as much spiritual as physical. There were things you didn't do, affronts that were unimaginable. Now it had all become a sort of affront. If she no longer enjoyed leaving the house, it was because some new shock always waited for her. One more thing had been destroyed or cheapened.

SHE preferred to stay indoors to savor what was preserved within the walls, even if most of it was invisible. Clara had been born in this house and, at sixty-five, could expect to die here. Her world was by now largely restricted to the innermost core, the Chancellor's original domain. It was a space thick with ghosts. She traced their movements by recollecting every story she had ever been told, every anecdote tied to the pictures and objects and pieces of old furniture for which the house had become a repository. By making sure that everything stayed in its place—by remaining faithful to what her mother and grand-mother had taught her—she kept the ancestors near at hand. For years she had repeated the stories to any visitor who would listen. Now that visitors were rare, she told them to herself, taking care not to omit a single detail.

Her role, all her life, had been to preserve and remember. A votary in an abandoned temple, she had been born to go through every scrap of paper, rummage in every drawer, make lists of relics left behind. The house was her museum; her mausoleum, finally. She had been buried here, together with all she loved, for as long as she could remember.

She thought ceaselessly about everything that had happened in these rooms. Might it have been on this spot that Daniel Webster stood as he argued a case? Or in this corner that Andrew Jackson had exploded into wrath against the southern nullifiers, in the middle of a game of whist? James Fenimore Cooper and Washington Irving and the magnificent poet Mrs. Sigourney had sat at the dinner table. Presidents, senators, military commanders, the most distinguished authors, and the most celebrated preachers of the gospel, all had trooped through, in the time of heroes and founders when the world was fresh.

Here was the north parlor where the man those people came to see—her great-grandfather, New York's state chancellor Reuben Hyde Walworth—held court for decades. Now it had become her sickroom.

She had come to the end, not just of her own life, but of everything to which those earlier lives had been dedicated.

There had been a family and there had been a nation. To her they had almost been the same thing. She carried the blood of the *Mayflower* pilgrims in her. Davy Crockett was somewhere in the family tree. Her mother's father had been a friend of President Lincoln, her paternal great-grandmother a cousin of Mary Todd. Her great-uncle had left his right arm on a battlefield in Virginia. Her grandmother had danced at President Grant's inauguration. On both sides of the family her people had warded off invading armies and established the laws of the new land. They had been among those who counted for something in the making of the country. Now that the family had almost reached, in her, its point of extinction, might not the country as well be close to its terminus?

And where had the family gone? How could a family vanish?

In the memory parade of ancestors—the settlers and warriors and justices and evangelists—something was missing. There was an episode never to be part of any inscription or memorial address. It lived in unlit corners. At times it made her feel she had really not been born, as if this half-life were a shadow cast by a disaster before her birth.

Her life had been, perhaps, an act of commemoration for a gigantic absence, for a missing father and a missing grandfather: the grandfather whose memory had been so thoroughly crossed out, and the father who died just seven months after her birth, exhausted before his time. Both were swallowed up in the same obscure storm.

It had been a long time before she was allowed to know why there was such a gaping hole in the family history. People had been good about not bringing up what was best forgotten. Recollections trailed off into silence. A day came when she realized how well she had been protected from the moment she was born. Everyone, starting with her mother, had shielded her as long as possible from information too jarring for her young mind.

They had almost succeeded in sweeping from the house all traces of quarrels and ravings, of murder and of judicial punishment that killed the soul if not the body. Around that blotted-out zone the pageants and observances—meticulous rounds of a social protocol never abandoned even in extremity—clustered like a form of healing.

The healing was also a concealing. Pieces of what had been left out were eventually to be found hidden in diaries, scrapbooks, letters, the old documents that her grandmother Ellen (she had written it in the diary that Clara inherited) had one night sat up reading, "stirring up the old miseries which have been dead for years." Of Clara's grandfather Mansfield Tracy Walworth, all that remained was a small shelf of books in matching format, bearing such incommunicative titles as *Warwick* and *Beverly* and *Lulu* and *Delaplaine*. They were novels whose opening paragraphs spoke of moaning winds and impenetrable gloom, bells tolling at midnight, ominously deserted metropolitan streets, cells in which unnamed prisoners were brutally punished. But their many hundreds of pages of clotted prose led only into strange impasses, spasmodic mood swings, hermetic interviews between people whose identities or intentions were never quite clear.

Concealed most carefully of all was the letter that Frank Walworth, the father whom Clara never knew, wrote ten days before his death. She read it many times in later years. It was as close as she could get to him. Each time it was as if she peered into a closed room in which someone was suffering horribly, and could do nothing to comfort him. Frank announced:

> When you read this letter, the last of the Walworths of Saratoga Springs will have been laid to rest. And as I now face the "Great Beyond" in the full knowledge that the crime I committed thirteen years ago brought me to this early end, at thirty-three years, I pen this message with the sincere hope that the youth of the generation that reads it will have learned the lesson I failed to grasp. The wages of sin is death—death to the soul and the body and the mind! . . . I today know the full

meaning of that verse in Exodus: "I the Lord, thy God, am a jealous God, visiting the iniquities of the fathers upon their children unto the third and fourth generations." . . .

As I make ready to meet the Great Judge of All, I would say that the verdict of the jury rendered in my case was a just one . . . I have come to realize, that for the crime I committed, my wife and daughter would also pay the price. In very truth, the wages of sin is death. Keep that in mind, when as youth of another generation, you attempt to take the law into your own hands. May God help you to keep the ten commandments of God, which are the basic law of all life and love and living.

FRANK HARDIN WALWORTH
October 19, 1886.

"Unto the third and fourth generations"—the family had not even gotten that far. Her father could not have foreseen that his only daughter would live out her life childless. With Clara's approaching end all these documents would pass beyond her control. Perhaps after her death a part of what had been so long wrapped up would be revealed, even if there remained the question of what exactly that revelation would amount to. Who, after all, was Frank Hardin Walworth, and what might her life have been if she had known the answer to that question?

In stretches of uninterrupted solitude she found herself tracing a path in a city strange to her, a city she had never dared to explore. Amid railroad smoke and avenues full of foul stenches and jostling anonymous crowds she followed the movements of two men—the large and menacing older figure with blazing eyes and a boxer's build—and, in his wake, the deceptively unemotional boy scarcely arrived at his full height, making his way through the clutter and noise as if oblivious to what was around him.

A stalker laid a trap and left messages. His designated target moved through the rounds of his hours oblivious that they were racing toward their close.

But who had really designed the trap? The whole city was a trap; time was a trap; the inward coiling of a family was a trap; each of the men was himself the trap in which he was caught. In those depots and eating houses and lobbies and stairways—those unlit halls and sparsely furnished bedrooms—no breeze entered. The immense city ground to a halt. She could not imagine a word being spoken.

One man approached the other, drawn to him as if sleepwalking. The sun had barely come up. In a moment, in a narrow room at the top of the stairs, they would meet face-to-face and her destiny would be written, or unwritten: erased by blood.

2

Room 267

I F any of the other passengers took special notice of the young man who boarded the train at Saratoga Springs that Monday morning—the second of June, 1873—they never stepped forward to say so.

Perhaps he sat in silence all the way to the city. Even if someone had bothered to look at him closely, they would likely have detected nothing more than a modish youth—just nineteen in fact—in a light gray overcoat suitable for the mild springtime weather and a soft felt hat in the Alpine style. Beyond that they might have observed that he was well-mannered but lacking in expression, his gaze somewhat withdrawn, his whole carriage almost absentminded.

For all the exuberance of his side whiskers, carefully calculated to give him the look of a young bravo, Frank Hardin Walworth was easy to miss in a crowd. A few days later—when Frank was being discussed on every front page in New York—a journalist would remark maliciously that "he appears just about intellectual enough to make a very ordinary dry goods clerk."

His mother, Ellen, would testify that Frank looked pallid and sick when she encountered him in the hall of Pine Grove that morning. She had spoken to him as he was going out the door. It was early for him to be up; usually, especially in recent months, he preferred to lie in bed late. She missed him at breakfast, and was told he had left word that if he wasn't back by supper time he wouldn't be back at all that day. She had no idea that he was going to New York, or that he was carrying a revolver in his pocket. She knew that he possessed one, though, and that he was in the habit of keeping it loaded in his room.

It was only some hours after Frank's departure that Ellen Walworth noticed the empty envelope he had left on his desk. The address was in the unmistakably emphatic handwriting of his father, Mansfield. That was when she started to worry, and set about trying to learn where Frank had gone. Her first thought had been that Frank was on his way to a meeting, probably prearranged, with his father; but she had no idea where to start searching.

She sent a telegram to her brother-in-law Clarence—Father Clarence Walworth, the parish priest of St. Mary's in Albany—who a few days earlier had invited Frank to accompany him on a yearlong tour of Europe. They were supposed to set sail within the week. More hours would pass before Ellen came upon the cache of letters from her estranged husband—letters she had not seen before, because Frank had been intercepting them for months. But she had seen others and knew what to expect.

ALMOST twenty-four hours would pass before Father Walworth received the letter Frank had written to him on Sunday afternoon, the day before he took the train to the city. By then Frank had already arrived in Manhattan. Clarence had been prepared for disturbing news by Ellen's anxious telegram.

The letter that Clarence received was all the more ominous for its lack of detail about Frank's intentions. The boy began by thanking his uncle for the very welcome invitation to go with him to Europe. But any such voyage, he explained, would be impossible unless he could assure himself of his mother's safety: "I am of the opinion that it would be neither safe nor wise to leave her unprotected against father's acts . . . I am going down to New York in the morning to try to see him . . . My trip will determine any question in regard to my going to Europe or anywhere else."

In further explanation he enclosed the letter sent to his mother that morning, only the latest of the many that Frank had kept from her. It

was a very long letter, and its tone was quite familiar to Father Walworth. For a time, in the aftermath of the couple's divorce two years
earlier, there had been a stream of such communications from Mansfield to Ellen: enraged, disordered, sometimes violently threatening
letters demanding money from his blocked inheritance, or insisting on
visitation rights with his children. It had been a relief when at last they
stopped coming. This latest was even more explicit in its threats and
was written, as Clarence had come to expect, in language that could
have been lifted straight from one of his younger brother's extravagantly melodramatic novels. (As it would turn out, it pretty much had
been.)

"Prepare yourself for the inevitable," Mansfield wrote from his
boardinghouse in the East Fifties. "I am getting over my wasting fever,
and shall be out of my room in a few days. I am going to call upon my
children; my heart is starving for their caresses . . . I will see them—
peaceably if I can, or with a tragedy if I must . . . Keep Frank Walworth out of my way. You have taught him to hate me . . . Beware that
you do not in any way arouse the frenzy which you have known to
exist since you left me . . . I am a broken-hearted desperado. I admit
it. Save this letter for lawyers and courts if you please. God is my
lawyer . . . that God who has planted love in my heart for my little
girls, and that says to the tiger bereft of its young, 'Kill!' . . . When I
know from the conduct of my little girls that you have taught them to
hate me, that moment two pistol shots will ring about your house—
one slaying you, the other myself . . . The God of justice demands it."

By the next morning there would no longer be any question about
where Frank had gone, but the information came too late to be of
any use.

THE train pulled into the newly built Grand Central Station around
half past two. It took Frank about thirty minutes to make his way
uptown to the boardinghouse where his father was now living, at
Fourth Avenue near the corner of Fifty-third Street. Frank had not
been there before; he had not seen his father since the previous
autumn. When the landlady, Mrs. Eliza Sims, came down in response
to the street-door bell, he inquired—in a manner she considered cool
but courteous—whether Mr. Mansfield Walworth was at home.

She was not sure. She had exchanged a few words with Mr. Walworth when she left a bucket of water outside his door around noon, and had heard him go out an hour afterward. She would go to his room to check if he had returned in the interim.

It took but a moment to confirm that he had not come back. "Can you tell him then," the young man replied, "to call upon me at the Sturtevant House. Tell him that his son wishes to see him."

"Are you his son, sir?"

"Yes, I am his son."

"Maybe you had better leave a note for your father, then."

"Yes, I guess I had better do so."

Mrs. Sims ushered him into her sitting room, where he wrote out the following message at her table: "I want to settle some family matters. Call at the Sturtevant House. If I am not there I will leave word with the clerk. FRANK WALWORTH." He did not seal it up but only folded it over and handed it to her, and wishing her good day strolled down toward Fifty-third Street.

Mrs. Sims went back upstairs to Mr. Walworth's room. Great heaps of manuscripts and books and magazines were spread over the room. During the twenty-eight months that he had been her tenant, he had applied himself ceaselessly to what he called his *literary labors*, the novels and reviews and unfinished scholarly works that kept him up sometimes for nights on end. His writings, if anything, were what he chose to talk about. Of his family he said not a word, although she was certainly aware that he was the son of the famous Chancellor Walworth. It was nothing for him to work for ten hours at a stretch on one of his serials—he would write even when, as was recently the case, he was bedridden with illness and had not eaten or slept—and messengers from the *Home Journal* or from his publisher, G. W. Carleton, were known to come and go at all hours to pick up his copy.

She was careful to deposit the note in plain view on the desk, finding a space for it without disturbing anything, for Mr. Walworth did not care to have anyone disarranging his papers.

ABOUT a mile and a quarter separated Mrs. Sims's boardinghouse from the sprawling Sturtevant House at Broadway and Twenty-ninth. The hotel, occupying the better part of a city block, had opened only two years earlier with a reception well attended by New York's social elite. It was among the most splendid of the establishments that in the prosperous years since the war's end had sprung up rapidly in the center of the city, each more imperially ornate than the last.

The lobby was swarming with Masons gathered for their annual convention. (Mansfield Walworth, who a year before had been confirmed as a Master Mason of New York's Grand Lodge no. 103, was among the many expected to attend.) It was an exceptionally busy time, and afterward no one at the hotel could quite remember when Frank showed up to register. The hotel's chief cashier, Hooper Barrett, thought it was about three; the bellman William Amos recollected it as closer to five.

Barrett, the cashier, was himself from Saratoga Springs, where his father was a justice of the peace and, by odd chance, lived next door to the stately Walworth place on upper Broadway. The cashier had met Frank several times before and knew his father, Mansfield, slightly as well. They chatted at the desk; Frank asked him if he would have dinner with him, but since Barrett did not get off duty for several hours, they agreed on a late supper instead. Beyond the fact that Frank's clothes were dusty and travel-stained, the encounter left no impression whatever on the cashier. Nor did their eight o'clock supper, in the grandiose dining room adorned with frescoes in what the management claimed to be Pompeiian style, give him any cause for anxious premonition. Frank said nothing about his purpose in coming to the city, nothing about his father. They talked, Barrett would recall, of "ordinary matters," and after thirty minutes said a perfunctory goodnight.

Frank went upstairs to his room, number 267. Some of the Sturtevant's three hundred rooms were spacious and luxuriously appointed, but Frank's was not among them. He had taken a room on the second floor at the rear. It was a small enough lodging, nine feet wide and twenty long, furnished with little more than a bed, a stove, and a washstand.

The next morning, amid the tumult, someone noted that Frank's bed was undisturbed. He had evidently sat up all night, waiting for an answer to his message.

MANSFIELD Walworth did not get back to his room at the boarding-house until around midnight.

He may have been in no great hurry to return to the "simply furnished room in the metropolis" that he described in his latest novel *Beverly*, a book in which (he acknowledged in one of his last letters) "I have made myself the unhappy hero." This fictional alter ego was the journalist MacGregor—"the patient toiler, the indefatigable man of will, the soul that aspires to the possession of the pure, the beautiful, the intellectual, the grand"—a writer of genius, abandoned by his treacherous wife and neglected by the world at large.

Walworth could not resist injecting into the convoluted mystery plot of *Beverly* some glimpses of his own sullen condition: "He looked very weary and care-worn . . . He was in pain, and its location was in that part of the head where so many literary men, when overtaxing their powers, suffer, viz., the back of the skull where the spinal cord meets the brain . . . And now the weary and gifted *littérateur* was about to launch his production upon the waves of public opinion . . . Quiet, rest for his brain, and warmth, were the luxuries which the convalescent hoped now to enjoy for a little time."

Apparently he found at least some rest for his brain beyond the confines of his little room. When he had left his lodging house that afternoon, he had made his way to Jones' Wood, a forested area along the East River north of Sixty-fifth Street. It was a popular resort, a last wild pocket on the increasingly built-up East Side. Once, according to local lore, the wood had been a rendezvous for pirates—a spot where they divvied up their booty and indulged in licentious revels—and it still had a reputation for rowdiness. On that warm June day it was crowded with German Americans—as many as twenty thousand, according to one report—celebrating the annual Turnfest, a traditional mix of gymnastics and choral singing that had been a New York tradition for nearly twenty years now.

Walworth may well have participated in the singing himself. He was a member of the Männerchor, a popular German choral group headquartered on East Fifty-sixth Street, three blocks from his lodgings; he not only spent quite a bit of his spare time in their company but took it upon himself to publicize their concerts in the newspapers when he could. He would certainly have availed himself of the food and drink plentifully available at the picnic grounds.

Evening found him in the company of his friend Michael Tuomey, a former city alderman who now kept a stable in the neighborhood. After a time they went around the corner to Dr. Kirscht's drugstore at Lexington and Fifty-third, a familiar haunt. Here they passed an hour or two in idle conversation, as they must have done on many other nights.

Tuomey, previously a wholesale liquor dealer, had served back in the 1850s in the administration of the notorious Fernando Wood and had taken his share of the public abuse aimed at Mayor Wood's corrupt ways. The *New York Times* had characterized Tuomey in 1858, amid a scandal involving the selling of tainted "swill milk" from diseased cows, as one of those Tammany aldermen "selected from among the dregs of the populace, prize-fighters, grog-shop keepers, bullies, and kindred characters." That same year Tuomey brought a libel suit against the publisher Frank Leslie for having published in his *Illustrated Weekly* a defamatory caricature of the alderman as "a rollicking Irishman, holding a dubious-looking black bottle in one hand and a shillelagh in the other." Tuomey's Tammany ties looked more disreputable than ever in the wake of recent revelations about the Tweed ring, whose career of election rigging and public theft had at last been sensationally exposed (although the deposed mayor Tweed had so far, thanks to a mistrial, evaded punishment and was currently enjoying a vacation in California).

LATER that week Tuomey allowed himself to be interviewed at length about what turned out to be his last evening in the company of Mansfield Walworth. What had they talked about? About writing, as was usual with the novelist, who had shown Tuomey a copy of the paper that had his latest story in it. The alderman took the occasion to ask him how many hours a day he devoted to his literary work, and Walworth said about ten, not counting the hours spent in arranging the publication of his compositions. They talked as well about the Männerchor— Tuomey also belonged to it—and the day's singing events.

The novelist's barber, Henry Ackerman, was another member of the singing group—he not only sang with Walworth in the chorus but had been giving him German lessons—and he too drifted into the drugstore in the course of the evening. Ackerman would declare that he considered Walworth not merely a client but a friend. There were others who wondered out loud, in the days that followed, why a man of Walworth's social standing had been reduced to having Sunday dinners with his barber. In any event the barber would tell a reporter, "When I heard of his death I was struck dumb—I was sick at heart," and reminisced about a Christmas dinner of ducks and geese that he had shared with the novelist.

On the evening of June 2 Walworth's heart was not really in the conversation, Tuomey observed. He would drop out of the talk for five minutes at a time, and his mood seemed positively gloomy. Walworth had enjoyed his afternoon in Jones' Wood—the cool breezes in the groves had refreshed him—but he felt a bit dull. Might he have been drinking? Tuomey, while denying that his friend had been habitually intemperate, acknowledged that he liked to take the occasional drink, sometimes when alone, and with his friends often. It could not be denied that he betrayed, at times, some slight traces of dissipation.

But Tuomey assumed that Walworth's pensiveness was more the result of his literary temperament than of inebriation. All that reading and writing had taken their toll. He was a person of great refinement, much esteemed as such by Tuomey and the other habitués of the drugstore whom he had befriended since moving into the neighborhood. Men of talent were, after all, known for their unfathomable ways.

Walworth was a fine-looking man, tall and robustly built, and his manners were impeccable, but in Tuomey's view "there was something in his countenance which shadowed the man with mystery . . . He was fond of retirement and loneliness to a great extent." He was more an observer than a talker—though he could talk brilliantly when he wanted to—and that night he seemed particularly wrapped in thought. Tuomey imagined he might have secret troubles. Merely to see him walk across Fifty-third Street every evening with the same preoccupied air suggested he was burdened with a hidden sorrow.

That night, in fact, Walworth did not feel like taking a drink. Mr. Robinson, another neighbor who had joined in the conversation, offered him one, but he declined. He had just one glass of root beer with Tuomey and went on his way around midnight. But before leaving the company, Robinson recalled, Walworth offered them some lines of poetry. He recited them with great feeling, although Robinson could recall only the last words: "Beware, take care." He repeated them twice and then said goodnight and went off toward Lexington Avenue.

At six o'clock the next morning Mansfield Walworth arrived at the Sturtevant House and asked for Frank Walworth. The clerk on duty objected that it was early to be calling, but Mansfield was insistent—"Oh, he will see me"—and wrote his name on a card to be sent up to room 267.

The elderly bellman William Amos made his way to the front desk when he heard the signal-bell ringing. As the clerk gave him the card to carry up, Amos had a quick glimpse of the stout, muscular man standing by the desk. Nearly six feet tall, and with a weightlifter's build, Mansfield cut an imposing figure. When Amos got to room 267 he rapped twice on the door; it opened only a little, and Amos handed in the card. The room's occupant, half visible in the doorway, told him to tell the gentleman that he was not up, or not dressed—Amos couldn't quite catch the words. He went downstairs and informed the stout visitor that the other gentleman would be down in a few minutes.

A few moments later the bell rang again. This time Amos found Frank Walworth fully dressed in his hat and overcoat. He sat cross-legged by the window and seemed thoroughly relaxed—"There was no excitement about him"—as he told Amos that the gentleman who was waiting could come up.

Back at the desk Mansfield Walworth—"I knew who he was by his card"—struck the bellman as equally calm. He followed Amos upstairs, and when Frank opened the door to the bellman's knock, Amos entered first with Mansfield close behind him. There was an uncomfortable pause. Amos had lingered a moment, as was customary, to see if either of the men wanted anything, but Mansfield shot him an unpleasant look, "as though he wanted me to go." The bellman left hastily without bothering about protocol. Mansfield had looked "very much displeased," for whatever cause.

Next door, in room 266, Josiah Moorehead, a retired businessman who resided permanently at the hotel, was having a rough night. He suffered from insomnia and had been awake for some time, since before the church clock had struck six. The light bothered him. He figured he would get up to close the blinds so he could try to get some sleep. Just then he heard someone knocking on the door of the adjoining room; it was the bellman, announcing, "Here's a card for you, sir, that a gentleman just sent up." There were further comings and goings on the stairs, which could only have further unsettled the bleary-eyed Moorehead.

In room 268, adjacent to Frank's on the other side, the cotton merchant Adolph Ebert had been asleep but was half woken by loud talking. He couldn't make out whole sentences, only a few words shouted with special emphasis: *home*, *mother*, *liar*. Then came a series of shots. Fully awake, Ebert tried the communicating door between his room and 267 but found it locked.

Josiah Moorehead, in room 266, had not heard any words being spoken before the first pistol shot. Not more than five minutes had passed since the guest had been shown into the room. Then, he recalled, came a cry of "murder"—then another shot, and another cry—and another, and a third cry. The cries were those of an utterly terrified man. There were four shots in all, in quick succession, "just like a telegraph operator sending a message." Moorehead heard a door slam and someone running into the hall; he wondered groggily if there were a fight going on among the servants. He pulled his trousers on and went out to investigate. He had the impression that someone had just headed downstairs, but failed to catch sight of him. Moorehead went in search of help.

Very agitated, Adolph Ebert ventured into the hallway and pulled the bell-rope. Only then did he look inside room 267, the door being ajar. He could not afterward testify very clearly as to what he saw. He was, he reiterated, much excited at the time. All he could say was that there was a body lying there.

A few moments earlier, before the shots, Charles Doolittle, the hotel steward, had been walking downstairs at a good clip. He had overslept a little and gotten dressed in a hurry, and was coming down to oversee the servants in their regular morning duties. On the third-floor landing he met the housekeeper, Mrs. Turner, and they were having a quick chat when the shots were fired. He heard a voice cry out but was unable to say afterward if the word *murder* had been pronounced or if it was simply an inarticulate cry of pain. The shots came so fast he couldn't count them. In almost the same instant he heard the bell in the office ringing furiously. (This would have been the agitated Ebert pulling on the bell-rope.) Doolittle ran down into the second-floor hall but for a moment could see nothing amiss. The smell of gunpowder pervaded the hallway.

Mrs. Turner conceived the idea that one of the guests might have committed suicide. She had her doubts about the gentleman in room 271, and so she and Doolittle went off to see about him. As they rushed through the hall they observed that the bathroom was occupied— perhaps the suicide had taken place in there. But whoever was in the bathroom turned out to be quite all right. Mr. Moorehead from room 266 had by now joined them, and he filled them in on what he had heard and seen. Doolittle went down to the office to find out what was going on.

The night watchman, John Harrison, was going off duty after his usual early morning rounds when he heard the shots. Some short time later the steward ran up to him: Mr. Doolittle had learned in the office that a shooting had occurred in room 267. Doolittle had glimpsed a young man in the office—in his excitement he only half observed him—who appeared to be dictating a telegram to Mr. Barrett the cashier. Barrett said something about someone having shot the young man's father, but the details were not immediately clear to Doolittle, or perhaps he was too much in shock to put the pieces together right away. He made his way as instructed to room 267. Not more than ten minutes had passed since the shots.

The door gaped open about twenty inches wide. Harrison the watchman entered first, with Doolittle and Moorehead following. The room was unoccupied except for the man lying on the floor, his feet jammed against the door, his head at a crumpled angle near the wash-stand. His arms were flung back, his legs were doubled up, and his left arm seemed broken. Someone had put a towel under his head, and it was soaked with blood. A black hat, with a crepe mourning band, lay near the body. Mansfield Walworth was not quite dead; he moved his head three times.

Mr. Doolittle ran to alert the hotel's resident physician, Dr. Samuel Childs, but found that the hotel's owner, Louis Leland, had already been notified by the watchman and had himself sent for the doctor before going up to room 267. A small crowd had by now gathered around the body. Doolittle meanwhile, on Mr. Leland's instruction, went around to the nearby residence of Dr. Walter Fleming, on Thirty-third Street, rousing him from his slumbers and asking him to come to the hotel immediately to assist in examining the body.

Dr. Childs had been whiling away the early morning hours in the hotel's reading room when Mr. Leland sent word to him of what had happened. By the time he got upstairs Walworth's pulse had as far as he could determine stopped beating. Childs arrived in time to hear a last heaving breath. The tiny room was awash in blood. A large pool had formed around the head and soaked into the carpet. A quantity of blood had splattered the washstand, filling the toothbrush dish and mingling with the soap in the soap dish to form a frothy red foam. The wall above the basin was likewise smeared with red. The murdered man's face, hands, and hair were covered with blood. The eyes were open and fixed.

Dr. Childs thought it a good idea to fetch some oilcloth to protect the bed before placing the body on it. While he was out on this errand, Dr. Fleming arrived. Fleming bent to examine the body and thought he detected a faint pulse. Someone told him not to touch the body until the coroner came, and the doctor exploded, "To save a life is worth more than all the coroners in the country!" Childs having come back with the oilcloth, Fleming managed with the help of Leland and Moorehead to lift the heavy body onto the bed. Fleming tore open the shirt and undershirt and in an instant satisfied himself that Walworth was dead. As he examined him he realized he had met the man before. The identification was confirmed when a bystander handed him the calling card that Walworth had sent up to Frank. It too was bloodstained.

Dr. Fleming probed the wounds as best he could under the cramped conditions. One bullet had entered the right side near the sixth rib. Another had pierced the left side, about two inches below the collarbone. Another had smashed into the jawbone. A fourth had fractured the left arm below the elbow.

MOMENTS after the shots, the bellman William Amos saw Frank Walworth walking quickly downstairs and heading straight for the hotel office, where his friend Barrett was on duty. The bell pulled by Ebert on the second floor had just rung.

Frank walked up to the desk and said, "Barrett, I have shot my father in my room, and want a policeman."

"You don't mean to say that you have shot your father?"

"Yes, I have shot him four times." (Or did he say "three times"? The point was to become controversial.)

Frank did not seem in the least excited. He told Barrett he wanted to send a telegram, and proceeded to dictate it to the clerk. It was at this moment that Doolittle, the steward, came downstairs to report the shots.

The telegram was addressed to Frank's uncle Father Clarence in Albany.

> New York, June 3, 1873. C. A. Walworth, Chapel Street, Albany: Have shot father. Look after mother. Frank Walworth.

Frank reached into his pocket and handed Barrett a roll of money, which came to about seven dollars. "I think this will pay my bill."

Barrett murmured that he was very sorry about what Frank had done.

Frank remained standing by the desk, apparently at ease. Doolittle remembered later on that he had been "quite cool and collected" and made no effort to escape. Frank's calm would quickly become journalistic legend: "Not the slightest paleness whitened his cheek, not a single tremor disturbed his lips, not a single waver was there in the glance of his blue eyes," according to one of many accounts.

He was the still point in the midst of a storm. The rest of the hotel was by this time in an uproar, the lobby and hallways swarming with guests, many of them Masons who were there for their convention, demanding to know what was going on. Leland had already ordered Frank's room locked to prevent any further intrusions before the coroner arrived.

The only difficulty was finding a policeman to whom Frank could surrender. The bellman was sent outside on that errand—"go quick as lightning," someone urged him—but he went up and down Broadway repeatedly without any luck. Finally it occurred to Barrett to summon one by telegraph, and in a few minutes an officer came into the lobby to escort Frank to the nearest precinct, the Twenty-ninth, at Thirtieth Street and Seventh Avenue. They managed to slip out before the reporters got there.

At around eleven the undertaker's wagon pulled up at the hotel. Packed in ice in a refrigerated coffin representing the most advanced mortuary technology, the body of Mansfield Walworth was carried down to Senior and Benedict's funeral parlor on Carmine Street. Here the coroner would make a more thorough examination to clarify the cause of death.

The telegraph wires already hummed with the news that the son of the great Chancellor Walworth—the well-known novelist Mansfield Tracy Walworth, author of *Warwick* and *Delaplaine*—had been gunned down in a Manhattan hotel room by his own son. As reporters, law officers, and lawyers mobilized rapidly, the Walworths of Saratoga, or what was left of them, were about to encounter a new and unwelcome kind of public exposure.

3

Another Sentimental Murder

"A most uncommonly shocking murder this morning at the Sturtevant House," wrote the attorney George Templeton Strong in his diary on Tuesday evening. It was a nightly ritual for him. Strong had been keeping his copious, sharply observant personal record of the New York scene for decades, long enough to have included in its pages a description of his trip up the Hudson to Saratoga in 1841, when as a young man of twenty-one he had called on Chancellor Walworth at Pine Grove to be duly sworn in as a member of the New York bar. He had marked as well the day six years ago when he had learned of Chancellor Walworth's death.

The Walworth murder—as unsettling as it was to Strong's sense of social order—was hardly the only thing on his mind that day. He noted that Captain Jack, the notorious leader of the warring Modocs in the West, had finally been captured and was likely (to Strong's undisguised satisfaction) to be hanged; and he devoted most of his entry to a detailed appreciation of the collections of the Metropolitan Museum of Art, then in its infancy and housed on West Fourteenth Street, waxing particularly eloquent about some ancient glass vessels from Cyprus which were "exquisitely colored with iridescence from partial decomposition or disintegration of the surface."

He had paid enough attention, however, to the events at the hotel to encapsulate the known facts about the killing in a neat digest: "Mansfield Walworth, son of the last of the chancellors and a kind of small littérateur who devoted himself to the concoction of dish-water little novels, received four revolver shots from his own son and was instantly killed. They had got into a hot discussion of some trouble between Walworth and his wife at Saratoga. The parricide, a boy of nineteen, went coolly to the nearest station house and gave himself up." Strong further noted, with considerable skepticism, that Frank had justified his act by stating that "he thought his father was going to draw a pistol on him." His own conclusion was pragmatic: "We shall have to make the carrying of concealed weapons a felony."

Strong had hit all the main points of the narrative that was rapidly being assembled by newspapermen all over New York City, with unsolicited corrections instantly supplied by upstate journalists who claimed to understand the background better. A terrible event had struck the family of "the last of the chancellors"; the murdered man had been, at the very least, a writer of irredeemable mediocrity; the crime was rooted in his marriage; and the son who had killed him had behaved "coolly" in the aftermath of his crime. As the story of the murder evolved through the retellings of scores of newspapermen, the evocation of the Chancellor's memory would, at least in some quarters, take on an obligatory, almost liturgical ring, a pro forma lament over the degradation of American tradition; the flaws of Mansfield Walworth's writing would come to seem only a minor aspect of the far more ferocious flaws of his character; and the "infelicities" of Mansfield and Ellen's marriage would provide a steady supply of sensational copy.

But it was the coolness of Frank that gave the city reporters their best hook. Here was an alleged crime of passion—"another sentimental murder," in the words of one newspaper—committed by a youth inflamed by the mistreatment of his mother. Yet the youth in question seemed to almost all observers curiously dispassionate, "offhanded," nearly contemptuous in his manner. His oddly matter-of-fact behavior gave just the right seasoning to the event: this was a disturbingly modern crime, in a modern hotel, committed by a modern kind of youth—refined, stylish, in some accounts irresistibly attractive ("he has the prettiest mouth I ever saw on a masculine face," one correspondent reported)—manifesting "utmost calm" and "utter indifference" amid the bloodiest circumstances. "The coolness and deliberation displayed by the youthful parricide," wrote the *New York Herald*, "over whose head scarcely a score of summers have passed, reveal a depth of depravity that we shudder to contemplate . . . A nameless horror takes possession of the mind." The *Evening Post* wondered if "modern society has produced a monster whose possibility we are bound to consider if we cherish any hope that those who come after us shall not lapse into barbarism." "The Thug in India," noted the *Sun*, "who considers murder a religious act, does not show more complacence than this boy at his act."

Nameless horror and endless fascination; to the loudly expressed repugnance of many, the young parricide had become a celebrity overnight. The newspapers seized hold of Frank Walworth and made sure that their readers could follow his movements from day to day, almost from hour to hour. With remarkable speed and in multiple editions, they tracked his movements from hotel to police station to cell 54 of the Tombs, along with the movements of those caught up with his fate. There was much to track. From the moment Frank fired off his telegram from the lobby of the Sturtevant, energetic efforts had been set in motion. As members of the Walworth family got word of what had happened, they moved quickly to contain the situation.

Frank's grandmother Sarah, the Chancellor's ailing widow, headed back east from Chicago, where she had been staying with her son, General Martin Hardin, a maimed hero of the Civil War. Father Clarence Walworth, the first to be informed, set out as quickly as possible from Albany, meeting up with Frank's mother, Ellen, who by then had already sought legal advice from Edward Beach, an attorney with close ties to the family. Together Clarence and Ellen took the night train from Saratoga. Clarence sent word to Frank's fifteen-year-old-sister, also named Ellen but known to the family as Nelly, a student at the Sacred Heart Convent in Kenwood, New York, to meet him in Albany, but by the time she got there he had already departed for Saratoga. He left a message at his residence for her to join him at Pine Grove; not wanting to unsettle her, he gave no further details. She presumed she was on her way to a farewell party for her brother Frank, who as far as she knew was leaving with Clarence for Europe in a few days. On the train from Albany to Saratoga she caught sight of a traveler's newspaper, with her father's name spelled out in boldface capitals. She fainted and had to be revived by other women in the car.

But there were forces closer to hand. The elderly Judge John M. Barbour, chief justice of New York's Superior Court and Frank's great-uncle, was informed of the shooting in the middle of a court session on Wednesday morning. Tottering from shock and needing assistance getting out of the courtroom, he gathered his strength and, rounding up a close associate, former district attorney Samuel Garvin, sped with him in a carriage to the Sturtevant, only to find that Frank was already in custody at the Twenty-ninth Precinct.

THERE was some question about how exactly Frank had gotten to the precinct. The clerk at the Sturtevant would testify that he had telegraphed for police assistance and that Frank had been accompanied to the station house by an officer. But the bellman William Amos said that "he went to the station house himself," the officer at the receiving desk was vague on details, and the first newspaper accounts seized on the irresistible image of the unperturbed young assassin walking out of the hotel and strolling in gentlemanlike fashion over to Seventh Avenue and Thirtieth Street to turn himself in.

Frank was said to have approached the policeman at the front desk—Sergeant Stephen Keating—and declared with lawyerlike precision: "My name is Frank H. Walworth; I have just shot and killed my father, Mansfield T. Walworth, in the Sturtevant House, and this is the pistol I shot him with—you had better have it," handing the sergeant a Colt revolver four of whose five chambers had been emptied. He showed the sergeant where the powder burns had singed his left hand. Keating managed to ask Frank, "What possessed you to do such a thing?" "Family trouble," he replied. Sergeant Washington Mullen was dispatched to the Sturtevant to verify the story. In the meantime Frank was searched and divested of a penknife. "Do you think I would commit suicide?" he asked. "You are mistaken."

At least one reporter, a correspondent for the *Sun*, claimed to have managed to get an interview at a point when Frank, unadvised by counsel, was still willing to talk unguardedly with the press. Asked what had led to the crime, Frank replied: "Family troubles. It's been going on for some time, and the story is a long one." If the interview can be taken at face value—there is no evidence one way or the other, but nothing inherently implausible about it—Frank let slip a good deal more than he was subsequently willing to concede.

> *Reporter*: "Excuse my asking the question" (here the prisoner looked hard at the reporter and smiled—his smile is very sweet), "but did you come here with the intention—why did you come here?"
> *Walworth*: "I came here to do what I have done."

Frank went on to describe the murder scene in detail: "I took out my pistol and pointed it at him. I said, 'I want you to promise that you will not threaten to shoot me or my mother any more.' . . . He said, 'I will promise not to do so.' . . . I said, 'Will you promise that you won't insult me or my mother any more? In the past you have done it with impunity, but you cannot do it any more.' . . . He said, 'I won't trouble you any more.' Then I said, 'You have broken your promises many times before. I am determined you shall keep them this time.' Then I shot him . . . The last shot I fired he was close up to me." Within hours Frank's account of what had occurred would undergo significant revision.

Judges Barbour and Garvin caught up with Frank at the Twenty-ninth Precinct. Barbour had little to say to him, but Garvin spent an hour in conference with the boy, instructing him not to talk to any more reporters and perhaps sketching out a possible line of defense. A reporter for the *Commercial* prevailed on the obliging Sergeant Mullen to let him talk with the prisoner, but Frank now "maintained an imperturbable demeanor" and stated "in a leisurely, drawling tone" that he really had nothing to say at present. He contented himself with murmuring something about "extenuating circumstances."

While still at the station house, Frank was formally questioned by Coroner Nelson Young, fresh from his examination of the body at the Sturtevant. A statement was drawn up which appeared within hours in every newspaper in New York: "I reside with my mother in Saratoga, my father having parted from her some years ago. My father is an author, and I have been studying law . . . My father has not lived with my mother since we left here three years ago, but he has repeatedly sent us threatening and insulting letters. It is only a short time ago since he threatened to shoot my mother and myself. I shot him because of this. Not long ago I met him in the street in Saratoga, and I then told him that if he did not keep away from us, or insulted my mother any more, I would shoot him. I also told him that there were bounds which I would not allow any man to go beyond with impunity, especially when my mother was being insulted."

The details of the shooting were essentially the same as what the *Sun* reporter had elicited from Frank, at least until he got to the last part. Mansfield, he testified, had promised not to molest the family anymore—but then "we began speaking on family matters . . . he used some very insulting language and put his hand in his pocket as though to draw out a pistol, when I shot him." Much would be made subsequently of the fact that Mansfield was known to carry a pistol—although he had gone unarmed to the Sturtevant. What seemed to many observers a clear case of entrapment—the victim lured to a hotel room and shot down without warning—was now implied to be a matter of self-defense. In any case Frank was not expressing any penitence about his deed. He ended by declaring, "I only regret this on account of the effect it will have on my family."

The formalities completed, Frank was hustled in quick order from the Twenty-ninth Precinct to the Tombs. His police escort, Officer Denis Leary, tried to draw him out on the murder, but Frank ignored him and puffed on a cigar. He talked only about the streets they were passing through as they approached the remnants of the notorious Five Points District; he said he had forgotten most of their names.

At length they arrived at the forbidding pseudo-Egyptian prison on Centre Street, a dank mausoleum built on landfill poured into the toxic muck of the old Collect Pond. Within its walls a shifting multitude of killers, thieves, drunks, prostitutes, and disturbers of the peace were crammed into some two hundred closely packed cells, with the second tier reserved for those charged with murder. Going through the gates, the clean-cut youth from Saratoga retained his composure. Afterward Leary told a reporter: "I have seen a great many murderers, but I never saw one who was so cool." The keeper who admitted him to the Tombs chimed in with a similar impression: "There was no excitement about him, and I tell you it's a rare thing to see a man come in here as easy and offhanded as he did."

The strangely detached assassin of his father, a boy accustomed to the comforts of a luxurious home, was to spend his first night in the Tombs in a cold and cheerless room furnished only by a bed and a chair. The room's previous occupant, an Irish immigrant named Robert Bleakley, had just begun serving a life sentence for the murder of his niece, a prostitute he claimed to have killed in a fit of insanity brought on by the shame of her fallen life (although some claimed it was more likely because she refused to share her earnings with him).

Frank slept peacefully, according to the prison guards who looked in at regular intervals to make sure he did not attempt suicide. In the morning he sat quietly on his bed and, having made it clear that he did not want to talk to anyone, was permitted to remain in solitude for several hours. There was little mystery about what he had done. The only mysteries were what was going on in his mind, and what would now be done with him.

At about ten o'clock on Wednesday morning Ellen Hardin Walworth, veiled and dressed in black, arrived at the Tombs by carriage to visit her son. There were some in New York who could still remember Ellen as the young woman of wit and charm who had graced the society of Saratoga and Washington in the days before the Great Rebellion, when her father-in-law was a national figure and her mother (the Chancellor's much younger second wife, Sarah) the incarnation of everyone's idea of a vivacious southern belle.

Ellen, now forty-one, had long since retreated from ostentatious circles. She had passed the war years at her family's home in Kentucky and weathered years of domestic upheaval after reuniting with her husband (and stepbrother) Mansfield—who had himself spent the war years apart from her, under house arrest in Saratoga on suspicion of spying for the Confederacy. After they formally separated, she had operated a well-regarded boarding school in the Walworth home at Pine Grove.

Certainly Ellen had never expected to enter a city in which the most intimate and horrific episodes of her life were splashed across newspaper headlines and hawked by miserable urchins on every street corner. Having successfully maintained a public silence for so long, confiding her troubles to no one outside a trusted circle, she was now exposed in the coarsest way imaginable. The failure of her marriage, the debaucheries and brutalities of her husband, the details of physical and mental assaults and indignities so revolting she would never willingly have made an open declaration of them—all this was the gossip of a city with no compunctions about wresting its quota of cheap entertainment out of her misfortunes. She had become a character in the sort of play she would not have seen fit to attend, the rankest Bowery blood and thunder.

The reunion of a mother with the son who had allegedly murdered to protect her safety and honor made for a potent scene. Many alternate accounts were rushed into print: "As Frank came into the room his mother sprang toward him, and clasping her arms around his neck, sobbed with grief. The son was greatly afflicted by his mother's sorrow, and for several moments was powerless to resist the influence of her woe. Tears came to his eyes and he was unable to speak." Here was a situation that journalists were well equipped to describe; they had only to consult the popular plays and novels of the day. A crude woodcut of the encounter became the cover of a popular pamphlet ("a full, impartial and thrilling account of that horrible tragedy"), its caption not relating anything that Ellen is likely to have said but what by the lights of contemporary melodrama she ought to have said: "'Oh! Frank what have you done! what have you done! Ten thousand times would I rather have died than that you should have raised your hand against your father!' wept the wretched mother."

The *New York Times* depicted Frank as weeping in his mother's arms, smoothing her hair, and murmuring, "I love you more than my life." "Young Walworth," the paper concluded, "even by the most trivial attentions, showed how deeply he loved and reverenced her." The horror of parricide—a crime, according to many commentators on the case, previously unfamiliar in American annals; a crime so rare as to be known only to the remote antiquity of Greek tragedy—was juxtaposed disturbingly with that mother love that was the central shrine of American sentimentality. "If Frank Walworth goes from his prison cell to the ignominy of the gallows," one sympathizer told a newspaper, "he will die a martyr to the religion of his life—a sacrificial offering to a divine love."

Not everyone, of course, was sentimentally inclined. The close bond between Ellen and Frank did not necessarily have anything to do with remorse or grief. Might not more sinister complicities be at work? A writer for the *Graphic* reported that he had observed the pair "laughing and in very excellent spirits." Both mother and son, after all, were creatures of privilege. Holding themselves superior to ordinary Americans, they might well believe that the laws did not apply to them. At the very least it could be assumed that, since Frank's present situation was so intolerable a contradiction of the status to which he had been born, the Walworth family must surely be exerting all its power to sabotage the workings of justice.

NOT only had Frank fallen from the heights, he had done so in plain view, and was now constantly on display as he had never been when he walked free. By entering the Tombs, he had become part of a roster of celebrated rogues who even behind bars were given continual press coverage. The doings at the prison could be relied on for entertaining copy, couched in a style of cynical humor at odds with the moralizing of the editorial page. The Tombs constituted a rowdy world within a world, a sleazy theater where corruption was presumed to be rampant, and where thieves and murderers were lionized as social luminaries.

Frank had entered quite a distinguished company of killers. He was lodged next door to a murderer named David Murphy who was awaiting execution, and found himself a close neighbor of the notorious Edward Stokes, the financier who had assassinated "Big Jim" Fisk, his rival in business and love, in the lobby of the Grand Central Hotel on New Year's Eve of 1871. Another Wall Street type, the stockbroker James C. King, was awaiting trial for the murder of a railroad detective slated to be a hostile character witness in King's upcoming divorce proceedings. Also in residence and much in the newspapers was William Sharkey, a Tammany ward heeler and "sporting gentleman," on trial for his life, following many delays and legal maneuverings, after killing a gambler named Bob Dunn in a Hudson Street barroom the previous September. John Scannell, a Tammany hanger-on somewhat lower on the totem pole than Sharkey, had ended up in the Tombs in the wake of a poolroom killing during the last election. Even Zack Simmons, a downtown numbers runner who had stabbed one of his competitors to death in a street altercation, found himself transformed into a kind of celebrity, one of the "Lions of the Tombs."

It was an open question whether either the wealthy Stokes or the politically connected Sharkey would be made to pay for their misdeeds. Skepticism was warranted. During Frank's stay at the Tombs, a party of several hundred well-wishers gathered there to congratulate Stokes on the success of his latest appeal (he would ultimately serve no more than four years for Fisk's killing); while Sharkey, once he had been convicted of murder, would manage to fend off the carrying out of his death sentence long enough to engineer a dramatic escape in women's clothing the following autumn. (He made his way to England and was never seen on American soil again.)

Corruption high and low was the common theme of the moment. New York was reeling from the exposure of the Tweed ring and its multiple frauds, even as Tweed himself continued to evade the reach of the law, while in Washington the Grant administration was awash in a tide of barely concealed graft; shortly the grubby details of the Crédit Mobilier scandal would begin to unfold. The impunity of the rich and powerful might elicit outrage or resignation, but it seemed a fact of life, and the desperadoes of the Five Points seemed positively upright in their straightforward criminality compared to the devious and hypocritical malefactors of the upper classes.

Frank Walworth looked to many like one more privileged character destined to escape justice, and for a crime of unparalleled hideousness. Certainly he did not lack for legal representation, and one paper ventured to insinuate that his lawyers "seem to be retained in advance." The family of Chancellor Walworth, who had once dominated New York's legal system, knew where to turn for the most reliable help in that line. It was not every murder suspect who had a Superior Court judge and a former district attorney on call; and for the leader of Frank's defense team, a figure even more commanding had been called in.

Before Frank saw his mother on Thursday morning, he had already received an important visitor in his cell. In the early hours of the morning he had been waited on by Charles O'Conor, perhaps the most famous trial lawyer in America, and it was soon announced in the papers that his services had been retained. O'Conor was a legendary courtroom performer, eloquent and sarcastic by turns, whose admiring colleagues invoked his "imperial faculties" of memory and analysis. Not all were admirers; for the acerbic George Templeton Strong, "he began his career as a low Irishman and worked his way up by energy, industry, and a talent for bitter vituperation . . . I fear he is a bad and mischievous man."

O'Conor was celebrated for having turned the tables on the choleric Shakespearean actor Edwin Forrest, in his divorce suit against his allegedly adulterous wife, by bringing Forrest's own misbehavior to bear against him with damning authority. A strident defender of Irish nationalism and the Catholic Church, O'Conor had likewise, before the war, been outspoken as an upholder of slavery and had made himself a mouthpiece for the many New Yorkers sympathetic to the southern cause: "It is not injustice," he had argued, "to leave the negro in the condition in which nature placed him, and for which alone he is adapted."

Now in his seventies, the lawyer showed signs of impaired health—"O'Conor's face is much shriveled," an observer wrote, "and his eyes look as though he had just got through a fit of weeping"—and in other ways as well seemed a man of another era. His impassioned defense of Jefferson Davis, when the Confederate president was arraigned for treason after the war, had done his reputation little good, and the fierce partisan—after a doomed run for president as a states' rights, anti-Reconstruction "Straight-Up Democrat"—was finding it a good time to distance himself from politics. He had never really accepted the war's outcome, feeling only (in a colleague's words) "aversion to, and distrust of, the new political authorities that were put in charge of the National Government." As a lawyer his prestige was undiminished, and he was already deeply involved in the efforts that would eventually bring Mayor Tweed to justice and restore some measure of probity to a city far gone in fiscal turpitude.

His ties with the Walworths went back decades. He had been in and out of Chancellor Walworth's courtroom in Saratoga countless times, and when the Chancellor, in what turned out to be his last hurrah as a political hopeful, had run for governor as a prosouthern Hunker Democrat in 1848, O'Conor had been his running mate. Some thought it astonishing, nonetheless, that so distinguished a man should stake his reputation on what looked like an unwinnable case.

Talking to the press, O'Conor was full of characteristic bluster. Frank was bearing up, not with unnatural coolness as accused, but "bravely and quietly, with a calmness that is certainly remarkable. There is not the slightest indication of fear, and scarcely of sorrow." And was this not strange under the circumstances? Not at all, O'Conor shot back: "It is the soldier spirit and blood that are in him." After all, his maternal grandfather Colonel John Hardin, who had been killed at the Battle of Buena Vista in the Mexican War, had been a great hero, "as brave as Julius Caesar." No cowering parricide, Frank was the plucky defender of his mother against the man for whom O'Conor reserved his strongest blast: "I knew [Mansfield] Walworth well . . . It was scarcely possible to conceive of a worse man; he was bad in grain, and his badness was the more contemptible because it was united to a character that was very frivolous and inane." Facts would come out at the trial, he promised, that would show just how bad Mansfield was: "No person justifies murder, but these circumstances are extenuating."

While O'Conor readied his client's defense, the press was doing a good job of trying Frank in advance. The city papers came down hard on him. "No life," declared the *Sun,* "was ever taken more intentionally." Even as they acknowledged that Mansfield Walworth was "savage, sottish, and licentious," and recounted what they knew of his rumored history of threats and violence, the New York journals had little sympathy to spare for his killer.

Whatever pleas on Frank's behalf had made it into print emanated not from editorials but from Frank's legal counsel or various friends and relations, not always identified by name. The attempts to justify or at least explain what he had done were jumbled and contradictory: he had acted out of derangement; he had acted in self-defense; he had responded with legitimate force to intolerable threats; he was pushed over the edge by the social humiliations to which, in Saratoga, his father's bad conduct laid him open; he had acted in the only way a son so devoted to his mother could act.

The same newspapers that were happy to dramatize the lachrymose side of the story in describing scenes like Ellen's reunion with her son were harsh when it came to cutting Frank any moral slack. The *Brooklyn Eagle* denounced the manner in which "the sacred name of mother is lugged in to heroize the blackest deed of modern times." The paper made light of Mansfield's misdoings, and hinted at premeditation: "His son and murderer parrots a pretty tale of provocation, as if he had learned it as a part . . . This sensational murdering must be stopped. The gallows, stern, sure and swift, is the remedy."

In a follow-up editorial, the *Eagle* continued to rail against "the introduction of the mother element into the Walworth affair": "He is said to have been spurred to it by the contemplation of his mother's suffering under his father's persecutions, and by the taunts of his companions, the hot-house products of New York tailors and Saratoga society . . . Evidently all the resources of bathos and sentimentality are at work in behalf of the dear parricide." The *Tribune* added a seconding voice to this line of attack: "A son avenges the wrongs of an injured mother—that will be the key-note of the defense when the prisoner is brought to the bar. We protest in advance against such resort to maudlin sentimentality."

The Nation advised Frank's unnamed friends to steer clear of "any of the attempts at whitewashing or exciting 'sympathy' . . . unfortunately entered on in some quarters." In the eyes of some commentators, these attempts at influencing public feeling amounted to conspiracy. A letter to the *Brooklyn Eagle* asserted that "secret means are at work to establish a public opinion in favor of what you justly style an unnatural murder by a brutal boy." The ultimate source of these "secret means" was no secret at all. Upstate, the *Troy Press* raged: "Will the young man be hung? Of course not. The grandson of Chancellor Walworth can never be hung. He belongs to a privileged class. Old friends of the late Chancellor will step in to save him, to save the honor of the name, as if the name could be more tarnished than it is . . . A rich man, or a man of good family, cannot be hanged. Else why is Stokes alive to-day?"

Back in Saratoga a very different sentiment prevailed. "The general conviction here," wrote the *Daily Saratogian* the day after the murder, "is that he was not entirely in his right mind when he went to New York, and that the deed was committed in a condition of partial insanity," and the next day the paper confidently predicted that "the defense of young Walworth will be insanity." In any event the *Saratogian* and its local readers had clearly rallied behind Frank and expected him to be exonerated of the crime—"if crime it shall prove to be." He was their boy, and they understood his character and motives far better than could the big city journalists: "As usual, when a tragedy of startling character occurs . . . the New York city journalists lose their heads. They seem to have lost their sense utterly since the Walworth affair, and in treating of it editorially all, save the *Times*, talk like lunatics." (The *Times* had avoided taking a strong position, on the grounds that not enough was yet known.)

The *Saratogian* would wage a ceaseless battle in defense of Frank: "It is our belief that young Walworth shot his father either in self-defense or in a momentary fit of insanity . . . We cannot believe that the shooting was premeditated." The defense of family honor, something of which New York urbanites took a rather jaded view, was a live issue in Saratoga, especially when the family in question was linked so intimately to the town's history. Saratogians knew Frank and knew his family, understood the long gestation of this event, and resented the intrusion of strangers into such delicate and difficult affairs. When an Albany paper, in a rare show of sympathy for the murder victim, wrote of Mansfield's "manly form and gentleness of manner," which it suggested would be "sadly missed at the summer resort of fashion," the *Saratogian* retorted: "The writers who thus describe Mansfield Tracy Walworth either never knew the subject of their remarks, or else they knew him very slightly, or they would not use such terms of one whose depraved and vulgar tastes and habits and brutal temper are well known here in Saratoga."

But what did New York City, in 1873, care about the family of Chancellor Walworth, or indeed about Saratoga itself as anything but an old-fashioned, overcrowded summer resort for people who lacked the social connections for Newport? Two days after the murder, the *Sun* audaciously hinted that the revered Chancellor Walworth— whom the paper described as "vain, conceited, loquacious, irascible, always overbearing, often grossly partial," and given to citing absurd precedents from Arabian and Hindu law—might well have shared some of the madness of his offspring. Noble old upstate families were the currency of comedy for tough-minded tabloid reporters, especially when their most distinguished scion turned out to be a "murdering whelp" dressed as a newspaper reader's idea of a dude, with boots and sideburns designed to demonstrate that everything was up-to-date in the greater Albany region.

Frank, a parricide for mother and family, was nothing but an embarrassing exposure of the secret decadence of such old monied lineages. Those self-nominated patricians who had for so long exercised a stranglehold on upstate politics, while flaunting their wizened teetotaling virtue in the face of the vibrant Gomorrah at the mouth of the Hudson, now looked like the creaky figurines in antique woodcuts. There was a certain satisfaction in seeing this foppish mother's boy from Saratoga, the spoiled product of boarding schools and starched cotillions, tossed among the worldly-wise pimps, whores, and confidence men of Manhattan.

Tʜᴇ coroner's inquest was scheduled for ten o'clock Friday morning, June 6, at the Twenty-ninth Precinct, but at the appointed time—with Coroner Nelson Young, District Attorney Benjamin Phelps, and a six-man jury punctually in place—there was no sign of Frank.

Rumors circulated through the large crowd that had assembled outside the building. Perhaps Frank's lawyers had advised him not to appear. Perhaps the boy had committed suicide. At exactly noon a coach drove up, delivering Frank, his police escort, and his attorneys O'Conor and Garvin. With what was described as "a careless, jaunty walk," Frank entered the building, a mob of spectators swarming in after him.

A reporter moving through the crowd attempted to give his readers an idea of what he overheard: "Why he's a nice looking young fellow at any rate." "I don't think he is. He looks just like what he is, a mean coward!" "Oh, no! There's no coward about that chap. He's true grit!" "It don't make any difference whether he's brave or cowardly, he had no right to kill his father." "He ought to have shot the old scoundrel years ago . . . If a woman's own son won't defend her, who will?" "I tell you, gentlemen, when a stripling like Frank Walworth does that, it is getting time for society to look after itself . . . We want fewer new trials, appeals, stays of proceedings, pardons, and such nonsense, and more of the hangman's rope." "That's so! You're right, sir. That's a fact."

It had been a sunny morning, but as the inquest got under way the sky rapidly darkened, and a violent storm broke out. Gas lamps had to be lit for the hearing to proceed. All eyes were on Frank, who preserved the same composure he had maintained all along, occasionally drumming with his fingers on the table, but otherwise watching with polite attentiveness as a succession of witnesses recreated the events of

Monday and Tuesday. Mansfield's landlady, Mrs. Sims, and various staff members and tenants from the Sturtevant contributed their fragments of knowledge, as the court set about establishing Frank's movements from his arrival in the city to his arrest the next morning.

The audience seemed more moved than Frank Walworth himself by the recital of what had happened. When Mansfield's bloodied calling card was held up in court, there was a perceptible shock among the onlookers, but no one detected the least tremor from Frank. Only once—when his neighboring lodger Moorehead clapped his hands four times to indicate the rhythm of the gunshots—did he seem ever so slightly rattled.

The nature of Mansfield's wounds were described in elaborate detail by the deputy coroner. Mansfield had died, in Dr. Marsh's estimation, of "shock and internal hemorrhage," but only one of the four bullets had been necessarily fatal: the one that had passed through the second and third ribs, penetrating the chest on the left side, six inches above the nipple, filling the left lung with blood and fluid and lodging finally in the second dorsal vertebra. The examining physicians had experienced "great trouble" in locating the fatal bullet. The victim had been otherwise healthy. One of the bullets—the one that passed through his face on the right side and pulverized his left jaw—had been left in place because removing it would have disfigured the corpse.

Finally it was Frank's turn to testify. He answered the initial routine inquiries in a firm voice: his name was Francis Hardin Walworth; he was nineteen years old; he was born and lived in Saratoga; he had no regular occupation. Now Coroner Young asked, "Have you anything to say, and if so what, relative to the charge here preferred against you?" After a quick whispered consultation with O'Conor, Frank addressed the court in clear tones: "I am guilty of no crime."

Pausing to let this sink in, he added, "I will make a statement." He reached into his pocket for a document which he proceeded to read aloud at a calm and measured pace, allowing the clerk—and the reporters—ample time to get his brief but dramatic narrative down correctly.

> My father treated my mother very cruelly for years, incensed against his own father for putting his little share of the property in trust, so that my mother and the family got something

out of it. My father kept writing letters to my mother full of imprecations against his father. He wrote to her among other things, "I will kill your boys and defeat the damned scoundrel in his grave, & cut off his damned name forever." He also threatened my mother's life, spoke of shots being suddenly heard from his resentment. About three years ago, he beat my mother cruelly. I was not present but saw the marks . . .

When I heard this, I loaded a pistol belonging to a cousin of mine, and have carried it. I supposed my father was armed at least when he intended to see us. My uncle Clarence Walworth has been as a father to us. He recently proposed taking me to Europe with him. I was troubled about leaving my mother without a protector. On Sunday last I wrote thus to my uncle, and that I must go and see my father & whether I could go to Europe or not could depend on that interview. In fact I wanted to get reliable assurance that he should not molest my mother during my absence . . .

I had no intention of killing him: when he came into my room I asked him to sit down. He did so. I spoke to him of his conduct and said, "Promise me that you will neither shoot my mother nor insult her or any of the family any further." He answered me, "I promise," but with a look which to my mind implied contempt, and the reverse of an intent to keep the promise. He had just before put his hand up to his breast, as if to pull out a pistol. I am unconscious of having fired more than three times. He closed on me rapidly. His grasp was upon me when I fired the last time. I do not think that he said anything during the whole interview except what I have stated.

When he had finished he folded the paper, put it back in his pocket, and sat down with no visible emotion—except perhaps a barely repressed air of self-satisfaction. "The reading," a reporter noted, "produced a most painful impression." Many in the crowded room afterward expressed revulsion at what they had heard, and the manner in which it had been delivered.

The whole affair had taken five hours. Frank seated himself again in the carriage and was whisked back to the Tombs to await the action of the grand jury.

THREE days later the grand jury rendered its verdict, recommending that Frank be indicted for murder in the first degree. The official document described in sonorous terms how Frank, with "a certain pistol then and there charged and loaded with gunpowder and one leaden bullet . . . then and there feloniously, willfully, and of his 'malice afore-thought,' did strike, penetrate, and wound in and upon the body of him the said Mansfield T. Walworth one mortal wound of the breadth of one inch and of the depth of four inches, of which said mortal wound he the said Mansfield T. Walworth . . . did instantly die."

4

≈≈≈≈≈≈

Early Life of a Chancellor

F RANK'S mother had not attended the inquest. She had left the
city the night before, taking a steamer up the Hudson to make it
back to Saratoga for the burial of her husband. Some had supposed
that Ellen would not attend Mansfield's last rites, but it was not her
way to neglect social forms no matter how little they mirrored inward
realities. As much as possible, everything would be conducted in the
appropriate manner.

On Thursday night Mansfield's body remained on ice in Mr.
Senior's funeral parlor on Carmine Street. At three in the morning the
refrigerated coffin was opened for inspection, and the body was found
to be frozen through. The late novelist—well-known for his dandyish
obsession with sartorial fashion—was dressed for the last time in a
plain black suit, and laid in a silver-plated coffin of black walnut. "His
face," a newspaper reported, "though somewhat disfigured and decom-
posed, still presented many traces of the manly beauty for which in his
early days he had been celebrated." A prayer was said over him, and
the remains were taken by hearse to Grand Central Station, to be sent
up to Saratoga, by way of Albany, on the eight o'clock train.

A large crowd gathered at the station in Saratoga to greet the coffin as the train arrived from New York, at just after three in the after-

noon. About a dozen carriages followed the hearse to Greenridge Cemetery. Eight of Saratoga's most distinguished citizens carried the coffin through the iron picket fence surrounding the little hillock in the center of the cemetery—the commanding position—where Chancellor Walworth was buried alongside his first wife, Maria Averill, the pious and much-mourned mother of Mansfield, Clarence, and their three sisters. Ellen, looking exhausted, leaned on Clarence's arm, while she held the hand of Frank's little brother, eleven-year-old Tracy. Her mother, Sarah—the chancellor's second and much younger wife—stood nearby, and other family members gathered around the grave as a brief Episcopal service was read. Perfect decorum was observed during the ceremony. A wreath of white flowers had been placed on the coffin. An observer noted that "the tone of the funeral was distant, but not cold," and added: "There were no manifestations of grief."

SARAH and Ellen, mother and daughter, stood together by the graveside—as they did six years earlier when Sarah's husband, the Chancellor, was interred in the fall of 1867—and fifteen years before that to bury Sarah and the Chancellor's first and only son, Reuben Hyde Walworth Jr., dead in his sixth month.

Sarah and Ellen were Hardins from the Kentucky-Illinois frontier. As they watched the dirt being shoveled over Mansfield's coffin, mother and daughter must have given some thought to how they came to be standing at this gravesite in this northern place, among Yankees who had once seemed an alien breed but with whom they had now become one. But only in a sense; there was a line of division that even twenty years of intermingling could not erase.

There were Walworths, with their own peculiar sense of history and identity, their special claims on the world as they found it, and there were Hardins. The Hardins married the Walworths and that was where the trouble began.

They had both married into the house of the Chancellor. It had all happened very fast. Sarah, widowed when her husband was killed in the Mexican War, had accepted the Chancellor's timely proposal and moved with her three children to Saratoga. Less than a year after her marriage, her daughter Ellen had become engaged to the chancellor's son Mansfield. Within a year of mourning the infant son of the Chancellor and Sarah, they were celebrating the birth of Mansfield and Ellen's firstborn, Frank. At that time Ellen had been only a year or so older than Frank was now.

Even if they may finally have come to feel as if they had been taken prisoner, in the beginning the Walworth home must have seemed like a place of refuge. Otherwise why would they have left the much-regretted country of their origins? For years they had all lived together within the confines of Pine Grove—still in its original narrower dimensions—and when that had become impossible, or intolerable, they had continued to share a closely connected life, inescapably chained to one another. Today Frank was on Murderers' Row in the Tombs, and Mansfield was being laid to something resembling rest near his father on the Walworths' mortuary hillock.

But what manner of people, finally, were these Walworths upon whom their lives had been shipwrecked in such unexpected fashion?

Becoming part of the Walworth family must have seemed an attractive destiny to embrace. Chancellor Reuben Hyde Walworth was an institution in himself—even if in truth he was, when Sarah married him, already past the high noon of his splendor. He was no longer even chancellor, ever since a New York State constitutional convention had (in response to widespread demand) abolished the post in 1848, although he would continue to be accorded the title out of respect for the rest of his days. And by the time he died of diabetes at seventy-nine, even his later career as a prestigious legal adviser was in abeyance. He had long since retired from the public eye and had become a kind of living relic of the now fondly recalled antebellum period. So much had happened in so short a time that to probe the roots of a career like the Chancellor's was to enter a world already quaint.

Yet was not the American world one in which quaintness was the fate of each succeeding era? So mercilessly did the Age of Speed erase the comforts and habits to which each generation had clung that the past became invisible almost before it could properly be seen. For a man to speak of his father's childhood was already to evoke a time not only of altered manners but of altered landscapes. Rivers thickened with the debris of new industries. Immense cities grew up along freshly dredged canal routes. Railroad cars erased the visual memory of abundant unfenced hunting grounds.

Consider, for instance, Pine Grove. When the future Chancellor Walworth—then a newly appointed circuit judge with three young daughters and a newborn son, a veteran of the War of 1812, fresh from serving a term in Congress—first acquired the place in 1823, it was a thickly forested property with a small Federal-style house one and a half stories high. The house was set in the midst of woods and groves that the Chancellor, as his fortunes steadily improved, would buy up lot by lot. Where the railroad would soon run was all trees. (The Chancellor, as it happened, had a good deal to do with the coming of the railroad, helping to clear the way for it with a legal decision allowing the overriding of private property rights in the public interest. The rail magnates were duly appreciative and gave him political support throughout his career.) The center of Saratoga Springs, spreading outward from the salubrious waters of High Rock and Congress springs, still seemed quite removed—with bogs and thickets to impede travelers—even if the distance between upper and lower villages was little more than a mile.

Reuben Hyde Walworth acquired his residence at just the moment when Saratoga's already considerable stature was on the verge of a phenomenal expansion. The village had for several decades been emerging as a place of national importance, in a nation short on gathering places for people from different regions. A handful of local entrepreneurs had systematically exploited the fame of the local springs, to which extraordinary healing and preventative powers had been attributed, and created an artificial and fashionable playground for a small but moneyed tourist class. It started with nothing but the foul-smelling waters.

WHEN George Washington visited in 1783 in the company of an Italian nobleman, Count Francesco dal Verme, there were no tourist amenities in the vicinity, merely, as the count observed, "three springs whose water is very cold and constantly bubbling . . . The water has a salty taste and smells of sulphur. Many use it for treating gout, dropsy, and asthma." That was sufficient recommendation. By 1793 the New York physician Valentine Seaman had published his *Dissertation on the Mineral Waters of Saratoga,* which mixed hard science with a mystic yearning for a natural panacea, "a water, in some neglected valley, whose solvent quality . . . may melt down the torturing stone, or whose penetrating influence may root out the scrofula from the system."

The emerging spa even had an appropriately atmospheric myth of origin, cultivated by locals even if lacking historical evidence. It told how the ailing Sir William Johnson, the legendary superintendent of Indian affairs who had married the sister of the Mohawk war chief Joseph Brant and carved out a sort of baronial fiefdom for himself along the Mohawk, was in 1767 carried by tribesmen in a litter over remote forest trails—"amid a wild and strange chant raised by the Indians to their deity"—to a bark lodge by a spring. The spring's waters healed the effects of a leg wound sustained in the French and Indian War, and Sir William was able to continue his journey on foot. These waters were said to be none other than High Rock Spring, around which the village would grow. The story helped give the place an indispensable patina of ancient and secret knowledge; the uncorrupted natives threading a path through "the land of crooked waters" was the stuff of poetry.

General Philip Schuyler carved a trail from High Rock to his estate on the Hudson in the early 1780s, and within a few years Gideon Putnam was operating a prosperous sawmill in Saratoga. From then on things moved quickly. Putnam built the village's first hotel in 1802, and before his death in 1811 had begun construction of the much more ambitious Congress Hall. This establishment—whose wide frontage and spacious columned piazzas set the style for generations of ever more grandiose Saratoga hotels, and which by 1819 boasted an orchestra and a billiard room—was adjacent to Congress Spring, by common consent sovereign among Saratoga's waters.

Saratoga quite rapidly became an unavoidable destination for travelers. In the same year that Walworth bought Pine Grove, the village received as many as twelve hundred visitors. John Clarke, a retired Manhattan businessman who enjoyed the distinction of having opened New York's first soda fountain, purchased the land containing Congress Spring and its neighbor Columbian Spring, and around them laid out Congress Park, a landscaped pleasure ground featuring pavilions and a running brook—and, in the fullness of time, a Greek temple and a sixty-foot water tower disguised as an Egyptian obelisk.

Congress Park became the center of Saratoga's social life. A visitor

from Utica in 1822 observed what had already become a ritualized feature of the summer season: "Got up early this morning and walked to
Congress Spring. The water rises in a square box and is dipped with
tumblers by youths who serve you in expectation of pay . . . There are
about 800 strangers at Saratoga, most of whom drink this water every
morning." John Clarke also set about bottling the water from Congress
Spring, creating a durable industrial operation which by 1830 was
shipping some twelve hundred bottles a day of the world-famous Congress Water.

In the tourist literature that was beginning to remap the nation
as a network of attractions—its tone typified by the title of Caroline
Gilman's *Poetry of Traveling in the United States* (1838)—Saratoga came
to represent a lyrical summit, an artificial preserve of civilized pleasures
to balance the sublime natural wonders of Niagara and the Catskills. It
was also becoming a place where the powerful of New York State and
the nation could expect to run into one another. By becoming part of its
core of property owners, Walworth had sealed his membership in an
exclusive club.

WHEN he arrived in Saratoga, Reuben Hyde Walworth was a coming
man at the turning point of an already very promising career. A preco-
ciously successful young Plattsburgh lawyer who had served with
honor in the militia during the War of 1812, he was emerging as a man
of some national distinction. Having cast his political lot with Martin
Van Buren and the so-called Albany Regency that would dominate
state politics for decades, Colonel Walworth had been elected to a term
in Congress and then, at thirty-three, gotten himself appointed circuit
judge for New York's fourth district, encompassing a wide upstate area.
For a farm boy (born in 1788 on his father's farm in Bozrah, Connecticut, and raised in Hoosick, New York) with little in the way of formal
education, he had not done badly, and expected to do much better.

Not that there was any cause for shame in his family origins. Anything but ignorant diggers of the soil, the Walworths saw themselves
as honorable and distinguished yeoman farmers whose roots were historic. Reuben's father would have taught him early on to cherish the
accounts of their English ancestors. The outstanding figure was Sir
William Walworth, the lord mayor of London who slew the rebel

leader Wat Tyler during the peasant revolt of 1381, coming to the rescue of Richard II. The family's motto—STRIKE FOR THE LAWS—commemorated this signal event. The Walworth coat of arms, which Reuben displayed in his courtroom, bore in its center the image of an "arm grasping a dagger sinister imbrued gules"—stained scarlet, that is, in striking for the laws. The image may have encouraged Judge Walworth on those occasions, in his circuit days, when he sentenced more than one wrongdoer to death.

The first of the American Walworths, William, had come over from London in the 1680s to help establish an agricultural settlement on Fisher's Island in the Long Island Sound. William would subsequently remove to Groton, Connecticut, where he enjoyed prosperity as a farmer and stockbreeder and fathered seven children. His sons, in the words of a later chronicler (the Chancellor's son Clarence, who inherited his father's taste for genealogical researches), "had money in abundance, which they spent freely in buying more land." Some of the land they acquired had formed part of the territories of the Pequots, before the tribe's devastation in the Pequot War.

In general the Walworths had little cause to complain about how the New World had treated them. The Chancellor's grandfather John Walworth enriched himself further in the West Indian sugar and molasses trade, and on his Fisher's Island property alone was possessed of "four negro servants, a herd of fifty horned cattle, eight hundred and twelve sheep, and a study of thirty-two horses, mares and colts" along with "seventy-seven ounces of wrought silver plate, and other valuable household articles."

IN their first century in the New World the bent of the Walworths seems to have been to reproduce themselves as prolifically as possible and to get hold of tracts of land commensurate with their numbers. No great dramas adhered to their name, only a long pastoral idyll of profitable accumulation. The coming of the Revolutionary War shook things up a bit, and during a few years many members of the extended family had a rough or at least perilously exciting time of it. Young Reuben, born seven years after the British defeat at Yorktown, grew up on endlessly repeated accounts of these battles and ordeals.

His father, Benjamin, fought at White Plains in 1776 and was present at the raid by the notorious half-Mohawk renegade Brant on Minisink in 1779. Family lore preserved the story of how he had passed unknowingly through a line of Indians waiting in ambush, the savages sparing him only to avoid revealing their presence. Reuben's uncle Sylvester was among those massacred in 1781 at Fort Griswold by British troops under the command of the traitor Benedict Arnold, on that ghastly day when "the wounded were thrown into carts, which, by their own weight, plunged, with their writhing freight, furiously down the rocky declivity toward the Thames." His uncle John and John's wife, abducted by Indians near the site of the Battle of Bennington, were taken by them to the British camp as prisoners. His cousin Samuel, who served with the Continental army in the Hudson Valley, died of wounds received in the war.

After the war Reuben's father married a sea captain's widow—there was a delicate hint in family accounts that they had been quite fond of each other even before the captain was lost at sea—and, giving up his earlier trade of hatter, retired to devote himself to his farm, his grist mill, and his growing brood. That was what you did if you were a man: you farmed, had a good many children, and led them with stern affection toward righteousness; if you had the gift and energy for it, you participated as well in the running of things, making and administering laws, upholding religion, and establishing necessary local institutions.

Reuben's mother, Apphia Hyde, the sea captain's widow, seems to have been a remarkable as well as long-lived woman. (She would outlive her husband by a quarter of a century, dying in 1837.) Known for a tenacious memory and a gift for storytelling, she gave her son his primary education in American political and military history, so much of which had unfolded during her lifetime. "Mrs. Walworth was a lady of uncommon intellect, the vigor of which she retained to her latest moments," a newspaper obituary (quite likely drafted by Reuben himself) noted. "Listening to her, one could almost fancy he was living over the scenes of border warfare." Reuben may have felt that he enjoyed a special legacy from his mother in his own much-vaunted keenness of recollection; in any event he would spend a good part of his later life exhaustively studying her family tree, producing in his two-volume *Hyde Genealogy* a work of unprecedented length in which her bloodline was traced back to the royal family of Scotland.

The little that would be remembered about Reuben's early life had to do with dogged perseverance. His schooling was at home, but he learned well, and focused more on his studies after an ankle injury from a capsizing hay cart temporarily disabled him for farming. From his half-brother William Cardell, the sea captain's son, he learned the rudiments of Latin, as much as he would ever need in his legal career. This Cardell was a man of some note: a teacher of French, a philosopher of language, and the author of well-received homiletic works such as *Jack Halyard, the Sailor Boy*, a bestseller by the desultory standards of his day. But at this date such enterprises were unlikely to bring in much revenue; to be an author was an accomplishment, perhaps, but scarcely a profession, and for all the prestige of his scholarship Cardell died penniless. Reuben by contrast always displayed a sharp instinct for the main chance. A sufficiently apt pupil to scavenge enough of his half-brother's learning to compensate for lack of college training, he also had the sense to make better practical use of it.

The contacts Reuben made when he went off to Troy to study law at eighteen would serve him well; his fellow students included the future governor of New York (William Marcy, formulator of the memorable Jacksonian dictum that to the victors belong the spoils) and the future chief justice of Michigan. After three years—during which time he slept in a bunk in the law office where he was studying—he established a partnership up near the Canadian border in Plattsburgh with an old legal acquaintance from Hoosick.

He seems to have made himself indispensable to such persons of property and influence as could be found in the Plattsburgh region, taking part in any available genteel amusements and cultivating a personal charm that would distinguish him from the common run of farmers and merchants. He wrote letters to young women, in an elaborate style copied from books and wielded with a certain roughness: "Friendship then, like the Mentor of Tellemachus, shall direct and control my every action. With this pole star for my guide though my little bark may be driven by the storms of Passion out of its proper course, I trust it will never get foundered on the quicksands of vice but will at last arrive safe at the port of happiness."

Plattsburgh was far enough out on the edge of things that his student days in Troy seemed by contrast a golden time. In 1810, on his twenty-second birthday, he wrote to a friend in Troy: "This day is the twenty second anniversary of my birth but it is the most solemncholly one I have ever known. I have been seated in my office alone during the whole day, excepting indeed the short visits of two or three clients and my mind has been so entirely vacant that it was but a few hours since that I recollected this was my natal day . . . Somehow there is a kind of dullness or stupor reigns here eternally and seems to pervade all classes." It was as unguarded a mood as he would ever commit to paper: alone with a vacant mind in an empty law office in the most boring town in America. Later he would learn to keep his schedule so full that there would be few opportunities for such moments. He was born not to mope but to succeed: "I had rather be called almost anything than a poor lawyer."

He had the knack for situating himself in the middle of promising developments. In Plattsburgh he began piling up titles: justice of the peace, master in chancery, supreme court commissioner. He became a Mason, an almost inevitable step at this time and place for anyone who wanted to be part of the inner circle of decision makers: the secret society attracted such a large portion of ambitious politicians and judicial figures that to some it seemed linked to pervasive collusion. He married Maria Averill, a girl of prosperous family, in 1812.

A new round of difficult days was in the offing. War had broken out between the States and England, and Plattsburgh, exposed on the northern border, would experience the ravages of a British raid in which many homes were destroyed or (like Reuben's) badly damaged.

IN the end the war would turn out to be a good thing for Reuben. At the opening of hostilities he was already regarded as a promising figure. Despite his relative inexperience, in the spring of 1814 he was appointed judge advocate in the trial of an English spy who had come to Plattsburgh disguised as a deserter. He conducted the proceedings to general satisfaction, and at age twenty-four passed his first sentence of death.

When the British returned in early September with the largest army ever to invade American soil, Reuben found himself in the thick of some chaotic action as a militiaman serving as aide to General Benjamin Mooers. Carrying messages under cover of darkness between the militia and the regular infantry, attempting to dismantle a bridge to delay the invaders before enemy fire proved too strong, participating in a confused series of retreats and rallies throughout a long night, he distinguished himself reasonably well in his first and only major experience of combat.

After the war he plunged, along with his former commander General Mooers, into local business—the two became cofounders of the Bank of Plattsburgh—and into state politics. New York had long been dominated by the seigneurial governor De Witt Clinton, with his lofty and not always credible claims to transcend party factionalism, but Reuben and Mooers sided with the upstart contingent of anti-Clintonian "Bucktail" Democrats, becoming part of a new establishment that would effectively run things—or at least a suitably large share of things—for decades to come.

The Bucktails—whom the Whig leader Thurlow Weed described as "Van Buren's pimps"—prided themselves on their plainspoken opposition to the aristocratic pretensions of Clinton and the great landowners who exercised singular power in New York's upstate politics. Reuben, who liked to describe himself as a self-educated farm boy, was ideal for their image. He was to prove as well a reliable party loyalist and an all-around asset. Walworth was a man of accomplishment but not an innovator or a leader; a workhorse, a detail man; a joiner, at home in committees and conventions, perfect for after-dinner toasts even after he gave up intoxicating drinks. He could combine a public image of perfect honesty and disinterestedness with a keen grasp of the intricacies of deal-cutting and mutual back-scratching.

In his single term in Congress (1821–22), he discovered perhaps that the constant rough and tumble of political life was not for him, but he solidified indispensable political ties. The radical Democrat William Leggett, in a piece of political invective remarkable even for that unrestrained era, characterized him as thoroughly corrupted by his associations: "Marcy, Walworth, Dickinson, and others of the Albany Regency . . . are a set of creeping, dissembling creatures, who have grown fat on the dripping of unclean Bank Legislation; a knot of cat-paced, sly-faced, cringing, artful fellows, who go about among the members of the Legislature, smiling, and bowing, and shaking hands with all they meet, and disclosing their schemes in broken whispers,

eked out with knowing shrugs and nods—they are men who strive to
turn all political questions into a lever to raise up and set in motion
their own nasty, selfish projects."

For the rest of his career he would remain closely associated with
the men whose acquaintance he first made in the 1820s. Through the
strings they pulled he would secure the judicial appointments—first as
circuit judge and then, in a sudden upward leap, as chancellor—that
gave him a unique authority in New York's legal world. He had come
into something much more agreeable to him than the political battlefield: a judicial domain in which he enjoyed something like absolute rule.

WHILE Reuben was in Congress firming up the political connections
that would serve him so well, his twenty-six-year-old wife, Maria, was
back in Plattsburgh getting religion.

It was not that either of them lacked religion in the outward practices of their lives. Churchgoing and Bible-reading went without saying. It was in church—the Presbyterian Church whose doctrines he
would uphold all his days—that Reuben first caught sight of her: a
teenager who would later describe her youth as pampered and frivolous, given over to the temptations of earthly goods and pleasures.

External observances, nevertheless, were but the shell of faith. It was
only now that Maria, already the mother of three daughters and a son,
Clarence, born during the first nine years of her marriage, awoke to a real
calling for the spiritual life. Reverend Samuel Whelpley of Plattsburgh's
First Presbyterian Church kept the young congressman apprised by letter of his wife's spiritual progress: "Your dear wife is all alive. She is seen
at every meeting. Her whole soul appears engaged with religion. I am
astonished when I look at her—to behold the regularity of her walk, the
steadiness of her zeal and the solemnity of her whole deportment to me
she appears to be ripening fast for heaven." Reverend Whelpley even gen-
tly suggested that Congressman Walworth ought to take time out, amid
the morally questionable welter of Washington politics, to examine the
state of his own soul: "Take courage from her example and see that she
does not outstrip you in the heavenly race."

A gift of the spirit was descending on Plattsburgh; or at least Reverend Whelpley and his fellow church members hoped that "the times
are about to change and that we shall soon be visited with a Revival."

There was a yearning among them to recapture the enthusiasms of a few years back, when Plattsburgh had caught one of the waves of religious excitement that had been periodically sweeping across America since before the Revolution.

Such revivals were longed-for visitations, but they had their dangers. In the main they could be channeled into affirmations of orthodox belief. But the religious freedom promulgated in the new republic was also a freedom to invent new creeds and new forms of worship. In upstate New York the upholders of orthodoxy had their work cut out for them. Especially in its western reaches, sometimes called the "burned-over district," the state was a breeding ground for anomalies and excesses, notorious for a tendency toward enthusiasm bordering on heresy. Heresy could take bizarre forms.

Already by the turn of the century, Reuben's own aunt Sarah had, with her husband, gone off to become a follower of the Quaker prophetess Jemima Wilkinson, living out her life at Jerusalem, Jemima's communal settlement in Yates County, New York. This happened just after Reuben's birth, but he must have heard rumors about the flagrant errors and delusions of Jemima's followers: how they considered that the prophetess had transcended gender and achieved a kind of hermaphrodite identity which precluded referring to her as either "she" or "he" but rather as "the Universal Friend"; how her followers, who included people of high social standing and considerable wealth, a prominent judge among them, had given her all their worldly goods; how the women washed her feet and then dried them with their long hair, as Mary Magdalene had done for Jesus at that house in Bethany that filled with the odor of precious ointment.

Walworth and the other members of his congregation were on the frontier in more ways than one. The border between faith and fanaticism was porous. Solitary readers immersed in sacred words might find fearful meanings in them. A wrong turn—in thought as in the wilderness—could lead toward an ominously transformed world. A string of false prophets of all sorts would continue in the coming years to emerge out of western New York—the murderer and swindler Mathias, the Mormon revelator Joseph Smith, the communalist preacher John Humphrey Noyes of Oneida, with his exotic notions of group marriage—demonstrating just how easily religion's defenses could be broken by means of the very methods and language of religion. Sincerity might prove the worst trap of all.

It was to the appropriate channeling of such dangerous currents that the great midcentury revivalist preachers—charismatic spellbinders on the order of Elder Jacob Knapp and, later, Charles Grandison Finney—devoted their energies. Themselves operating independently of any particular established church, they addressed and converted multitudes, taking over whole cities for weeks on end with the fervor of their sermonizing. Such preachers might be recognized, at least in private, as fanatical, but they were fanatics on the right side of the line. Even the most conservative churchmen saw the need to provide outlets for the overflowing of religious emotion, while taking care not to let things spin out of control. Any degree of emotion might be tolerated, even encouraged, as long as it did not distort doctrinal rigor.

And so, in Plattsburgh, if a servant girl eavesdropping on revival talk among the women sprang up suddenly from her chair and—"struck under deep conviction"—cried out asking what she should do to be saved, begged them all to pray for her, and found no comfort in their repeated assurances, this was taken as a sign not of despair but of promise: "We feel as though we were on the eve of a glorious work." The local worshipers lived in an atmosphere thick with anticipation, studying friends and neighbors for traces of authentic feeling: "Our Sunday evening conferences . . . are solemn, animated and impressive. Deacon Platt . . . comes forward with confessions, enters fully into the spirit of our meetings and appears all alive. Mr. Trowbridge is also very much engaged—Mr. Nutting sighs—Mr. Winchel groans." At a recent meeting, Reverend Whelpley informed Walworth, "we had a melting time. Jesus, we trust, was present at the feast."

"All alive," "a melting time"—this was code language for the initiated; and a reminder for Reuben, caught up in the mundane skullduggery of the national capital, of the inner life of the community he had left behind. Alert to that reminder, he would take care to join the functions of lawmaker and magistrate to those of church elder and moral proselytizer. Again and again he assumed a leading role in the successive movements that swept the state in an era of religious ferment: the campaigns to make the Bible universally available, to establish Sunday schools, to foster absolute temperance, to rigorously enforce the observance of the Sabbath.

But even when involved in religious affairs, Reuben Hyde Walworth had a way of making them seem a branch of politics and law. All his activities were part of a ceaseless effort toward the rectification of social contracts, the maintenance of order, the sniffing out of whatever tended to corrode or slacken the invisible bonds that kept his world together. Visions were not his province. Where others saw flaming chariots about to break through the clouds, or heard voices of judgment proclaiming the imminent return of the Bridegroom, he was conscious merely of the inexorable working out of long-established precedents and procedures.

He had a satisfactory explanation for everything. If the Sabbath must be faithfully observed—even by canal and railroad workers who by working Sundays were eroding old practices—it was because history demonstrated that "the morals of the people soon became corrupted where the Sabbath . . . is spent by the mass of the people in secular employments, profane revelry, irreligious sports, or in traveling on business or for pleasure." In a keynote address to the National Sabbath Convention, he cited the overthrow of the Stuarts as God's punishment for James I's "impious declaration in favor of Sabbath sports in Lancashire," which had led inexorably to "dancing assemblies and other revelry, archery, vaulting and other sports of like nature." The Chancellor—as an accomplished vaulter who even late in life liked to jump over chairs in his sitting room—could certainly understand the temptation of such sports. He was not, however, in the habit of succumbing to temptation or of excusing those who did.

The practical details of religious morality might easily take on the tone of contract law. When, early in his legal career, he sent a donation of a hundred dollars to New York's mayor Cadwallader Colden for the relief of cholera victims during the epidemic of 1819, Walworth stipulated that help should go only to those who had proven themselves worthy of it. Any who had brought hard times on themselves through vice and idleness need not apply—nor even their loved ones, however blameless: "It is . . . my wish that no part of this trifling sum which has been honestly acquired by industry in my profession should be given even to the family of any who have not always supported a character for honesty, industry, frugality, and temperance." In a culture where, all around him, dilemmas of sin and moral culpability and redemption were being resolved through agonies of prayer and torturous self-excoriation, it is hard to imagine him doubting his own elect role. An innate self-assurance—or was it a sustained nervous excitement?—carried him through the jolts and eddies of morality and law.

NEVER were legal and religious roles so fully blended as when, in his days as a circuit-riding judge, it became his duty to pass a sentence of death. His pronouncement in one such case—that of the murderous Thayer brothers of Buffalo—did more than anything else to spread his celebrity among the general population. This was among the most sensational crimes of an era when sensational crimes provided a supremely popular form of public entertainment. Sermons and political speeches were ordinary fare by comparison with the high drama of a criminal trial culminating in the spectacle of a public execution. Hanging days, with their carnival atmosphere, left a disturbing aftertaste in towns turned upside down by the unruly mobs who flocked to them from the surrounding countryside. Public hangings were already coming under challenge for promoting what a contemporary described as "rioting, drunkenness, and every species of disorderly conduct," and within a decade would be phased out in favor of executions within prison walls.

In the meantime they drew extraordinary numbers of spectators. A crowd of thirty thousand was said to have witnessed the death of the Thayer brothers in June of 1825. Judge Walworth had passed sentence on them two months earlier for their murder of John Love in Erie County, and printed accounts of the trial were as a matter of course hawked at the hanging. A ballad was already in circulation.

> *Three brothers bent on crimes and blood,*
> *In bold defiance of their God;*
> *More monstrous than the savage fiend,*
> *Have murdered Love, their nearest friend.*

The Thayers were a troubling instance of local boys gone bad, a clan of farmers who according to subsequent reports had "cultivated habits of idleness," devoting a minimum of labor to working their land and preferring to consort at taverns and other "lounging places." Starting to rely dangerously on credit, they finally saw no recourse but to murder their boarder, John Love, from whom they had borrowed a good deal of money. The crime was as squalid and ugly as it could be. Love was lured to one of the brothers' houses on a pig-slaughtering day, so that his blood might mingle indistinguishably with that of the pigs. One of the Thayer boys distracted Love with conversation while another, lurking at a window, shot him through the head. As the shot did not finish him off, the brother who had been doing the talking helped him on his way with a meat ax. An orgy of spending with the victim's property and cash quickly brought the brothers under suspicion.

An eyewitness account suggests what kind of spectacle such a "hanging bee" provided: "When each brother had been placed by the sheriff so as to stand under the beam and on the fatal drop (which was made to swing back) and directly under the hook to which the rope was attached, their white caps were drawn down over their faces. Then the awful silence was broken by the terrible wailing of the three brothers, which grew more loud and intense each moment until the sharp sword of the sheriff severed the rope that held the scaffold. The noise did not cease or lessen even then until their heels had left the platform and they had dropped to the length of their ropes. The screams of the Thayer brothers were echoed a thousand fold by a simultaneous and involuntary exclamation from the thousands of spectators who till then had stood as if almost breathless and silently gazing on the awful scene."

No doubt the reporter brought to this description all the lurid repertoire of gothic fiction, but then so did the spectators. They knew what was in store and relished every detail as if it had been choreographed. In the case of the Thayers, the scene was all the more impressive for the fact that, as the crowd knew, it was being witnessed by the brothers' father. The old man, assumed to be complicit in concealing the crime, had been spared the death penalty; but being forced to watch doubtless made for a more satisfactory punishment. Such was the impact of this event that it proved to be the last public execution in Buffalo. Walworth was not, apparently, present to witness the carrying out of his sentence, but his words of judicial condemnation would be made available in at least six separate published accounts of the trial.

To the thousands present on the day would be added many thousands more who could relish the details after the fact.

These pamphlets—souvenir programs of capital justice—neatly combined the most solemn morality, revolving around questions of penitence and hopes of divine mercy, with the most irresistibly bloody particulars of slashed throat and smashed skull. Their covers bore images that spoke with blunt force: three black coffins for the Thayer brothers, or, on another broadside, three hooded figures hanging with snapped necks side by side. Walworth's final address at the trial helped make his reputation—it was anthologized in a popular textbook of elocution—and decades later a prominent lawyer would opine that "some of the language used by him in pronouncing sentence upon the prisoners . . . is not excelled in legal history."

Walworth's remarks found favor in part because of the sensitivity with which he acknowledged his own emotions. It was perfectly in order to sentence the young killers to hang, but to have done so with indifference would have called Walworth's own humanity into question: "To be compelled at one and the same time to consign to the gallows three young men, who have just arrived at manhood . . . presses on my feelings with a weight, which I can neither resist nor express." It was not, he stressed, in order to cause pain to the condemned prisoners or their families that he would use "strong language to express the enormity of [the Thayers'] guilt"; his purpose was simply to bring them to contrition and repentance.

With gathering force he recalled the details of Love's murder to the Thayers: "You stole upon him unperceived and aimed a deadly rifle at his head, and with the fatal axe, you mangled and murdered your victim, mingling his blood with that of your butchered swine." And now Walworth's tone became that of a thundering sermon: "Wretched and deluded men! In vain was the foul deed perpetrated under cover of the darkness of the night . . . You forgot that you were in the presence of Him to whom the light of the day and the darkness of the night are the same." The Almighty, the judge went on to specify, possessed the power to prevent expected snow from falling, or to melt the snowdrops before they settled on the earth, in order to expose the crude grave in which Love's body had been concealed. God had intervened directly to bring about the exposure of their crime.

After a final reminder that in the afterlife the Thayers would have to extend their bloody hands toward their Savior for forgiveness, Walworth delivered them to their fate.

> Then the Judge pronounced their dreadful sentence
> With great candidness to behold:
> You must all be hanged until you're dead
> And Lord have mercy on your souls.

Walworth's address may have struck its readers as heartfelt and stirring, but he was hardly breaking new ground. Point for point he harked back to a centuries-old tradition of funeral sermons, and in fact just a few months earlier he had delivered nearly identical pronouncements in a case a good deal closer to home. In this instance, however, the outcome did not have the same uniformly positive effect on Judge Walworth's reputation. A house servant of his old Plattsburgh associate Benjamin Mooers had been arraigned in October 1824 for the murder of her newborn child. Peggy Facto, a French Canadian and Catholic, was accused of strangling the infant with "a certain string . . . of the bredth of one inch and of the length of two feet" and afterward burning the body. The child's father, one Francis Labare, was described as fully complicit in the act.

Facto's trial on January 19 lasted only half a day. Her swift conviction was followed by an address in which Walworth used the same tone and often the identical phrases as he would apply in the case of the Thayers, harping again on the theme of an ever-watchful God: "Wretched and deluded woman! . . . Little did you imagine when you tied around the neck of your struggling infant the fatal string with which you deprived it of existence, or when you placed its body upon the fire, that He would cause the senseless cord and the scorching blaze to come up as swift witnesses against you." He sentenced her to be hanged in two months' time, and added that her body would be turned over to the Medical Society for dissection.

Later the same day her lover, Francis Labare, was tried. Facto, who had said nothing at her own trial, testified that he had taken away the newborn child and returned without it, and then "came towards her with a knife & threatened her life if she had said anything about it." Labare, however, was promptly acquitted.

At this point events began to diverge from their expected course. Walworth's sentence met with condemnation from many locals, including close associates of the judge. Rumor spread of evidence that would exonerate Facto, and the *Plattsburgh Republican*, a newspaper sympathetic to Walworth, felt obliged to condemn "a catch-penny pamphlet, bottomed upon some pretended new discovery of evidence, which is probably some old woman's story . . . We should not have entered upon the subject, but for the ungenerous & stupid remarks of a driveling pamphlet." Facto's employer, Benjamin Mooers himself, however, evidently believed her innocent, feeling perhaps that Labare bore sole or at least primary responsibility. Walworth continued to maintain that "the woman was perfectly abandoned and depraved and that she had destroyed this child and probably the one the year previous, not for the purpose of hiding her shame which was open and apparent . . . but for the purpose of ridding herself of the trouble of taking care of them."

Beyond the specifics of the case other factors were involved, among them a growing opposition to the death penalty and a feeling that in any case women should not be executed. There was enough local pressure that Walworth was obliged to forward to Governor De Witt Clinton a petition for clemency, even joining his own name to the list despite his absolute conviction of Facto's guilt and his strong belief that "her execution would have afforded an example beneficial to the community." Governor Clinton declined to exercise his prerogative and upheld the sentence; Walworth's remarks had left him with no doubt of Facto's guilt. Clinton was also inclined to think that those "enlightened and benevolent men" who objected to the death penalty were perhaps prevented by their own elevated and well-meaning character from grasping just how powerful a deterrent an execution could be for the depraved and crime-bent sectors of the populace: "If terror loses its influence with them, then indeed the life of no man will be secure."

The *Plattsburgh Intelligencer*, the paper that had led the opposition to Facto's sentence, published a mordant account of the ribald and light-minded atmosphere in which it was carried out, with the execution cavalcade followed on foot and in wagons by a crowd in which women predominated, "females of various ages from the decrepitude of the grandmother, down to the rosy cheek'd maiden in her teens, all eager to witness the rare show." Bad roads had not prevented a huge body of out-of-towners from assembling, and the condemned was regaled with a lively tune as she was borne to the scaffold, "either the 'Soldier's Joy' or some other equally calculated to excite a gay feeling and a brisk movement." A Catholic priest accompanied Peggy Facto to the gibbet, where she again declared her innocence. Afterward the *Republican*, in denouncing the claims of the rival newspaper, found it necessary to reaffirm Walworth's wisdom and integrity: "Every person of candor who attended the trial must admit that the judge summed up the testimony in the most clear, dispassionate and just manner: he explained the law in its true spirit, and gave the jury an impressive admonition of the important duty which devolved upon them."

It was not, however, as a hanging judge that Reuben Hyde Walworth was to be best remembered. Capital cases were not within his purview in the realms of equity law of which in 1828 he was appointed master. The chancellorship was a position unique to New York, one of the state's many legal and political peculiarities. It gave him peremptory authority—essentially one-man control save for appeals made to the state's Court of Errors (of which he was also a member)—over such things as the disposition of wills, the adjudication of property rights whether in regard to wilderness waterways or fugitive slaves, the settling of disputed contracts and messy divorces, the guardianship of the orphaned, the deranged, and the habitually intoxicated. He came to the post very much in the shadow of his recent predecessor James Kent, esteemed as one of the greatest figures in American legal theory for his role in disentangling a distinctively American practice from the inherited mass of British law.

Walworth made no such claims for himself. He accepted the position in a self-deprecating speech: "Brought up a farmer until the age of seventeen, deprived of all of the advantages of a classical education, and with a very limited knowledge of Chancery Law, I find myself at the age of 38 suddenly and unexpectedly placed at the head of the judiciary of the State." Aaron Burr—who had weathered duels, scandals, and accusations of treason to find himself in old age a gray eminence of the upstate political establishment—remarked archly that if Walworth insisted on publicizing his lack of qualification, people might well wonder why the devil he had taken the job. A humorous poem improvised by Walworth's future running mate Charles O'Conor suggested that the question was indeed in the air.

> Here am I, at thirty-eight,
> Chancellor of the Empire State;
> And like the fly in amber beer
> The wonder is how I got here.

However he managed it—and it was rumored that Governor Nathaniel Pitcher had turned to him only after several other justices had turned down the post—Walworth had now been admitted to the highest reaches of American political life. At a celebratory dinner he hosted at Pine Grove in the wake of this appointment, the guests included John Quincy Adams, Andrew Jackson, and former chancellor Kent.

For five years as circuit judge he had traveled from town to town, often on horseback, with an energy that all found remarkable. As chancellor he would remove initially to the state capital at Albany; but within another five years, in 1832, he arranged to relocate once and for all to his home in Saratoga. Here Walworth turned Pine Grove itself into his courthouse. Nothing exemplifies the coziness of the Chancellor's position more than his ability to turn his back on the capital and exercise his power from his parlor.

By now he had five children, three daughters (of whom the eldest, Mary Elizabeth, had just married a merchant named Edgar Jenkins) and two sons born after them. Clarence, at thirteen, already showed great intellectual promise. He had been sent to a boarding school in Massachusetts (the future Williams College) and seemed well on the path to a legal career as outstanding as his father's.

And then there was the youngest, three-year-old Mansfield, born December 1830 in Albany. In the family Bible, next to the notice of his birth, someone (his mother Maria perhaps) had inscribed: "Little rascal." An outburst of parental affection, or an early note of understated anxiety?

5

~~~~~~~~~

Spa and Courtroom:
The Chancellor in His World

CHANCELLOR Walworth had selected a place where he could be seen to best advantage. Saratoga was a public space where superior specimens from all over—what passed for the best in the nation—could parade themselves. The spa preserved an exclusive air, even if it was a democratic kind of exclusiveness: anyone could get in if they could afford it. A tourist with the price of a ticket could mingle with these luminaries—senators and generals, actors and singers—and feel part of their world.

Often the parade was literal. The rounds of life at Saratoga were punctuated by ceremonies—set to the music of Congress Hall's resident band leader, the African American composer Frank Johnson—designed to make leisure seem like more than merely lazing about. Americans had a hard time justifying open idleness. They were more comfortable with a ritualized program of group activities, an active and collective pursuit of health, moral uplift, and the self-conscious display of polished manners.

The ritual of rituals was the early morning confluence of visitors gathering to drink the waters of Congress Spring. This was an occasion the Chancellor regularly attended in season, making himself part of a spectacle retailed by guidebook after guidebook in only slightly varying terms: "To this spot, perhaps more than any other on the globe, are seen repairing in the summer mornings, before breakfast, persons of almost every grade and condition, from the most exalted to the most abject. The beautiful and the deformed—the rich and the poor—the devotee of pleasure and the invalid—all congregate here for purposes as varied as are their situations in life." Early on, Congress Spring began to be touted as a sort of swirling epicenter of human diversity, a Chaucerian pageant of juxtaposed extremes: "The pale emaciated and lame; pampered epicures and spare gentlemen with red pimpled noses . . . a continually changing crowd from all the various classes ages & conditions."

In the summer of 1839, New York's ex-mayor Philip Hone, a self-made businessman who had fashioned himself into a connoisseur of cultivated leisurely pursuits, caught a glimpse—in between gorging on "champagne, and ice-cream, and blancmange"—of Saratoga as it meant itself to be seen. Here was an American spa worthy of its legendary English models Bath or Cheltenham, hosting a throng that encompassed "antiquated belles of a by-gone generation . . . fine married women and lovely girls . . . and men uniting as in one brilliant focus the talent, intelligence, and civic virtues of the various parts of the country."

Most travelers were impressed less by the fine patriotic pageantry than by the tantalizing social opportunities of a world swarming with "hosts of cheerful pretty faces of the softer sex, and hordes of young aspirants to their good graces." Saratoga in high season offered a novelistic bustle full of competing plot-lines cribbed from British novels like *Humphry Clinker* or *Sense and Sensibility*, with scope for assorted comical supporting roles and tastefully muted erotic possibilities. The Virginian Elizabeth Ruffin, one of the many Southerners who flocked to the spa in the summer months to escape (it was said) the feverish miasmas of their homeland, amused herself by cataloging the varieties of couples on display, focusing on "the oddest and most ill-matched."

BUT as the tourist seasons rolled by, the impression of vital exuberance and cultivated elegance gave way soon enough to a notion that the resort was already past its prime. Disillusionment set in quickly; some of the earliest surviving accounts are already laments for the vanishing of the old order. Perhaps, indeed, the old order had been little more than a creation of promotional pamphlets. When the young George Templeton Strong visited the place in 1841, he saw only "a mean little country town, ambitious of looking as much like a city as it can." Philip Hone himself was disturbed by the presence at Saratoga—along with the talented, intelligent, and virtuous—of "humbuggers and humbugged."

A company of strangers played at being acquaintances in a common national drawing room, and being strangers they were forever at risk of being preyed upon. Elizabeth Ruffin's brother Edmund (who would later distinguish himself for his fierce devotion to the Confederacy and would blow his brains out after Appomattox) was horrified on an 1827 visit to find that a supposed gentleman he had been socializing with was a "blackleg," one of the racing touts who thrived on an already heated-up culture of gambling.

Saratoga was a paradise for those petty thieves, confidence men, and tricksters of doubtful identity—"pickpockets, sharpers, loafers"—who flourished where social encounters could be so easily managed, where (in the words of the peripatetic social observer Nathaniel Parker Willis) "a game at billiards or a chance fraternization over juleps in the bar-room is, in fact, the easiest and most frequent threshold of introduction to ladies." Newspapers warned darkly of fortune hunters—"fellows who possess a pretty good gift of gab, can muster a fine rig of clothes, and money enough to pay for a few weeks' board"—expert at seducing the daughters of merchants and plantation owners.

The anonymous reporters assigned to cover Saratoga for the city tabloids took unmistakable relish in besmirching the would-be aristocratic surfaces of spa life. Numbed by a succession of carefully stage-managed balls and receptions, they delighted in uncovering a hint of murk amid the crowd straining at high-class decorum. Even here, in the halls of overstuffed hotels and on their epic verandas, in the very boudoirs of marriageable women who had come from all compass points to this Elysium, ruthless eyes calculated the odds for theft and seduction. Charmers with false visiting cards insinuated themselves into America's most reputable families. Intricate confidence games were set in motion over apparently casual games of billiards with the sons of newly moneyed manufacturers. The bubble world found itself infiltrated by forces from the outside, the same forces that (along with industrial accidents and freaks of nature) provided the most thrilling items in the local paper, the *Saratogian*: murders, robberies, abductions, attempted rapes.

The commonest, although infrequently acknowledged, threat was not mayhem but terminal boredom. The Saratoga experience often approximated a narcotic trance. It was like a rest home for chronically overbusy Americans, deliberately warding off any hint of genuine excitement: "Life at the Springs," a newspaper chronicler reported, "is a strange succession of agreeable nothings, to which we become more attached than can well be imagined at the outset." Just how agreeable depended on the traveler. Some were quite happy to be ravished by "festoons of wreaths" and "a pavilion sparkling with lamps and perfumed with flowers." Others ended up finding—at the center of the precisely timed strolls and balls, the carefully programmed and endlessly discussed regimens of diet and bathing, the rounds of backgammon and checkers, the laboriously contrived displays of finery, and the equally contrived efforts to approximate witty conversation of the sort found in novels and plays—a devouring ennui. "There is nothing in the whole compass of yawns like a Saratoga yawn."

But the dream was hard to kill. The popular essayist George William Curtis, strolling the streets of Saratoga in 1852, paid homage in a sweeping verbal tableau to a place already defined chiefly by nostalgia for its past: "We stroll down the street to Congress Hall, we make a pilgrimage to the piazza, which was the Saratoga of our reading and romance—to Congress Hall, across whose smooth-columned piazza we pass, to pay the tribute of our homage to the spot where so much love beat in warm hearts and blushed in beautiful cheeks." It is the ballroom of the departed, a place of ghostly farewells suspended in time. The actual Saratoga is nothing compared to the disembodied recollection it will leave in "the young, feminine fancy" of a visitor—herself an imagined being, a stranger glimpsed in the crowd—long after she has gone home. Only then will the United States Hotel stand revealed as "a transfigured palace of fairy . . . the nearest hit we Americans can make to Boccaccio's garden."

Within this fairyland, in the seasonable months, from the 1820s to the 1860s, Chancellor Walworth would continue to walk down Broadway to Congress Park in the early mornings, and pay his respects to neighbors and visitors as they lined up to take the water from the dipper boys. He would look in at the ever more immense hotels: Congress Hall, Union Hall, the United States, each with its own clientele looking down on the others, Democrats favoring one, Whigs another. Southern planters and wealthy Cubans flocked to the Pavilion; clergymen preferred the teetotalling Union Hall. Consulting the registers, he would inform himself as to which friends and acquaintances of distinction were newly arrived in Saratoga, so that he could invite them to Pine Grove. "And then," in the recollection of a lawyer acquaintance, "he liked to saunter in parlors and ball-rooms to scan for a moment the Vanity Fair as it flitted before him."

ONCE settled again (after the Albany hiatus) in Saratoga with his family, Walworth set about making Pine Grove his permanent base of operations. The north parlor was converted into a makeshift courtroom. There was a raised desk for the Chancellor, equipped with a tumbler of water (the quantity of water he consumed during court sessions was legendary) and a poker for the fireplace, and a single long table for the lawyers in attendance. The shelves along the wall were lined with leather-bound law books, with strips of green baize to protect them from dust and ashes. The Walworth coat of arms with its dagger insignia hung framed on the wall. Thus he made his own home the hub in and out of which flowed a constant noise of lawyers and litigants, politicians and industrialists, suppliant orphans and quarreling heirs. Fusing his judicial office and his home into a single entity, the Chancellor confirmed that all aspects of his existence were part of the same job: the tireless exercise of his faculties.

Whatever he had set out to do he had done, depending on neither luck nor privilege. His career to date—although he would scarcely have been so arrogant as to say so—could withstand every kind of moral scrutiny. Vices? He had abstained from liquor since an early age and had joined forces with others to make total abstention the law of the land. Sloth? His existence had consisted of nothing but purposeful movement, with only minimal rest periods in between. Wrath? He was personally the kindest of men; any trace of harshness in his character was limited to the legitimate requirements of his judicial calling. Vanity? His religion kept constantly in his view the end of all things and the final dissolution of transient baubles.

He did permit himself an appropriate level of social enjoyments, savoring as a connoisseur the protocols of the Springs. He was a man for every occasion: to romp with an infant or to pronounce a eulogy; to mobilize a campaign for moral purification or to welcome visitors to a midsummer ball. Puns amused him. He liked to show off his undiminished skills at running, jumping, and horseback riding. Yet even his frolics were purposeful, taking their place within the invisible boundaries that patterned all of life. He had committed no act that he could not, if called upon, explain and justify. He held no opinion for which he did not have a basis stretching as far back as the creation of the world.

Mortal life was but a way station between primordial chaos and the faithfully anticipated afterlife. The thought of what past times had been like—the border wars, starving times, Indian attacks—made Saratoga's relative comfort and stability all the more unlikely. From out of the still-uncleared thickets of the Chancellor's childhood emerged, in memory, vagrant old men who had spent their lives in mountains and virgin forests, and whose secrets of survival were embedded in endless strings of stories about weather and killing. Nor had that wilderness gone away. A permanent disorder hovered at the edges of the Chancellor's only provisionally ordered world. Cults formed along the seams. Stretches of lawlessness persisted in the gaps between settlements, or in the narrower gaps within families undermined by spirituous drink, or—darkest and nearest of all—within that interior wilderness in which minds surrendered to the dissembling commands of mania, and souls gave themselves over to frenzies of delusional enthusiasm.

It required constant and rigorous action to combat the universal tendency toward slipping, slackening, and generally giving way. The words of the old primer had never been lost on him: "For Satan finds some mischief still for idle hands to do." He had organized around himself a domain in which, at least in principle, there was no time for evil, or dishonor, or disorder. In a life with no idle hours, what harm could come?

Every minute was spoken for. After an evening spent playing backgammon or chess with his guests, while spinning out a stream of delightful conversation—savory recollections of the War of 1812, perhaps, or the quarrels of Mr. Clay and Mr. Calhoun in the Seventeenth

Congress—he would at length retire to his study. There, while the rest of the household slept, his candle would burn until three or four in the morning, a sign of wonder and respect for nocturnal wayfarers: the Chancellor's light shining in the dark like a beacon of reason and benevolence. In the midnight silence he pored over legal precedents, or wrote letters urging the need for a Bible in every American household, or drafted a speech calling for a ban on the sale of wines and liquors, or outlined a campaign to purchase slaves so that they might be shipped back to their African homeland.

The next morning he took his place downstairs in the north parlor to face the assembled lawyers and litigants. Here his power was unchallenged, even if a good many of his judgments would later be overturned on appeal. In the courtroom he was a tough master. Untried and thin-skinned advocates entered with extreme caution. They had already heard the stories about how Reuben Hyde Walworth earned the nickname "Raw Hide Walworth." New York lawyers learned early in their apprenticeship to dread the sarcastic interruptions and barrages of questions that could wreck the presentation of a carefully prepared argument.

For Walworth's defenders, these already legendary outbursts were nothing more than the brimming over, as it were, of a mind too rapid to tolerate preamble and circumlocution: "Through the activity of his mind," in the words of Charles O'Conor, "through its anticipatory traits . . . he would seek to see the end from the beginning, and learn the argument before it was made." For O'Conor, the Chancellor's "extremely troublesome" manner sprang "not from vanity or superciliousness, but from the quickness of his perceptions and the uncontrollable activity of his mental forces." The key word seems to have been *uncontrollable*. An opposition paper, the *Daily Plebeian*, tempered its savage criticism of the judge's courtroom manner by noting that "this habit of his seems to be almost involuntary." Indeed, the *Plebeian's* description of Walworth's "many digressions and wanderings from the questions at issue"—his way of losing himself in whatever hypothetical speculations "his active and vaulting imagination suggests as likely to arise upon a given or fancied state of facts"—begins to sound like the symptoms of a neurological disorder.

To outside observers it had a rather comic quality, and, after all, courtrooms were expected to be arenas of entertainment. Newspapers would have been lost if they could not fill their pages with transcripts of trials and judicial hearings, and thick volumes rolled off the press containing anecdotes both serious and comic about the doings of judges and lawyers. For downstate visitors to his courtroom, Walworth qualified as a sort of grand rural eccentric. Philip Hone, spent a morning observing the Chancellor—"his habiliments not remarkably neat, pantaloons drawn half-way up to his knees, drinking most intemperately of water (his only drink, as he is president of the teetotalers)"—at work at Pine Grove in the summer of 1840. Hone acknowledged that Walworth's abrupt manner "must be a stumbling-block in the way of young counselors," but found in the atmosphere of the courtroom a refreshingly "colloquial" reminder of simpler times. The Chancellor, he noted, "does a great deal of the talking himself . . . It looked very like a schoolmaster and his pupils, only the boys were a little too big to answer the description of the latter."

Thus twenty years passed in the preparation of countless thousands of legal judgments. A wife was forbidden by her husband to attend the church of her choice. A husband was deemed to have been exposed to sexual temptation because of his wife's unjustifiable absences from the home. The unpredictable behavior of a local sheriff landed him in an asylum. An heir was debarred from his property rights by reason of mental defectiveness. As "guardian of the interests of infants, lunatics, idiots, drunkards and their families," there was no family business so intimate that the chancellor was not called on to delve into it. But mostly his hyperactive mental forces were applied to the ceaseless parsing of the direst of infinitesimal details: bales of cotton lost in shipwrecks, a dyemaker's landing wrongfully appropriated by ferryboat operators, a mill keeper inconvenienced by the construction of a dam, a landowner resisting the building of a railway, the clauses of a tortuous will unraveled (as in the 1835 ruling by which Walworth made Henry James's father a rich man). The cases are preserved in the fourteen thick leatherbound volumes of Paige's *Chancery Reports*.

Perhaps, caught up in those details, the twenty years seemed to him like no time at all. He had always exhibited a capacity to feed on material that to others was the very essence of tediousness. An acquaintance said he had "little susceptibility to poetry," but to him poetry may have resided precisely in the fine print of deeds, wills, and contracts. At any rate nothing deterred him from proceeding tirelessly with the work before him. Yet it did seem that, for all his labor, the pile of unfinished business never got any smaller. In fact the more he worked, the bigger the pile got: there were six hundred causes in arrears while his decision remained pending. The word got around that his courtroom was a place not to resolve business but to be kept forever waiting for the resolution that never came. The judge so impatient that he could not let a lawyer finish a sentence nevertheless exacted an infinite patience from those awaiting his final judgments.

6

≈≈≈≈≈≈≈

The Two Brothers

THE Chancellor had become a famous man of sorts. His name was a seal of legitimacy for any enterprise benefiting "the general cause of humanity and religion." A group of settlers in Wisconsin—temperance enthusiasts—named a county after him in 1836. He continued to play genial host at Pine Grove to men of all nations and denominations, from the Nestorian bishop Bar Yohannan—an exotic visitor, robed and thickly bearded, who appalled the chancellor's wife, Maria, with his constant smoking, and was regarded with awe by some local Protestants who took him for a descendant of the lost tribes of Israel—to the Irish Catholic Jeremiah O'Donovan, who was touched by Walworth's sympathy for the sufferings of the Irish even if "he sticks as fast and tight to Protestantism as Prometheus did to the mountain."

By 1838 his three daughters were all married off, not gloriously but respectably, Mary Elizabeth to a merchant of middling success, Sarah to a local lawyer who duly received a sinecure at the Court of Chancery, and (the best catch of the lot) Liza to the minister of Schenectady's First Presbyterian Church. The Chancellor's ambitions for his family centered now on his two sons, born after the girls: Clarence, at eighteen just graduated from Union College in Schenectady and clearly marked for a career in law, and eight-year-old Mansfield, the "little rascal" who might well be expected to follow a similar course. The extended Walworth clan, Reuben's brothers and cousins and nephews, when they were not lawyers or judges were physicians, military officers, or ministers.

Nothing went as it was supposed to. His sons, each in his own way, spoiled their father's plans for them. The Chancellor made a world for them to inherit and they turned out not to want it.

Clarence, it was true, at first followed the path laid out. For the rest of his life he preserved the Polonius-like directives his father had imparted when sending him to boarding school: "Strive to be first in your class, first in your school, first in every situation in which you may be placed . . . Study mineralogy and botany for your amusement in your leisure hours . . . but learn writing, arithmetic, English grammar, Greek, Latin, French, composition and declamation, or the habit of public speaking, as the foundation and only sure means of making yourself great and respected and useful in after life."

The Chancellor need hardly have worried. Clarence was made for studying: Latin grammar held no terrors for him, and Greek and Hebrew would follow. Years later, half-blind, he was still chasing down the Hebrew equivalents of Greek terms to clarify his thinking. "From his point of view," his niece and biographer Nelly Walworth wrote, "words were as the food, clothing, weapons, tools, vehicles and housing of human thought." Unlike his father, he had a taste for poetry. Listening to a classmate recite an ode of Horace, hearing it for the first time with the proper quantitative lilt, he remarked, "Why I could dance to such time as that!"

A rambunctious boy who gathered bullets from the ground at the battlefield of Saratoga and who once smashed the church windows and got an unforgettable licking from his father in consequence, Clarence grew into a youth noted for his beauty, a graceful dancer, a clear-voiced and passionate singer. Through exercise he combated his tendency toward physical frailness. At his father's urging he spent a whole summer as constantly as possible on horseback, just as the Chancellor had done in his days as circuit judge.

As for "the habit of public speaking," Clarence developed a lawyer's flair for argument and persuasion. He acquired early on a reputation as a natural orator in an age when oratory was chief among American arts, and every politician, lawyer, and preacher aspired to Shakespearean music and Ciceronian gravity.

THE Chancellor must have felt much pride in his boy in those days: a boy during whose boyhood he had, in truth, often been absent, away in Washington or working the circuit. Young Clarence had spent a good deal more time with his mother. He would recall going in winter to the meetinghouse where Maria was so often in attendance, bringing her a foot warmer and nestling up to her as she sang hymns. Of her intensely personal relation to God, he had an intimate and daily awareness. His father's accomplishments, by contrast, took place in a realm where he never felt quite at home. Clarence went off dutifully to study and then practice law, but it was religion that kept finding him.

In those days academic administrators encouraged their pupils to attend the revival meetings conducted by itinerant preachers. These periodic shake-ups were considered advisable for students otherwise at risk of sinking into the vices of drinking and card playing—not to mention more serious mischief like defacing Bibles or setting school buildings on fire. Clarence, whose own wild streak was attested to by some of his classmates, had witnessed if not participated in such things. A good revival could melt the toughest cases. Classes would be suspended for days as a wave of prayer and Bible study at all hours swept the school.

It was never enough simply to attend church and observe the outward forms of religious observance. Each individual, for the salvation of his soul, had to undergo a personal conversion, as Clarence's mother had done in Plattsburgh in 1821. Clarence's turning point came when he was eighteen and about to graduate from Union College. Elder Jacob Knapp had brought his revival to Schenectady, and all through the summer of 1838 preached with such success that shops were closed and a large part of the populace stopped what they were doing to heed the call. In the warm weather, with windows open, the sound of prayer reached into every dwelling in the city.

Jacob Knapp was a freelancer, something of a wild card—he had stood trial for alleged financial malfeasance, although the charges were never brought home—but the established churches tolerated him because his converts could then be divided up among the local congregations when Knapp went on his way. A skeptical observer in Saratoga

remarked of him: "He is a great man in his way. That is, a great
fanatic." For Clarence, no matter what theological disagreements he
later had with Knapp's brand of Christianity, the experience of conversion was "real, substantial, and lasting." To say anything more
about it, he added, would intrude "upon those sacred privacies which
do not belong to the public."

He went on with his intended career, moving up to Rochester to
practice law for the first time, but here again a traveling preacher
stirred his depths. This was the great Charles Grandison Finney,
famous for laying out the case for salvation "like a lawyer arguing a case
before a court and jury." With Finney, logic was heightened by an
unerring sense of theater. At a crucial point he would lift his finger
toward the ceiling and let it trail slowly downward, tracking the fall of
a sinner. By the time the sinner landed in Hell, Finney's forefinger was
pointing directly at the floor in front of him, while the audience craned
forward to catch a glimpse of the eternal fires.

But Clarence, no matter how moved by the emotional force of
Finney's preaching, had already shifted away from evangelical Christianity toward a more congenial worship. By his own account it was his
love of music that did it. The chance to become a chorister at an Episcopalian church near his law school had led him to the denomination
in which he was finally confirmed by Bishop Benjamin Onderdonk.
To be a congregant was not enough, however. In 1842, at age twenty-
two, informing his father that he intended to give up law and study for
orders in the Episcopal Church, he enrolled at New York's General
Theological Seminary.

Giving up law cannot have caused him much regret. Whatever his
aptitude for the profession, he had little tolerance for what went on in
and around courthouses. His standards were perhaps too pure for the
era in which he found himself. Not long after being admitted to the
bar, he was accosted outside his father's courtroom by a business magnate who offered two thousand dollars—the cash smoothly fished out
from a breast pocket—to expedite a case. Clarence responded with an
angry outburst: "You dirty dog! You blackhearted rascal! What do
you take me for?" The scene remained vivid to him in his old age. It
may have been the moment when he realized how completely he must
detach himself from his father's world.

He had only a glimmer of what awaited him. The seminary was in the throes of theological upheaval. Episcopalians were beginning to feel the influence of England's Oxford movement, with its call for a return to the precepts and practices of the Primitive Christian Church, and its affirmation of the Apostolic Succession, according to which the present-day church was connected to Christ's apostles through a chain of direct transmission. The argumentation of Newman, Pusey, and the other Oxfordians was intricate, but the effect on some minds, especially young minds impatient with the bland respectability of mainstream religion, was like lightning. Bishop Onderdonk, the seminary's president, encouraged these tendencies, and more conservative church members were getting nervous.

LEAVING behind his father's realm—walking away from the brutal wranglings and sly collusions of capitalists and politicians—Clarence stepped into a parallel world. He began to absorb "that peculiar atmosphere which all who came to the seminary must necessarily breathe." This hothouse of spirituality was made for him. Disciplined study and inner passion blended strangely in a space in which the most minute questions of logic and etymology—the fine points of hermeneutics and Hebrew grammar—were inseparable from profound and tumultuous emotion. The labyrinthine paths of the domain he had entered could not be negotiated without stringent adherence to the exact meaning of words. This was not the verbal trickery of the legal world, in which relentlessly self-interested parties maneuvered constantly for advantage by exaggerating and misrepresenting and milking for emotion. Here his own eternal life, the fate of his soul, was at stake. No fudging was permissible or possible.

The young seminarians carried their fervor from room to room, restlessly debating points of doctrine among themselves. A friend across the hall spoke to Clarence of "baptismal regeneration" and he found himself overwhelmed. Could a ritual act effect a spiritual event? "I remained for a long time sleepless during the night revolving the question, and unable to dismiss it." Later he saw this as "the entering wedge" of a new belief. He and his classmates began to feel they inhabited another plane of being.

Clarence would remember always the night when his fellow student

Arthur Carey—the most spiritually vibrant of their band—read to him from the Gospel of John, beginning with the words "Let not your heart be troubled." Suffering already from vision problems that made it difficult for him to read, Clarence could only surrender to the words as they were recited: "Believe me that I am in the Father, and the Father is in me." In that moment the words opened to reveal a greater reality. The two of them were enclosed in it and borne up by it. Carey continued reading to the end of the gospel. For Clarence it was like hearing the full force of the words for the first time. His friend's voice, he would recall, "was low and sweet, and had a quietness of suppressed feeling in its tones which was magnetic . . . I see Carey's kindly face before me and his hair glowing like gold in the lamp-light."

His letters home made clear how radically the seminary was changing him. "I do not look upon myself as having *any interests* on earth to advance," he told his parents. "I am hired body and soul to the service of Him from whom I ask nothing on this side of the grave, but His love. If in another world He shall please to give me a voice and a harp and that 'new song' and a place near enough to see Him, I am content." No interests on earth to advance? This was a far cry from even the most enthused of revivalists. Relatives and family friends in the city kept an eye on him, worried about theologically dangerous tendencies. But he was already beyond their reach. When his sister Eliza pressed a history of the Reformation on him, he found in its pages not the inspiration she hoped for but an indelibly negative impression of Martin Luther as "a religious and political agitator . . . as much marked by duplicity as by audacity." When the well-meaning Mrs. Codwise of St. Mark's Place took him to hear a celebrated anti-Papist preacher, Clarence was appalled: "I never heard such bitterness, hatred, and bigotry concentrated into one sermon."

He had entered a world hidden to the Mrs. Codwises, and within that world obscure transformations were taking place. Young men looked into each other's souls and spoke in a kind of code. They threaded their paths with caution in an atmosphere of surveillance and conspiracy-hunting. Scandals erupted. The "holy and lovely" Arthur Carey, whose gospel reading had so impressed Clarence, had been ordained only after a grueling examination by eight clergymen unhappy about his views on the Council of Trent and the doctrine of transubstantiation, and even after they reluctantly cleared him the ceremony was interrupted by the protests of two prelates who accused him of being "imbued with the errors of Rome" and then walked out of the church in the midst of the liturgy.

Worse was to follow. Rumors had already begun to spread about the seminary's director, Bishop Onderdonk, who had supported Carey so firmly. Under the influence of wine, it was hinted, the bishop had behaved with gross inappropriateness toward a number of young women. In December 1844 the bishop stood trial before an ecclesiastical court on charges of "immorality and impurity." The testimony was devastating. Published accounts of the trial bore all too troubling a resemblance to the lurid novels that had begun to flood America, sprawling gothic serials like George Lippard's just-published *Monks of Monk Hall*, with its portrayal of lubricious clergymen (in company with bankers, landowners, and corrupt politicians) taking foul advantage of the young women who fell into their hands. Here, for instance, according to the evidence presented, was Bishop Onderdonk, evidently intoxicated, fresh from having "grossly insulted" one woman as he accompanied her home in a carriage, waiting to greet her sister as she went downstairs to investigate: "I sat down on the centre of the sofa. He sat down near me; and in an instant, as quick as thought, he thrust his hand into my bosom, very low . . ."

Found guilty on six counts, the bishop was allowed to keep his title but was permanently suspended from ecclesiastical duties. Clarence was less appalled by Onderdonk's misdeeds—"maudlin familiarities indulged in by a half-conscious man overheated with wine"—than by the fact that the other bishops had gone public with them. Unable to indict Onderdonk fairly on theological grounds, the orthodox faction had sabotaged him with the immorality charges, and had used the resulting scandal as an occasion to crack down on Romish tendencies at the seminary. But by then the ethereal Arthur Carey was dead of a fever, buried at sea off Cuba where he sailed in the hope of recovering his health, and Clarence had dropped out of the seminary for good.

WORSENING eye problems were only a pretext for his escape. Heading north in 1844 toward Lake Champlain, he joined forces with another heterodox seminarian, Edgar Wadhams, on the Wadhams family farm near Ticonderoga. There they attempted to found a monastery on the Cistercian model, practicing ritual in an open-roofed log-house cloister and reading to servants and local children from the liturgy and the lives of the saints. In early spring they made a voyage to Montreal, eager to see a real Catholic city, and—having been "brought up in the barrenness of Protestantism"—were overcome in Notre Dame by the robes, the chanting, the bursts of organ music. For Clarence the sensory richness of Catholic ceremony was the other side, the outer casing, of an ideal of extreme ascetic discipline.

Within weeks Clarence was off on the ferry downriver, leaving a note for Wadhams (still reluctant to commit himself fully to Catholicism) in which he declared his decision to go over to the Roman Church: "In a few minutes I shall be gone—and oh . . . how wildly something beats within! It seems as if I were about to separate from everything I love, and my poor heart, faithless and unconscientious, wants to be left behind among the Protestants." He had made an appointment in New York with the Redemptorist convent on Third Street. The shabbiness of their building pleased him: "Everything was new and poor. I liked it all the better for its destitution." In short order he made his profession of faith. He had already decided to take orders; he would sail to Europe in August to undergo his novitiate at St. Trond in Belgium.

Having informed his parents by letter, he made a farewell visit to Saratoga. His mother was bitter. The intensity of Maria's conversion two decades earlier had not abated, and now she confronted an equal and incompatible intensity in the son who had sung hymns with her and brought her foot warmer to the church. There was no way to bridge the gap. They said their last good-bye in Albany. As he watched his mother through the window of the departing Saratoga train, he saw that she had buried her face in her arm in a posture of grief.

As for the Chancellor, he made one last improbable effort to keep Clarence in the family fold, by offering him a job as probate clerk in his court, with an excellent salary—unless, of course, Clarence preferred to abandon his parents and friends. Whatever his decision, the Chancellor assured him, he would continue to pray for Clarence's happiness now and in eternity, even if he turned out to be "the means of rendering the residue of my life miserable, if not of abridging its duration." The response was a foregone conclusion. Clarence was not free to accept his father's kind offer: "I am persuaded the voice of God calls me elsewhere."

It was not happiness that he was looking for, Clarence explained. He was abandoning a life of wealth, independence, and warm social ties in favor of "a life among strangers ... poverty and perpetually recurring humiliations and mortifications." He was embracing a faith held in contempt in America. But Jesus had suffered no less. To the dry resentful tone of his father's letter Clarence responded with a passionate outcry: "Here is then on one hand, the call of God, and on the other the cry of flesh and blood. Which shall I follow? Clearly I must follow God, although my heart should break in the meanwhile ... Farewell! then, dear Father, and forgive me all the grief I have ever caused you, and especially this last of all. *It is I who give you the wound, but I strike through my own flesh.*"

A few days later, on August 1, 1845, Clarence sailed with his fellow seminarian James McMaster and another distinguished convert—Isaac Hecker, a former resident of the utopian settlement Brook Farm and a familiar of Emerson and Bronson Alcott—toward his new life with the Redemptorist Fathers. Abandoning the "stifling village circle" of Saratoga, the machinations of railroad magnates and upstate lawyers, the unruly noise and slanging arguments of American democracy, he prepared to enter a realm of obedience and silence.

WHILE Clarence was immersing himself in the tracts of John Henry Newman and feeling out a path toward the forms and rituals of the Primitive Church, his younger brother, Mansfield, was beginning to savor the prerogatives of a chancellor's son. Just entering his teens, the "little rascal" was already showing signs of blossoming into an imperious young dandy.

Ten years younger than Clarence, Mansfield regarded his older brother more as a parental figure than a sibling. When he was four, his mother gave birth to her last child, Fanny. But Mansfield's little sister died at five, and so from the age of nine Mansfield found himself in effect an only child surrounded by elder authorities. When he came to write novels, they gave him an occasion to offer a series of variations on the same essential self-portrait: the protagonist was always an isolated hero of rare genius and moral worth whose qualities had gone somehow unappreciated by those around him, and who managed just barely to restrain his seething resentment at that neglect.

A fugitive glimpse of Mansfield at twelve survives, thanks to a chance encounter with a young lawyer who would later make a record of their meeting. In the summer of 1843, L. B. Proctor had traveled to Saratoga to be sworn in by the Chancellor as a solicitor in chancery. Surprised to learn from a local resident that his destination was not a courthouse but the Chancellor's own home, he proceeded to stroll over to Pine Grove. Court was in session.

At the front gate Proctor met a boy whose appearance immediately impressed him: "His form, set off by a fashionable dress, was exceedingly graceful and attractive; but it was not his form and dress that chiefly attracted attention; it was the bold, buoyant, intelligent expression that presided over his handsome face. There was something in the restless though penetrating and semi-impudent glance of his eye that indicated a haughty, arrogant nature, and an ill-regulated mind."

Mansfield, who was just back from boarding school, wasted no time asking the stranger his business, and inquired where he hailed from. When Proctor indicated Cayuga County, the boy asked if he knew an acquaintance of his at Auburn, whom it turned out Proctor did know somewhat. "When you see him again," said Mansfield, "tell him you met an old school-mate of his at Saratoga." "What name shall I give him?" "Mansfield Walworth. I think he'll remember me, for I gave him a thrashing just before we left school."

Proctor, taken aback by the boy's contemptuous tone, proceeded to introduce himself further, thinking to establish his own respectable credentials. Mansfield cut him short: "Perhaps I have no desire to make your acquaintance. You should have thought before you proposed to *honor* me with an introduction." Then, assuming the tone of a jaded insider, he went on to give Proctor a tip on how long he could expect to wait to have his business expedited: the attorneys John Collier and Daniel Dickinson were arguing a case before his father, "and they are both endless."

Going into the courtroom, Proctor then watched as the Chancellor exercised his role with the usual mix of homespun dignity and peremptory interruption. Only decades later, long after Mansfield's death and with the clarity of hindsight, did the lawyer have occasion to linger over his impression of the judge's younger son: "His remarks and manner had something in them approaching to the *bizarre*, blended with a kind of repulsive sarcasm which he intended for dignity." He had come to think of him as "an instrument strangely attuned, jarring with wild contrasts"—Roderick Usher as a twelve-year-old boarding school bully, precocious and defensive.

THE Chancellor seems not to have approved of thrashing, although Clarence recalled undergoing harsh punishment after breaking the church windows as a boy. By 1847, at least, Chancellor Walworth had gone on record with his belief that "corporal punishment, as a means of moral discipline . . . is pernicious in its tendency. It frequently has the effect to harden the offending child." Parents and teachers must, of course, insist on absolute obedience to all reasonable demands. But violence should not be necessary except as a last resort "to correct deliberate and malicious or perverse disobedience."

In his statement on the subject the Chancellor did not indicate whether he had ever encountered such malice or perversity in his own family.

Afterward many would opine that a little more corporal punishment might have done the young Mansfield a world of good. A writer for the *Utica Morning Herald*—claiming, like so many upstate journalists, an inside knowledge of the family—asserted that the Chancellor's absorption in his public career allowed young Mansfield to run wild and become completely spoiled: "He was not only ready for the spasm of profanity, but for bloody fight when occasion required, at least with a weaker party, for like all tyrants, he combined cowardice with arrogance." The Chancellor's loss of control over his son, the *Herald* writer ventured, bore an eerie resemblance to the plot of a book "long since gone out of print," Mary Shelley's *Frankenstein*. In this reading, Mansfield, the ultimate spoiled child, had gone on to become a monster of exceptional proportions.

There is no knowing what befell Mansfield at home in his earliest years. A close friend of the family recalled him as having been the Chancellor's favorite child. But at least one contemporary—an anonymous writer who was one of the few to express much sympathy for Mansfield—suggested that the Chancellor had "ruled his household with a rod of iron . . . and in the gloomy family home the Puritanical ideas which found favor in the days of our grandfathers were strictly enforced." It was precisely this rigid upbringing, the writer concluded, that would trigger Mansfield's subsequent pattern of behavior: "The boy who when at home was afraid to call his soul his own became the fastest young man in the college."

Mᴀɴꜱꜰɪᴇʟᴅ's early sense of entitlement had everything to do with who his father was. His sarcastic airs were fed by a keen appreciation of the family's status, even if later he would chafe at being forever iden- tified as "the Chancellor's son."

The years of his early childhood were precisely those of his father's unquestioned glory. Now, as he entered adolescence—reaching an age when he was likely taking a more conscious look at what that glory really consisted of—a series of unanticipated upsets altered his father's position in fundamental ways. Within five years the Chancellor's pub- lic career would peak. By the time Mansfield graduated from Union College in 1849, his father's long judicial dominance was over.

For an exhilarating moment in 1844 it looked as if Reuben Hyde Walworth was about to realize his highest ambition. A vacancy opened on the Supreme Court, and President John Tyler wanted to find a New Yorker to fill the post. Walworth, out of the political fray in any direct way for decades, seemed generally acceptable; but Senate Whigs resisted, hoping their man Henry Clay would win the next election and give them a more palatable option.

Indeed, the Whig leader Thurlow Weed suggested in a letter to a political colleague that Walworth's own partisans had mixed motives for wanting him on the Supreme Court: "He is recommended by many distinguished Members of the Bar of the State *merely because they are anxious to get rid of a querulous, disagreeable, unpopular Chancellor.*" The nomination had already run into trouble when Walworth's chief backer in Tyler's cabinet, Secretary of the Navy Thomas W. Gilmer, had the misfortune to be blown up along with seven others during the cata- strophic testing of an experimental cannon on board the USS *Princeton* on February 27. Whatever the reasons, Walworth was finally rejected by the Senate. A rumor—or perhaps only an inevitable joke—circulated to the effect that he had lost Tyler's support because his constant harping on his ancestor Lord Mayor Walworth had offended the president, proud of his descent from the rebel Wat Tyler.

Walworth had been elated at the prospect of this honor and could not have been much comforted by a letter from Clarence, in his monastic Ticonderoga retreat. Clarence encouraged him to look on the bright side: by not getting the appointment he was saved from the temptations and hazards of increased wealth and worldly honor. The pleasures of this world, he reminded his father, could only diminish his "eternal gains."

THE failed nomination brought to the fore some long-standing complaints about the Chancellor. His obtrusive courtroom manners and his backlog of unfinished legal business were now a matter for public debate. Editorials questioned the "one-man power" he exercised over much of the state's legal system.

It was an earlier wave of judicial reconfiguration that had brought Walworth to power in the first place, back in the 1820s when Van Buren and his Bucktails had revamped the state's supreme court and established the circuit judge system in which Walworth had made his mark. Now there were calls for further and more radical reforms. It was a deeply unsettled moment. The state's politics had been in turmoil for years over the so-called Anti-Rent Wars, pitting tenant farmers against the landholders who (through a virtually feudal system unique to New York) controlled immense tracts of upstate farmland. The war was at times a hot one; in August 1845 a band of antirenters dressed as Indians killed a deputy sheriff in Delaware County—hardly the first such violence—and Governor Silas Wright declared the county to be in a state of insurrection. Reformist Whigs threw in their lot with radical antirent forces, and the upshot was a state constitutional convention that quickly became an arena for the playing out of local and national conflicts. Both Whig and Democratic parties were by now split into factions over the issue of slavery, and it took some last-minute collusion between supposedly hostile elements to block a move that would have granted suffrage to Negro males.

One thing the convention did manage to accomplish was a thorough remolding of the state's judiciary system. Judges were now to be elected; the legislature (whose members had up to now participated in the state's supreme court) would no longer play a judicial role; a new legal code (affecting, among other things, married women's property rights) was to be established; and, not least, the court of chancery was to be done away with altogether.

To some, such changes seemed harbingers of a radical apocalypse. The cranky lawyer hero of James Fenimore Cooper's ultracranky novel *The Ways of the Hour*, published in 1850, railed interminably against the election of judges and the imposition of the new state legal code, viewing them as part and parcel of an intolerable wave of change: "pro-nigger, anti-gallows, eternal peace, woman's rights, the people's power, and anything of that sort, sweeps like a tornado through the land."

In any event Chancellor Walworth would soon be out of a job. As a consolation he was named to the committee overseeing the drafting of the new code, an appointment that struck many as incongruous. The state senate, according to an editorial in Horace Greeley's *Tribune*, could hardly have chosen a better way to evade the reformers' intentions than by turning to Chancellor Walworth, who had "made his rules of practice so tedious and voluminous, and his court so useless, injurious, costly and perplexing, that it was declared in Convention to be an intolerable, unbearable nuisance, and as such, with its masters and examiners in Chancery, forever abolished and abated."

Even though Walworth's political and business associates would see that he never lacked for employment, he had—without his noticing exactly when it had happened—become an emblem of a waning era. To be exposed to such unrestrained and mocking attack, and then to be stripped so abruptly of his position, might have unnerved a man less sure of himself, but if Walworth was affected he gave no public sign.

One further public humiliation awaited. For the first time since his brief term as congressman, Walworth ventured into the political arena, accepting in 1848 an invitation to run for governor of New York. Nominating the gray but supposedly reassuring Walworth was a desperate measure to shore up a party in disarray. The struggle over the extension of slavery (heightened by the acquisition of new territories in the Mexican War) had split New York's Democrats into opposing factions. When the national party convention in Baltimore degenerated into a chaotic fight over seating credentials, the antislavery Barnburners walked out; the conservative Hunkers who remained nominated the reliably partisan but thoroughly unexciting Lewis Cass to run for president against the Whig candidate Zachary Taylor. The Barnburners—regrouping under the banner of "Free Soil, Free Speech, Free Labor, and Free Men"—brought Martin Van Buren out of retirement to contend with Cass and Taylor on the Free Soil ticket. In November, the Democratic split would ensure the election of Taylor, who although a slaveholder was also widely admired as the greatest military hero to have emerged from the Mexican War. However much the conflict over slavery extension may have been exacerbated by the war, Americans could still unite around a patriotic triumph like the Battle of Buena Vista.

Walworth was too regular a party loyalist even to consider backing anyone but Cass. As far as slavery went, he acknowledged its evils, but (as he clarified in a statement released to the press) he relied upon "philanthropists at the south" to bring about gradual emancipation, a slow and delicate process that could only be delayed by northern agitation.

Slavery as an essentially philanthropic issue had been one of the many causes that had occupied the Chancellor over the years. He had long been associated with the Colonization Society and its program of freeing slaves through purchase and sending them to Africa to found Christian colonies. For a time he had worked energetically as a public spokesman for the society. The English antislavery activist Edward Abdy had observed him at a crowded New York meeting in 1833, denouncing freeborn blacks as "a wretched and degraded race" and suggesting that no virtuous woman would allow her child to marry a colored person.

Walworth's speech enraged Abdy: "Mark the Chancellor's logic: 'My daughter will not marry you, because you are degraded: therefore you deserve to be degraded, and if my voice has any weight, shall be degraded, because my daughter will not marry you.' ... The more I saw and heard of this odious and disgusting antipathy, the more convinced I felt that a civilized nation, thus tattooed and crippled in mind, is, in point of moral dignity, below those savage tribes that merely paint the body or compress the skull."

Abdy spoke a language the Chancellor could scarcely have understood. For Walworth colonization was true emancipation, not to be confused with "that *unconstitutional* and dangerous emancipation contemplated by a few visionary enthusiasts, and a still fewer reckless incendiaries among us." He had written this in 1836, already foreseeing the time when such incendiaries might "*arm one part of the Union against another*, and light up the flame of civil war in this now happy land." As always he represented himself as the voice of light and reason warding off forces of fanaticism and brutality. But by the late 1840s he had been put on the defensive by abolitionists like Gerrit Smith, a colleague from the temperance movement who finally broke with him in a public letter: "You cannot legalize robbery and murder. Much less can you legalize slavery,—that infernal compound, the numerous horrible elements of which include both robbery and murder."

Walworth was also a spokesman for those close ties between northern and southern elites that were cultivated so assiduously at Saratoga. The spa was a favorite resort for Southerners, and a perfect spot for cementing the business relationships that encouraged a wide tolerance for slavery among New York merchants and industrialists. Southern visitors brought with them an aura of romantic traditions and admirably antique codes of honor. Young Mansfield would grow up admiring the poetry he found in southern ways—a poetry of duels and assignations and Byronic pride—so much more appealing to him than Yankee calculation and litigiousness.

But to a growing number of New Yorkers—enough to swing, if not to win, an election—it looked as if the compromising reasonableness of Reuben Hyde Walworth and his colleagues had crossed the line into active and irredeemable collaboration. An opposition newspaper declared: "That precious band of politicians, headed by Marcy, Walworth, and Croswell . . . have not only ruined the *party*, but they have ruined *themselves*. Their political honesty has long since vanished, and upon their banner, written with the blood of *Slavery*, they have inscribed the doctrine of SLAVERY NOW AND FOREVER."

ALONG with his running mate Charles O'Conor, a far more strident defender of slavery, the ex-Chancellor went down ignominiously in the gubernatorial election, coming in a poor third as the Whig candidate Hamilton Fish swept to victory on Zachary Taylor's coattails. The honorary degree Walworth received from Harvard that year may have palliated his defeat. But the diminution of his public glory had been accompanied by a succession of private blows. As he was running for governor, his rebellious son Clarence was being ordained as a priest in Belgium; his daughter Mary Elizabeth, after the untimely death of her

merchant husband, had moved back into the household with her children; and Walworth was mourning the death of his wife, Maria, which
occurred in April 1847. During her long and painful illness, it was said,
she had stared at Clarence's portrait, unreconciled to his conversion.

The force of Maria's early turn toward religion had been sustained
throughout her life. As the Chancellor's wife she cultivated a flair for
fine furniture and household adornments, but she was better known
for the peculiar intensity of her spiritual life. When she died, a local
minister recollected years later, it had the effect of "the breaking of that
alabaster box of precious ointment which was poured upon the Savior's feet, and the odor of which filled all the house." Dr. Sprague, for-
merly her minister in Albany, exalted her as a nearly saintly model in
his eulogy: "Many of us knew,—I, myself, knew well,—when she
resided here, that she had, in a pre-eminent degree, her conversation
in Heaven . . . She lived habitually, as seeing Him who is invisible."
Reverend Alfred Chester, a cousin of the Walworths who delivered
her funeral sermon in Saratoga, spoke of how the dying Maria had
pointed to a corner of the room to indicate the spot where she had
received assurance of her salvation from Jesus: "He told me he would
be my advocate. Isn't he precious?" Others recalled her care for the
poor and sick, for victims of drunkenness and degradation, for
orphaned children whether white or black.

Of what her death meant to her seventeen-year-old son, Mansfield,
some trace would persist in the succession of saintly mothers in his fiction, caring tirelessly for the weak and the outcast, the wrongly accused
and the oppressed. She could be glimpsed, perhaps, in the mother who
rescued an orphaned black stable hand in *Hotspur*, or the matron in *Lulu*
who displayed a true Christian tolerance despite belonging to the Presbyterian church—a church Mansfield would otherwise depict as a nest
of joyless, judgmental backbiters. The death scene in *Hotspur* must
surely have been an evocation of Maria's passing: "In a dim and silent
chamber of that silent manor house, the pale, suffering, holy mother was
dying . . . Struggle, oh! chestnut branches in your convulsive grief—sigh,
oh! grass of the fields, bowed down and desolate, and whisper in grief, oh!
encircling evergreens—for the eye which reveled in your beauty, and in
your wonderful formation found the hand and the power of her God, is
fast closing upon you forever." The mother's dying words would again

be a rebuke to the censorious and narrow-minded: "The lonely and deserted are all God's children. He loves them all. Let no one dare revile or persecute or shun the lonely of any grade or any rank."

Whenever this saintly ghost floated through Mansfield's imaginings—tolerant, forgiving, seeing past the trivialities of dogmatic prejudice and class distinction—there would be an eerie sense of psychic intrusion. Some internalized version of his mother strove from beyond the grave to untangle the confusions of his narratives, and bring some peace to the deeper disorder those confusions mirrored.

THE family—all but Clarence, still in Europe, and well embarked on his career as a Catholic missionary—assembled to hear Reverend Chester's discourse on "The Union of the Redeemer with the Redeemed." It was later printed as a chapbook of which Mansfield would take pains to acquire a copy in later years. Chester took as his text the declaration of Jesus before his disciples at the Last Supper, in the Gospel of John: "Father, I will that they also whom thou hast given me be with me where I am." But what, Chester asked, could it mean to be with Jesus in the afterlife? In what kind of body could we share his company? And in what form would he be perceptible to us? What kind of exchanges and relations could possibly occur in that sphere of being?

To give the answer meant going back to the beginning—to the Creator dwelling in Heaven amid obedient angels, at "the seat of empire." Suddenly God was troubled by an outbreak on the newly created world: "The voice of daring rebellion was heard." But instead of the instant annihilation that such insubordination merited, God's infinite mercy instead sought a pardon attainable only through the sacrifice of his own son. The son would descend to Earth, become a man, make of men his companions. He would not only redeem them; he would honor them eternally with his company, just as he promised that the disciples should eat and drink at his table. What the Savior promised to the redeemed, in Reverend Chester's telling, was no less than "the pleasant and friendly intercourse of the family circle."

And to preserve the friendly intimacy of that circle, he will take on the same form as those he has redeemed. What form that is we cannot know; we have not been told; even if we were told, we probably could not grasp it. Yet can we really believe that even if Christ assumes the same form as us, he will really be the same as us? Even in the brilliant daylight of Heaven some trace of sin will still be visible, "like the scar of a healed wound." And nonetheless the Savior will consent—will condescend—to take on that form, and we will share with him—what? Not merely the contentment of safety and happiness but an infinitely greater joy "such as thrills through the bosom of the glorified Son of God."

God the Father will look at us, in our resurrected form, with the same emotion he feels for his own Son. As for the Son, it may be that his intent all along was to secure for himself eternal companions— even if he can still see the scars of their wrongdoing.

Even in Heaven, it can be assumed, the scars will be eternal.

7

~~~~~~~~

Hardins and Walworths

IN the autumn of 1850 Reuben Hyde Walworth went to Louisville, Kentucky, to attend to some legal business. Since losing his post—but not his title, which clung to him respectfully for the rest of his life—the Chancellor had done a great deal of traveling. Relieved of judicial duties, he embarked on a busy private practice, fed by a stream of government business courtesy of former colleagues and associates.

In Louisville he met Mrs. Sarah Hardin, a thirty-nine-year-old widow who had lost her husband in the Mexican War, in the same year that Walworth had lost his wife.

Mrs. Hardin made enough of an impression on him that when he got home he at once wrote her a proposal of marriage. She responded with equal promptness. The whole transaction unfolded rapidly. It was managed, not perhaps with reckless speed, but with the practicality of experienced traders who understood the terms and conditions on both sides, or imagined they did.

The bland refinement of Sarah's initial reply—it might easily have been adapted from a handbook of etiquette—scarcely concealed an impatience to get on without fuss: "I feel highly flattered and much grateful that one who I respect and esteem so highly should choose me from the world to be a friend and companion . . . If the impressions received on so transient an acquaintance be as lasting as they were bright and beautiful I know of no good reason why matters should not terminate as favorably as you desire."

A few more letters sealed the deal. Reuben was clear enough about his needs: "The requisites I desire in her who is to be the partner of my bosom are gentleness, amiability of temper, benevolence, mental culture, and a decided Christian character or personal piety as distinguished from mere formalism in religion." With regard to all but the last of these traits, he told Sarah, their single encounter had been enough to set him at ease—although he had made some additional inquiries just to be sure. On the matter of religion she undertook to adjust, as best she could, her Episcopalian ways to his more austere Presbyterianism. She knew all about the Presbyterians; her mother had raised her in that church, and she had only recently stopped being a member.

To the Chancellor it must have seemed a belated windfall to be rewarded in his sixties with the charms of an entrancing widow twenty-three years his junior—a year younger in fact than his first-born daughter. Sarah was a woman of taste and experience, livelier and more intellectually curious, certainly, than the devout Maria. Though not in the least irreligious, she appears to have been more inclined toward attending fancy dress balls and mingling with the politically powerful than toward having private conversations with her Savior in the corners of rooms—as if life were really here to be enjoyed rather than endured as a way station in the shadow of the final judgment.

SARAH came of what she saw as a robust and heroic line, settlers of the country as the Chancellor's forebears had been, but in a region—western Kentucky and eastern Illinois—that remained to a degree unsettled. The touch of wilderness was still on them. The Hardins—just like, on Sarah's side, the equally tough and determined Smiths and Logans—had always been explorers, settlers, Indian fighters. They didn't just live in places; they founded them. The model was established by the old patriarch and namesake Colonel John Hardin, who after distinguishing himself in the Revolutionary War—at Saratoga, in fact, under General Horatio Gates—set off into the wilds of Kentucky, marched out with the militia along the Wabash, and took arms against the Kentuckys and the Miamis whenever required, finally getting himself shot down by some renegade Potawatomi while engaged, it was said, on a peace-making expedition. The place where he fell became Hardin County.

A glimpse of Sarah on her native ground survives in the memoir of a young preacher, one Truman Marcellus Post, who passed through Jacksonville, Illinois, in the early days when it was—in Post's high-falutin phraseology—"a new world, socially embryonic, genetic, in a period demiurgic, constantly engaged with primordial problems." There he observed memorably disordered scenes of "trading, horse racing, carousing, gambling, and fighting of all kinds," and met, among such local society as there was, the "rather crude and roughly dressed young Kentucky lawyer" John Hardin and Sarah, his "brilliant young wife, a dashing Kentucky belle, afterwards known to the country as Mrs. Chancellor Walworth."

This was the era when Stephen Douglas and Abraham Lincoln were relatively obscure local figures; Douglas was a guest at the same party, where Post met the Hardins, and, through her cousin Mary Todd, Sarah would become closely acquainted with Lincoln. Sarah's husband, the seemingly crude young lawyer John Hardin, would vie with Lincoln for advantage, momentarily forestalling his fellow partisan's ambitions; and, on one occasion that attained legendary status, he intervened when Lincoln and a political rival were on the verge of fighting a duel and brought the parties to a tranquil resolution.

Hardin—who built the first brick house in Jacksonville and went on to serve as a Whig congressman—was also a warrior in the family tradition. He served with distinction in the Black Hawk War, and through cool judgment was said to have averted a bloody mob attack on the Illinois Mormons following the murder of Joseph Smith, ensuring that the Saints would be expelled more or less peacefully from the state. The versatility to be at once soldier and politician was a trait of this dynasty. Everything that needed doing the Hardins could do, with a certain humor and riproaring delight. "We all recollect," proclaimed one of Hardin's eulogists, "the great display of his legal ingenuity, the power of his sarcasm, his inimitable wit, the originality of his manner, and his soul stirring eloquence." While Chancellor Walworth had been noted at times for legal ingenuity and sarcasm, his public discourse would not often, or indeed ever, be called "soul stirring."

His wife treasured the rough-hewn love poems John Hardin had written out for her—

I remember when boyant with health and with joy,
Her presence first caught my eye
When her bright witching smile which no ill could alloy
Cost my heart full many a sigh.

—and after his death wrote despondently to her sister: "My heart dies within me and I still have the feeling I had when first I knew the sad tiding that my husband had fallen on the field of battle, how can I live, how dark and lonely will be the journey of life." But during the couple's long separation after he embarked on his Mexican expedition, she wrote to him in tones of deep discontent: "Life is too short to be wasted in the way you are living, but I hope you enjoy it . . . I suppose you are writing a book from your writing so few letters and they so short."

For his daughter Ellen, born in 1832, John Hardin was an object of "unbounded devotion." She recalled following him everywhere, learning from him about every tree and pond and bird, keeping company with his hunting dogs on expeditions into the woods. He taught her to ride when she was five years old, becoming, according to her brother Martin, "a good & fearless rider." When she was eleven her father lost an eye and shattered part of his face when the breech pin of his gun exploded while he was hunting alone. He walked for many miles in extreme pain and distress back to the family farmhouse, where what was left of his ruined eye was extracted. Unobserved by the adults, Ellen remained in a corner watching the whole operation. She held her breath, deeply impressed that her father did not utter a sound despite his evident agony. She determined that she would not cry out either.

BY the autumn of 1850 Sarah and her brood—Ellen, now nineteen, and two younger sons, Martin and Lemuel—could cling at best to their sense of pride and history. Times had been hard for them after the heroic death of her husband at the Battle of Buena Vista. The late Colonel Hardin's end was indeed something to remember. He had shouted "Charge bayonets! Remember Illinois!" to his regiment of infantrymen up to the moment when, unhorsed and overwhelmed by a company led by Santa Anna himself, he took a bullet in the neck and five Mexican lances through his body—not before squeezing off a last pistol shot to bring down one of his attackers. So at least his daughter would describe the scene decades later. But the glory of the family name was overshadowed by money troubles and the death of Lizzy, the beloved youngest child.

Ellen at nineteen was bookish and flirtatious, her head filled with heroic stanzas out of Byron and Scott and Plutarch, whose *Lives* were, she later recalled, "like a long continued fairy story to my young imagination." For all their rugged frontier ways, the Hardins had a strong literary bent. Ellen's paternal grandmother, notwithstanding the ferocious rigidity of her Calvinism, kept close at hand the poems of Burns and the essays of Addison; her father, a graduate of Kentucky's Transylvania University, immersed himself in Guizot's history of European civilization and Thiers's account of the Peninsular War; her mother, as Ellen recalled, took an interest in her youth in the philosophy of Locke and Comte; and the conversation of her uncle Abram Smith, a slave-owning Mississippi planter, was steeped in the language of Shakespeare: "I have never met anyone who had the great dramatist at such ready call."

Her brother Martin, never much of a reader, recalled simpler pursuits, the joys of prairie dog hunts and spear fishing and learning how to throw a Bowie knife. He remembered too the fears that clung to the lives of children: the terror of a ghost chasing after them in a cemetery— "as I have learned since it was a crazy woman"—or the sinister aura attached to a solitary doctor who practiced mesmerism on a Negro girl "and made her say and do things she could not possibly know or do if she had not been under the control of some other person." A fear of ghosts lingered with him so powerfully that as an adolescent he visited dissecting rooms in order to cure himself of timidity.

Ellen was an exceptionally attractive young woman, intense and willful, and her social life was already strewn with broken engagements. On extended stays with her uncle in Mississippi, she would absorb what she later described as "the beautiful patriarchal life" on his plantation. She made the most of whatever refinements the supposedly backward South had to offer, keeping up to date on the cultural excitements of the day: in Saint Louis she went to hear Jenny Lind sing and thrilled at Shakespearian performances by the great stars of the day: Edwin Booth, Edwin Forrest, Fanny Kemble, Charlotte Cushman.

Even after her father's death she seems to have been shielded from rough edges by the circles in which she moved. Her best friend, Mary Duncan, was the daughter of Illinois governor Joseph Duncan, and the bloodlines of her acquaintances charted the crisscrossing alliances of a budding regional aristocracy. (Her grandmother, after the death of her first husband, married Henry Clay's younger brother.) As she moved from house party to house party within that cultivated orbit, borne along in a world of antebellum gaiety that she would always miss, she could remark to her mother with blithe optimism: "I sometimes think I must be one of fortune's favorites, I find some kind friends who are interested in me wherever I go."

There was another member of the Hardin household: their slave. Dolly—known as Dolly Smith (from Sarah's maiden name) and later as Dolly Walworth—was not technically a slave, since Illinois law recognized only a form of indentured servitude with a fixed term, but she had been acquired as an infant and was given over to the Hardins under terms indistinguishable from slavery until her eighteenth year. She accompanied the family when Sarah went north to live at Pine Grove with the Chancellor, and—whatever the ambiguities of Illinois law—her status on crossing the state line changed automatically to that of a freewoman. New York had decreed the gradual abolition of slavery in an emancipation law of 1817, and by the late 1820s the institution no longer existed in the state.

Ellen and her brothers felt that Dolly's fortunes were intimately linked with theirs. In old age Martin remembered her as his "great friend," and her name figured in virtually every memory of childhood. Her comings and goings, in the years when the family became increasingly fragmented, would figure in their letters and diaries as events signaling the arrival or departure of good and secure times. A skilled and literate woman, Dolly would play a crucial if mostly obscured role in keeping the Hardins together through very rough times. If Ellen reminisced nostalgically in her old age about slavery as "a bond of mutual interest and protection between whites and blacks," her intense and lifelong relationship with Dolly was perhaps what she had most clearly in mind.

WHEN the Chancellor came courting, did Sarah see chiefly an opportunity to escape from premature widowhood into a place of national prominence—the place her late husband would surely have achieved if not cut off early—by marrying the great and famous Walworth? Or was their brief first meeting really as "bright and beautiful" as her letter indicated, a lightning bolt sufficient for her to uproot herself and her family? After that initial encounter in the fall, they did not see each other until their wedding the following April. "It is rather strange," Sarah wrote to him on March 7, "that we should have kept up the interest in each other with so short an acquaintance to begin with and so broken a correspondence, living so widely separated we do not hear of each other." Two days later, she wrote again: "Would you know me if you were to meet me on the street unexpectedly. I do not believe you would."

Reuben and Sarah's wedding on April 19, in Harrodsburg, Kentucky, was the union not simply of two individuals but of two families. Henceforth Sarah, Ellen, Martin (once he got back from boarding school in Illinois), eleven-year-old Lem, and "indispensable Dolly" would all become residents of the "plain, low, old fashioned frame manse" that greeted Ellen when they arrived at Pine Grove. She had perhaps expected a more elaborate dwelling. But what first impressed her was the transition from the bright open light of the prairies to the sense of being enclosed by the "sublime yet somber" pines that towered over the Chancellor's home. Closer to the house, providing it with comfortable shade, was a cluster of elms, and it was the elms that at first seemed to offer emotional refuge. The pines for a long time seemed a more alien presence: "When the tall and swaying pines sang their melodies in the midnight hours," she recalled years later, "a mysterious influence pervaded them."

The migration was not without its culture shocks, for all the Hardins. Sarah had written to the Chancellor before their wedding, "A cold climate and a free state is not altogether congenial with my tastes and habits." (She had, however, already determined that her brother's Mississippi plantation was "decidedly the last place to raise children, our boys are running wild here.") The children, in Martin's recollection, had been "educated to despise the Yankees," and Ellen complained early on that northerners were "so outrageously conceited and selfish that they think it a moral impossibility for anybody from the other side of the Alleghenies to be refined or proper in any respect." Nothing had prepared her for the first Abolitionist speech she chanced to hear: "the ravings of a fanatic combined with the most contemptible and villainous sentiments and principles that I ever imagined a human being would utter." The Yankee world was frosty, hypercritical, and tolerant of public insults that would not have been abided where she came from.

Ellen might have seen herself as something of a creature in a fairy tale—or perhaps in one of the ghost stories that the servants used to tell by the fireside back in Jacksonville, the ones that had filled her with "delightful terror"—transported to another life, to a palace in another country, with different ceremonies and perplexing codes. Having lost her father at fifteen, under circumstances that had been recited to her in all their barbaric horror as a heroic saga, she had now lost her mother to the arms of a sixty-three-year-old widower infatuated with his young bride. Martin later wrote that his mother's remarriage filled him with resentment: "I was so deeply hurt by this that I came near running away & going West." Ellen said nothing about the matter, but it was only after wrestling with anxiety about how she might take it that Sarah had broken the news to her.

The Chancellor's energies were undiminished in his retirement, and to live in his house, as his daughter, was indeed to have entered a different kingdom. Long afterward Ellen would describe his blue eyes as "the most brilliant I have ever seen in a human face." He had been used to exercising control over those around him for so long that his unquestioned sway seemed a comfortable fact of nature. He had created a world around himself—a seat of empire, however tranquilly maintained and however miniaturized.

THE calm nurtured a rebellion. Ellen had entered the arena where that rebellion was to be played out. At some point, months or perhaps years later, it may have occurred to her that she had walked into a trap.

The death of Maria and the withdrawal of Clarence had exposed an ominous gulf between Mansfield and his father. The superior youth of twelve who liked to brag about thrashing his schoolmates had gone on to Union College, his brother's alma mater, even though Clarence—alert to his brother's evident flaws of character—had warned the Chancellor about sending Mansfield there: "It is almost a moral impossibility . . . to pass through it uncorrupted."

Clarence's instincts were accurate. Mansfield, as a journalist would later recount, "went through the usual routine of college dissipation, stabbed one of the students, and gained a notoriety among the worst of the class." The stabbing incident was attested to by a Union classmate who claimed he had received the cut when intervening in a fight between Mansfield and another boy; the wound, he said, "narrowly missed a vital part." By the time he graduated from Union in 1849, Mansfield had acquired an unshakable reputation for drunkenness, debauchery, and general indiscipline.

He had not yet done anything flagrant enough to disgrace the family—the stabbing incident had been hushed up—but, among those close to the family, an indelible impression had already been created of moral weakness and potential danger. That despite his unreliability Mansfield graduated at all, and went on to get his law degree from Harvard, may well have had something to do with Reuben being a long-standing trustee of Union (regarded at the time by some as a sort of diploma mill) and the recent recipient of an honorary degree from Harvard.

His father already felt betrayed by Clarence's escape from his influence. Now the Chancellor confronted a son who seemed fated not merely to disappoint but to embarrass him. Indeed the whole family circle was concerned about Mansfield. They must have surmised for a long time that something was not quite right. The little rascal was maturing into what at times looked like a little demon, a creature of overweening pride, violent outbursts, abrupt shifts of mood. If some trauma had wounded him indelibly, no record of it survives. At nine he had lost his sister Fanny, his only youthful companion in the family. At seventeen he had lost his mother; but by then he was well along his errant way.

Naturally they hoped. The boy had not gotten a grip on himself. He needed to settle on a direction in life. The law did not appear to rouse his ambition much. He announced that he would devote himself to literature; or perhaps—on another day—he would join the army.

Certainly Mansfield was not without gifts. He was physically strong, the very picture of health. His faculties of memory and articulation seemed exceptional. His imagination was abundant, excessively so. From boyhood he had scribbled poems and stories, acted out plays, entertained neighbors and servants with wild comic improvisations—except that they had a tendency to turn wounding and disrespectful.

He had always been a handsome child, a fact of which he was only too aware. Mirrors held an attraction for him. As he approached maturity he expended elaborate care on his appearance. The combing and trimming of his dark curly hair was a matter for serious aesthetic consideration. He became as knowledgeable about clothes as a fashionable tailor, and managed the nuances of his wardrobe in a way that his father—noted for the countrified sloppiness of his attire—could only regard as foppish. Still, he could be a charmer.

ELLEN, at least, was charmed, enough so that any thoughts of the beaux she had left behind in Mississippi and Illinois seem to have receded rapidly. She had felt uprooted after the move to Saratoga. In her twenty-one-year-old stepbrother she found hints of a world she could imagine being part of, a world with enough aura of the forbidden to exert, however covertly, a seductive fascination. Mansfield was, she wrote to her friend Mary Duncan just after meeting him, "a strange boy as ever lived." But she was already sure of his appreciation of "the good and the beautiful." A month later she told Mary, "I wrote so much of brother Manse because he is the person who interests me most at present . . . if you knew him well you could not help loving him." In final commendation she added, "He is so free from all Yankeeism."

For a long time he had fancied himself a southerner at heart: a cavalier equally adept at lyrical flights and roguish mockery, disdainful above all of parsimonious and pettifogging northern ways. Saratoga in season was a fine school for southern manners, and Mansfield had already had occasion to gamble and carouse with the best class of the young plantation heirs. He adored the writings of Edgar Allan Poe, whose exquisitely modulated frenzies he would do his best to imitate. The nationalistic fervor of the emerging secessionist hotheads was something he could admire for its sheer unrestrained boldness. If he had fought no duels, he had certainly dreamt of them.

The art of courtship was part of that tradition, and Mansfield brought to it something more than his father's businesslike straightforwardness. "It is always dangerous," he would later write, "for two beautiful and gifted representatives of the sexes to be brought intimately and alone together, no matter what may be the ostensible necessity for such communion." He had, he was convinced, a flair for making the most of such danger. Ellen was to be drawn into a world of shared poetic delights, and perhaps also of shared instincts for rebellion.

The aspirations of their private world could seem at once erotic and transcendently religious. They found a way to live adjacent to, but apart from, that more rule-bound and coarsely material reality in which the Chancellor and his new wife pursued their domestic happiness. In their own version of the conjugal, Mansfield and Ellen would not only mimic but surpass their elders.

Was it not an exquisite kind of undermining to carry on their courtship in secret—nearly brother and sister as they were—in tandem with the mating of their parents? In the late summer of 1851 it became apparent that Sarah was pregnant. In his old age, the Chancellor might yet beget another male heir worthier than Clarence or Mansfield. In December Ellen told Mary, in confidence, that she and Mansfield considered themselves engaged.

In the meantime something else had happened that was to have unforeseen consequences for all of them. Clarence came back to America. In the three years since his ordination in Belgium he had worked arduously as a missionary priest, propagating the faith and ministering to the faithful in England and Ireland. Now he had returned as one of a contingent of American converts determined to advance the cause of Catholicism in a country where it still came under fierce attack. He became a frequent visitor in Saratoga, and it would become clear over time that Clarence did not intend to remain the isolated religious renegade in the family. His American mission extended into Pine Grove. In Mansfield and Ellen he found apt listeners.

Three years of immersion in religious life had made Clarence a different person. He commanded respect as a figure of charismatic eloquence, capable of eliciting deep feeling from any audience. "He was dramatic without being theatrical," one witness commented. "His voice

was the best preaching voice I ever heard." In the presence of his radiant assurance and sense of otherworldly purpose, the rest of the family
might well have felt themselves a distracted and unworthy lot, consumed with mundane anxieties.

For Mansfield, to whom Clarence had always been held up as a model,
his brother must have been more than ever an object of envy. It was not
enough that Clarence exuded an aura of sanctity. He also displayed easy
authority in areas of art and literature where Mansfield was often a
bluffer, and social graces and worldly knowledge acquired while Mansfield had been stuck at home. And Clarence had returned in triumph:
having dared to defy his father's wishes and embark on a life of his own
choosing, he was now welcomed back to Pine Grove with deference.
Ellen was clearly impressed by him. Seeing the two brothers side by
side may have given her a clearer sense of Manse's rawness.

Mansfield had always been a person of sudden slippery changes of
course. His newest goal, apparently, was to become Clarence. He too,
he announced, would be a Catholic. Perhaps he too would join the
priesthood. He would go to study precisely where Clarence had studied. But under Clarence's influence Ellen also was turning. The returning missionary had unloosed unpredictable forces in the household. In
long sessions he practiced with intimate fervor the skills he had been
honing these past years. Soon it was no longer a secret that Mansfield
and Ellen were serious in their drift toward Catholicism, and the rest
of the family began to exert pressure.

Sarah begged Ellen not to place herself "in the power of those abominable priests." Her brother Martin wrote to her from school: "I
received a letter from mother day before yesterday, which made me
very uneasy. She said you had been reading a good many books on the
Roman Catholic religion, and had nearly persuaded yourself that it
was better than that of your parents . . . Remember your mother, your
brother and all of your friends are much opposed to that religion." He
added, "Do not listen too much to what Manse tells you, for he is
rather enthusiastic in whatever he turns his mind to."

Sarah too was wary of her younger stepson. Even Clarence, she told
Ellen, was skeptical about the idea of Mansfield becoming a priest. For
Sarah it was just a piece of feckless bravado: "I believe the whole affair

is gotten up by him . . . to amuse his friends with the idea he is going to do something his father has never done. Just as he has always been talking of going into the army and all that kind of stuff." The would-be priest, she disdainfully informed her daughter, had spent the morning socializing with Dolly and the other servants, to their great enjoyment as far as she could judge "from the peals of fun and laughter that came up from the kitchen." Why, she begged Ellen, did she not encourage Mansfield to seek some honorable and useful employment? "He is fast bringing his poor old father grey haired with sorrow to the grave."

The Chancellor wrote angrily to Clarence about the situation, stopping just short of accusing him of deliberately fomenting trouble in the family. But he reserved most of his outrage for Mansfield. His younger son was free, of course, to espouse whatever religion he thought right, but to the Chancellor it was transparent that the priesthood was not his vocation. He was quite willing to forgive past misconduct and give Mansfield an allowance while he found his way in a legal career; but, in the meantime, "nothing is gained by his continuing here in idleness, disturbing the peace of my family and bringing disgrace upon me." At length he poured out the full measure of his disappointment.

> He has no capacity for trade and cannot be trusted with money, for as he never learned to earn anything he wasted whatever funds he can get in to his hands . . . I had hoped, after you so grievously disappointed my expectations, that Mansfield would have tried to be something; so that I might have one son to depend upon in my declining years. But I have now given up that hope and all I attempt to pray for is that he may try to do something for his own support and that he will not become entirely useless even to himself.

The exhortations came too late. Mansfield and Ellen formally converted to Catholicism in February. Sarah did her best to reconcile herself to what had happened, but could not at first manage it. "Your conversion to Romanism has been so sudden," she wrote to Ellen, "your conduct so strange, so unnatural, so out of character with yourself altogether. I cannot look upon it in any rational light, but only as a queer headstrong notion you have taken up and are determined to carry out, to show your independence." That she was going to marry Mansfield also took some getting used to. Her brother Martin offered cautious approval: "I think he will make a smart and honorable man if he once gets settled." Back in Jacksonville, Ellen's strict Calvinist grandmother signaled her unhappiness.

It is not recorded what the Chancellor thought of the marriage. Had he conveyed to Sarah all she was entitled to know about Mansfield, the troubling details that might have made her hesitant to let her daughter marry him? Ellen had not been in the household long. How much could she have known about Mansfield's early history? Doubtless a great deal of intimate and potentially disturbing knowledge had not been brought to her attention. On the Walworth side there was perhaps the hope that a good woman might turn the budding prodigal around.

But as always the Chancellor had other preoccupations—his wife's pregnancy not least among them—and in the meantime domestic events moved forward with restless urgency. Perhaps there simply was no time for the sort of conversation that might have clarified everything he knew or sensed about his younger son, in the unlikely event that the father was inclined to that sort of conversation. Most such things, in most families, were after all left in silence. In April the Chancellor celebrated the birth of a son, Reuben Jr.; and on July 29 he attended the wedding of Mansfield and Ellen at St. Peter's church in Saratoga, with Clarence officiating. Ellen was ill—"so deathly sick that I can scarce hold my head up & am afraid to go to bed & give up," as she scrawled in a note to Mary Duncan—and barely made it through the ceremony.

The *New York Herald* published an account of the occasion under the headline "Marriage in High Life," noting that "the fashion and beauty of Saratoga were present to witness the imposing scene." In the evening the Chancellor opened his home for a lavish reception, with William Henry Seward and other luminaries of the New York political world in attendance, and an honored appearance by Washington Irving. The distinguished author had extended his stay in Saratoga—where he had relieved bilious symptoms and found his "mental faculties refreshed, invigorated and brightened up"—to participate in the festivities.

A few days later the bridegroom and bride—whatever her condition—set out for a honeymoon trip to Niagara Falls.

8

〰〰〰〰〰

Sorrows and Joys of
Married Life

REUBEN Hyde Walworth Jr. died in October 1852 at six months
of age. "The Chancellor," Ellen wrote to her grandmother,
"made an idol of the little fellow and is almost heart broken at his loss."
He would sire no more children.

Frank Walworth, Ellen and Mansfield's first child, was born in
August of the next year. The eight years that followed—the years of
childhood that Frank spent growing up at Pine Grove—would to an
outside observer have seemed fairly uneventful, even claustrophobic.
Ellen continued to have babies: another son in 1855, three daughters
between 1856 and 1859. She was often sick, and her correspondence
was punctuated with allusions to long convalescences.

She appears to have had difficulty forming close friendships in
Saratoga. When she reached out it tended to be to other Catholic converts she had come to know, a loosely knit network of those who had
come under Clarence's inspiring influence. Married life seems to have
overwhelmed and muted her. The exuberant young devotee of theater
and poetry became harder to discern in letters that, filled as they were
with the tedium of housekeeping and child-rearing and with constant
struggles against her own and others' bouts of illness, hinted that what
was most important might have been left in silence. The implications

of some of what was happening may not yet have been entirely clear to her. "I do not go out of the house or yard except after dark," she wrote to Mary during her first pregnancy. "Manse is so sensitive of me being seen, especially by young men."

Her mother, Sarah, on the other hand, cultivated an elegant social life both at Pine Grove and elsewhere. The Chancellor still enjoyed showing off his new wife at occasions like the grand dress ball at Saratoga's Union Hall in August 1855, where Sarah shone among "three or four hundred of the most beautiful women who have ever graced any festal hall," in the words of the *Saratogian*. But it was to the social life of Washington that Sarah was increasingly drawn. The political circles to which she had access there were more congenial than the narrower cliques of Saratoga. In the capital she pursued a new-found interest in the preservation of American historic sites, an interest that would in time consume her daughter as well. In 1856 she became vice president of the newly formed Ladies Mount Vernon Association, which a few years later would purchase Washington's neglected home and, as things turned out, help to protect it during the Civil War. All this social prominence came with a price tag in ball gowns and the other paraphernalia of Washington's inner circles.

The Chancellor had not noticeably cut back on his activities—could hardly have afforded to, given his wife's lavish spending. As a chancery judge, Walworth had received a relatively meager stipend. Now as a lawyer he was beginning to rack up considerably higher fees. To some it began to look as if he had mastered the art of making work for himself by extending and complicating the matters entrusted to him. The complaints became vocal during the long and Byzantine progress of the notorious "Spike suit," a case seemingly designed to test the outer limits of complexity in the administration of patent law. Involving the rights to a peculiar hook-headed railroad spike leased by the railroad magnate and upstate political fixer Erastus Corning from the manufacturer Henry Burden, it had already been dragging on for a good many years when Walworth got involved in the wake of the U.S. Supreme Court's 1853 ruling in favor of Burden.

Appointed by the Court to assess the damages due in what some at least considered a reasonably clear-cut case of patent infringement, Walworth would preside over a process so inexplicably prolonged that all participants ended up feeling like hostages. William Henry Seward, representing Corning, wrote to a friend in 1854, when the case still had years to go, of an autumnal visit to Saratoga for yet another hearing: "We are here again. The Chancellor, and the case, and the parties are the same, and all the rest is changed . . . Sheep are feeding in the park, and the statuary that was there has fled, and the music is fled . . . Even the lawsuit has lost its magnitude . . . There is no life left in it. A child could almost do all that I have to do in it, and yet it goes on."

"I wish you would explain what this everlasting spike suit is about," Sarah Walworth asked Seward at one point, "I don't understand it." "Indeed, madam," he replied, "I should be very much ashamed if you did. I have been engaged in it for several years, and I don't understand it yet." The Chancellor's management of the case did little to clarify things. His assiduous, if not obsessive, attention to procedural detail multiplied difficulties and redundancies. Hearings were postponed. Testimony was duplicated many times over. Years went by and witnesses grew old and died, and still the matter remained unresolved.

A lawyer for Burden later described the case as "a series of interminable delays, which threw Jarndyce vs. Jarndyce, of *Bleak House* fame, quite in the shade." Dickens's 1853 novel of an epic and unfathomable lawsuit, devastating the lives of those involved in it unto the second generation, had provided a perfect epigraph for the proceedings: "The Lawyers have twisted it into such a state of bedevilment that the original merits of the case have long disappeared from the face of the earth . . . It's about nothing but Costs, now." The seasons passed, and the Chancellor's fees piled up.

Caught up in the toils of the Spike suit—tracking the interminable and lifeless details of this legal labyrinth—was a reluctant Mansfield. Having gotten his law degree from Harvard in 1852, and passed the bar three years later, he had been enlisted as his father's clerk in the case. Since his son seemed perennially unable to fix on a course of action, the Chancellor had chosen one for him. It was a role in which Mansfield found himself unappreciated and, he would later claim, often unpaid.

As a licensed lawyer with a growing family, it would have been appropriate for him to establish an independent career for himself. Not to do so marked him as something less than a man. But he couldn't seem to pull his life together; nor could he even manage to move out of Pine Grove to set up a home for Ellen and the children. They lingered in the narrow precincts of the family dwelling, coexisting with their elders in an atmosphere doubtless thick with frustration and unvoiced anger.

Mansfield had a weakness for get-rich-quick schemes. With a partner he invested in some land in Saratoga with a view to discovering some new mineral springs, but the effort fizzled early on. At one point he convinced Ellen that they should start a new life in the western territories. He would go out there, alone, and see for himself what opportunities were to be found. The trip took several months and he got as far as Minnesota, but he came home having found nothing, and they did not relocate. Ellen reported to her father-in-law, with whom she increasingly saw eye to eye regarding Mansfield's need to shape up: "I am glad he has seen the country for himself as he will be better satisfied hereafter that it is not all enthusiasts would have us believe."

THE year after their marriage—before the children started coming—had been a period of intellectual excitement for Mansfield. Their conversion to Catholicism, in the wake of long discussions with Clarence, had been like an initiation into higher spheres. Religion became a great romance. His father's Presbyterianism was narrow and provincial by comparison with the sophistication of the ancient church, its robes, its colors, its rituals. While the Chancellor called for total abstinence from drink, the Catholic Church not only tolerated alcohol but incorporated it into its rites. A visit to Pine Grove from Cardinal Bedini, the apostolic delegate of the Vatican—clearly impressed by Clarence's missionary successes—drove home the comparison. The cardinal represented the superior world to which Mansfield felt he naturally belonged, but to which (unlike his brother Clarence) he had so far been denied entry.

In the ferment of that year Mansfield did something that astonished and gratified him: he wrote a novel and got it published—quite likely with Clarence's help, as the publisher was a specialist in Catholic religious literature. Although *The Mission of Death: A Tale of the New York Penal Laws* was framed as a historical novel in the mode of Walter Scott, it devolved for the most part into a baldly schematic piece of Catholic pleading, centered on the martyrdom of a missionary priest in eighteenth-century New York, a figure who in Mansfield's account might have been modeled on Clarence at his most charismatic.

The novel opened with a word-picture of colonial New York, designed to display Mansfield's literary mastery: "The silver lamps of heaven were lighted one by one above the glistening spires of the provincial city; and as their increasing lustre dispelled the gloomy shades of night, distant sounds of festal merriment came swelling from the tranquil bosom of the bay, as if to accelerate the loitering footsteps of the tardy reveller." If he could do nothing else as a writer, he could manufacture paragraphs of that sort without let-up. He was drawn to such language like a drug, and to some degree his intoxication proved salable. Inflated, poeticized, oratorically cadenced language was the common music of the age. *The Mission of Death* went through twelve printings, according to a reference book published some years later—if one can trust a figure whose ultimate source was probably Mansfield.

Any success the book had was probably connected with its usefulness as a tool for Catholic teaching. It read as a sort of child's introduction to the catechism in the form of a storybook adventure. Fugitive Catholics hid out in a New York depicted as a bigoted police state, where the authorities hunted down priests with bloodhounds, just as in *Uncle Tom's Cabin*. Its undigested didacticism might have been lifted from those conversations during which Clarence had instructed Mansfield and Ellen in Catholic doctrine. Mansfield thought nothing of writing a scene in which, for example, two young women passionately debated the concept of transubstantiation for seven or eight pages: "And may not the Almighty Creator of all things, if he desire it, leave the taste, the color, the smell, and the appearance of bread, and yet change himself into the essence of it which is below all these?"

The story also resonated with suggestions of the Walworth family's own inner tensions. A Catholic priest, a convert of great eloquence and intellectual power, was hunted down and executed at the instigation of a fanatical Presbyterian. A younger Catholic, the priest's disciple, found love with a beautiful girl who likewise came over to the faith. There were passages that hinted at an atmosphere in which the religious and the erotic were inextricably mingled, as perhaps during the courtship of Mansfield and Ellen: "Harry had offered her his hand in his own manly way, assuring her that his sense of propriety and duty as a Catholic had not suffered him to indulge the desire of possessing her, until the delightful moment when Agnes made him acquainted with her abjuration of Protestantism."

Mansfield could now take pride in a new identity: he was an author. But for the rest of the decade he failed to write a second book. He anguished instead over the petty legal business that kept him from exercising his real talent. His father had imposed on him something like indentured servitude. And his wife, who ought to have backed him in his attempt to break free, ended up all too often sounding just like his father. She too spoke of monetary responsibility and reliable sources of income. However reluctantly, she judged him and found him wanting. She began to irritate him. Only through their sexual relations did he find a way to keep her from dominating him as everyone else in the family had sought to dominate him. Child followed child, and the times between pregnancies dwindled to the briefest of intervals.

Ellen nurtured her own literary ambitions. Reading had always been fundamental to her sense of the world—nothing was quite real until it had been described in a book, and the world at its most entrancing was a more brightly colored version of what had already been written. Mansfield had wooed her with poems and stories. At some point their encounter must have seemed to her the most real thing that had yet happened to her: real, that is, because it resembled the sort of higher reality she had hitherto found only in poetry. It was in poetry— disillusioned poetry—that she would later try to describe what those early days had been like, when she had inhabited

> the sweet heaven of our love,
> Where I so fondly trusted thee,
> And thought no outer joy could move
> Thy soul from that sphere's ecstasy.

But doubts had insinuated themselves even before the wedding. In a letter to Mary Duncan a few weeks before the ceremony, she had written of Mansfield's "noble intellect," not to mention his "Catholic zeal ever growing," but had ended with a desperately unpunctuated acknowledgment of her misgivings: "I know that in commencing life with one so young, inexperienced as Manse, I shall have to take upon myself part of the burden and I can now see very plainly trials and difficulties to encounter and either to be endured or overcome but my body and heart are young and strong and courageous and almighty God will give me grace as I need it so Molly dear I shall place myself by Manse's side hoping and fearing yet ready to meet all things with him and for him and happy in the thought that our hearts may ever be united in aspiration and strivings after something better and holier than anything we can gain upon earth with our struggles and labors."

She continued to unburden herself to Mary in the first years of her marriage, amid the round of pregnancies and deliveries, constant illnesses and convalescences. Motherhood was the stated theme, the pleasures and difficulties of marital love the barely articulated bass line. "Married life," she wrote in the third year of hers and on the eve of Mary's own wedding, "has its own peculiar sorrows as well as joys; and they are sorrows that bring bitter tears and sharp heart aches too intense to be revealed to any but the Unseen One . . . But I do not mean to speak of these sad things now. Perhaps, you will escape them, dearest. God grant you may!" She advised Mary to expect little out of marriage and recognize that she had no right to demand more. Anything extra should be gratefully appreciated as an unlooked-for bonus. But it was important to learn to do without.

Her closest tie was with Frank, her firstborn, her "noble, beautiful boy." She suffered over weaning him—"it seemed so like tearing myself from him to deny him the nourishment that had sustained his little life"—and as he grew she wrote of "his affectionate disposition which leads him to say unprompted so often in the day 'I loves you dear mama' or 'I will help you up the steps mama' or 'I don't want you to be sorry.'" "It was *maternity*," she told Mary, "that, as it were, renewed my existence . . . It enkindled a spark of love next to Divine, (even nearer than the *wife's* love), which has glowed and burned, and will continue to burn with greater and greater intensity through all time and eternity; until it shall be merged into that Divine Love of which it is a part."

She let Mary know that Mansfield was part of this circle of domestic happiness: "Frank is a great little prattler now, and has won his father's heart, as you would suppose nothing could win him except . . . modesty forbids!" The following winter, now the mother of a second son, she wrote: "I must tell you what a fond father Manse has grown to be. He makes a perfect idol of Frank, thinking that nothing ever was or can be equal to him, and pets and notices Johnny much more than he did Frank at his age."

But Mansfield played a shadowy role in her letters, a creature of not quite defined dissatisfactions and enthusiasms, capricious, easily offended. He was a creature too of absences, increasingly lengthy, explained or otherwise. In New York City he found a world more to his liking, where he could trade as it suited him on his father's name—and it often suited him, since the Chancellor's name opened most doors—but could amuse himself in high and low society without being spied on by family or neighbors. He sought out connections in the world of book and magazine publishing and found for once a milieu where he could fit in quite easily. Manhattan literary life, in its more unbuttoned reaches, offered a thoroughly comfortable theater for his expansive impulses. Going back to Saratoga and the family could seem like a penance. After a time he took rooms in Manhattan, where he could steal away for writing and who knew what else, leaving Ellen and the children at Pine Grove under the Chancellor's care—or more precisely under her mother's care—for long stretches.

CLARENCE visited often at Pine Grove, despite the missionary labors that took him all over the eastern United States. His energy for preaching had for a long time seemed boundless. But evidently, he had reached a crisis point in his ecclesiastical life. The band of American converts with whom he was associated, led by the brilliant Isaac Hecker, had after long deliberation broken away from the Redemptorist order and, with hard-won Vatican approval, reconfigured themselves as the Paulist Fathers. But Clarence—for reasons that neither he nor anyone else ever adequately explained—chose just this moment, when they were struggling to establish their independence, to abandon his fellows. He renounced his membership in the new order, accepting instead a position as parish priest at St. Mary's Cathedral in Albany; and he compounded his rejection by criticizing the Paulists to important members of the American Catholic hierarchy. Some of his former companions regarded his behavior as an incomprehensible betrayal—later commentators would speculate that his envy of the less privileged but more naturally gifted Hecker played a part—and he himself within a few years came to regret having dropped out. In 1860 he wrote to the Paulists from Albany requesting to rejoin them: "I cannot find in my present life that which looks like my vocation . . . My element is not here . . . If you think the old horse can be of any service, I offer him."

During all this period Clarence never relaxed his missionary interest in those nearest to him. The family had come to rely on the firmness of his convictions. He could clearly be a most persuasive man. Sarah and her son Martin were wavering already in the direction of Catholicism, and Dolly as well eventually converted. The daughters born to Ellen in the same period, Ellen ("Nelly") and Clara, received Clarence's special attention, and under changing circumstances he would play an increasingly central part in their lives. One day Mansfield would come to feel as if his role as father had been usurped by his older brother.

THE Chancellor still maintained considerable involvement in public affairs. He kept in constant touch with his old political cronies, happy to play the role of elder statesman. He was rumored to be under consideration for a cabinet post in the Buchanan administration. But these days his political views attracted as much contempt as respect. As the slavery issue continued to widen the gap between political opponents, the forces with whom Walworth was most closely allied were now clearly identified as the "doughfaces" or "hard-shells" of the North, effectively prosouthern elements who, as Southern secession loomed closer and then became a reality, would rally in vain to prevent the outbreak of war.

As the South made good on its threats and began to pull out of the Union, Chancellor Walworth once more projected himself onto the national stage. A Democratic convention held in New York on January 31, 1861, in support of peaceful relations with the six states that had just seceded, gave the old guard a last moment of visibility before the inauguration of Lincoln swept them from the seats of national power. The Whig politician James S. Thayer thundered, to enthusiastic applause, that "when the hand of Black Republicanism turns to blood-red . . . we will reverse the order of the French Revolution, and save the blood of the people by making those who would inaugurate a reign of terror the first victims of a national guillotine!"

The Chancellor, who received a tribute of resounding applause when he rose to speak, sounded a more plaintive note. He spoke of his youthful experiences in Plattsburgh during the War of 1812, recalling the British bullets falling like hail on his home and the sight of fellow citizens shot down at his side. But this was as nothing compared to the horrors of a civil war in which the combatants were joined by blood ties. He likened the seceding Southerners to the American patriots who had led the Revolution, and affirmed, "It would be as brutal, in my opinion, to send men to butcher our own brothers of the Southern States as it would be to massacre them in the Northern States." Any form of conciliation was preferable, if a man wanted to have a clear conscience in his dying hour. Jefferson Davis would remember Reuben Hyde Walworth affectionately as a voice for moderation in the face of fanaticism.

The war had taken the family by surprise, no matter how aware they had been all along of the underlying issues. Those issues had long since become a part of the landscape. The threatened showdown had failed for so long to materialize that it had lost its urgency; and they had their own affairs to think about. Even Martin, who had graduated from West Point in 1859, seemed complacent, although he had come closer than the rest of the family to the incipient violence when Robert E. Lee appointed him to his staff in the wake of John Brown's raid on Harpers Ferry. Lee ordered him to ride around the countryside looking for signs of any of those thousands of adherents that Brown had supposedly enlisted to follow his lead.

But now—in January 1861—Martin was stationed at Fort Umpqua in Oregon and wrote home to tell of the exotic life he was leading in the wilderness. He spoke of superstitious Indians called "Diggers" living on fish and roots, and speaking "a jargon called 'chinook.'" Of what was happening on the other side of the continent he professed to have only a vague notion: "The news is very meagre we have no idea what is going on in the east until such a long time after it has happened we had about as well not hear at all. We are not much excited and consequently are not so very anxious about what is going to happen as those who are in the midst of it."

9

~~~~~~~~~

Civil Wars

A T the beginning of February a group of mostly elderly delegates, among them many close associates of the Chancellor's, were holding a Peace Conference in a last-ditch effort to avert the madness of war. They were still at it when Abraham Lincoln—exhausted after a long and secretive journey amid rumors of assassination attempts—arrived in Washington on February 23. A group of the conference delegates met with the incoming president and tried to elicit a definite statement from him on whether he would give way to the South's demands. Lincoln restricted himself to declaring in general terms that the Constitution needed to be enforced and obeyed "in every part of every one of the United States," but added: "In a choice of evils, war may not always be the worst."

On March 4 the Chancellor and his wife attended Abraham Lincoln's inauguration in Washington. In the days that followed, the Chancellor was still managing to persuade himself that war would be avoided. "There is great rejoicing here," he wrote to Sarah, who had returned briefly to Saratoga to look after Ellen, "among all parties except a few rabid abolitionists who want civil war and bloodshed."

On April 12, at four thirty in the morning, Confederate gunners in Charleston, South Carolina, began firing on Fort Sumter. The first cannon shot was fired by Edmund Ruffin, who years before as a tourist in Saratoga had complained about the indiscriminate mingling there of quality people and riffraff.

That it would come to this had always been the final possibility, beyond which it was impossible to imagine. Now that the cataclysm had arrived, a man of the Chancellor's age and prior associations had little further to contribute. He was a worn-out reminder of decades of useless compromise. The world as he understood it had been swept aside in an instant.

Having made his last stand, the Chancellor went home to Saratoga Springs to resume his legal work—the Spike suit was still rolling along on its convoluted course—and to devote himself to the genealogical studies that had become his chief preoccupation. For years he had been gathering information about his mother's family, and his immense *Hyde Genealogy*, painstakingly compiled in charts whose complexity and tiny multicolored lettering bore tribute to his scrupulousness, would, he felt sure, prove his most enduring accomplishment.

As the country in which the Walworths and the Hardins lived broke in two, the family as well was whirled apart. Afterward they would never quite reassemble. Nothing in fact would ever again go quite as they intended it to.

ELLEN, pregnant again, was at Pine Grove with the children. In June she would give birth to her sixth child in eight years, Mansfield Tracy Walworth Jr. But she had already determined that she would not be staying in Saratoga.

The difficulties of her marriage were well known within her extended family, and long suspected by a community in which Mansfield's dissolute ways and long absences were no secret. Just how bad things were at this point in their life together would never be fully aired by her—even in later legal documents and trial testimony she would speak only in the most general terms of the period before the war—and any letters or journals in which she detailed what she had experienced in her marriage did not survive, probably by design.

But if she brought no public complaint, she did act. After conferring with her mother, Ellen announced that once she had recovered from her latest delivery she would take the children to Kentucky, where her mother's father and many other relatives were still living. The prospect of war may have encouraged her to make her move; whatever her political loyalties, she was a Southerner who would always feel somewhat isolated and estranged in Saratoga. There was to be no formal separation; she would simply withdraw as discreetly as possible from the vicinity of her husband. Neither then nor at any point during her long Kentucky residence did she ever contradict the idea that Mansfield would rejoin her at a later time, as soon as circumstances permitted.

Ellen went to live in a spacious house that her younger brother Lem, just at the beginning of a career in law, had bought outside Louisville with his mother's help. Bird's Nest, built on thirty-six acres and surrounded by peach and apple orchards, was a comfortable retreat, with its ivied piazzas and landscaped gardens. Here Ellen headed by train in August, accompanied by her five children: Frank and his much-loved brother Johnny, the little girls Nelly and Clara, and three-month old Mansfield Jr. (ever after known as Tracy). She had left behind in Greenridge Cemetery her firstborn daughter Mary, dead in her second year.

Sarah, once she had straightened out the details of her daughter's relocation, returned as quickly as possible to Washington. There she would end up spending much of the war. As a cousin by marriage of Mary Todd Lincoln, Sarah was drawn both by the Washington society that welcomed her as an insider and by the weight of the events in which the city was caught up. She had already become closely involved in the building of the Washington Monument—a fantastic saga of political maneuvering in which the anti-immigrant, anti-Catholic Know-Nothing Party attempted to seize control of the monument's administration and succeeded in delaying its completion for many years—and would now grapple as well with the emerging need to protect Mount Vernon from the mischances of war.

Washington was virtually a city under siege, surrounded by secessionist Virginia to the south and proslavery Maryland to the north, and with a good portion of its own population sympathetic to the besiegers. "I can scarcely realize the strange situation I find myself placed in," Sarah wrote to Ellen in late April. "Here is the President, the Cabinet, with the great Chief of the Army, shut out from the rest of the world . . . Truly we are living history now . . . In after years I shall be able to describe to my grandchildren these scenes. I can tell them the afternoon Fort Sumter was taken I was riding out with Mrs. Lincoln and her little boy gave me his picture."

When Union troops crossed the Potomac confidently on July 20, expecting the first major battle of the war to be an easy win for the North, Sarah was among the many spectators who waited for their return. The mood was festive at the outset. By evening the word was out that the troops were coming back not in victory but in panicked retreat. "It was midnight," Sarah told Ellen, "when the routed army staggered across Long Bridge into the city, and by morning the defeated soldiers were pouring into Washington." It would later be rumored ·that Confederate spies, chiefly the notorious Rose Greenhow, had assisted the Union defeat by relaying crucial information on the timing of the advance to Confederate general Pierre Beauregard.

Martin had come back from his Oregon posting and in July joined up with the Forty-first Pennsylvania Volunteers. His brother Lem, just twenty-one when the war broke out, had not yet determined what course he would follow.

MANSFIELD too was in Washington. The Chancellor, anxious to find something useful for him to do, used his influence to get him a job as a clerk in Adjutant General Lorenzo Thomas's office. Charged with the processing of military communications, the office had undergone rapid expansion since the southern states began to secede. It had also been obliged to replace the many loyal Southerners who had left the staff and headed home. Quite aside from the southern channels open to Mansfield through his Hardin family connections, his new post offered him a prime source of confidential information.

He seems to have had difficulty keeping such information to himself. On a ten-day visit to Ellen at Bird's Nest—it was the first time he had seen his wife in a year—he found time to cultivate the local society in Louisville and evidently talked a good deal about what was going on in Washington. A hint of his talk turned up in enemy correspondence. In September a Confederate major general, David Twiggs, wrote to the rebel secretary of war in Richmond, LeRoy Pope Walker, about some interesting tips he had picked up from an informant. A Mr. Ford of Memphis—he had served with Twiggs in the Mexican War—had conversed with Mansfield in Louisville and apparently learned quite a bit both about a possible leak in the Confederate camp and about the state of Yankee war planning.

The powers at Washington were in close contact, according to Mansfield, with someone on the staff of the Confederate general Charles Dahlgren. (Dahlgren was already under something of a cloud since his brother John worked for the Navy Department in Washington.) This staff member had apparently relayed to Washington whatever they needed to know about the present state of Confederate defenses in the New Orleans area. The Federals were gathering this information—according to Mansfield, who claimed to have gotten his facts straight from the secretary of the navy—in view of an imminent Union invasion of Louisiana.

There was no indication in Twiggs's letter that Mansfield had been selling secrets or working in any capacity for the Confederates. In fact Mansfield had, around this time, offered his services to Major General John Frémont as a spy for the Union, vaunting his wife's southern connections as a rich potential source of intelligence. He assured Frémont that through those ties he had made "important discoveries concerning the attack on Washington." But Mansfield's offer was turned down. He would later claim that his efforts to help the Union had been blocked by General Randolph Marcy, an influential figure in the military, out of a grudge having to do with a southern lady named Mrs. Augusta Morris.

Augusta Morris, "a gay, dashing, and sprightly widow" as the *New York Herald* would describe her, had installed herself at Brown's Hotel and insinuated herself into Washington social circles. Marcy, according to Mansfield, had been among the many men drawn to her charms, and the Chancellor's son had taken it upon himself to inform Secretary of State Seward (with whom, after all, he had been acquainted since childhood) about this "undue interest." Of Mrs. Morris's southern loyalties there was no question at all, but that was hardly unusual in Washington in the first days of the war. In any case—and this put his charge against Marcy in a different light—Mansfield was himself intimately acquainted with "little Mrs. Morris."

Mansfield's loyalties were characteristically elusive. To Frémont he had represented himself as a potential Union spy, who could make valuable use of his marital connections for intelligence purposes. To his cousin John Barbour, on the other hand, a young lawyer who had found wartime employment on Seward's staff, he bragged that he had obtained a secret commission from General Beauregard. During a visit to Saratoga, Mansfield, in a theatrical gesture, paraded in front of his cousin in his Confederate uniform. Family ties did not inhibit Barbour from relating the incident to Seward.

At four o'clock on the morning of February 7, 1862, Mansfield was in the company of Augusta Morris at Brown's Hotel—in bed with her, according to some sources—when secret service agents under the authority of General George B. McClellan knocked on the door. Both were arrested on charges of suspected treason. They had been swept up in a broad investigation of espionage and sedition in the capital, spearheaded by the railroad detective Allan Pinkerton. It was Pinkerton who had guarded Lincoln as the president-elect journeyed incognito through seditious Maryland on his way to the capital, and now on McClellan's orders he had formed a secret service dedicated to assessing the rebels' military strength and more particularly to rooting out Confederate operatives in Washington. Mrs. Morris—thought to be part of Rose Greenhow's network of socially connected spies—was the primary object of Pinkerton's concern that morning, but Mansfield was taken in custody as well on suspicion of complicity in her treasonous activities.

They were taken to the Old Capitol, a brick building that had once, in the aftermath of the burning of Washington during the War of 1812, provided a temporary meeting place for the Congress, had subsequently been a boardinghouse where both John C. Calhoun and Rose Greenhow had resided, and was now serving as a military prison. Rose Greenhow had been confined in the filthy and overcrowded facility since the previous October, along with a mass of captured Confederate soldiers and—in the wake of Pinkerton's espionage operation—a growing contingent of political prisoners accused of varying shades of disloyalty.

Three days after his arrest Mansfield wrote to Ellen in Kentucky to tell her what had happened. He had been taken prisoner, he said, "for unknown cause." After offering some ambiguous counsel about Ellen's welfare—"endeavor to manage or act, under the circumstances, regarding your matters, according to your best judgement for you know I can be of no assistance to you now"—he launched into a lament that had some of the grandiloquence of his fictional heroes: "I have struggled hard but it seems in vain. In this dark hour, when I cannot struggle for you I expect you to be strong, firm in faith and assured of my constancy to truth to the end. Put on that character which belongs to you from a noble and faithful ancestry and leave me in your prayers to the Eternal God of truth." It was as if he had assumed the mantle of martyrdom he had attributed to the renegade Catholics of *The Mission of Death*: "No services of religion" he told Ellen, "are heard within the square bounded by the tramp of the sentinels: but the heart conscious of noble purposes communes with its God and feels that He ordereth all things well." Mansfield, who had not been the most reliable of husbands, struck a patriarchal note in his letter. "Teach my children to think of me and speak of me daily," he exhorted Ellen, and added a special message for his firstborn: "Tell Frank that I think of him every day and that he must love you more while I am detained away."

As his imprisonment wore on, Mansfield's condition grew worse. He had an attack of measles and wrote to his sister Eliza of having visions of their dead mother. He seems to have gotten it into his head as well that his son Johnny was dying: "All is sickness and sorrow and there is no night but his still small voice will whisper of Heaven."

Mansfield's arrest was an embarrassment that some political opponents were only too happy to publicize. The *Troy Times* went to press with it before the staff even knew precisely *which* son of Chancellor Walworth had been arrested, saying only that they deemed it probable that it was Mansfield, whom they characterized as "a sort of—*nothing*: a wild, reckless, impetuous, dare-devil fellow, without much principle or any reputation." They also noted—by way of clarifying the doubtful loyalties in question—that "the Chancellor married a Southern widow some years ago, and Mansfield's wife is her daughter."

Stung by the implied insult to her own family, Sarah fired off a letter of protest to the more sympathetic *Syracuse Daily Courier*, accusing the author of the piece of "not knowing who I am," and launching into the best defense of Mansfield she could muster, calling him "one of the most accomplished and intelligent young men in the state of New York. Mr. Walworth has published some literary works which have met the approval of the most cultivated people." More to the point, Mansfield was "now a Union man," and his alleged disloyalty amounted to nothing more than the kind of sentiments espoused not too long ago by other Democrats, many of them enjoying positions of power: "If he has been arrested, it is from the determined rancor and misrepresentation of enemies here, which some few indiscretions on his part have made for him."

The arrest was also a minor headache for the government. Given his father's prominence and the breadth of his political and social connections, there were many prepared to take up Mansfield's cause and make him a symbol of the new regime's tyrannical high-handedness. New York papers, both upstate and in the city, were already full of references to the "reign of terror" inaugurated by Lincoln and his Black Republicans. What made matters more awkward was that no clear evidence could be found against Mansfield, beyond the Confederate uniform stored in a trunk in his room. Pinkerton doubted that he had anything more than a social connection with Augusta Morris, and in any case, after the initial wave of arrests, the government wanted to weed out the more innocuous political prisoners in the Old Capitol. Many, including eventually Augusta Morris and Rose Greenhow, were sent back to the South on signing an agreement not to cross the line again. Suspect Northerners were asked to swear an oath of loyalty to the federal government.

For reasons known only to himself, Mansfield initially resisted this option. The Chancellor, eager to bring the discreditable episode to an end, complained bitterly about his son's "folly" in refusing to take the oath. Mansfield had made things worse by writing letters from prison that made it "impossible for the Secretary of War Stanton, Dix and others of my friends to do anything for his relief at present." The old man had now reached the lowest point of his public and private life. "I am broken down and desperate," he confided in Sarah, "at news of my country and the troubles of my own family, and I fear that my mind will give way under it before long. But I shall endeavor to hold up my head before the world as long as I can although I cannot see any bright spot for the future this side of the grave."

Rumors of Mansfield's recalcitrance leaked out and found their way into southern newspapers. The *Savannah Daily Morning News* reported on his case, noting that "there is strong suspicion that Mr. Walworth has a secret commission as Major in the Confederate army, in the handwriting of Beauregard. He has nevertheless been offered his freedom on three distinct occasions, by the commission, on condition that he will take the oath of allegiance. His firmness in refusing is unaccountable to his friends." In prison Mansfield found himself playing the heroic role that had hitherto eluded him. The part of the unjustly condemned man was perfectly suited to his habitual sense of grievance.

When his prison mate Jesse Wharton—another who had refused to take the oath of allegiance—was shot dead by a guard on April 20, allegedly for standing in a window against orders and making disorderly remarks, Mansfield took it up as a personal cause. Once released from the Old Capitol, he would publish a description of the incident: "I was beside Lieut. Wharton in the room when he was shot, heard the altercation with the sentinel and the charges made by the dying man. I was his friend, and when the fellow-prisoners left him with his wife he requested me to remain with him and her until he died." (No other accounts of the incident placed Mansfield anywhere in the vicinity.) Wharton—who had been cashiered out of the army in the 1850s for drunkenness and dereliction of duty, and arrested subsequently as a Confederate spy—had not, according to Mansfield, been of a quarrelsome disposition. A moment before the shooting he had just closed a Bible, in which he had been looking up his mother's favorite passage. However justified Mansfield's protest may have been—prisoners and guards gave drastically different versions of the shooting—he could not help making it as stilted and unpersuasive as a passage from one of his own novels.

He would soon have plenty of time to work on his fiction. In late April, having given way on the oath of allegiance, he was delivered from prison after nearly three months of confinement. Released on parole in the custody of his father, he was ordered to spend the duration of the war in Saratoga Springs and to report daily, via the Chancellor, to the

Department of War. He would not see his wife or children again until the war was nearly over.

THE marriage had split apart into two domains: the world of Pine Grove, where father and son would labor over their respective projects, Reuben his genealogy of the Hydes, and Mansfield his novel *Lulu*, a potpourri of lawsuits, poisonings, and thwarted loves; and the world of Bird's Nest, where Ellen would struggle, under increasing pressure, to keep her children fed and healthy.

There had occurred for her, she would write years later in her diary, "a revolution in the change from New York to Kentucky, from the dependent wife and daughter to the isolated woman with her little children." With no support from her husband she was living in genteel poverty, eking out a living from the soil as the war went on and relying on sporadic handouts from her father-in-law. Sarah was the primary mediator between the two worlds of Saratoga and Kentucky, although Martin and Lem also came and went between the two homes as circumstances dictated.

For Ellen it was a homecoming that was also a sort of exile. Kentucky was a border state just barely remaining within the Union. Rebel raiders flourished in the back country, and the state's governor, Thomas Bramlette—a Hardin relation and an old family friend—maintained an uneasy alliance with Lincoln's government. In her isolation Ellen had ample time to contemplate everything that separated her from the family into which she and her mother had married.

Her older brother had taken his stand unambiguously with the North. Just as Mansfield was released in April, Martin was being promoted to lieutenant colonel. In August he led a brigade in the Second Battle of Bull Run and was badly wounded in the chest and shoulders as the Union forces were routed and forced back toward Washington. It was there that his brother Lem found him among the wounded, and on September 3 transported him to Pine Grove to recuperate. Five weeks later the brothers returned to the capital. Martin was now a colonel; Lem still had not yet chosen a side in the war, at least as far as anyone knew.

In the fall Lem headed to Pine Grove again, taking with him two of Ellen's children, Nelly and Johnny, to visit their grandparents and enjoy the supposedly healthier climate of upstate New York. Ellen never saw Johnny again; he died of a sudden illness at Pine Grove in early December. Her mother sent Ellen a rambling letter intended to console her with the thought that her lively seven-year-old son "could only have been happy in contemplating nature and it would have been an awful responsibility for a mother to lead his mind from that to a higher and nobler worship of God." Perhaps, she suggested, God had intervened because he had foreseen that Ellen would fail. In any case Ellen must remember the sufferings of others—"your bleeding country . . . the sad hearts of poor bereaved mothers who have sons dead upon the battlefield"—and not allow herself to wallow in grief.

Staying for long stretches in the capital, close to the front lines, Sarah had a more visceral sense of what was going on in the fighting than her husband back in Saratoga. The Chancellor kept well away from Washington. From a distance he registered his despondent view of "this unnatural and horrible civil war that unprincipled politicians and demagogues have inflicted upon the country." "The troops are being slaughtered as usual," he went on, "without any results, and without any credit to have engaged in fighting under incompetent officers." The old man resented his wife's long absences and complained of servant troubles: "You had better come as soon as you can; it is very lonely here above stairs and there is an Irish carnival in the kitchen every night."

The Chancellor made every effort to keep Mansfield usefully occupied, throwing legal work his way, however little enthusiasm his son showed for such drudgery. He tried as well to channel Mansfield's literary instincts into a more acceptable channel. At some point a plan had been broached—whether by Mansfield or his father—for a multivolume history of the chancellors of New York, beginning with the revered Robert Livingston and culminating, inevitably, in Reuben Hyde Walworth.

This was a project the Chancellor could support energetically, and he continually encouraged Mansfield to proceed with his researches, feeding him leads and sources, giving him contact information for all the scattered individuals who could provide crucial papers. ("General Graham who was the particular friend of Chancellor Jones will be able to give you a history of the latter part of his life . . . And I believe the oldest son of Chancellor Sanford lives in New York . . . His widow and youngest son I believe are still living in Poughkeepsie.") Mansfield did follow through on some of these leads—they were a perfect excuse for the kinds of social invitations he loved to cultivate—but no evidence survives that much or any of the often-discussed history ever got written.

IT made, at any rate, a good cover story. In response to the queries of friends and relations, it felt much more acceptable to say that one's son was at work on *The Lives of the Chancellors* than on *Lulu: A Tale of the National Hotel Poisoning*. The incident alluded to in the subtitle of Mansfield's second novel was a widespread outbreak of intestinal illness at the famous Washington hotel on several occasions prior to and during the inauguration of President Buchanan in 1857. Buchanan fell badly ill and his nephew died, not the only fatality. Mansfield had been among the hotel's guests at the time and had himself, he assured his readers, succumbed to the "severe and mysterious illness." Further investigation would lead to the widely accepted explanation that the root of the malady was contamination due to a broken sewage line. But Buchanan's presence, and the hotel's popularity with Southerners, encouraged an alternate theory that abolitionists had conspired to kill the president and many of his supporters. Without laying so specific a claim of responsibility, Mansfield declared in his preface that poison had definitely been at work, and cited the opinion of the distinguished Mobile physician Henry Le Vert that the poison was indubitably arsenic.

There is no telling how long Mansfield may have been working on the book; perhaps ever since he had gotten sick at the National Hotel. That its composition had often been interrupted and recommenced was suggested by the book's misshapen plot, in which the poisoning of the title turned out to play a belated and almost irrelevant role. At every point in the abruptly zigzagging intrigue Mansfield displayed, not for the last time, a staggering slovenliness about pulling together the details of his fictional world. He may have been incapable of planning a book from beginning to end; or perhaps he was too impatient to work things out in advance. But if he could not plot, Mansfield was at pains to demonstrate on every page that he could *write*, whether he was launching into ornate descriptions of seascapes, enlivening his dialogue with bouts of ungainly punning, venturing trenchant asides on politics and law, or making room for any random dream scene or stray bit of oracular poetry.

Much of Mansfield's authorial energy seemed to have gone into burnishing the portrait of his hero Harry Carter, introduced as "a gay, talented youth of nineteen, remarkable not only for his rare manly beauty, but also for an indescribable charm of manner and conversation, which gained for him many admirers, and when he chose to exert himself, secured for him life-long friends." This was only the warm-up. The qualities of Harry Carter unleashed cosmic perspectives in Mansfield, perspectives on which he could enlarge for pages at a stretch: "Like the far-reaching sea, his heart . . . was broad enough to love the world, and discover beauties in every clime beneath the sun . . . Like the ocean, his soul too possessed deep, deep recesses, and weird caverns, where delicious melodies stole soothingly along coral aisles, and beautiful thoughts were stranded like sunken jewels on golden sands."

But out of those deep recesses and weird caverns emerged a hero whose chief gift seemed to be for seduction, and whose chief hobby was the tireless cataloging of women's wardrobes and physical attractions. "Our hero," Mansfield wrote, "possessed a ready flow of eloquence and a magic power of utterance which seldom failed to fascinate the being upon whom he concentrated his powers of persuasion." His protagonist was generally to be found lecherously contemplating one female character or another: "His eye had detected every point of beauty in the graceful attitude and outline of her plump little figure . . . Her closely-fitting merino dress . . . revealed to advantage her slender waist, full rounding shoulders and bust; and a perfect little foot, cased in a dark gaiter boot, appeared stealthily from under its blue folds, as if stealing a brief glimpse of the fire light during the distraction of its dear little mistress." Once Mansfield became embroiled in cataloging women's clothing, it was difficult for him to get back to the story. Harry Carter's discovery of some feminine footwear belonging to the lovely Lulu sparked a typical rhapsody.

> In the top basket was an almost finished gaiter of scarlet silk . . . Its lovely proportions and size attracted the eye of Harry Carter at once, and he approached to contemplate it with the interest of a foot connoisseur.

"This must be Lulu's foot," he muttered to himself daintily raising the unfinished gaiter from its blue receptacle, and turning it over in every direction studiously and admiringly. "That is a lady's two and a half if I am not much mistaken; yes! two and a half is the number I'm sure, and that is a mighty small foot for one of her height and figure—and such admirable proportions, too . . . Ah! how slim and graceful it is; how the curved line of beauty is developed in the hollow of the foot and the high instep. I wish Bess had such a foot. Why can't all girls have these perfect developments of charms?"

As Saratoga residents would come to know, when Mansfield sat down to write he was likely to take the opportunity to settle scores and vent animosities. In *Lulu* Mansfield described Saratoga, mockingly renamed Tattletown, as divided between two social factions: the high-church Reds, like Mansfield, who favored "fine linen, brocade silks, diamonds, turkey and oysters, dancing, whist, champagne, and a spirit of fun"; and the dismal, hypocritical Blues of his father's Presbyterian persuasion, restricted to the old-time American regime of "calico, plain black silks, cameo breast-pins, veal pot-pies, the game of fox and geese, tea parties, lemonade, and a spirit of prayer." Every despised member of the Blue set was paraded past the reader in thinly disguised caricature, a series of mean-spirited portraits—focusing especially on physical blemishes and marks of age—entirely unrelated to the book's wisp of a plot.

The caricatures included in all likelihood his father, who appears to have been the model for the Honorable Judge Carter, here given the Supreme Court seat the Chancellor had been denied in life. The judge was depicted as a philanthropist famous for supporting programs of moral reform "at home or in distant lands," prone to grow teary-eyed over newspaper accounts of poverty, but indifferent to any sufferers who actually showed up at his doorstep: "He regarded the poor-house system as entirely superseding all Christian precepts in regard to alms." The echo of Ebenezer Scrooge could only have been deliberate.

When he narrated Harry Carter's ultimate union with the elusive Lulu, Mansfield offered up what looked like an intensely self-flattering version of his courtship of Ellen. Like Ellen, Lulu was "a devoted

Catholic," and their love affair was dressed up in hints of high meta-physics, as the hero contemplated "her lovely soul eyes beaming with intelligence and heart." But mostly Mansfield wanted to talk about his power over her, not hers over him. Re-creating "the meeting of two bright intellects brought in contact for the first time," he described how "language with its indescribable influence revealed to her the deep enthusiasm of his heart; and his keen sense of the beautiful and romantic in life appeared to her each instant." To recollect the seduc-tive force he had once wielded with his own poetically charged speech set him off into ever more unrestrained raptures: "And she, the earnest loving woman that she was, could not restrain her impulse to be with him, and hear his ardent enthusiastic language, and drink at that foun-tain of precocious intellect, which seemed to purify, and render clear, all subjects of thought."

She had given herself to him completely; such was the indispensable end point of his otherwise erratic narrative, the one thing that had to be made clear to the reader. She, with her "matchless shoulders" and "exquisite figure," her intellect and her soul eyes, had been forced to sur-render: "That wild, eager, impulsive heart that could dare anything which men called danger, and yet could love with the vehemence of a woman, now poured forth in broken accents, while his strong frame quivered, the most burning words of passion that ever came from mortal lips." Told as Mansfield told it, the story seemed more like a gloating anecdote for one of Saratoga's smoking rooms, dressed up in fancy language.

READING *Lulu*, one would hardly know there was a war going on. Mansfield was serving his period of loosely enforced house arrest well away from the battlefields where Martin continued to fight, and well protected from the shortages and dangers with which Ellen and the children had to reckon. If he had not been dependent on his father, and if he had not been addicted to complaint and resentment, Mans-field might have seen himself as fortunate in his reclusion. Despite a falling-off in summer population—the Southerners who had been a mainstay of the tourist trade had begun to keep away even before the attack on Fort Sumter—Saratoga was having quite a comfortable war.

The social rounds went on undisturbed amid the fighting. While New York exploded into the violence of the draft riots, and even neighboring Troy contended with angry mobs, Saratoga was enjoying a presentation of *tableaux vivants* at Congress Hall, as "some of the ladies of the hotel" got up a series of displays including "Gypsy Scenes," "Guardian Angels," and—a concession to the times—"Wounded Soldier." A local retailer under the boldface headline "Stoneman's Cavalry Raid Outdone!" announced that he had "surrounded and captured the largest and best selected stock of dry goods ever offered in Saratoga," a peerless assortment of shawls, cashmeres, hosiery, and new-style ladies' skirts. There was fresh money in town: the businessmen who were enriching themselves on the conflict—Cornelius Vanderbilt the most prominent among them—found the spa a convenient retreat and meeting place, especially with the novel amusements that were on offer.

The gaming house that John Morrissey had opened in the summer of 1861 announced a new and rowdier era. Gambling had always been going on in Saratoga, but now it was to become central to the town's identity. Morrissey himself was an emblem of how much Saratoga was changing. An illiterate street brawler from Troy, he had gravitated to New York City, where he became a leader of the Dead Rabbits gang and an enforcer for the Tammany establishment. Heading to California during the Gold Rush, he earned a reputation as a professional gambler and prizefighter before returning east to work for the corrupt administration of New York's mayor Fernando Wood.

By the time Morrissey set up shop in Saratoga, the brutal street fighter had evolved into a debonair impresario adept at political maneuvering and at home with the most refined company the spa could offer—those at least who were willing to venture into a gambling hall. Within two years he expanded his Saratoga operations by opening a thoroughbred racetrack. Soon, with the help of New York stockbroker William Travers, the local racing scene had become a national attraction; Mary Todd Lincoln made an appearance at the first Travers Stakes in 1864. Within three years Morrissey would move his gambling operations to a newly built casino in Italian palazzo style, set down in Congress Park itself. He would serve two terms in Congress and end his days as a state senator.

WHILE Mansfield was enjoying his enforced leisure and keeping his distance from wife and children, his brother Clarence, having temporarily rejoined the Paulist order, was performing frequent service as a chaplain on behalf of the many Catholics in the Union army. He was also ministering to the legions of Irish immigrants in the shanties and tenements of New York City—a fourth of its population was Irish by this point. When New York's draft riots broke out in the summer of 1863, he found himself in the thick of the disorder.

Nothing in his experience could have prepared him for the foundering of civic order and the uncontrolled destruction that followed. Irish mobs—hostile to emancipation and incensed by a conscription bill that allowed the well-off to buy their way out of fighting for three hundred dollars—took over the streets for four days and nights until crushed by federal troops and the hard-pressed city police, many of them Irish as well. In Virginia the arch-secessionist Edmund Ruffin celebrated the "wide-spread & bloody riot in the city of New York," hoping it foreshadowed the imminent social collapse of the North. Up in Saratoga, the *Daily Saratogian* asked, "Is Mob Violence to Rule?"

A good many of Clarence's own parishioners were doubtless among the rioters, but this did not protect him when, with his Paulist superior Father Augustine Hewitt, he went into the streets to try to calm the crowds. Father Hewitt was clubbed unconscious, and Clarence only just managed to drag him out of harm's way into a vacant house, thus avoiding the fate of Colonel H. T. O'Brien, who under similar circumstances was seized by the mob and beaten to death on Second Avenue.

In the wake of the unparalleled outbreak Clarence delivered what was evidently one of his most powerful sermons. The riots, he reminded the faithful, had been like an earthquake: "When one suddenly feels the earth rising and sinking and swaying to and fro beneath his feet, when he can no longer trust the very ground on which he stands, the illusion of a whole life is dissipated . . . To feel that any one who hated us might come and burn our houses over our heads with impunity, or beat us to death upon the pavement,—this was something new and startling." As he looked at the worshippers before him, Clarence acknowledged that he might well be looking at some of those who had burned orphanages and hanged Negro bystanders from lampposts: "I do not know how many, if any, of those before me are implicated in it. I thank God I do not recognize any. I am glad to believe that most of you feel the same horror that I feel . . . It was an awful week."

As the war went on, Sarah spent more and more time with her daughter and the children at Bird's Nest, and she would write back to Saratoga as gaily as she could about the life they were living there: "Tell Manse Nellie has had some views taken of the place for him. She intended to have all of the family in one of the pictures, but the artist fell off the platform and broke his instrument." Her talk was all of strawberries and grapes and peaches, of "tomatoes larger than hen's eggs."

The war lurked somewhere in the background, a constant threat even as they passed their days in genteel tedium, posing for daguerrotypes or enjoying fresh cole slaw for dinner. "The guerrillas have been within twelve miles of Louisville," she wrote in June 1863. "They think here Grant will be obliged to raise the siege of Vicksburg soon. If so Kentucky will be full of troops." Each of Sarah's letters home—after the smattering of family news and the updates on the fruit harvest—ended with a request to send money: "It takes more to travel with than it did and I have been obliged to spend some. I can't get home without more than I have."

Having already survived serious wounds, Martin Hardin fought on, earning distinction at the Battle of Gettysburg. On December 13, 1863, he rode out with his lieutenant colonel to examine the depot at Catlett's Station, Virginia, with a view to building blockhouses to defend the railroad against partisan attack. As he made his inspection five horsemen in slouch hats and Union overcoats rode close by. Just as they passed, the supposed Federals—probably rebels associated with Colonel John Singleton Mosby's irregular cavalry battalion—whipped out concealed revolvers and fired on Martin and his lieutenant. Martin was shot in his left arm and thrown violently to the ground as his fatally wounded horse collapsed under him. The attackers rode off unimpeded through the cedars: "they disappeared," wrote Sarah to her husband, "as effectively as if they had gone into the ground." After the incident Martin had written to his mother assuring her he was out of danger; by the time she received the letter his wounded arm had been amputated. This time he went to Bird's Nest to recover.

By early summer—even though to Sarah's eyes he was not well ("he keeps going to forget his misfortune, tho I think he feels it very much")—Martin was back in action, commanding a regiment at Spotsylvania and again at Bethesda Church, and earning a promotion to brigadier general. His mother, who had pulled strings on behalf of her son's military career from his earliest days at West Point, took credit for procuring the promotion through her tireless social networking: "I have succeeded in the object which has kept me here for the last month . . . I have had kind and influential friends, or I could not have accomplished what I have done." The position, she felt, would "in some measure pay him for his services and sacrifices in this unhappy war."

Martin made his way to Pine Grove to pay his respects to the Chancellor. There is no record of what, if anything, he had to say to his brother-in-law, who was presently basking in a certain degree of literary glory. *Lulu* had been issued by G. W. Carleton, a publisher whose name was a byword for low-grade sensational and sentimental fiction, and was enjoying some success. It had even gotten some appreciative reviews, although these tended to emanate from newspapers closely associated with the Chancellor's old political associates in the Democratic Party. The *Albany County Democrat* paid tribute to Mansfield's "lively and attractive" imagination while taking care to remind its readers that he had been "one of the 'victims' or 'subjects' of Secretary Stanton's arbitrary arrests during the reign of terror at the seat of government in the early stages of the 'rebellion.'" Now Mansfield was deep in *Lulu*'s equally convoluted follow-up, *Hotspur: A Tale of the Old Dutch Manor.*

By now Martin knew from Ellen how brutal and debauched Mansfield's behavior had been in the period before their breakup, and how absolute had been his failure to provide support for his wife and children. He may also have had some inkling of how worried Mansfield was that he might yet be called up for military service; he had written to the Union authorities arguing that New York had no claim on him because he was a legal resident of Kentucky (despite the fact that he had not spent more than a few weeks there during his wife's three-year residence at Bird's Nest) and that in any event he was, as a former prisoner of war, ineligible for the draft.

Martin went on to Washington to spend time with his mother.

Sarah had accepted an invitation to visit the army—"I may never have another opportunity to see the ground now rendered famous . . . In imagination I could see the battle of Bull Run where D. [Martin's nickname] received that fearful wound"—and had stayed on in the capital. Her reluctance to go back to the role of the Chancellor's wife at Pine Grove was fairly evident. She maintained close ties to the administration's social circles and kept her husband posted on the war of which he had managed to avoid any direct experience: "There are forty thousand sick here and the sight of the wounded and dead is a heart-sickening scene." Martin remained in the capital as well, as Washingtonians prepared for Jubal Early's Confederate raid that never came.

In late November Martin was back at Bird's Nest, this time to celebrate his recent marriage. (He had by now formally converted to Catholicism, and it was Clarence who officiated at the ceremony at Pine Grove on November 15.) Lem was not present to greet his brother's bride; he had finally made his move, joining up with the partisan band of John Hunt Morgan, who conducted raids harassing Union forces in Kentucky and rode as far west as Indiana. Like his brother, Lem had been wounded in the fighting, receiving a bad leg injury at the battle of Crockett's Cove in Virginia in 1864. Both brothers had sometimes recuperated at Bird's Nest, but—doubtless through careful arrangement—never at the same time.

Now Lem had gotten away altogether. Ellen—who in the latter days of the war employed her time sending gifts and letters to captured Confederates—had helped to dress him in women's clothes, and in that disguise he headed for Canada, sending word that he had arrived safely a week after Martin's wedding. He mailed the family a photograph of himself on crutches in Montreal.

FRANK Walworth was now eleven years old. Circumstances had cast him in the role of caretaker, looking after his sisters and younger brother in place of the father he had not seen in three years. During that time he had experienced the loss of his brother Johnny, his closest sibling. For Frank the war had been a period of social restriction and, in some ways, limited activity. But the absence of his father, and the chaos of a war always hovering somewhere in the vicinity until it reached out to maim someone close to him, also gave him unexpected leeway. Frank doubtless enjoyed more freedom in the back fields of Bird's Nest than in the regulated corridors of the Chancellor's house. He had grown close to his uncle Lem and was by now as much the product of Kentucky as of Saratoga.

In the final months of the war, no longer feeling pressured by the terms of his house arrest, Mansfield sent word that he would be arriving soon at Bird's Nest to be reunited with his family. Of this momentous six-week visit, the first time Mansfield and Ellen had been together in three years, no account survives. If the reunion was intended to bring the couple back together permanently—as if all that had occurred in the war years was no more than an uncomfortable reverie—it failed in its effect. Ellen for the time being elected to stay on in Kentucky, to look after her remaining children and oversee the fruit orchards that sustained them. As for Mansfield, he went back to Pine Grove, to withdraw into the rhapsodic interior spaces of his latest novel.

> There was an indescribable aspect of loneliness over this superb and wide-reaching manor, under the frown of the pale snow clouds, and breathed over by the chill moaning wind. No human figure moved upon the scene. The great piazza of the mansion, with its tall, solemn pillars of white, wreathed with bare and leafless vines, was utterly deserted. No face looked from the windows, and the only sound from the great house was the occasional low, grating noise of the window shutters on their iron hinges, as they moved slowly back and forth in the rising or receding force of the cold, shifting wind. The evergreens about the house were dark and gloomy in the frown of the approaching storm.

Mansfield and Ellen might for the moment be apart, but their marriage was not nearly over. It would take seven more years, and a tortuous series of reunions and separations, to reach the breaking point. The public disaster of the war was to be followed by descent into a private hell.

10

~~~~~~~~

The Disinherited

IN April 1865, just as the nation was absorbing the end of the war
and the assassination of Lincoln, word reached the Chancellor at
Saratoga that his son Clarence lay dangerously ill at the Paulist rectory
in New York City. Despite his always fragile health, Clarence had
driven himself to maintain a schedule of near constant preaching
throughout the war. But now it appeared that he had undergone a
complete and sudden collapse. Doctors diagnosed him with what was
then called "brain fever" and would later probably have been described
as a nervous breakdown.

His father, himself a good deal frailer now, undertook the journey
to the city and brought him back to Pine Grove, where Clarence
stayed on through months of slow recovery. In July Clarence wrote to
the Paulists, to let them know that he had decided to leave the order
once and for all and return to St. Mary's as parish priest: "For myself
I scarcely know what to look forward to. Sometimes I think my time
is up." But the thought of death, he acknowledged, was "less startling"
to him than it had previously been.

Reuben and Clarence, the aging father and ailing son, had ample
opportunity to talk about the state of the family, Ellen's long absence

in Kentucky, and the expectations of the Chancellor's grandchildren. Now that he had delivered to the world his massive two-volume *Hyde Genealogy*, the Chancellor had more time to think of present concerns and future prospects. He and Clarence must have cast an uneasy eye in the direction of Mansfield, who was dividing his time between Saratoga, New York City, and Albany. To judge from their occasional spare correspondence, the father addressed his younger son with the weary politeness of someone who had given up any hope of reform or improvement, while continuing to inquire after the progress of the *Lives of the Chancellors*. The project had become Mansfield's calling card, a certificate of his scholarly seriousness, regularly invoked whenever his name was mentioned in the press.

Mansfield was in fact making something of a name for himself, although in ways that could not have impressed his father much. G. W. Carleton was sufficiently pleased with the sales of *Lulu* to keep Mansfield on his list of writers, in company with such popular favorites as Marion Harland (*The Empty Heart*), Mary J. Holmes (*Tempest and Sunshine*), and T. S. Arthur (*Light on Shadowed Paths*). So *Lulu* was followed by *Hotspur*, and *Hotspur* by *Stormcliff*: more masked riders, more hidden passageways, more secret wills, more prophetic old women, more imperiously beautiful young heiresses, above all more heroes racked by a sense of thwarted genius and unjustifiable mistreatment.

The sort of thing that came easily to Mansfield was apparently just what thousands of American readers were looking for. They may not have been precisely the sort of readers he craved—the sort whose endorsement might shore up his belief in his own brilliance—but there were enough to enable him, like the hero of *Stormcliff*, to persevere in his chosen path: "in the still hours of the night to devote himself to his favorite pursuit, literature . . . to furnish such composition for publication as should secure him fame among men of letters."

If truly distinguished men of letters had not exactly come flocking around Mansfield, he could at least carry off, on the verandas of Saratoga and in the lesser byways of literary Manhattan, the swagger of a successful author. Some little celebrity, then, he had achieved, if not much money to go with it. Actually to profit from writing took a lot of doing, especially for someone whose tastes in refreshment, entertainment, and especially clothing were as exacting as Mansfield's.

From the beginning he had worked at every detail of his appearance with the scrupulous attention of an actor. "He was fastidious and proud of his handsome person," an anonymous biographer would write, "and fond of exhibiting himself in the streets of our large cities." For years he had lifted weights and been a regular visitor to the gymnasiums that were another German American contribution to American urban life. The kind of figure he imagined himself cutting became part of the description of his fictional protagonists, like the hero of *Hotspur*, "five feet and eleven inches in height, and gracefully moulded in form and limb as the mythical Adonis," or of *Stormcliff*, "as attractive a picture of neat and muscular manhood as the eye ever meets outside of the artist's canvas and the sculptor's marble."

The spectacle of his own public self was Mansfield's most carefully elaborated artwork, and after his death a multitude of witnesses would come forward to testify to his physical grace, his wit and erudition, his courteous refinement. Members of the family circle saw another side of the author of *Stormcliff*.

IN the summer of 1865, Ellen allowed herself to be persuaded to come north with the children to spend the summer at Pine Grove. There is no record of whatever suggestions and evasions and negotiations might have preceded that decision. At first she found herself, as she later testified, "on very pleasant terms" with Mansfield. It was not long, however, before the mood shifted drastically.

It was the first time in years that Ellen had seen her husband on his home ground, and at length. His behavior, always unpredictable, had become even more disturbingly erratic. In the midst of a conversation he would abruptly change the subject, launching into a confused tirade while throwing his arms about violently. In sudden fits of anger he kicked savagely at pieces of furniture. Sometimes he would pick up a small object and crush it in his hand.

Chancellor Walworth, delighted once again to have the company of his daughter-in-law, invited her out to one of the hotels one evening, in the company of several other friends. On returning at about ten, she went up to her husband's room and, finding it unaccountably locked, knocked to be admitted. As the door opened, she found herself looking at Mansfield's pale enraged face and yanked by him suddenly and forcefully into the room as he cursed her and shouted, "I will show you how you will leave me of an evening again!"

He shook her "with great violence" and dragged her through the room and into the adjoining bedroom, smashing her repeatedly against the furniture, finally ripping her clothes off. Some hours later, after he had fallen asleep, she managed to creep out of the room. It is hard to believe that no one else in the house was aware of a disturbance throughout the long night. Badly bruised, Ellen left Saratoga soon after and returned again to the shelter of the Kentucky home for another autumn and winter.

This was the first such incident about which Ellen would later give legal testimony. She implied that it was in the summer of 1865 that her husband's behavior began to show marked signs of deterioration—but likewise she noted that "he had been in the habit of acting in a very violent manner for a great many years." It was only now, perhaps, that the violence became so acutely physical, that verbal tirades and emotional storms became brutal beatings. Once again she kept her distance from him and bided at Bird's Nest. The family held to the official line that it was only a matter of time before the couple was permanently reunited, either in Saratoga or Kentucky.

Ellen's mother, who presumably knew the whole story, counseled her a few months after the attack in August that "women, especially cultivated women, have an intuitive perception of propriety and what is acceptable on all occasions." Appearances were still being preserved, despite the already unorthodox arrangements of the marriage of Mansfield and Ellen. That winter Mansfield was living most of the time at a boardinghouse on Madison Avenue in New York City, where Ellen visited him briefly around Christmas. During the following spring the family once again reunited at Pine Grove, the most complete reunion since the war.

But by July Ellen was back at Bird's Nest, undergoing the extremely painful removal of her wisdom teeth, apparently a botched procedure; "the dentist," Sarah wrote the Chancellor, "had liked to have torn out her jawbone." Sarah herself was recovering from an unnamed illness, "the same disease I had last summer." In the same letter she wrote at length about the abundant harvest of fruits and berries, the most untroubled theme available to her: "It does one good to walk out and see the fruit growing . . . There is a feeling of humble dependence on our creator whose almighty power has provided all these good things for us." She did not allude to the fact that, during the springtime reunion with Mansfield, Ellen had gotten pregnant again.

In Saratoga, in late August of 1866, the Chancellor summoned the energy to preside over an elaborate ceremony at High Rock Spring. The opening of a modernized and refurbished pavilion at the spring, in which the healing waters flowed freely for the first time in more than a century, became an opportunity to salute the end of the war and the restoration of profitable tourism in the postwar era. "The venerable Walworth" rose to the occasion with an oration that revisited the geology and early history of the spring in exhaustive detail.

He dwelled on his own age: "The whitening of the head of him who now addresses you, by the snows of seventy-eight winters which have fallen upon it, admonishes him to recollect that he can enjoy with you this valuable addition to our health-preserving fountains only for a very short period." His thoughts were now of the future generations, from all regions, who could enjoy the waters now that the war had ended, and hoped they might continue to enjoy them "without disturbance from the withering curse of sectional agitation . . . until the thundering Cotopaxi shall cease to burn, and the cloud-capped Chimborazo be sunk in the ocean." As the Chancellor finished what was to be his last speech, the band struck up "The Star-Spangled Banner."

Mansfield's latest novel *Stormcliff* had been published in July, to decidedly mixed reviews. Even the *Home Journal*, a paper to which Mansfield regularly contributed, although it praised the author's "boldness and freedom from conventional laws," noted that "more frequently he illustrates the nearness of the ridiculous to the sublime." He had been expected to join Ellen at Bird's Nest, but stayed away even as her term approached.

"Manse," Ellen explained to her mother in February 1867, "writes me that he is very sick, in bed . . . He has been suffering with his head & very nervous all winter." She said she was worried he would not get there before she went into labor, but hoped he would eventually make it to Kentucky. She supposed, based perhaps on previous observation, that his condition would improve once he got there. At least on paper she managed to sound quite relaxed. The children were all well, and

Lem's wife, Annie, had just had a baby who was proving "a famous little fellow." "Although I feel anxious about Manse's being sick in New York," Ellen added, "I think it is only one of the spells like he has had before." Eight days later her daughter Reubena—Ruby to her family—was born, as healthy and happy a baby as she would ever have.

Months went by, and still Mansfield did not come. Sarah had settled in at Bird's Nest for a long stay, and Dolly was in more or less permanent residence too. It had become the domain of women and children. There were long walks among flowering orchards and hot afternoons without newspapers, because Lem was in the city most of the time now in his law office, leaving the women to their own devices out in the country. Sarah sent her husband a stream of letters that detailed the infants' joys and ailments while repeatedly anticipating Mansfield's arrival, and wondering if the Chancellor would not accompany him: "I do not know any way you can spend your time more pleasantly than with us."

Mansfield showed up finally in late July—without the Chancellor, now too ill, with diabetes and other ailments, to stir much from home—and stayed on until autumn. Perhaps, as Ellen had hoped, the Kentucky climate did his head some good. The visit—his last to Bird's Nest—was interrupted when word came from Saratoga in late November that the Chancellor was about to die.

AT the end of that summer, as the season was winding to a close in Saratoga—the horse races finished, the itinerant rakes and gamblers drifting back to the metropolis—two lawyers had paid a morning call on the dying judge. Charles O'Conor, Walworth's running mate in the 1848 election, had gotten wind of his failing condition and asked James Gerard, another veteran New York attorney, to accompany him on what was likely to be a final visit.

They strolled past Congress Park toward the north end of Broadway. Pine Grove seemed a quaint cottage compared to the newly built grandiosities vying for attention along Saratoga's broad avenues. "We opened the little white gate," Gerard would recall, "and entered the portal of his dwelling. There was an air of melancholy around the place. The very trees looked sad and drooping . . . He came into the room, and his bending form showed that disease had made its mark upon him." The lawyers wished Walworth well and exchanged pleasantries and gossip. But as the Chancellor warmed to the conversation, Gerard was astonished to find that the old man's vital spirits could still be roused—not by legal or political affairs, but by the intricacies of the family tree whose branches he had spent so many years tracing.

Gerard listened with amazement to Walworth's monologue on "the *genealogy* of many families of the old world and the new, with whom he was in any way connected." Gerard had pictured the Chancellor spending his retirement reviewing old law cases: "I never had an idea that there stood before me one of the greatest genealogists of the present day. I soon found it out from the animation and intelligence with which he spoke on the subject, and it was surprising to hear him, even in his day of sickness, discourse upon the subject with all the energy of a herald-at-arms, as he produced and read off a history of his own ancestors and traced one of the families with which he was connected back to Malcolm 3rd, King of Scotland, whose father, Duncan, was murdered by Macbeth."

Those ancient ties of kinship tied the old man to life. The record of ancestral interrelations had become more real than the shadow existence he had led in these last years. The nation's best days had passed, and his expectations for the future of his line had collapsed as well. Clarence would have no heirs; Mansfield, it seemed clear, would leave behind chiefly the memory of disgrace. When the Chancellor dared to look forward instead of backward, he saw an eminent line trailing off into darkness.

Of what final value, then, had been his mental labors, his feats of memory and argument? He had never allowed a single detail to fall by the wayside. The code that made sense of it all—that in some way made manifest an underlying order—was, after all, in genealogy. The genealogical thread unseen by others had to him been constantly visible. "His memory," a friend recalled, "reached beyond the personal knowledge of individuals to their relations and connections in life, their marriages and intermarriages, their family history, genealogies and chronologies. Often it happened that strangers on being introduced to him for the first time would be astonished to find that he knew more of their families and family connections than they did themselves." The skein told him where he came from and of what larger entity he made part. In the knowledge of all the twists and turns of that thread, time itself was abolished.

As the lawyers took their leave of Pine Grove, they must already have been rehearsing phrases for the Chancellor's eulogy. It was a death long expected, and when it came, on Thanksgiving day, the ceremonies and speeches and commemorative writings that followed had all the expected gravity and polish. A parade of mourners accompanied him to his rest on the high ground of Greenridge Cemetery, led by dignitaries of the Masonic Order as pallbearers.

Chancellor Walworth's life, in Charles O'Conor's summation, had been "glorious, happy, and eminently useful," and O'Conor ventured to suggest that "if perfection could be claimed for any, it might be claimed for him." He had been a success story of the Republic. In the course of his career he had participated in public life in all aspects: legal, military, financial, political, educational, religious. He was a reminder of the days when it was impossible to separate those spheres: they were all one thing, a unitary system whose intertwining orders he had spent his life defining, by word and deed. There was no detail that did not signify, or that existed in isolation from the main body. He had been a lover of connections and a fighter for order. It was only by banding together that men made things solid and kept them that way. Freedom was never a solitary occupation. Men lived within compacts.

The Bible on which he was sworn in as a Masonic Grand Master was said to be the same on which George Washington had taken his oath of office. His duty since birth had been to the American Republic, and of what did that Republic consist if not the sum total of all the codes of criminal and civil law, worked out into their minutest details, as they applied to the hierarchies and manners of ordinary society and the distinct and appropriate roles of the sexes, decorum of speech and gesture, all the way down to the maintenance of physical health through exercise, diet, and total abstention from intoxicating liquors?

Once there might have been a few naysayers to suggest publicly that on a more fundamental level his life might be judged a failure. From time to time, in former years, some had volunteered that he had been for all too understandable reasons a one-term congressman and an unsuccessful candidate for governor; a Chancellor decried for wounding sarcasm and time-wasting pedantry; a prolific author of tracts, orations, and pamphlets that few had ever finished reading in view of their belaboring of minutiae and their unvarying tone of pious self-congratulation; a moralist more concerned with observance of Sabbath restrictions than with the soul-shaking question of the nation's ultimate destination; a politician who had allied himself with a faction notorious for its small-minded pursuit of profit and petty advantage, and who in the nation's hour of danger had broken only reluctantly if at all with those forces dedicated to appeasing the Slave Power; a legal practitioner who, for all his much-vaunted probity, had managed in his retirement to create, through his management of the Spike suit, a new byword for legalistic obfuscation; nothing more, finally, than a paltry and superfluous functionary, of whom the best that might be said was that the young nation had already known far worse.

But at this moment no such voices would be heard, not in public at least. His old political enemies had nothing to gain by raking over half-remembered quarrels and factional disputes. The Chancellor could be comfortably and unanimously eulogized as a man of incomparable integrity and unquestioned accomplishment.

His memory was a last token of how things had been before the war, in an era that now seemed already somehow less commercial, less brutal: the pastoral period of what had become an industrial empire. It was enough to picture him as an old man continuing to trot about the streets of Saratoga on his sorrel Araby, in the riding habit he had worn for half a century, so weathered in his latter days that it made him look like the humblest of countrymen. Here died a homespun gentleman whose least quirk or crotchet embodied the old ways that now seemed attic curiosities, all the more admirable for being utterly out of date.

Only in private could the dissenting versions and alternate accounts of his career begin to leak out. George Templeton Strong noted in his diary: "Died at Saratoga, his residence, old *Walworth*, last of the chancellors. He left the bench with an exalted reputation for learning, ability, and integrity, but his record since then has been less brilliant. He married a splurging Western widow (Mrs. J. J. Hardin) for his second wife. It's said that her fast, expensive ways demoralized the staid, strait-laced, rather puritanical old fogy; threw him off his bearings, and made him rapacious, if not corrupt. He was referee in several great cases, among them the very important patent case of Burden and Corning.

In this case he is said to have bled the parties heroically, demanding a thousand or two on account of referee's fees whenever he found himself a little short, and to have pushed the process of depletion till the parties decided to abandon the suit. Such is the story, whispered about and disbelieved at first . . ."

MANSFIELD had headed for Saratoga as soon as he learned of his father's condition. Ellen, delayed by making arrangements for the care of the children, arrived a day after the Chancellor's death. (To Dolly, who had not been able to come, she wrote a note that implied more than it said outright: "We all regretted very much that you could not be here with us as we paid our last services to our dear old Chancellor who with all his peculiarities was ever a kind friend to you and me.") The rest of the family circle had already gathered. The three elder sisters were there. The widowed Mary had been staying at Pine Grove since her husband's untimely death; Sarah had come down from Albany with her lawyer husband; and Liza—the sister whom Mansfield had come to regard as a domestic enemy, and whom he would savagely caricature in his fiction—was there with her husband, Jonathan Backus, pastor of the First Presbyterian Church of Schenectady and, as it turned out, coexecutor of the Chancellor's will.

The other executor was Clarence. During his extended convalescence at Pine Grove following his breakdown, Clarence had spent many hours with the Chancellor discussing the final disposition of the paternal assets and the question of what to do about Mansfield. Now someone—it is likely to have been Clarence—had to inform Mansfield of the terms of the will the Chancellor had drafted the previous July. It would have been merciful to go straight to the point, sparing his brother the suspense of perusing the whole document in order to learn his fate.

The Chancellor's testament was long and extremely detailed. While making generous provisions for his widow, he had earmarked each of his possessions—each book, print, painting, curio, pitcher, and teakettle—for specific individuals. From this protracted inventory Mansfield would have learned that his stepmother, Sarah, was to retain, for instance, an engraving of the trial of Charles I and a set of the novels of James Fenimore Cooper; that his son Frank was to have a family coat of arms, a copy of Froissart's *Chronicles* with the account of Lord Mayor Walworth's killing of Wat Tyler, and a history of the Mexican War with an account of his other grandfather's death; that the faithful Dolly was to receive a legacy of fifty dollars cash; that Ellen, along with her brothers, was to receive a portion of the grounds of Pine Grove.

It would indeed have been cruel to make an expectant heir sit through such a reading, waiting with increasing anxiety for the mention of his own name. It came up first in an oblique fashion. Clarence was requested to "prepare or cause to be prepared under his direction . . . a biography of myself." If Clarence should choose to employ Mansfield in this task, he was directed "to give to his said brother Mansfield or to his children the profits arising from the publication including the copyright." Given what Mansfield already knew about the economics of American publishing—and what he could guess about the public's interest, at this late date, in the details of his father's judicial career—this clause could not have inspired much optimism.

What followed was worse. The Chancellor's specific legacies to Mansfield were enumerated, and it was a very short list: copies of Alison's *History of Europe* and Hammond's *Political History of New York*; an agate seal bearing the Walworth arms; an enameled portfolio, previously the property of Mansfield's mother; and—an item that was to be a continuing source of friction—"the cabinet purchased for him by his mother, together with the collection of minerals, shells and other curiosities in and on the same." That was all.

There should have been a further item, detailing the allotment of Mansfield's due share of his father's financial and real estate holdings. For this he would have waited in vain. Instead there was a stipulation that a portion of the estate—amounting to about 23 percent of its value—be given to Clarence in trust, to be paid out as he saw fit for the support of Mansfield, his wife, and his children. At thirty-seven, Mansfield had become the ward of his elder brother.

The Chancellor may well have made threats to cut Mansfield off. It would be surprising if he had not, especially when it was finally brought to his attention that Mansfield had conspired on more than one occasion to sell out his father's professional secrets to interested litigants. The details of these breaches of legal confidence were never made public, but within the family they may have been what made

Mansfield once and for all an outcast. Nonetheless Mansfield's astonishment that the disinheritance had come to pass seemed genuine. It was certainly explosive, even if stage-managed with the self-conscious melodramatics that constituted his natural language.

An unnamed relative of the Walworths—evidently getting his information from Mansfield's sister Liza Backus—would later detail for an upstate newspaper how Mansfield raged after finding out the details of the will. Standing in front of the Chancellor's body—it was laid out in the library, flanked by walls of law books—he delivered a blasphemous harangue. He cursed the day of his own birth and called on God "to avenge his upas tree, as he called it"—that legendary poisonous Malay tree that William Blake had made the symbol of a hidden, murderous wrath: "In the morning glad I see / My foe outstretched beneath the tree." Mansfield vowed that from now on the object of his life would be to make sure that his father lay uneasy in his grave. Ellen said nothing publicly about any such declarations then or later, recalling only that the kicking of furniture and smashing of small objects reached a crescendo at this time.

Mansfield took his place among the mourners at his father's grave. But the night of the funeral he got drunk and tried to break into the sleeping quarters of the local female seminary. The police were called out and discreetly removed him from the scene, apparently before any of the young women were molested. The family managed to keep this incident out of the papers.

Mansfield's choices had suddenly become drastically more limited. He found himself placed under a restraint he had not anticipated. The prospect of his father's death had been a promise of long-deferred freedom, the chance to assume his proper place in the world as he came at last into the inheritance that was to set all things right. He had borrowed extensively against that inheritance, and was now obliged to put up most of his remaining possessions as collateral to the Jennings Brothers of Saratoga to keep his head above water. If he did not pay his debts within a year, they would be authorized to seize the lot, including his entire library of a hundred or so books, among them the *History of Europe* and *Political History of New York* that his father had taken care to leave him; a gold watch he had bought only a year ago, perhaps in unjustified expectancy of profits from *Stormcliff*; an iron

The Walworth children: (*front row*) Frank; (*middle*) Reubena, Clara; (*back*) Nelly, Tracy, unidentified friend. Courtesy of Walworth Memorial Museum.

Mansfield Tracy Walworth.
Courtesy of Walworth Memorial Museum.

Chancellor Reuben Hyde Walworth.
Courtesy of Walworth Memorial Museum.

Ellen Hardin at sixteen.
Courtesy of Walworth Memorial
Museum.

Ellen Hardin Walworth in
mourning, probably in the 1860s.
Courtesy of Walworth Memorial
Museum.

Ellen Hardin Walworth late in life (after the murder).
Courtesy of Walworth Memorial Museum.

Frank Hardin Walworth
as a child.
Courtesy of Walworth
Memorial Museum.

Frank Hardin Walworth shortly
before the murder.
Courtesy of Walworth Memorial Museum.

Frank (*left*) after his release from prison,
with Tracy, his brother.
Courtesy of Walworth Memorial Museum.

Clarence Walworth.
Courtesy of Walworth Memorial Museum.

Pine Grove in its original condition. Courtesy of Walworth Memorial Museum.

The Walworth Mansion.
Local advertisement.

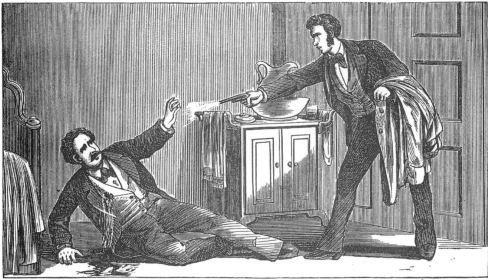

With frightful coolness, young Walworth sent four bullets into his father's body.
Mit furchtbarer Kälte schießt der Sohn vier Kugeln in den Körper seines Vaters.

An illustration from *The Walworth Parricide*.

safe; a rocking chair; a stained wood washstand; a suit of gray clothes and a brown overcoat; and, again, the "mahogany cabinet of shells & minerals and curiosities in the Chancellor's parlor, Saratoga Springs."

He consigned as well a framed set of engravings of Thomas Cole's *The Voyage of Life*. For Mansfield this famous allegorical series—four paintings showing the progress of the soul from the joys of infancy and youth to the perils and portents of maturity and old age—must by now have taken on a very personal significance. Had he not been that angelic child launched under serene skies into peaceful waters by a maternal angel? In his youth had he not experienced to the full the visionary ecstasy suggested by the ethereal palaces that beckoned above the horizon in Cole's second panel, that radiant celestial aperture promising something like the conquest of the universe? Now he had arrived at the third grim stage. Under an apocalyptic sky the terrified voyager found himself alone. The angel he prayed to was no longer visible, and he struggled to control his battered craft as it slipped toward the murky rapids.

11

The Look of a Wild Beast

"**S**HE is adrift; her husband is insane, she can do nothing for him."
This was Ellen, a few years later, trying to cast her life into the
form of a novel. It must have seemed to her that she had been drifting
for years: away from Mansfield and then back to him. For years in
Kentucky she had lived apart. Divorce in her world was an almost
unthinkable last resort, but often their situation had amounted to
divorce. Yet time and again they had somehow found themselves back
together, and even his brutal outburst in the summer of 1865 had not
ended things between them. She had borne him another daughter, the
golden-haired Ruby, although Mansfield had not even laid eyes on the
child until she was five months old.

But Mansfield had surpassed even his earlier frenzies. The attempted
assault on the female seminarians was only one flagrant instance, and in
the recriminations over the Chancellor's will, other members of the
family—Liza Backus doubtless among them—could have dredged up
plenty of other evidence of Mansfield's ever more erratic behavior.
While Ellen had been down at Bird's Nest, the rest of them had kept a
closer eye on him and would have had much to tell her, not least about
infidelities that were locally notorious, although their particulars were
never published or even written down.

Mansfield was dead to Ellen, putrescent, interred in her broken heart; this was the gist of "Alive, Yet Dead," a poem she wrote in March 1868. She had acquired the habit of recording her feelings freely in verse, and over the years a sizable sheaf piled up. The poems formed a sort of closet autobiography, carefully trimmed of names and specific circumstances, memorializing her most despairing moments. In many she seemed to sum up what her dealings with Mansfield had amounted to.

> *He took her heart and tossed it up and down*
> *As 'twere some trifling toy to please a child.*

"Alive, Yet Dead" amounted to a mortuary farewell to the "brilliant eyes" and "sunny curls" and "gay words" and "strong manhood" of an idealized love, evoking moments of erotic bliss—

> *O lordly head that I so oft*
> *Have pressed with rapture to my breast*
> *While 'mid your clinging curls so soft*
> *My fingers found a loving rest*

—before passing final judgment.

> *For you one grave is dug most deep,*
> *And there you lie all stark and cold,*
> *Corruption's horrors round you creep,*
> *My shattered hopes, those worms so bold,*
>
> *No resurrection from that grave . . .*

It is a matter of assumption that the poem's subject was Mansfield. From this period of her life, and for the next several years to come, Ellen left virtually no letters or diaries. But something certainly changed for her. Long afterward, in the wake of another tragedy, compiling a list of the crucial turning points in her life, she wrote: "1867—The year in which my heart was broken."

In any case she withdrew from her husband again. Not to return to

Bird's Nest, that place of exile where she had been out of touch with the rest of the world and consumed by the cares of child rearing. Her mother, Sarah, drawing again on her Washington connections, found Ellen a clerical job in the Treasury Department. She would rent an apartment in Washington and send Frank to Georgetown College. The older girls, Nelly and Clara, would continue their education at the Kenwood convent, with Clarence nearby to look out for them.

For Ellen, this period in Washington was the beginning of her emergence from a long silence. She began to make herself at home in the political world that was her mother's base of action, and find her way toward an understanding of what it took to make things happen in that world. Soon she would be attending the same balls, the same receptions. Being a social ornament was no longer something that came naturally to her, but she would work at it. The incisive intellectual conversation for which she had been noted in her youth was once again to be exercised. No longer living under the shadow of her husband, she made an impression as a woman of unusual seriousness and independence.

Frank too apparently thrived. Years afterward a writer for the Georgetown alumni journal would recall him with evident sincerity as having been "universally liked, as a boy whose qualities of mind and heart gave him well-deserved prominence," notable for his capacity for warm friendship.

As for Mansfield, he entered into a kind of hibernation. Whether willingly or not, he had taken up residence with Clarence in Albany. After Mansfield's recent behavior, his brother doubtless felt that close observation was in order. Holding undisputed power of the purse, Clarence was well positioned to nudge his brother toward a more disciplined mode of life.

Under Clarence's supervision he seems to have avoided scandal. To some he expressed satisfaction at the new orderliness of his life. Clarence allowed him to work in peace, unlike his wife who had had a bad habit of disarranging his papers. He spent his days at the New York State Library, deep in research for his next novel. An assistant librarian who aided him in his researches and came to know him quite well was mightily impressed: considering him "as brilliant a man as I

ever knew . . . I never can be made to believe that he beat his wife or
abused her or wrote threatening letters." On the contrary, Mansfield
struck him as the most polite and cultured of men, a man who "never
drank, never smoked, never chewed, never swore, and was as nearly
perfect as any man could be." He was slow to anger; he had tolerated
insults that the librarian would have knocked a man down for. The
nature or occasion of the insults was not specified.

It was to this librarian that Mansfield complained about his wife
disturbing his manuscripts. She had even, he claimed, deliberately
torn up his notes and hidden his works in progress. (Given Mansfield
and Ellen's frequent long separations, it is not clear when she was supposed to have done this.) The real trouble between the couple, the
librarian deduced, had to do with Ellen's fierce southern temper—she
had "the spirit of her people." Mansfield himself had pretty much
adhered to "southern principles," so much so that he had made himself
unwelcome in Saratoga, but the incompatibility of temperament
between husband and wife had finally made things impossible. Mansfield's own nature, according to his admirer, was by far the gentler.

His new novel called for quite a lot of library work. Mansfield had
always enjoyed splashing evidence of his erudition across his pages, but
never on the scale of *Warwick; or, The Lost Nationalities of America*.
Ancient religions, lost languages, mythological keys to geologic secrets;
as if all this were not enough, *Warwick* was also larded with discussions
of Anglo-Saxon historiography, Spanish literature, varieties of apples,
and the veterinary care of horses. This last theme arose only because the
book's title character was a horse—a horse who, although introduced
with great fanfare, turned out to play a marginal role in the story's
unfolding. This was no more unaccountable than any other ingredient
in Mansfield's usual olio of perplexities.

The implications of *Warwick*'s story were inescapably personal.
The novel concerned a scholarly and virtuous man, Constant Earle,
deprived of his rightful inheritance by his elder brother and condemned to make his way in the world as an author. In the meantime
the sinister brother Montrose—as gifted as his sibling but morally
warped—wallowed in the luxuries of a palatial home comprising both
an unequaled menagerie of exotic beasts ("the long-lipped bear of the
Terai . . . the gyal of Upper Assam . . . the muntjak or barking deer of

India") and a vast private library, "the paradise of a *littérateur* ... a dream of luxury and ease."

The two brothers, good and bad, were almost mirror images, alike in their physical strength and agility, alike in their mastery of foreign tongues and recondite lore, alike in their quest for the power to be drawn from ancient knowledge—in this instance from the mysterious talismanic inscription on the back of a portrait of their dead mother. Montrose would spend most of the book vainly conniving to wrest away this portrait—Constant's sole legacy—with a view to deciphering the cryptic message, which turned out to hold the key to the buried gold of lost Atlantis, a trove vast enough to give its discoverer a controlling influence over the global economy.

But before the betrayed younger brother, having been cheated out of his own inheritance, could inherit the infinite wealth hidden at the earth's core, he must submit to a long process of purification by suffering. He would be forced to labor as a legal copyist and as an underpaid tutor; he would write a masterpiece—nothing less than "the harbinger of a new literary millennium"—only to have it stolen and published under another man's name; he would fall in love with a mysterious veiled woman who then vanished without warning; in his rat-infested garret he would be tormented by the noises of cartmen and vagrant children and clanking machinery until "at the junction of the brain and spinal cord a painful sensation came daily and nightly to disarm the scholar."

A moment would arrive when not even the thought of his dead mother leaning toward him from "her seat beside the great white throne of God" was enough to rescue him from his demons: "There is a mental night when the soul is alone and dark; when God the great central light is hidden; when moans come up from the valley of death; when the unanchored heart drifts silently upon the black sea, aimless, fearful, encompassed by despair."

Over hundreds of pages Mansfield allowed his hero to revert continually to this zero degree of consciousness, a compound of rage and self-pity and helplessness: "Why struggle? For what? A name?" He relived his own humiliations as his father's law clerk as he recounted how Constant's "resolute and earnest pen marked down summons and complaints, demurrers and decrees, deeds and mortgages, leases and charter-parties, bonds and judgments, and all the legal paraphernalia and technical phraseology by which property is transferred, contracts solemnized, and litigation carried on."

But Mansfield was preparing a wonderful payoff for his protagonist. Constant's purloined book would be recognized as his and proclaimed as the greatest work of the day. He would gain unique access—along the lines of the Count of Monte Cristo, but on a far more grandiose scale—to the Atlantean treasure-house, hidden far down in the depths of Kentucky's Mammoth Caves. And his veiled lost love would return to him, revealed as New York's wealthiest and most intellectually accomplished heiress, ready to bestow a fortune he no longer even needed.

The heiress could hardly help surrendering to him, given his physical and mental attractions, cataloged here at greater length than Mansfield had previously allowed himself. He dwelled on the "delicate finish to every limb," the "symmetrical rounding of his arms," the "slender, effeminate hands, white and soft, and graceful as a girl's," the ankles "perfect as those of an Apollo," the "perfection of elegance in the long, slim feet," all of it an indication that Constant Earle "had sprung from a pure and cultivated race of men." Even the wicked Montrose, having drugged Constant to rob him of the all-important portrait, could not refrain from admiring his unconscious brother: " 'Beautiful as Picus!' he muttered, noting the fair, clear complexion of the drooping face. 'No wonder women love you. I would myself.' "

And then there were the eyes, to which he continually reverted, the large blue eyes "soft and lustrous as a gazelle's," "magnetic in their influence," evoking at one moment the tortured gaze of "Christ scourged at the pillar," at another the glance of the Hindu god Krishna, "exciting the imagination, and breathing music from the eyes." To see them was to be lost forever: "The woman who once had gazed into the lustrous eyes of Constant Earle was forever blinded to all other male beauty." The point could not be made too often, at any random narrative moment: "The personal beauty of Constant Earle, and his magnetic sympathy in the mental and physical order, gave him dangerous power in the society of women. He could fascinate female intellect without effort, no matter how exalted the type."

Mansfield had never allowed himself to get quite so lost in his reveries of loss and power, the "alternate exaltations and depressions" to which natures like his were susceptible. But *Warwick*'s overlay of ancient inscriptions, ominous caverns, and subterranean gold mines proved attractive to a larger crowd than he had previously drawn. The image of Constant Earle dangling by a rope over a bottomless abyss had struck some kind of responsive chord. Informed by Carleton that the book was doing unexpectedly well, he had a handbill printed up to let the world know of his triumph.

UNPRECEDENTED SALE OF AN AMERICAN NOVEL!
35,000 COPIES
OF
WARWICK!
SOLD SINCE THE 1ˢᵗ OF MAY, 1869

An extravagant array of pull quotes was drawn from such sources as the *Albany Knickerbocker* ("brilliant, scholarly, and absorbing"), the *New Orleans Times* ("not far behind the productions of Ouida"), and the *New York Citizen* ("one of the ablest and most comprehensive of satirists . . . Neither Orpheus C. Kerr, Artemus Ward, Mark Twain nor C. H. Webb, can for a moment be compared with Mansfield Tracy Walworth"). In Saratoga, where "parlor, piazza, bedroom and Congress Park were alike noticeable as resorts for the *Warwick* readers," he relished the unaccustomed role of local celebrity. He would now be identified in the press not as "the Chancellor's son" but as "the author of *Warwick*." A journalist who met Mansfield in Saratoga at the height of *Warwick*'s success described him as being "constantly pointed out as one of the lions of the Spring."

This journalist was much taken with Mansfield—remembering him as an "agreeable, honest-looking and unassuming man" who "looked you squarely in the eye when speaking"—and ingratiated himself by comparing the climax of *Warwick* with the work of Poe. Mansfield modestly replied that "if he thought he could ever write anything worthy to be compared with Poe he should consider he had attained sufficient glory for any man." He then invited the interviewer home with him, to a domestic scene recorded here for the nonce as an idyllic scene of domestic merriment and tranquility: "I never in my life beheld a pleasanter family group than the Walworths presented." He described carefree afternoons on the lawn in the shadow of the pines, surrounded by little boys and girls who enthusiastically listened in on discussions of "literature, philosophy, and religion." In particular he recalled Ellen laughingly recounting how Mansfield had woken her in the night to tell her he had finally figured out how to resolve the cliff-hanging climax of his novel.

ELLEN had only recently come back once more into Mansfield's life. Political reshufflings had led to the loss of her Treasury Department job, and she needed urgently to find support for herself and the children. She had no illusions that the success of *Warwick* or anything else would prompt Mansfield to help with that support. She had determined therefore to come back to Pine Grove, now Sarah's domain, and let rooms to boarders in the summer of 1869. Her mother and Clarence backed her completely in the plan. Mansfield was outraged that the ancestral home should be converted into a hotel.

It was a rough summer for the family, and perhaps for the boarders as well. Mansfield continued to lavish any money he had on the upkeep of his own appearances, all the more essential now that he was so much in the public eye. Yet he took it as an affront if anyone else tried to help out his offspring. Learning that one of his sisters had sent over a gift of clothing for the children, he went on a rampage, screaming curses as he searched through the house for the gifts and ripped them apart when he found them. "At that time," Ellen would later observe, "his appearance was very remarkable, as were also his words and gestures."

Pressed further to describe what Mansfield looked like during these fits of rage, she added: "He was always extremely pale and had the look of a wild beast. I cannot imagine any other expression like it."

In these familial comings and goings, Frank had stayed at a distance. He had been at school in Georgetown all during Ellen's employment at the Treasury Department. When she lost her job he broke off his studies there and returned to Louisville, where he resumed reading law under the supervision of his uncle Lem. His father was becoming a remote figure in his life, a figure of whom he heard nothing good.

Ellen persisted in her plans to run Pine Grove as a summer boardinghouse, but there were also the autumn and winter to get through.

She stayed on at Pine Grove until October, while Mansfield rented rooms on Twenty-third Street in New York City from a Mrs. Montross. He begged Ellen to join him there, and she finally gave in, going down to the city with all the children except Frank. On the day of her arrival, she became so ill—and perhaps so ill at ease—that within days she left for her brother Martin's home in Buffalo. There she recuperated throughout the winter. Mansfield stayed where he was, grinding out journalism for the *Home Journal* and other papers, and beginning to draft his follow-up to *Warwick*, an ambitious fictional journey through Russia and Persia.

By the end of the year Ellen, although still not fully recovered, was back with Mansfield in New York. It proved an untenable arrangement. When, in bed one night, she told him that Martin had invited her to visit him in Buffalo, he began to scream at her—"Bitch! Fiend!"—and to drive his fist into the pillow where she lay. She felt her life was in danger.

Yet she managed to open Pine Grove for the summer season and keep the family's affairs running with apparent efficiency. It was clear to her mother that the marriage could not continue, and even Clarence, to whom divorce was an unpalatable solution, acknowledged a real physical threat to Ellen and her children. He knew of a clerical position in the state government in Albany that might be just the thing to keep Mansfield gainfully occupied, away from the temptations of New York City and in a position to care, if not for his family, then at least for himself. Ellen put this proposition to her husband in October of 1870, while they were still at Pine Grove. The usual curses and threats followed. Ellen begged him to stop the abuse and not compel her to divorce him. He replied with theatrical bravado, "I am McFarland!"

IT was a double sort of threat, alluding to the year's most sensational trial. Daniel McFarland was a New York lawyer whose drunken brutalizing of his wife had led her to divorce him; she had then become engaged to Albert Richardson, a prominent young journalist who had covered Civil War battles for the *Tribune*. On November 25, 1869, McFarland had ambushed Richardson at the *Tribune*'s offices, fatally shooting him. Richardson lingered long enough to be married by Henry Ward Beecher to the former Mrs. McFarland, an aspiring actress and writer who now went by the name Abby Sage.

McFarland's conviction seemed inevitable. But when he came to trial in the spring of 1870, the prosecutors (including Noah Davis and Samuel Garvin, both to be prominently involved in the trial of Frank Walworth) found themselves up against a team of defense lawyers who turned the case on its head. McFarland's wife had, they implied, begun her affair with Richardson before the marriage ended; and the knowledge of this was argued to have driven her husband mad, turning him into "a man overtaken by sorrow and calamity brought on by the unholy, reckless, and lawless passion of a bold, bad libertine, a wife-seducer and child-robber sent into eternity by a husband and father wronged when a great sea turned away his reason." The jury voted for acquittal.

For Ellen, reading Abby Sage's trial testimony about her husband's behavior must have been like seeing her own life written down: "He would lock himself in the room with me and give way to such terrible furies that only extreme pride and self-control prevented me from making my misery known . . . He told me that he kept loaded pistols with which he would at any moment shoot me." For Mansfield—another lawyer given to drink and brutality, and ridden by a powerful sense of personal grievance—the case must have likewise presented a compelling interest. The defense lawyers' pitying description of the wronged husband's descent into madness could have been taken from one of his own novels.

In McFarland's fate he could discern as well a hint as to how he too might finally triumph. To wave the McFarland case before Ellen was to say that not only could he do whatever he liked, but—wronged and maddened as a lawyer might argue him to be—he would get away with it too. "Hardin shall not rob me of my wife and children!" he went on. If Ellen left him, he told her, he would kill her brother Martin. Beating her with closed fists, he grabbed hold of her with both arms and flung her on the bed. While she lay unconscious he continued to beat her, injuring her arm so severely that she could not use it for weeks afterward.

FRANK was in Saratoga for part of the following summer. He was of an age to enjoy the spa's social opportunities more than before, and made himself well liked among the locals. He may have been spending time with Corinne Bramlette, the fifteen-year-old daughter of ex-governor Bramlette of Kentucky. Bramlette was Sarah's cousin and had helped Lem reestablish himself after the war. A regular visitor to Saratoga in the antebellum period, the governor was now once again summering at the spa with his daughter and his second wife, and renewing his close ties with Sarah and the family.

In the course of the summer Frank made a significant acquisition. A friend of the Walworths having died, his widow entrusted Frank with her husband's Colt revolver, as a memento.

It was only at this time, apparently, that Ellen decided it was time to take Frank into her confidence. She wanted him to know what she had endured, and continued to endure, at Mansfield's hands. When she showed her son the severe bruises on her arm he went pale, and Ellen noticed "a pinched look on his features expressing severe suffering"—a look so unusual and extreme that she began to worry about her son's health. Not raising his voice, Frank murmured, almost without expression, "This must not be." After that, Ellen would claim, she rarely spoke to him about Mansfield.

A few weeks later, just at the end of the season in Saratoga—"still suffering," in her words, "from the effects of these bruises and beatings"—Ellen asked Mansfield to allow her to go upstairs and sleep with her children rather than with him that night. He leaped at her, shouting—"I'll show you damned Hardin what I can do for you! Take that, and that!"—and spat repeatedly in her face. As she begged him to stop he raised clenched fists over her head and—"to her great terror"—bellowed, "I'll blow your damned brains out!" The screaming continued until the house servants came running to her assistance.

When she left Pine Grove she was pregnant with her eighth child.

SARAH had taken a large apartment in New York City on Fifty-second Street, and it was here that Ellen came to live after Pine Grove was closed for the winter. Mansfield came too. It was intended to be a provisional arrangement. Ellen was still talking to her husband about how they could set up a permanent home for themselves and their children, but in view of all that had happened it is hard to know how real this prospect seemed to her. Her mother, her brothers, Clarence, and the other Walworth in-laws were by now well aware of the situation and were already conferring privately about what was to become of the marriage of Ellen and Mansfield, and how this would affect the disbursement of the trust fund managed by Clarence and Reverend Backus. Mansfield was not privy to these discussions but could clearly sense that his fate was being decided behind his back.

Frank, now seventeen and still studying in Louisville, came north for a prolonged visit around the holidays. It was toward the end of his stay that matters exploded beyond repair.

On January 13, 1871, around eight in the evening, Ellen and Mansfield were having what was intended by her as a calm discussion about where and how they would live. This immediately set Mansfield off. Waving his arms "wildly and rapidly up and down," cursing and screaming, he accused Ellen of conspiring with the rest of the family to have him taken back to Saratoga. As she threw up her hands to shield herself from his blows, he grabbed her hand and caught one of the fingers between his teeth, grinding down until he had bitten through to the bone.

Her screams of pain and terror brought Sarah, Frank, and the rest of the household bursting into the room, and Mansfield turned his attention to Sarah, attempting to beat her before Frank seized hold of him and prevented him from doing any further harm. While Sarah and the others looked after Ellen's wounded hand, Frank remained face-to-face with Mansfield. Looking him in the eyes, with his arm firmly on his shoulder, he said to him, "Be quiet, father." Mansfield seems to have calmed down. Frank stayed in the room all through the night and into the next day. Mansfield remained in the room until dawn. There was no further violence or outburst from him, evidently no discussion of any kind.

For ten days Ellen stayed in her room. Many nights Frank slept just outside her room, his pistol loaded and ready to hand. The rest of the family was given word of what had happened and made their way to the city, Martin from Buffalo, Clarence from Albany, the Reverend Backus from Schenectady. They served as a buffer between Mansfield and Ellen to make sure no further harm would come, although he was permitted to see her with others present. She did not say anything to him about her immediate intentions.

On the morning of January 26 she made her way with the children

to the Hoffman House, the hotel where her brother Martin was staying, and announced her decision to divorce Mansfield. When the legal
papers were drawn up they would provide a detailed account of what
she had undergone: "This plaintiff faithfully discharged her duties as
wife of the defendant and at all times treated him with kindness and
forbearance but that defendant her said husband commenced shortly
after said marriage a course of harsh tyrannical treatment towards her
which continued with slight intermissions until she finally separated
from him . . . The defendant utterly neglected and refused to support
and provide for plaintiff and her children . . . She has been almost
entirely dependent upon her own property and her relatives for the
support and maintenance of herself and her children and . . . the defendant during this time has been chiefly supported by the said relatives
and friends of this plaintiff and by this plaintiff."

Once Mansfield understood what had happened he went to the
Hoffman House at about four in the morning with a pistol in his pocket.
Martin Hardin—still suffering very much from the massive wounds,
including the loss of his arm, sustained in the war—was woken by violent knocking. Several lawyers whom he had engaged were on the premises, working through the night on Ellen's divorce papers. One of them
opened the door, and Mansfield strode in. Reaching for his pistol, he
went over to Martin's bed and demanded to know where his wife was.
Martin asked him to be patient and to allow him to get up and put his
clothes on. He did not take his eyes off his brother-in-law as he
stepped into his trousers, and then made a dash for the door, holding
it shut from the outside while Mansfield hurled himself against it until
he forced it open. Waving the pistol, he pursued Martin down the cor-
ridor of the hotel. By now people were crowding into the hall, and a
moment later a policeman arrived and took Mansfield into temporary
custody.

He never saw Ellen again, but he would continue to find ways to
make her life a misery.

12

~~~~~~~~~

Frank Is Sick

Fᴏʀ a time Mansfield did not know where the fugitives had gone. He must have suspected that it was not only Ellen's relations but his own who were making sure he had no contact with his own wife and children. For several months they went from home to home—a few days with Judge Barbour and then with Martin at the Hoffman House, up to Albany for nearly a month with Clarence, and then for another three weeks with Mansfield's sister Liza Backus and her husband in Schenectady. But Ellen did not intend to hide out indefinitely. As spring approached, she went with her mother to Pine Grove to open the house for the new season.

The Walworth family seat—Sarah's property now—would provide a very public haven for Ellen and her children. Six months pregnant and still suffering from the effects of Mansfield's last assaults, she set about making a new and independent life for herself. "After ten years of peace, of struggles, of agonies, of experiments," she wrote years later about this turning point, "a change and a revolution in the return to the New York Homestead and the determination to remain there at all hazards as a proper refuge for the children."

She had already been moving in that direction when she began to take in boarders two years earlier. Now her plans were more ambitious.

She would turn the house into a private school, the Walworth Academy, a small but exclusive establishment in which she would do much of the teaching. Without a pause she set to work organizing things for the coming fall, canvassing for pupils and writing letters requesting endorsements from influential people like the abolitionist Gerrit Smith, the Chancellor's old colleague in the temperance campaign. To Smith she confided that she had been "very unfortunate in my domestic relations," had been obliged to divorce her husband, and that her income amounted only to some five hundred dollars, the rest having been "entirely exhausted in former years of struggle & suffering."

If she had little cash in hand, she could turn to a wide network of distinguished potential patrons—all those contacts in the legal, political, and cultural worlds of whom she had made careful note through the years of being Colonel Hardin's daughter and Chancellor Walworth's daughter-in-law. She pushed the project forward rapidly. The Walworth Academy opened in October of 1871 as an all-boys school—"endeavoring to inculcate correct moral principles, gentlemanly habits and refined manners"—and by February the school was hosting a Washington's Birthday celebration featuring recitations in Latin, French, and German, readings from Whittier, Poe, Longfellow, and Tennyson, and a piano solo by the German professor's wife. The next autumn girls were admitted as well. The local press praised Ellen's "ladylike manner and urbane ways," well suited for transforming ungainly boys into polished gentlemen. She had her school, and she had what was left of her family circle around her.

That she had made this happen was extraordinary under the circumstances. Her daughter Margaret, born in June, was sickly from birth, not improbably as a result of Mansfield's extreme physical abuse during those last weeks in New York. The infant died the following January, without her father ever having a look at her. "God took her in her innocence," Clarence wrote to Dolly, who for the time being had taken a job as housekeeper for another family in New York City, "and undoubtedly she has in this way escaped a great deal of trouble . . . Of the poor children's father I can give you little information, except that he is in New York. The least said about him the better."

To four-and-a-half-year-old Ruby, Dolly sent affectionate letters that the little girl preserved carefully, a small whisper of kindness in an atmosphere whose underlying anxieties even a small child must have sensed. Before the death of infant Margaret, Dolly wrote: "You must not think that I have forgotten you because I don't come home . . . you can take a good deal of care of the little baby for you are a great big girl . . . I am sending this five dollars to you and tell your mama to get you a nice pair of Rubber Boots to keep your feet dry this winter." Dolly hinted at her own sense of isolation: "They is no little children in this house and seames very strange to me for I never lived in a house without children befor."

Through the spring months the divorce proceedings continued. The decree of separation was pronounced in April, with Mansfield ordered to pay alimony and child support amounting to a total of $1,100 a year, a sum he would have a hard time paying without a drastic reduction in the luxuries to which he was accustomed. The agreement also stipulated that neither party was free to remarry.

MANSFIELD had moved to Eliza Sims's boardinghouse on East Fifty-third Street. At the urgent pace his straits now demanded, he was writing novels for G. W. Carleton's fiction mill and journalism for the *Home Journal*, a long-established purveyor of light reading run by Morris Phillips. Phillips would relate in a newspaper interview that Mansfield had always been "a welcome guest" in his home, a "genial, well-bred, courteous gentleman," a "model of refinement in the society of ladies." He knew nothing of his family affairs. As for Mansfield's style of life, Phillips believed he was neither dissipated nor extravagant: "He lived in cheap apartments uptown, and took his meals at cheap restaurants downtown." The elaborately dressed dude of earlier years was now apparently obliged to cut back; though "neat and cleanly in his dress and habits . . . he was almost too economical."

As with most of Mansfield's literary acquaintances, Phillips's friendship with the author seems to have been of the most limited sort. It was a business arrangement, and one of which Mansfield took considerable advantage, pressuring Phillips to promote Mansfield's novels. Mansfield was in the habit of drifting fairly often into the offices of the *Home Journal* and of G. W. Carleton. The writers and editors who crossed his path claimed by and large to have found him perfectly acceptable in manners and behavior, although none seems to have been inclined to push the association much beyond the occasional superficial chat.

Eli Perkins, a popular lecturer and humorist who had done some first-hand reporting on the Crimean War, received regular visits from Mansfield, who was researching the Persian background of his new novel *Delaplaine* and found it convenient to drop by to look at Perkins's photographs and draw him out on his experiences in Central Asia. "He was extremely proud and ambitious for fame as an author," Perkins recalled, but the lecturer reckoned that "his books were read only by people who could not think for themselves." Even his publisher didn't bother, apparently. When Mansfield ventured to ask G. W. Carleton which he thought was his best book—*Lulu* or *Hotspur* or *Stormcliff* or *Warwick* or *Delaplaine*—the publisher answered with brutal frankness: "Why, I never read any of them. I published them, but never read them." As for Mansfield's private life, according to Perkins it was "an enigma to everyone."

A female journalist who met him at the *Home Journal* office—the newspapers discreetly left her unnamed—pried a little further into his personal business when Mansfield expressed admiration of a young woman they both knew. Was he perhaps courting her? Mansfield looked "excessively pained" at the inquiry and replied, "Don't you know that I cannot address any lady, that I cannot marry?" The journalist had read in the papers a public declaration by Mansfield that he had left the Catholic Church, supposedly because of his opposition to the recently promulgated doctrine of papal infallibility, and she had supposed this freed him to remarry. "Pardon me if I have made a mistake," she told him. His face was flushed as he launched into a rapid monologue.

> You have made no mistake. I am glad you have spoken. I wish to tell you the truth. I consented to the divorce from my wife by the advice of our families, but I believe I did wrong. I wish to live with my wife, and hope to be reconciled to her. She left me because I was a poor struggling young author. She wanted me to practice law, and I knew my only road to success was in authorship. The family sided with her ... Now I am just

beginning to make money with my books perhaps she may be induced to live with me.

All the while he spoke, she recalled, he pressed his hand to his forehead and seemed so distressed that she changed the subject as quickly as possible.

While expressing such sentiments in New York publishing circles, Mansfield was engaged on other fronts. His financial situation had thrown him into a panic, and—communicating through her lawyer—he pressed Ellen to agree to amendments to the initial divorce decree. He asked her to allot him two-thirds of the property now held in trust by Clarence, with Ellen and the children getting the remaining third; to relieve him of any future support payments after the initial payments already agreed upon; and to grant him immunity from any future legal actions to get more money out of him. After all, she had Pine Grove, the help of the whole family, and now a potentially profitable school; he had a rented room and the miserable life of a struggling author. She acceded to these changes, even if they were plainly not in her favor. The terms of the settlement were further amended to grant him monthly visitation rights to see his children, although only in the presence of Clarence.

There was a delay in her signing off on the agreement. Her lawyer, Charles Whitney, informed Mansfield that any tardiness on Ellen's part was owing to reasons of health. In fact she was still gravely ill from a pregnancy and delivery made more difficult by the injuries she had sustained from her husband's beatings. It was at this point that Mansfield became enraged. He did not consent to be delayed or deterred.

Ellen had taken herself beyond the reach of his influence—the influence he liked to imagine in the pages of his novels as magnetic and irresistible—the influence he had finally imposed by means of closed fists and bared teeth. It was an affront to his deepest sense of who he was. She not only had escaped from his control but had evicted him from Pine Grove, his ancestral home. Like the disinherited hero of *Warwick*, he was now truly "an outcast and a wanderer." She had enlisted his own family against him. Lawyers had been appointed to harass and pauperize him. He had not, finally, been able to break her, and that seems to have reduced him to helpless astonishment.

Whether what followed was a deliberate campaign of intimidation or the uncontrollable overflowing of a deranged mind was a question later much debated.

I T was during the negotiations over the amendments to the divorce settlement that the letters began to arrive. They came sometimes every day, sometimes many in a single day. At first the insistent theme was Ellen's refusal to follow through on the arrangement to which, Mansfield reminded her, she had already assented: "Why do you not sign the papers which your lawyer says he sent to you? Is it not an honorable settlement, and was it not signed by me promptly? I waited weeks and weeks patiently, but your lawyer said the doctors wouldn't allow you to attend to any business or sign it . . . Already $250 of my precious money gone to my lawyer. Jesus Christ! Aren't you going to sign the agreement your lawyer sent you? You are a demon, keeping me from success by wasting the precious dollars and tormenting me after a settlement has been agreed upon."

The fate of his latest novel preoccupied him. This was a few weeks after the birth of his daughter Margaret. Mansfield's own literary delivery was to his mind equally troubling. The book's publication had been delayed, allegedly because of a paper shortage, but evidently it was becoming clear that the much-heralded successor to *Warwick* was proving a commercial disappointment: "Great God, woman, let me go to my work. The hardest time for *Delaplaine* is here. In six weeks the fate of the book is told." If she did not give in to his wishes, he would go before the American public to reveal the facts of the case, regardless of scandal. "But," he added, "that is not my only resource; there is murder and suicide also!"

The threats began in earnest. At ten in the morning on July 7 he wrote to her: "That same pleading, ever-present determination is working me up to the final tragedy. I go down in five minutes to see if my lawyer has received and filed the agreement signed. But my superhuman second sight tells me that you have again prevaricated, and that Chancellor Walworth's younger son must be a murderer and a suicide. So be it! . . . You are pushing your doom . . . All the intensity of hate in my life is centered on you. Listen for the crack of the pistol!" And again the next day: "I cannot hold out longer. The pistols are loaded. If you succeed in getting the $950 from the trust estate of my father I shall shoot you, stamp out your life with my boot, and shoot myself if your mother is not near. If she is near I will use the second shot on her body and the third on myself, behind the ear."

At moments he sounded as if he were rehearsing a future legal argument along the lines of the McFarland case: "Murder for $950, you ask? Why? Because you robbed me of my young; and now, in my miserable agony, on the loss of all that makes life tolerable, you remorselessly seek to knock from under a despairing wretch the last plank on which he can succeed." He made it clear he was shadowing her, lying in wait so he could attack just as McFarland had ambushed Richardson at the *Tribune* office: "I went to Judge Barbour's to kill you; that door chain alone saved you. If you do not sign the papers your lawyer says he sent you . . . I shall shoot you. You are dealing with a despairing, demoniacal murderer, or whatever despair makes a man. Sign damn quick."

It made sense to threaten Ellen, since he could be sure that neither Clarence nor anyone else in the family would help him out. If Ellen could not be persuaded, she must be frightened into changing the terms of the divorce settlement. But she continued to delay, and Mansfield continued to find himself liable for lawyers' fees at the very moment when, he was convinced, a little more advertising might pump some life into the sales of his novel: "You damned dishonorable bitch! $200 more of the precious money gone to my lawyer . . . Oh! I am crazy for just a few dollars to push my book *Delaplaine* into success, and *Delaplaine* is dying—dying! Two years more of my life wasted! Oh! Jesus on Calvary!"

The letters were often very long, a sustained howl fusing obscene insult and self-pitying melodramatic soliloquy: "You are delaying, bitch of hell . . . The hopeless wretch grasps his pistol! You take from the hopeless author his last hope . . . Sign the papers you agreed to sign long, long, long ago, and I will let you go, bitch, dragging my heart-strings after you. But let go my sweet darling precious money." In an aura of stage thunder he struck his attitude, a caped avenger vowing destruction to his enemies: "You have miscalculated Mansfield Tracy Walworth as others have done."

As the legal negotiations dragged on into late July, the flood continued unabated. Mansfield reached for new threats, more fearful images: "I am a hungry demon, and I am longing to lap my tongue in salt blood. You are making your grave by delay. But we shall lie so peacefully side by side in death. O sweet death! Sweet death." The letters were not working, and that awareness stirred him to new levels of outrage: "You robbed me of my children and you want to rob me of my pittance . . . I am in earnest, God damn you. Do the words sound tame on paper? Hog's bitch, I will murder you for depriving me of my sweet, darling money. Hist! hist! hist! Let that ring through your damned inhuman ears. The broken-hearted wretch will drag his torturer with him to hell." Many of the letters contained bullets or small packets of gunpowder.

When the details of the divorce were finally settled, the letter writing ceased for a time. But Mansfield would continue to find fresh inspiration for his correspondence.

FRANK was now permanently settled at Pine Grove with his mother. He studied law with a local lawyer and took German lessons from the scholar Otto von Below, whom Ellen had hired for the Walworth Academy. Afterward Ellen would testify that Frank had never really been the same since the morning when she had shown him the marks of Mansfield's beating and had observed for the first time on his face that "pinched look" of "severe suffering." But he led the life of a privileged youth, partaking of the parties and outings of the spa, playing a little whist with the gunmaker Benjamin Amsden, enjoying a regular game of billiards with Dr. Charles Grant. His friends and relations all—or so they would attest—saw him as a good-natured, lively, helpful sort of boy, free of the vices otherwise rampant in a booming town more notorious than ever for its freewheeling ways.

A group photograph survives of the Walworth children in the period following the divorce. Even if one did not know the background, it would not seem like the image of a happy family. Frank at this point might have been eighteen; Nelly, fourteen; Clara, thirteen; Tracy, ten; Ruby, five. Each stares off in a different direction. Nelly, blank-gazed, seems almost unaware a picture is being taken; Clara's mouth is twisted as if mirroring some inner quarrel; Tracy has a look of wounded resignation that belies his age; and even Ruby, large for her age and clutching a commensurately large doll, shows no hint of babyish insouciance. Frank, in an elegantly cut dark sailor suit, lies sprawled in the front row leaning languidly on an ottoman, his oddly cross-eyed gaze seeming to sail just over the camera into some sky hidden to all but him. The handsomest of the children, he carries himself as if auditioning for the play scene in *Hamlet*—"Lady, shall I lie in your lap?"—with more than a little self-consciousness and just a trace of arrogance.

Frank found out about the letters soon after they started coming. He made it his business to get to them before his mother did. One day, Ellen came upon him when he was reading one of the early ones. She observed that he was "most violently affected," and surmised that he had been out in the sun too long. The next day he gave her the letter to read, and she understood his reaction. As far as Ellen was made aware, the flow of letters halted in August 1871. The last she received, written on the stationery of G. W. Carleton and Company, was in the same vein as the rest, alternating between death threats and self-pitying accounts of Mansfield's literary career: "Now sign this paper, and I will try to bring this tortured brain once more down to literary work . . . God damn you, Ellen Hardin. It is in me to succeed at books if you leave me alone and take the apprehension of law-suits from me. Sign this paper or a tortured author will kill you, by Jesus . . . I do not believe in any God, but I believe there is a devil, and that devil is you . . . So hard, so hard is an author's fate."

By waylaying the letters, Frank took it on himself to relieve his mother of the stress of constant harassment. Instead he put the burden on himself. She did not, she was to claim, understand why he continued to show the same disquieting symptoms as when she had first shown him the marks of Mansfield's abuse. For her own part she had never been busier. Despite the decline and death of her infant daughter and her own frequent ill-health, despite the legal complications stemming from her divorce and the settling of her financial rights, despite her husband's ominous messages, she had started a successful school from scratch. But to establish herself as an educator—no matter how draining the running of the school would continue to be—was not enough for her. The break with Mansfield had freed to her to realize intellectual ambitions she had set aside early in her marriage. She wanted to plunge into history, literature, science, even politics, to make up for the decades squandered on a union that should not have happened.

It was an altogether new life she was leading. She was released both from her agonized coexistence with Mansfield and from the shadow life in Kentucky to which she had resorted as an escape. Bird's Nest was a place, had she stayed there, for gradual and in some ways pleasurable self-erasure; a place of balmy fruit orchards and exquisitely prolonged afternoons apt for listening to the silence and reading over cherished old poems, the volumes of Scott and Burns her forebears had passed on to her. But it was inescapably a backwater.

At Pine Grove she established a platform for a world she could call hers—a world of action, of decisive interventions. Here she could impose herself as a free agent for what seemed like the first time. The price for such a world was uninterrupted activity. There was nothing like leisure in the hours she filled with purposeful busyness, as she managed every aspect of the school and reached out to an ever-widening pool of powerfully placed individuals who could help her realize the ambitions she was just beginning to formulate.

The right of a woman to pursue such ambitions was a conviction that had grown in her through twenty years of misery. She had absorbed the message of crusaders such as Lucy Stone and Elizabeth Cady Stanton, even if she had not embraced their more radical political positions. From the doctrine of woman's rights she took what she needed and discarded what seemed repugnant. She took, beyond all else, a sense of entitlement to the shaping of her own career. Toward that end she pushed herself at times to the brink of exhaustion. Never again would time hang useless on her hands. Nor would she permit herself to be what she had been— the slave of a moral weakling. Anything like despair or regret would be relegated to the poems and journal entries she wrote in secret.

After giving most of her adult life to motherhood, Ellen was peering well beyond the needs of her immediate family. She had allowed Clarence to convince her that Nelly and Clara were better off for the moment at the Sacred Heart Convent at Kenwood. The thought that they would be well away from any disturbing incursion by Mansfield must have weighed with her. Close to her she kept her younger boy Tracy, just entering his teens and showing hints of a nature perhaps too sensitive, and Ruby, her favorite and everyone else's. Too young to understand much about the family's upheavals, Ruby became for the rest of them the hopeful embodiment of all that had been lost: tranquillity of mind, a sense of trust, a confidence in the future.

As for Frank, Ellen relied on his strength, physical as well as moral. He had grown into a powerful young man, adept at every sport and with a temper quickly aroused by any perceived slight. He was now the only man in a position to protect her at home, and she was inclined to overlook any signs of disorder or debility. Afterward, though, she would recall any number of worrisome incidents.

ONE morning one of the younger children came to her and said, "Frank is sick." Upon entering his room, she found him stretched out on the bed, pale and unnaturally rigid. His face seemed "convulsed." Again she thought of sunstroke, and gave him some laudanum. There were other such occurrences—at least three or four—that made her seriously worried; and other changes, less violent but nonetheless quietly unnerving. He had been outgoing and often merry; now he became "quiet and abstracted." When he came home he did not go in to see the other children and play with them as before. His memory had always been outstanding, yet he began to forget the simplest things. He would go upstairs to fetch a hat or a jacket and then come down without it. The family would tease him about it and call him absentminded. Likewise he would go out on an errand and come home having completely forgotten what he had set out to do.

At night he had gotten into the habit of carefully locking up the house, a reasonable enough thing to do; but having gone upstairs, he would come down and do it all over again, checking to see if the doors were really locked, locking and unlocking them sometimes many times over in a single night. After he settled down finally in his room, Ellen would on occasion hear him call out to her in "distressing" tones, and when she went to investigate she would find him once again stiff and pallid, his face locked in a convulsive stare. He would come to with a start. In the morning the maids would report they had found strange discharges on his pillow, stains of a brownish yellow, as if intermingled with blood.

Others began to notice the changes as well. Professor von Below observed that Frank was forgetting the German he had already mastered and becoming "gloomy and morose." Joseph Hill, the lawyer with whom he had been studying since coming back to Saratoga, similarly observed that at a certain point he stopped making any headway in his studies.

Indeed, he no longer chatted as he had been accustomed to; he would come into the office and sit there doing nothing for an hour or two, then get up and go home, claiming he felt ill. Dr. Grant, with whom Frank liked to play billiards, remembered being impressed one afternoon when Frank racked up the balls in reverse order, putting the red where the white should go, as if he had forgotten the rules of the game.

A few days later he went very still in the middle of a game until the doctor said to him, "Frank, it is your turn to play." He said he was ready, but in a voice the doctor later described as "strange and unnatural." He then played a stroke with such force that the ball fell to the floor. At that point he dropped into a chair, breathing heavily and his face twitching violently. He seemed to have gone into a trance. When the doctor tried to rouse him, he opened his eyes and began to put his coat on, saying he had to get home. Then he began to take his coat off again. On another occasion the doctor and Frank were riding in a carriage when Frank again lapsed into a trance, staring blankly ahead of him and muttering the word *faint* repeatedly in a mechanical tone. The doctor touched his arm, which was rigid, and had the impression that Frank was about to strike him.

Others would come forward to recount similar incidents, none more than momentarily puzzling at the time they occurred. He had paid a visit to his friend Charles Pond at Union College, and woken up in the night crying out, and in the morning there had been a rusty stain on his pillow. Another day, when Charles went walking in the woods with him, Frank turned on him out of the blue and knocked him to the ground. Then, as if nothing had happened, he asked Charles if he wanted to have some tea.

13

~~~~~~~~

The Last Warning

A LL this time Frank was continuing to read and to hide away his father's letters. A few were addressed directly to him. As for those sent to Ellen, Frank had already, early on, gathered a bundle of them and entrusted them to her on condition that she would promise not to read them. Afterward he concealed from her the fact that they were still coming. The last letter he allowed her to see was dated August 7, 1871. A week later another was delivered, and perhaps it was this one that persuaded Frank to keep all future communications from Mansfield strictly to himself. Writing again on Carleton's stationery, Mansfield seemed to be trying to shape his ferocity into something like literary form. He seemed also to want to identify, once and for all, the source of his deepest rage.

> Publication House of Carleton & Co.,
> Under Fifth Avenue Hotel,
> New York, August 14.
>
> Listen to these terrible words. They will show you how keenly and fiercely I feel the humiliation of Reuben H. Walworth's will, and what a Scot, the descendant of King Malcolm, will do when all has been taken from him. Reuben H. Walworth

always hated me from my cradle. He always hated any one who was high-spirited and would speak out their thoughts. He always liked cringing hypocrites, like Eliza Backus and Clarence Walworth. Although he saw my ambitious spirit he hated it because it would not toady to his favorite Yankees. Hence from my cradle he persecuted me and headed me off in every pursuit or speculation. I could not please him in anything because I would not whine to him about his favorites. Everything that I ever wrung from him, even my pay in the Spike case, was wrung from his fears. The only reason that he did not omit my name from his will altogether was that he respected my talents and hoped I would write his life. He knew nobody else would. But he has stung me into madness and broken up my family by placing me in the humiliating position of being under a trustee, and that trustee my brother, who has neither ambition nor heart. From his grave he glares at me and says:—"Ha! ha! You were always proud and high-spirited, but by my will I have put in your side a thorn for life. You have no dignity under it, and it will sting you to your grave. The only ones of my name who have any dignity under my will are your sons, Frank and Tracy, who will bear my name to posterity." Now, Ellen Hardin, knowing that I am helpless under that will, if you will persist in trying year by year to see how much of that trust property you can get out of me by threats of law, by personal blandishments to my trustees, or by any other means; if you doubt and will not see that I ought to have something for my entire life, whether he intended me to or not, then mark what will be the finale of my vengeance upon that dead scoundrel dog who has made me so pitiable before men and before you. I will—so help me the demons who wait upon the persecuted and the proud spirited and the revengeful—I will, when stripped by you of my property (and you mean it at last), plunge my dagger into Frank and Tracy's heart, and cut off the Walworth name forever. God damn him, he has elevated them and degraded me, and you gloat over it. I have not one single firm right under his will. This you believe, and this has been the cause of your despising and abandoning me. With cold calm purpose you contemplate my eventual beggary and humiliation. I will kill your boys and defeat the damned scoundrel in his grave and cut off his damned name forever . . . If I can't have anything, I'll have revenge.—I have lost nearly everything which makes life tolerable.

Frank may have imagined that he was now the sole interceptor of his father's messages, which, although their frequency tapered off somewhat after this grand blast of August 14, would sometimes arrive in sudden large batches. At one o'clock in the morning on July 10, 1872, for instance, he addressed to Ellen what he said was the third letter he had written in the last four hours, undertaking to "hush your God damned woman's rights pretenses with a bullet . . . I'll suck your blood yet." He was still scanning the newspapers for inspiration: with one letter he enclosed a clipping about a particularly brutal murder of a wife by her husband, and in another he told her he would kill her on sight in the same way that Stokes had just killed Fisk in the lobby of the Grand Central Hotel. He would kill Frank as well, not only because she had taught Frank to hate him, but because Frank was not really his son but the offspring of an adulterous love. Ellen, he was now persuaded, had cheated on him from the beginning; she had married him only for the power of his family name and for the money and property she imagined he would inherit.

Mansfield was in fact writing to others as well. The letters eventually made public represented only a small portion of his immense outpouring. He wrote to Judge Barbour, threatening to shoot him on the street if he came between Mansfield and Ellen, and to the now openly despised Clarence, promising to kill him as well if he egged on Ellen against him.

His sister Liza Backus—for whom he nourished a particular animus as the very type of the religious hypocrite, painting her in one of his novels as an avaricious murderess—was singled out by him to receive a curious communication (written the same productive July night he had written the three letters to Ellen) that was later taken as indisputable proof of his madness.

My Dear Sister: I have conceived the great secret of my existence. I was not born as men are, but was let down from heaven in a basket. All who have preceded me are impostors. I am the true Messiah. It will cause a great commotion on the earth when I am summoned, for I shall be a soldier-king and have in heaven—the home of my Father-God . . . You, of course, are not merely my sister, but during our terrestrial intercourse you have manifested such kindness for me that I shall make you one of the queens of the earth . . . Keep this secret until I am announced by the sound of 10,000 trumpets, then fall down and worship me, for I am M. T. Walworth, the true and eternal son of God.

But this could equally have been the undiluted voice of Mansfield the maker of boarding school scandals, Mansfield the cut-up reducing the servant girls to convulsions of laughter. It could also have been another way of planting the idea of his madness as a justification for use in some future trial. It is possible that Mansfield was mad enough to fancy himself a sane man feigning madness.

A sane man, that is, given to lacerating quirks and prankish, wounding humors—but had not that always been his bent? Baiting his pious sister with blasphemies was just as good a joke as informing Ellen that he planned to set up his mistress in an apartment next door to the Walworth Academy. He amused himself by putting an announcement in the *Home Journal* that the Walworth Academy had been named "after the celebrated author Mansfield Tracy Walworth" and that the author had presented the school "with a rare collection of fossils and shells." Judge Barbour, who recalled this bit of effrontery, added that these were "things which he did not own"—even if Mansfield could have cited the exact line of his father's will that left him the fossils and shells, if little else.

If he had cared to establish his sanity, he could have pointed out that at the very time he was firing off his letters to Ellen, a reputable publisher was paying him good money for a novel—*Beverly, or The White Mask*—expected to have wide public appeal. It was a novel, as it happened, about a man very much like himself doing, although with a markedly better outcome, very much the same kind of things that

Mansfield had been doing. His hero MacGregor was a man of genius, of course—"a man of varied gifts, an orator, a brilliant conversationalist, a fine writer, and a natural-born leader of men"—but he lived in poverty after being abandoned by his wife. Obsessed with money and social position, lacking faith in his literary abilities, she had nagged him with "sarcasms and complaints" until "he retaliated upon her in words" and then finally "withdrew into his sanctum altogether in the evenings, and devoted himself to the literary culture so essential to the man who aspires to the rank of a great journalist." He was not merely the descendant of Scottish kings—a title Mansfield could also claim, on the authority of his father's *Hyde Genealogy*—but of Scottish visionaries: "He never failed in his mental predictions. To men he never mentioned his gift of second-sight. But he possessed it, and he knew it. Twenty generations back he traced his pedigree to the seers of Scotland."

When MacGregor's wife (in the novel she did not even merit a name) sued him for divorce, he gave in—broken as he was—without a struggle, and allowed her to obtain custody of their child. She had betrayed him, or at any rate she had permitted a stranger "to escort her to boating excursions, and to walk with her often upon the streets." His letters to his own child had not been delivered—"the demon-heart of the mother had prompted her to destroy the letters, that thus the child might grow up devoid of any knowledge of, or affection for, her father"—and when the child died, he was not even informed. All this could lead to only one resolution.

> The cruelty of the mother who would not even invite him to the death-bed of his only child . . . transcended almost his powers of belief. "Such a woman is worthy of death," he said fiercely, with all the tiger in him roused, "and I will be the agent of the avenging God to slay her."

Amid the usual farrago of any plot devised by Mansfield—lost wills, men in black masks, treasure hunts in the Amazon jungle, mystical Hebrew inscriptions, extravagant pleasure domes nestled in obscure corners of the Hudson Valley—MacGregor reverted continually to his theme of revenge. But his fictional counterpart in the end, with much difficulty, resisted the murderous impulse.

Day after day he struggled with himself to keep his hands clean of the blood of the false-hearted demon-wife who had robbed him of all. He shuddered at the violence of his own tumultuous thoughts, and realized that they tended to murder and insanity. He struggled fearfully for self-mastery.

In his novel, at least, self-mastery won out, just at the moment when the hero was at last given an opportunity to take vengeance. But though MacGregor was "terrible as the old chieftains of the Highlands" when roused, his clemency was "without stint, boundless. He had forgiven the woman who had wronged him."

The narrative of *Beverly* was further complicated by the infusion of an otherworldly element in the person of a mysterious little girl—known only as Dream-child—who materialized, literally out of nowhere, in MacGregor's apartment one lonely evening. "Limbed and formed with all the ethereal gracefulness of a fairy, with her golden hair waving in silken softness upon her shoulders," she had the appearance of a girl of four. In *Beverly*, Dream-child exerted a force far beyond her frail physical form, a force emanating from her eyes: "Larger and more luminous they beamed upon him, losing nothing of their infantile gentleness, while holding him with magnetic power."

For the lonely bachelor, the little girl became "his entire family," and he stayed up by her bedside "talking her to sleep with all the skill of a mother, and all the wealth of expression and narrative which had been peculiar to him in his boyhood, when he had fascinated his school-fellows with his tales of wonder." But she was not like other children. When he saw her standing in the sunlight flooding into the apartment one morning, he had the uncanny illusion that she was literally melting into the light: "For a moment he thought her wavy hair had dissolved into sunbeams, and that she would vanish . . . She seemed to be the central sun, from which the rays were emanating . . . He seemed to realize what theologians call a *spiritual body*." He was overcome by the fear that she would suddenly disappear, and reassured himself in an episode that blended most oddly the spiritual and the corporeal: "'I thought you were turning into sunlight,' he said, as he put his arms about her and tasted the pink moisture of her lips. 'No,' she replied, 'I was only taking a bath.'"

The child was in fact a seeress whose second sight was triggered by physical contact with others: If "the little elf" sat in a person's lap, she could read that person's thoughts. If her governess slept in the same bed with her, she dreamed the same dreams as the child. And when MacGregor asked her to impart what she knew to him, "the communication she gave him sent the blood coursing through his veins like fire."

At the novel's end Dream-child did finally vanish into a beam of sunlight. But however ethereal this novelistic apparition, Ellen, if she read the book, could hardly have failed to be reminded of blonde-haired little Ruby, just four when Ellen had left with the children—in which case *Beverly*, with its hints of "physical contact of the most intimate and perfect character" between adult and child, might have seemed either a revelation of further layers of perverse fantasy or a confirmation of an all-too-real transgression.

THE chaos of Mansfield's mental state was known within the family circle, among those who had been receiving his letters, and likewise to those friends and advisers in whom Ellen, Clarence, Judge Barbour, Liza, and the rest had confided. Elsewhere his reputation, at least as far as the press was concerned, remained more or less untarnished. He continued to be identified as "the author of *Warwick*" and continued to make the social rounds. On a Sunday in February 1873, a newspaper reported, he turned up at a "musical entertainment" hosted by the wife of Charles O'Conor, and joined with the other guests in a lively rendition of the "Laughing Chorus" from Offenbach's operetta *The Brigands*, which had just completed its New York run.

His spirits seemed buoyed by a recent upswing in his literary fortunes. A professor at the College of New Jersey (later Princeton) had contacted him in May 1872 requesting information on his work for inclusion in a massive reference work on American writers. When the book eventually came out as *A Manual of American Literature*, Mansfield had the pleasure of seeing himself presented as a highly successful novelist (the sales figures had been provided by himself) and as the author of a forthcoming *Life of Chancellor Livingston*, first in the six-volume *Lives of the Chancellors*.

More to the point, he had been paid a thousand dollars for his newest novel, *Married in Mask*, which was to run as a serial in the *New*

York Weekly, published by the booming fiction house of Street and Smith. The publishers were well pleased with his work and intended to offer him a similar deal for his next novel. As with other New York associates of Mansfield, Francis Street would testify that he was "very affable, agreeable, courteous, and cheerful . . . He looked like a quiet gentleman and not a hungry author." In fact *Married in Mask* showed signs of improving skill; the narrative was more tautly managed, and Mansfield was beginning to let his urban surroundings enter his writing more fully than before. The plot was as dreamlike as ever, but this time it distilled some sense of the world beyond the page, in however cracked a form.

Abandoned children inhabited a labyrinthine hideout constructed within a manure heap not far from where the docks went up in flames. A detective spent twelve years searching for an abducted girl who would finally be impersonated by an actress when the time came for her testimony at the murder trial of an Italian foundling who had, somehow, become the son-in-law of New York's most famous and most reclusive financial genius. The girl had by this point in the novel been abducted not once but twice, leaving behind two quite different sets of inconsolable parents, while in the meantime crucial evidence had been destroyed in two quite separate dock fires. The missing link between a sordid waterfront knifing and the apparition by the millionaire's bedside at midnight of a masked burglar not more than twelve years old would turn out to be the abortive struggle of Venetian patriots against Austrian oppressors. Perhaps only foreign refugees, masquerading as quack doctors and street musicians, had the knowledge and ability to interpret the last crucial message, scrawled on an envelope that slipped from a secret shadower's hands as he lay back in a rowboat, slowly bleeding to death from a bullet caught in crossfire. The piece of paper, blown by the harbor wind, drifting through every neighborhood of lower Manhattan and dropping down among pushcarts and the debris of carriages overturned in collisions, was retrieved by a beggar and hidden thoughtlessly in a schoolboy's pocket in a vest that would never be worn again, thus burying forever between layers of cotton the birth name of the heiress who could be identified, at last, only by the whiplash scar hidden under her bridal veil.

Here in full flower was the "crazy imagination," as Eli Perkins labeled it, of Mansfield Walworth: "From the most trivial circumstances he would write up the most gorgeous descriptions and produce the most wonderful, never-could-happen situations." This was a useful gift in the emerging age of the dime novel, and to some it seemed that Mansfield had at last found a remunerative niche for himself, if he could rise above his personal worries. But those who knew him at all well sensed that the author had troubles no publisher's advance could heal.

He lived in fear. He carried a loaded pistol with him at all times, and worried constantly about being attacked on the street. Francis Gerry Fairfield, another *Home Journal* contributor who had spent several years researching what he called "nervo-psychic phenomena," came to know Mansfield with sufficient intimacy to detect in him the signs—his compulsion to place his hand on his chest in moments of excitement, for instance—of an epileptic disorder. In the early spring of 1873, as the two writers were standing outside the Fifth Avenue Hotel, Fairfield noticed that Mansfield was repeating Fairfield's remarks before responding to them, and then repeating the last words of his own replies: "His eyes were faded, he was pale, and talked like a man in a dream; but recovered suddenly, and was himself again."

From time to time he went to Saratoga. The doors of Pine Grove were closed to him unless he would conform to the terms of the visitation agreement, something he had not shown himself willing to do. He had not seen any of his children for over two years now. But one day in the autumn of 1872, as he sauntered along the main promenade near Congress Park, he found himself face-to-face with Frank. The meeting was apparently accidental. Mansfield, to judge by his own final communication, made what he considered a sincere attempt to engage his son in friendly conversation. Frank told him outright that if Mansfield did not keep away from Pine Grove and leave Ellen alone, he would shoot him. "There are bounds," Frank told him, "which I will not allow any man to go beyond with impunity, especially when my mother is being insulted."

THERE were witnesses to this encounter, occurring as it did in the middle of the street. Word of Frank's challenge to his father—on top of the boy's other troubling behavior—may have been what prompted Clarence to approach Ellen with his proposal. Frank had finished his studies at the Walworth Academy in May, and the following year planned to study law in Albany. But Clarence suggested a different plan, broaching it to Ellen on a visit to Saratoga on May 29: what if Frank accompanied him on the yearlong voyage around the world for which all preparations had been made? The sights of Europe and Asia would broaden Frank's perspective and clear his head of the domestic anxieties evidently preying on him. Clarence could keep a close watch on him to see if his nervous symptoms showed any signs of worsening; and, assuming he knew of the exchange between Frank and Mansfield, he might have argued that the danger of a further and perhaps catastrophic meeting between father and son could be averted. Ellen agreed to inform Frank promptly of his uncle's invitation.

As it happened, on the Saturday after his mother told him of the offer, Frank intercepted one final letter from Mansfield. His father had written it at seven o'clock in the morning on May 30. By Mansfield's standards it was a short letter, and Frank could see at a glance that nothing had changed.

> Prepare yourself for the inevitable. I am getting over my wasting fever and shall be out of my room in a few days. I am going to call upon my children; my heart is starving for their caresses. Make the interview as easy and pleasant as possible. I cannot stay from them much longer. I will see them— peaceably if I can or with a tragedy if I must. Their little faces haunt me, as they are mine. Popish cruelty must bend to the demand of a father's breast, or the Walworth name goes out in blood. Keep Frank Walworth out of my way. You have taught him to hate me, and his presence or obstruction in any way will only excite fatal exasperation. I want to see my little girls and come away peaceably. Beware that you do not in any way arouse the frenzy which you have known to exist since you left me. There is a reasonable way to deal with me. I shall have my rights under that decree, with no further legal delay or expense . . . I am a broken-hearted desperado. I admit it. Save this letter for lawyers and courts if you please. God is my lawyer; not the remorseless, brutal god that you and Eliza Backus and C. A. Walworth worship, but that God who has

planted love in my heart for my little girls, and that says to the tiger bereft of its young, "Kill!" You are an infamous wretch to keep me for more than two years from the little hands and hearts that love me. Your only excuse was my poverty and misfortune. When Frank refused to speak to me in the streets of Saratoga I said to myself, "She is teaching them all to hate a broken-hearted father." Then all is lost, and the tragedy must come.

For a moment Mansfield seemed to express a grudging respect for Ellen: "I know that you have no personal fear, no more than I have, but we both must die when that discovery comes that you have estranged my young children from me." He was, he wrote, willing to spare her life if he was convinced she had not turned his children against him. Otherwise her fate was sealed, a fate extending perhaps beyond the grave into some afterlife answering to Mansfield's specifications: "I shall die with a feeling of luxury and rest to come; but you will have to attend me to the spirit land. The God of justice demands it."

Frank gave his mother no hint of what he had read. He went fishing with his brother Tracy, came home about six in the evening, and went to bed early. As far as anyone knew, the European plan was unaltered. He slept late the next day, Sunday. In the morning he packed books and clothes and put his room in order, and then went "swinging in the grove," a carefree boyish pastime. When his friends Charles Pond and Wally Barbour called at the house in the afternoon, the three went for a walk in the woods. On the way they stopped at the home of a neighbor, C. W. Smith, and Frank asked him if he could lend him some money, just for a day; he was going out of town and would be back by Tuesday. Smith was short on cash but told Frank to stop by Monday morning and he could give him fifteen dollars. Then the boys took off for the woods. They were going to gather flowers; but after Frank had picked a few, he said he wasn't feeling well and went home. At the house he asked his mother for some note paper; he was going to write a letter to Uncle Clarence; she had no idea what it was about.

When the other two boys dropped in on Frank later, they found him asleep. Roused, he told them that he might be going to New York on Monday; as indeed, after picking up the fifteen dollars from Mr. Smith, he did. On the way to the station he ran into his whist partner, Mr. Amsden the gunmaker, who asked him if he was up for a game that afternoon. Frank asked him if the next day wouldn't do just as well.

ON May 29, 1873—the same day that Clarence was discussing Frank's future with Ellen—something else had happened that would turn out to have a considerable impact on that future. The New York State legislature passed a law revising the legal definition of murder. Murder in the first degree—a capital offense—was redefined as murder perpetrated from "deliberate and premeditated design." The word *deliberate* had been added. A second degree of murder, distinct from manslaughter and self-defense but not resulting from deliberate and premeditated design, came into effect; it was not liable to the death penalty but carried a mandatory sentence of life at hard labor. The purport of the new law was discussed in many New York newspapers the next morning. It is not known whether Frank—a law student who was still, at least ostensibly, keen to get his degree in Albany—read about it, and if so whether he read about it before or after reading his father's letter.

14

∿∿∿∿∿∿∿

The Trial, First Week:
"Idiocy as a Profession"

T HE secret history of the Walworths ended at about twenty past six on the morning of June 3, 1873, when Frank strolled into the cashier's office of the Sturtevant Hotel and made his startling announcement to Mr. Barrett.

As secrets go, it had been a fairly open one. The end of Ellen's marriage was a matter of legal record. In Saratoga the gist of her story was well known—she had been frank about her "unfortunate" circumstances in canvassing for support for the Walworth Academy—even if she had certainly not enlarged in public on the intimate causes of the divorce. Even among intimates Ellen had done nothing to defame her husband; in the words of a relative, she "would allow no one to speak ill of Mansfield Tracy Walworth in her presence." But her assistance was hardly required in blackening his reputation; Mansfield's wayward behavior had been fodder for gossip in Saratoga and beyond for years. In the wake of his death an upstate paper described him as "a somewhat noted outlaw."

But until the shots at the Sturtevant, none of the rumors about him had appeared in print. His wartime arrest had been a minor item barely noticed in the midst of cataclysm. He had continued to move through the world receiving the token respect due to a more or less respectable citizen. To the extent that Mansfield had any sort of publicly acknowledged identity in 1873, it was as a novelist. In the judgment of most reviewers, and notwithstanding all the puffery of advertising, he was not a very good writer—in fact he had at times been mocked as the prototype of the comically bad writer—but his parentage still made him important enough to rate an occasional mention. As for Ellen, her reputation was almost exclusively local, as a respected educator with a historic pedigree and social connections to all the best families of Saratoga.

Now they had become characters in a serialized story not too different from the ones Mansfield had been writing for the *Home Journal* and the *New York Weekly*. That story was itself—as indicated by headlines like "Another Horrible Murder in New York"—an episode within a larger ongoing story. The New York Murder was hardly a new phenomenon, but newspapers had been focusing on it with particular zeal since the shooting of "Big Jim" Fisk by Edward Stokes in the lobby of the Grand Central Hotel in January 1872—one tycoon gunned down by another over a sordid woman and some equally sordid business dealings.

One of the striking characteristics of New York Murders was that their perpetrators did not appear to suffer much punishment. Notoriously, Edward Stokes was still in the Tombs a year and a half later with his fate unresolved. His first trial had ended in a mistrial, and even after he was finally convicted in January 1873 his lawyers launched an equally drawn-out appeal to overturn the verdict. Stokes's appeal was granted in early June, just days after Frank Walworth's arrest.

On June 14, in the wake of the decision on his appeal and ten days after the death of Mansfield Walworth, Stokes—dressed in a summery new suit—was visited at the Tombs by several hundred well-wishers. Such gala social occasions were not unheard of at the prison in those days. After greeting guests all day long, and with the help of his father and brother attempting to reply as well to a flood of letters and telegrams, Stokes was finally hustled back to his cell—redolent with the bouquets sent by admiring females—supposedly too tired to receive any more visitors. A reporter quoted his disdainful reaction to the gawkers who had joined the crowd: "One would think that this was a palace and I was a king, from the way they carry on."

Much in evidence at the Tombs that day were some of the other celebrity murderers—Sharkey, Simmons, King, Scannell—evidently pleased with what the decision might bode for their futures. Frank did not join in the festivities: "Young Walworth is very quiet . . . He thinks that his stay will be short, therefore he does not complain. In the afternoon he walks up and down the tier on which he is confined, coolly smoking a cigar."

Frank's shooting of his father would have stirred outrage at any time, but his timing had been particularly awkward. He now found himself the designated target of a long-simmering discontent. In the period since the Fisk killing, a succession of other accused murderers had come before the public, and the apparent unlikelihood of their receiving the full measure of punishment had become an affront. In November 1872 the *New York Times* ran—under the headline "Killing No Murder: What Becomes of the Man-Slayers in New York"—a rundown of every murder known to have been committed in the city since January 1870, calculating that only 42 out of 118 perpetrators had been convicted, and that a good number of these had received reduced sentences. Many others escaped indictment altogether. "Only three times in the last four years," the *Times* complained, "has the death penalty been inflicted in New York." In a related story the paper accused defense lawyers of flouting the law by the cunning deployment of legal delays: "For months and months, men who have imbued their hands in human blood are permitted to lie in prison until their offense is almost forgotten. When at last they are put on trial, important witnesses are often found to be missing, so that a full presentment of the case for the people cannot be made."

What the paper failed to mention in any of these alarmed articles was underscored in a letter to the editor by a member of the state legislature: if hanging was "played out," it was because, in the numerous cases where it seemed an excessive penalty, juries were understandably reluctant to impose it and fell back on lesser charges such as manslaughter. The revised murder law of May 30, 1873, with its mandatory life sentence for second-degree murder, now allowed them a different option. Frank, as it happened, would be the test case of the new law. For its provisions to apply to him, of course, a jury would have to determine that he had not deliberated his father's death. That might prove difficult, especially in the face of the statement he had allegedly made to the *New York Sun*: "I came here to do what I have done."

ELLEN and the rest of the family were certainly acquainted with the savage liberties to which American newspapers felt entitled. No family so active in politics and government could plead ignorance of the workings of the press. In his day, Chancellor Walworth had gotten his share of both special favors and freewheeling vituperation. But there were lines not usually crossed—the lines separating home life from the public sphere. If a man ran for office or campaigned for a cause, he knowingly made himself a potential target for abuse and mockery; but what went on in private between him and his wife and children was not under ordinary circumstances a matter for the press to discuss.

Murder changed all that. Frank had opened up the whole domestic history of the Walworths for mass consumption. Reporters accustomed to trawling among the lives of saloon keepers and hired Tammany toughs found it a refreshing change to rifle—with the license only a violent crime could give—through the hidden past of such a distinguished family. Here was life imitating the "sensation novels" of Wilkie Collins and Mary Elizabeth Braddon, which had so successfully found matter for melodrama in the guilty secrets of apparently respectable families. That the victim had been a sensation novelist himself made the story all the more diverting.

Nothing could really have prepared Ellen and her family to read under bold headlines the story of their lives, reduced to a few coarse paragraphs. They had been brought down to a common level from which, until that point, they had done all they could to distance themselves. The newspaper stories stripped their lives of all traces of sensitivity and cultivation and made them grotesque woodcuts fit for a theatrical poster advertising *The Colleen Bawn* or *Lady Audley's Secret*. Their home life had been spent among carefully chosen books and works of art. Now its journalistic simulacrum was set down amid the notices for carpets, gas fixtures, and Doctor Weaver's Improved Extract of Fire-Weed.

Not only were their lives turned into a play, but the play had a chorus of reviewers, raking over the motives, moral worth, and appropriate final destinies of each of the personages. Long before the trial began, Frank had been tried and sentenced by editorialists and readers all over the country. Little that they wrote was in his favor, even as they alluded ominously to the admiration he had supposedly stirred among the irresponsible masses.

But if the newspaper stories were a form of degradation, the family had no choice but to assist in their concoction. The papers got inside information about the most intimate details of the family's story right from the start; Judge Barbour, Liza Backus, and other relatives and acquaintances named and unnamed were cited as sources. Charles O'Conor, as part of his hastily worked-out defense strategy, was likely doing his best to orchestrate a press campaign calculated to place Frank's act in a more favorable light. If the crime was unthinkable, so had been the provocation: the boy had acted under intolerable pressures, and letters from his late father would be forthcoming that would "startle the entire community." By the time Frank's trial opened on June 24, newspaper readers had been given a tantalizing hint of coming attractions.

THE trial kicked off with startling suddenness. New Yorkers were not used to such speedy judicial action. The previous Saturday, the Tammany hireling William Sharkey had at last, after nine months of delay, been convicted of murder. A restless crowd had gathered at the General Sessions court on Monday, June 23, to hear Sharkey's sentencing, and only on learning it was to be held behind closed doors did they drift over to the courtroom where a hearing in Frank's case was scheduled. Anticipating nothing beyond a delaying action in the Walworth trial, they were surprised to learn that the juror pool was in place and that the proceedings would begin the next morning. Only twenty days had passed since the murder, scarcely time, one would think, for O'Conor to organize his defense.

The doors of the Court of Oyer and Terminer were scheduled to open at ten in the morning, but curious crowds had begun to gather long before. Frank's defense team—consisting of O'Conor, ex-Judge Samuel Garvin, Edward Beach, and General Henry Davis Jr.—faced off against walrus-mustached District Attorney Benjamin Phelps and his assistant, Daniel Rollins. To the trial-fanciers who haunted the courts like first-nighters at the playhouses on the Bowery, the legal talents on both sides were familiar faces. Grizzled veterans whose careers stretched back well before the Civil War, most of them had been acquainted with Chancellor Walworth and the Saratoga judicial world, and a number, along with presiding judge Noah Davis, were prominently involved in the gathering legal campaign against the corruptions of the Tweed ring. O'Conor was unquestionably the star of the bunch.

Ellen, wearing deep mourning and holding twelve-year-old Tracy by the hand, was among the first to enter the courtroom. O'Conor, who despite his long involvement with the Chancellor had not known her personally before getting involved in Frank's case, escorted her to a seat at the front. Other family members and friends accompanied her. The audience craned to catch a glimpse of Ellen's veiled face. Later she removed the veil, but her bare features gave little away. Then and throughout the trial observers were struck by her extraordinary self-control and stately immobility. To some her air of detachment seemed unnatural.

Moments later Frank, in a black broadcloth suit whose lapels set off a white vest and a blue necktie at just the fashionable angle, was ushered in. Nodding to his mother and briefly taking her hand, he seated himself among his lawyers. His demeanor lived up to the image the newspapers had already disseminated, or perhaps the reporters merely saw what they expected to see: he was "cool and haughty as ever," "looked perfectly unconcerned and indifferent," and displayed "his usual self-possessed manner." An anonymous pamphleteer went further in characterizing Frank's presentation of himself on this stage.

> His hair was carelessly brushed back from his forehead. As he took his seat he looked around at the audience in as unconcerned a manner as though he himself were endeavoring to see where the prisoner was. Indeed, there was just the least bit of bravado about his manner during the entire day ... Whenever ... the Clerk bade him rise, he did so quickly, always being careful to thrust his right hand partly under the lapel of his coat and throw back his head in a way that said plainly as actions could say it to the audience, "You see, gentlemen, I'm not the least bit frightened." ... His coolness and general air and jaunty don't-care-a-snap way of acting naturally led one to believe that instead of looking upon himself as

a person whose life was in danger, he was sure of being lauded for what he had done.

The *Brooklyn Eagle* underscored what was evidently a common perception: "A disdainful, haughty look rests upon his features continually. His general appearance conveys the impression that he is an excessively egotistical and conceited youth, who imagines he is a moral hero." Frank's habit of smiling to himself as if savoring a private joke furthered the impression of him as a "vain, thoughtless youth."

Judge Noah Davis took his seat at 10:30 sharp and began examining potential jurors. A jury was assembled with remarkable speed. The effort to find individuals who had heard or read little about the case was complicated by the weeks of insistent newspaper coverage. Several did acknowledge some prior knowledge, and observers were struck by how readily the defense went along with certain jurors who admitted to an unfavorable impression of Frank. O'Conor apparently wanted the trial to proceed rapidly. He may have wanted to forestall any notion that the defense would indulge in the delaying tactics that had made the Stokes and Sharkey cases notorious.

The panel assembled by day's end constituted a cross-section of working-class New York, numbering a plumber, a butcher, a brewer, a machinist, a grocer, and various representatives of the building trades among its members. The foreman was to be Joseph Horton, a jeweler with a shop on John Street. Horton, the first juror selected, was one of those who admitted to a slight bias against Frank, although he affirmed without hesitation that he could examine the evidence impartially. Commanded by the judge to "stand up and look upon the juror," Frank affected nonchalance but was observed to blush.

THERE was a rush for seats the next morning, but Judge Davis saw to it that strict order was maintained in his courtroom. Even more of the family had turned out than the day before: the increasingly frail Sarah, Father Clarence, Ellen's brothers Lem and Martin, Judge Barbour, Liza and her husband, Reverend Backus, and all of Frank's siblings, even little Ruby, at six just barely grasping what was at issue. A number of Frank's Saratoga friends had come down as well.

Laying out the prosecution case, Rollins focused on the heinousness and rarity of the offense. He reached far back in history for examples: the Persians, he told the court, "had no penalty for parricide, for they did not believe that a Persian would commit such a crime. Among the Chinese the whole family of a parricide was exterminated, and his very dwelling place razed to the ground." Paying courtly homage to the eminence of Frank's legal team, he acknowledged that ordinarily he would feel hesitant in entering the lists against Charles O'Conor. In this case, however, he felt no doubt that the jury would agree with the state's case: "Thrice is he armed who hath his quarrel just."

Walking the jury through the details of the crime, Rollins emphasized the long distance Frank had traveled from Saratoga to the city; the coolness he had displayed at every point before and after the murder; the decisiveness with which he had arranged his meeting with his father; the number of shots he had fired at such close range, arguing against anything but a sustained murderous intention; the business-like fashion in which he had fired off his telegrams after the deed was done, not to mention the fact that he had managed to pay his bill in the midst of the excitement; the damaging statements he had made to the press and at the coroner's inquest.

Rollins spelled out the nuances of the new homicide law, while declaring that it would not apply to the present case: the state was prepared to demonstrate that "every act and expression of the prisoner showed overwhelmingly that the crime was premeditated murder." Finally he warned that they could expect to hear from the defense a moving account of a wicked father and a brutalized mother; but they must not surrender to sentimentality. Such weakness could only encourage crime.

Frank remained apparently unmoved by the prosecutor's forceful recitation of the most dramatic details of the crime: the cry of "Murder!" echoing down the corridors of the hotel, the four bullets slamming into the body of Mansfield Walworth. "He looked," wrote the *Tribune*, "as one listening to the rehearsal of a stage tragedy looks." Some present, however, thought the defendant betrayed more anxiety than previously.

The prosecution proceeded to fill in the evidence of what had happened on the morning of June 3. Things moved forward at a clip. "The astonishing and unusual quickness with which the entire jury in this was obtained," the *Tribune* noted, "argue a like promptness and celerity in the progress of the evidence, and the District Attorney makes his examinations very brief and pointed." Mansfield's landlady Eliza Sims, the hotel clerk Hooper Barrett and other employees and residents of the Sturtevant, Dr. Childs, and Sergeants Keating and Mullen of the Twenty-ninth Precinct again went through their paces. Bellman William Amos provided an isolated moment of levity when, after describing the glaring look Mansfield Walworth had shot him when he was slow to leave room 267, he was asked by O'Conor how severe a frown it had been. "He did not look as cross as you do now," Amos replied to the amusement of the audience.

O'Conor kept his interjections to a minimum during this preliminary review. He spoke up only when Sergeant Mullen ventured to repeat some things Frank had said to Coroner Nelson Young just after being taken into custody at the station house. To admit a statement that Frank had made without "the usual and proper warning" and without an official recorder to take it down, O'Conor objected, was "a most dangerous innovation." Evidence of the facts was one thing; what certain people might recollect of the prisoner's comments was another. Nonetheless Davis permitted the testimony. According to Mullen, Frank had said that he was a law student, to which Young had replied, "Well then, I suppose you know what is right"—meaning, in Mullen's interpretation, that Frank could be assumed to understand his rights. Young went on, in Mullen's recollection, to ask Frank why he had come to New York.

> "To do this."
> "To kill your father?"
> "Well, to settle this family difficulty."

Coroner Young was then called to the stand himself to verify this account, and to present full details of the inquest and Frank's statement on that occasion. The prosecution rounded out the morning with full details of the postmortem, thus closing the presentation of the state's case. George Templeton Strong, who remained deeply unsympathetic to Frank, observed in his diary that "his counsel will find it a hard case to befog."

In the late afternoon Edward Beach opened for the defense. He spoke for an hour and a half but gave little precise indication of what legal arguments were going to be presented. It amounted more to an establishing of mood. He acknowledged the unparalleled nature of the crime, which had shocked families everywhere, parents and children alike: "No child, nurtured as a child, brought up with care and taught to love and reverence his parent, could read that first announcement without a thrill of horror." Yet every heart must have sensed that at the root of such an otherwise inexplicable crime must lie "a dread and deplorable mystery." Surely the jury must react the same way. Looking at Frank and wondering how he could have decoyed his father to a hotel room and shot him to death in cold blood, they must surely feel instinctively that this young man could not be guilty: "He stands before you in the first flush of early manhood, with no sinful excesses charged to his account, exhibiting none of the sins of practiced depravity and guilt."

Beach proposed to tell the jury how these things had come to pass. He was intimately familiar with the background of the case. He had grown up in Saratoga and had known the Chancellor and his family from his earliest days. "You all have heard of Chancellor Walworth," he said, "and it is almost incredible for you to imagine or believe that such a son as the deceased, Mansfield T. Walworth, could have sprung from his loins." Yet the jury would be shown a series of letters from the deceased to his wife and to his brother—letters "demoniacal in their purport and terrible in their threats." In these letters the jury would find motive enough for what Frank had done. Without reading the letters, they could frame no adequate conception of Mansfield's character: "You could only say that he was a very devil in himself, and sent by the archfiend to persecute his wife and children."

He would, he promised, give further instances of Mansfield's repulsive behavior, and was just launching into one such incident—the attempted assault on the female seminarians in Saratoga on the night of his father's funeral—when the district attorney objected that the defense counsel was going beyond the matters at issue and introducing hearsay evidence. Judge Davis having sustained the objection, Beach continued with a more restrained account of Mansfield's career, outlining his marriage to Ellen, his constant withholding of support from Ellen and the children, and the marriage's dreadful final days at her mother's home in New York City: "What she suffered during that time no tongue can tell." He would have liked, he added, to spell out the reasons for Mansfield's being paroled to Saratoga by the government during the war, but was afraid the court would object.

He asked the jury to imagine the effect of such an upbringing on a young and impressionable boy. Mother and son had lived in constant fear because of the father's torrent of obscene threats. "Gentlemen of the jury, look upon the prisoner and you will see in him one whose young life has been oppressed . . . Instead of a youth animated with the aspirations natural to his age . . . he presents before you a moody, silent, and abstracted look, bearing, and demeanor, which not all the love and devotion of a mother has ever changed." He had come to the city not with malice in his heart against his father but with the blind hope of persuading him to cease his persecutions.

Yet in the moment when Mansfield had made the promise demanded of him, Frank could not help perceiving "the lying demon in his face." He knew his father to go about armed, and saw him reach as if for a gun; his own reason capsizing, he drew his weapon and fired. "Some men call this parricide, but it was Providence." Mansfield, by brutalizing his wife and thereby perverting his son's nature, had crafted the weapon that would punish him for his affronts. Frank's nature was of the noblest; he had never had an intent to murder, and without such intent there was no murder.

All day long Frank had maintained the same apparent calm. But as Beach delivered his account of what Mansfield had inflicted on Ellen and the children, he dropped his face into his hands and began to sob.

On Wednesday morning the courtroom was even more jammed. Some in the crowd were women recognizable to the press as the regular matinee audience for such events, "old stagers in the murder trial line of spectators, two of them having attended, it is said, every murder case held in this city during the past ten years." But a large contingent of Frank's well-wishers had also turned up to see his side of the case laid out. Frank, after his display of the previous evening, had regained his composure.

The defense's main order of business this morning was a series of witnesses attesting to Frank's excellent character. Relatives and friends who constituted a gallery of upstate distinction—among them Reverend Backus and his wife, Liza, Chief Justice Barbour, a pair of Saratoga lawyers with whom Frank had been studying, Frank's German tutor Otto von Below—purveyed remarkably similar remarks that might be summed up in Judge Barbour's description: "Generally he has been noticeable for his amiability, pleasant temper, mildness of demeanor, and great affection for his mother." Phelps intervened only to ask each of the witnesses if he was aware that Frank had been carrying a pistol for the past two or three years; none claimed any knowledge of this. All the talk of Frank's mildness and purity led one journalist to an impatient summary: "Most of these witnesses testified that he had no vices, while some seemed to regard him as immaculate."

The note of immaculateness was sounded by Father Clarence, the last of these witnesses: "His character is as near perfect as may be." Shifting into a narrative mode, Clarence proceeded to offer a condensed version of the outward facts of Mansfield and Ellen's marriage. He refrained rigorously from any lurid particulars. He told of the couple's separation after the Chancellor's death during the eighteen-month period when Mansfield was staying with Clarence in Albany. He alluded to the Chancellor's will, without commenting on why Mansfield's inheritance had been placed in trust.

He then gave a somewhat more detailed account of the week preceding his brother's death, telling of his invitation to Frank to accompany him to Europe, and of the letter he had received from Frank on the afternoon of Monday, the second of June, with the enclosure in Mansfield's writing. He related how, just before receiving these letters, he had gotten a worried communication from Ellen, who had found out that Frank had left Saratoga and was afraid that he was going somewhere to a prearranged meeting with his father. Thinking the meeting might be in Albany, she had asked Clarence to try to locate him at a hotel where she thought him likely to be staying. Finally he told how, after these hours of confusion, he had the next morning received Frank's telegram from the Sturtevant House.

NOW Ellen was called to the stand. This was the dramatic moment the audience had been waiting for. A woodcut of Ellen in the witness box, in her suit of mourning, her veil drawn back to reveal her firmly set features, became the emblem of the trial in *Frank Leslie's Illustrated Weekly*. Ever since the beginning of the trial she had sat, inscrutable, in the front row next to her son. Now, as she delivered her opening statement and answered O'Conor's questions, she spoke so softly she could scarcely be heard, and O'Conor was obliged to repeat most of what she said for the benefit of the court.

Her initial testimony presented the barest skeleton of her story: her marriage to Mansfield in 1852 and the births of their eight children, from Frank in 1853 to the ill-fated Margaret in 1871, the various changes of residence and periods of separation, the final divorce. Her account was a record of comings and goings, absences and reunions with no clear motive: "In the summer of 1861 I went to Kentucky near Louisville, my brother Lemuel going with me, and all of my children; lived there until 1867; my husband did not go there with me . . . He promised to meet me there; where he went I do not know." After the Chancellor's death, she testified, "we discussed the question of a future residence but came to no understanding about it . . . In November 1870 I went to my mother's house in Fifty-second street, New York, Mr. Walworth being with me, and we remained there until the final separation on the 26th of January, 1871." Here O'Conor entered the divorce papers in evidence, noting the amendment by which she had forfeited her support payments and granted visitation rights to Mansfield.

The period after the divorce was painted in a similarly restrained fashion, of which this bit of understatement was typical: "Mr. Walworth addressed me very frequently by letter after our separation." The spectators were impressed at Ellen's apparent reluctance to express any rancor toward her late husband: "Though she had been so brutally treated, so vilified by him, yet, in this hour, when his mouth was closed in the grave, she was too noble, too generous to utter a single syllable against him willingly." Finally she recalled the week before the shooting, the otherwise harmless details of Frank going fishing with his brother Tracy, rearranging his books and clothes, going swinging in the grove, and sleeping late the next day. She described meeting him in the hallway on the Monday morning, observing to him that he was up early and getting from him "some casual reply" as he went out the door. She remembered going into his room a bit later on, finding an empty envelope addressed in her husband's writing, and promptly sending anxious telegrams to Clarence and Justice Barbour.

The empty envelope was entered in evidence just before the court took its midday recess.

After the break Ellen took the stand again. O'Conor now revisited the question of the divorce settlement, and the amendment to it by which she had relinquished her alimony. Under O'Conor's questioning—which gave the impression that he had to drag it out of her—she revealed that in all the time since then, apart from two payments from Mansfield totaling $350, she had supported herself entirely by the proceeds of the Walworth Academy. She acknowledged that she had had the amended settlement in her possession for some time before signing it, a fact that would have considerable bearing on the evidence to which the defense was building up.

O'Conor asked Ellen if Mansfield owned any loaded firearms. "He invariably had a loaded pistol in his room," she replied, "and he generally carried it with him when he went about." O'Conor then held up Frank's pistol and asked her if she recognized it. She identified it as the one that had been given to Frank by Mrs. Adams, a family friend from Buffalo.

The lawyer now embarked on a course of questioning to which the district attorney immediately objected. O'Conor started to ask Ellen abut Mansfield's habits with regard to getting up in the morning, but Judge Davis quashed this as irrelevant. O'Conor argued that it was important to establish that both Mansfield and Frank habitually slept late, and that their encounter at such an early hour of the morning may in consequence have been marked by mental confusion and unnatural haste on both sides. The judge decisively rejected this line of reasoning, and for the present no more was heard of it.

However germane the question of early rising might be to the defense case, Mansfield's letters were a good deal more important. If O'Conor could not get them introduced, he would lose the most dramatic and persuasive evidence at his disposal. Statements leaked to the press had promised that the letters held the key to the whole affair. The frequency and context of the letters, and their possible influence on Frank's conduct, had been established through Ellen's testimony; she had told of finding in Frank's desk the cache of letters he had concealed from her. On the stand Ellen had been shown a letter, apparently from 1872, and had identified it as Mansfield's, but the text had been made available only to the judge and the prosecution team.

This was hardly enough for O'Conor. It was the jurors who needed to be given an earful of Mansfield's full-blown style. All he had to come up with was a persuasive argument for their admissibility. At least one letter—the final one that Frank had enclosed in his letter to Clarence on the Sunday before the shooting—was clearly relevant, and with Judge Davis's assent was read aloud. It was by no means the bloodiest or most obscene of Mansfield's letters, but the lethal threats were explicit enough.

The rest of the afternoon was devoted to two and a half hours of legal parrying, as the lawyers and the judge considered what part of the remaining letters the defense would be permitted to share with the jury. O'Conor led with a very long argument in favor of reading the letters in their entirety, on the grounds that their overwhelming impact—an impact that did much to explain Frank's subsequent behavior—would be lost if only snippets were admitted. Beach seconded O'Conor, further arguing that without the letters the jury could not determine the state of mind of both men on the morning of June 3. The prosecution sought to present Frank as a calm and deliberate murderer; the letters would allow the jury to fully conceive the emotional turmoil that must have gripped him. Rollins objected that no evidence should be admitted if its only purpose was to defame the character of the dead man. Frank, not Mansfield, was on trial.

After further discussion the judge delivered his decision at some length. The real issue, he thought, was the nature of the threats themselves. Mansfield's threats had all been contingent on some course of action on Ellen's part: if she denied him his rights or prejudiced his children against him, he would kill her. As far as Judge Davis was concerned, such threats would not have been sufficient under the statutes even to arrest Mansfield, much less shoot him in self-defense. The judge was persuaded that Mansfield had been fully aware of this in writing the letters: "It almost seems evident that he purposely contributed this form to them in order to prevent himself from being prosecuted." If O'Conor could cite legal precedent he would hear him, but for the moment he was inclined to exclude any letters or portions of letters except for such as threatened Frank directly. On this note the session ended.

THE atmosphere in the courtroom on Friday morning was one of palpable excitement. Frank for the first time seemed almost cheerful as he greeted family members and friends, giving the court momentarily the air of a social reception. Perhaps, just as someone at a wake will for a moment forget the occasion, Frank entertained the illusion of welcoming guests to a particularly well-attended party—a circumstance for which he was certainly better prepared than the one in which he now found himself. Spectators jostled for space, and journalists noted the unusual number of women in the crowd, "with heads craned forward with curiosity that never slacked." Once the proceedings began, however, a total silence reigned.

Judge Davis had thought further on the question of the letters and was now inclined to bend the rules a little. Ordinarily he would have excluded anything but direct threats, but given the case's gravity—and in view, too, of some legal quibbles regarding benefit of the doubt that had arisen recently in the Stokes trial—he ruled that any letter allowed at all could be read in full. "The importance of this victory for the defense is almost inestimable," the *Tribune* commented.

O'Conor's moment had arrived. His renowned vocal technique served him well as he proceeded to read the unexpurgated text of Mansfield's letter of August 13, 1872, the most flagrantly theatrical of all, with its melodramatic opening—"Listen to these terrible words"—and its recitation of the sins of his father: "From my cradle he persecuted me and headed me off in every pursuit or speculation." Not even the hints in the press had prepared the audience for the final burst of rage: "I will kill your boys and defeat the damned scoundrel in his grave and cut off his damned name forever." The reading of the letter "caused profound sensation" in the courtroom, even if both Frank and Ellen remained aloof. For one observer, "the sentiment of the crowded Court from that moment began to turn in favor of the mother and the son, particularly in favor of the latter."

In the wake of this coup de théâtre O'Conor called Ellen back to the stand. O'Conor asked her about Mansfield's desire to see his children. Had she objected? No, she said, as long as he saw them in Clarence's presence. She had not even known he had any wish to see them until the fall of 1872; nor did he make any attempt to see them thereafter.

Now O'Conor asked her what had caused the breakup of her marriage. Phelps objected and was sustained by the judge. O'Conor came at the subject from a more specific angle: "When you lived together in Fifty-second street, did any acts of personal violence take place?" Judge Davis interrupted before Ellen could answer, asking O'Conor what he was aiming at. The attorney wanted to show, he said, that Frank was aware of the violence even if he did not witness it. The judge excluded the question, and O'Conor tried again. "We don't wish to detail the acts of violence," he told Davis, "but to show there was violence. Frank was in the room, and we desire to show the effect produced on the mind of the boy, that the effect was serious; and from that moment forward there was a change in his character." From that time Frank had gone from cheerful happiness to moodiness and distress—but not all the time, O'Conor was careful to qualify.

"Do you allege insanity?" asked the judge.

IT was a question O'Conor had hoped to avoid. The defense had not yet declared its intentions in regard to this issue. He managed a guarded reply: "We intend to allege that his mind was so affected that he was not sound at the time of his interview with his father." Beach chimed in: "We shall furnish evidence showing the state of his mind was such that he was not responsible."

Davis advised the lawyers that they had better put these questions to one side until expert testimony had been presented. But who better, O'Conor argued, than the boy's mother to give expert testimony on Frank's state of mind? The testimony of experts could not be called on until some basis in fact had been established. The judge agreed it was the usual practice to present some such evidence before turning to experts. But the real issue, Davis dryly observed, was a more basic one: "You have not said yet that you contemplated putting in the defense of insanity . . . If the counsel will plainly avow that they intend to interpose the defense of insanity, so that all of us will understand that that defense is before us, I will allow you to pursue whichever line of testimony you think advisable."

"If it has not been avowed," O'Conor replied, "I know no words by which I can more plainly avow it." He was evidently stung by the judge's implication that he had deliberately misled the court, and gave ornate expression to his discontent. He had been brought out of retirement much against his deepest wishes to take part in this trial, only to have his motives questioned: "I deeply regret that at this late day, after my long labor at the bar, it should have become necessary, in your Honor's judgment, to address certain remarks calculated to convey the idea that it was desired by me to gain some undue and irregular advantage in the trial of this case."

"I did not intend any personal imputation upon anybody," Davis fired back. "I do say, however, that it is the duty of counsel to avow their points of defense."

The exchange grew testier.

O'Conor: "If your Honor will give me a form in which to avow it, I will do so. I have said it twice."

Davis: "Go on, then. We understand now that that is your defense."

The district attorney chose this moment to attempt an ironic interjection about the defense plan, at which O'Conor exploded with calculated theatricality: "Are we to be put on trial again? If so, I would like to have something like an arraignment, when I can have an opportunity to prove my honor and fidelity and fairness in endeavoring to save this young man from an imperfect trial."

"Your trial is over, sir, and you are acquitted. Go on, sir!" Davis told him sharply, and O'Conor resumed his questioning of Ellen. There were many lawyers present in the courtroom—this was, after all, an all-star professional line-up—and they continued to whisper about the implications of what had just happened. Many of them, noted the *Tribune*, "imagined that the action of Judge Davis looked not unlike a trap to catch the counsel for the defense in a frank avowal of their plans before they were ready to announce them."

O'CONOR turned his attention to Frank's recent behavior. Under his questioning, Ellen described the symptoms her son had displayed after he first became aware of Mansfield's violence toward her, and the subsequent recurrence of those symptoms. She talked about Frank's memory lapses, his compulsion to check repeatedly whether he had locked the house after dark, his cries in the night, his fits of rigidity and pallor. Members of the audience could hardly help glancing at Frank as he listened attentively to his mother's testimony: "At times he was prostrated, and he gave up his exercises in the gymnasium, and would lie around the house. Previous to the first occasion of his knowing the trouble that existed, he was an unusually active boy, and after that he was in the habit of sitting from one to three hours apparently abstracted."

O'Conor asked Ellen whether she could give the jury any indication that Mansfield had been unable to control himself. When the prosecutor objected to the question, O'Conor insisted that Mansfield's mental state was relevant because madness was often inherited. The letters would show clearly that their author could not have been sane. Judge Davis instructed him that if he wanted to prove "a vein of insanity in the blood" he would have to offer competent evidence to that effect.

To this O'Conor readily acceded; the letters would be offered as additional, not exclusive, evidence of Mansfield's insanity. With the judge's consent, Ellen now launched for the first time into a more specific account of her husband's personality, beginning with his relatively harmless tics: engaging in rambling and disordered monologues, kicking the furniture, breaking small objects in his hand. Before she had a chance to address more serious behavior, the judge called a recess.

At the afternoon session O'Conor led with a direct question about Mansfield's "peculiar acts of violence" toward her, but Judge Davis felt the discussion was going too far afield. They were here to try Frank for murder, not Mansfield for insanity. Perhaps this line of questioning could be more appropriately resumed later on.

Balked, O'Conor reverted to the consideration of Frank's condition. Had he ever suffered any accident that might be relevant? He had indeed, Ellen remembered, fallen from a railroad car once when he was about seven, and years later received a blow to the head while playing baseball.

O'Conor showed Ellen a pistol. Did she recognize it? Yes, it had been a gift to Chancellor Walworth from its inventor, Samuel Colt, and had been passed along to Mansfield. This was the pistol recovered from Mansfield's lodgings, and O'Conor informed the court that five of the chambers were loaded. District Attorney Phelps cross-examined Ellen, but his questions shed little new light.

The rest of the day belonged to O'Conor. Judge Davis had finally consented to let the lawyer read, in their entirety, a selected group of the letters—ostensibly to suggest the possibility that Frank had inherited his father's insanity—and for the next two and a half hours the voice of Mansfield was allowed to speak without hindrance, as if from the grave. O'Conor did not hold himself back. His resounding voice could be heard in the corridors outside. The question of inherited insanity was not necessarily uppermost in the minds of the listeners. They were too occupied in taking in just how intolerable a presence Mansfield had been for anyone within his circle of domestic influence. The stunned silence of the audience gave way at times to nervous laughter at the enormity and downright absurdity of what they were hearing.

Some letters were suppressed as "entirely too filthy to be repeated," but what O'Conor read aloud was quite enough to create an atmosphere of mad and obscene theater, as a dead witness broke through the boundaries of ordinary propriety. The *Tribune* was troubled by the idea that the trial's many female spectators might have more of an appetite for such material than might be readily acknowledged: "Imagine the blasphemies to be heard on an average of eight or ten seconds, and the picture is complete! The sounds became so painful after constant repetition as to be nearly insupportable, and yet through it all the ladies at the back part of the room sat drinking in all the filth and profanity as coolly as the men, occasionally dropping their faces on their fans as if shocked, and then looking up again as the dangerous shoal was passed, until the next rock appeared to view."

Frank turned pale and asked for water. At other moments, however, he covered his face with his hands as if to conceal his amusement at the content of the letters. Evidently the attempt at concealment failed: "On Friday", one observer noted, "he actually got laughing while some of his father's letters were read, which shocked the audience very much and embarrassed his counsel." Even Ellen at one point was said to appear inadvertently amused, or at least jarred into a sort of nervous laugh. But in the midst of O'Conor's reading she left the courtroom leaning on the arm of "a colored woman," presumably Dolly.

When the reading of the letters was concluded, the court adjourned until Monday. Judge Davis had been willing to go on, but O'Conor pleaded exhaustion: "I can stand up, but that is as much as I can do. The day has been very hot, and I am very wearied." The session had been, in the *Tribune*'s words, "sensational to the last degree."

Now the newspapers would fill their columns with a faithful reproduction of Mansfield's letters, giving them a wider and more fascinated readership than any of his other writings had commanded. At a moment when forces of censorship were moving toward a new ascendancy by way of antiobscenity laws and Anthony Comstock's relentless crusade for public decency, Mansfield's letters gave the press a legitimate opportunity to offer up ribald and offensive language, and they made the most of it. These "ravings of an excited maniac," with their repeated exclamation marks and their swear words and blasphemies replaced by long dashes, made an extraordinary impact in the pages of the *Tribune* and the *Herald* and the *Sun*, giving the pages themselves a violent and disordered air.

O'Conor had wished at a minimum to provide convincing evidence of Mansfield's insanity, and he had certainly succeeded. The *Nation*, which had taken a sharply unsympathetic view of Frank from the beginning, acknowledged that the letters "have unquestionably done a good deal to alter the complexion of the act in the popular eye." "Could the letters be published in all their abominable filth and ribald abuse," the *Tribune* observed, "the ground of Mr. O'Conor could scarcely be encroached upon."

Yet beyond any question of madness, the letters seemed an affront almost as unthinkable as what Frank had done. If Mansfield was insane, he could not help himself. Yet the letters seemed to attest to a perversely triumphant will, a deliberate sin that was most particularly a *literary* sin: "It seemed as if the imaginative talent of the dead author had been turned from its legitimate current, and most powerfully exercised in the invention of epithets filthy beyond description of the woman who had borne him so many children."

The horror of parricide had been supplanted by something if not worse then certainly more grotesque. The barely suppressed laughter in the courtroom carried the queasy suggestion that the human traits expressed in Mansfield's letters represented a defilement even greater than murder. His words embodied an ultimate trampling on human dignity, the reduction of suffering—Ellen's, Frank's, even Mansfield's—to a species of brutal comedy.

Reporters and editorialists could scarcely find words to describe their reactions. What Mansfield had written was laughable, to be sure, and the *Tribune* allowed itself a touch of dry humor in titling its account of them "An Author's Letters Home." But the humor left an unpleasant aftertaste. In the end the letters made people angry. They had been insulted; it seemed as if Mansfield ought to be punished for what he had done by subjecting them to the contents of his brain. But of course Frank had already taken care of that.

Nonetheless a need was felt to get back at him somehow, by mockery if no other means presented itself. The *New York Times*, which had striven to maintain a dignified tone in its coverage of the murder and trial, published a long editorial the next morning—under the headline "Idiocy as a Profession"—which gave free rein to an evident desire to kick the dead author. The tone was one of frustrated, jeering rage. The source of the rage appeared to be, not what Mansfield had done to his family, but what he had done to the sensibilities of the *Times* and its readers.

"Genius is proverbially said to be closely allied to lunacy," the article began, "and that the latter is the near relation of idiocy no one denies. Herein we have the key to the conduct of the late Mansfield Tracy Walworth. He desired to be a genius, but finding that impracticable . . . he boldly decided upon idiocy as the sort of thing best adapted to meet his views. As a persistent idiot, Mr. Walworth was signally successful." Sensing the only appropriate way to punish Mansfield, the *Times* proceeded to demolish his pathetic claims to creative ability: "The public has hitherto judged him chiefly by his novels, which were in all respects beneath contempt. His letters to the lady who had the misfortune to be his wife are now in evidence . . . They are modeled in style upon the worst forms of Bowery melodrama, and they show that the writer was as ignorant of grammar as he was of decency."

The point of the editorial was to strip Mansfield of any claim, even posthumous, to membership in the community or the least shred of human respect: "Mr. Walworth is dead, and it is eminently proper to speak as well of him as truth will permit. Were he, however, in full possession of his bodily health and mental mucilage, it would be only paying him the tribute he deserved to treat him as the most successful and incontestable idiot of the age . . . That this idiot was addicted to the infamy of writing filthy, blasphemous, and cowardly letters to a woman, in order to terrify her into giving him money, has been sufficiently established." Nonetheless the *Times* did not allow itself to be swayed with regard to Frank's fate: "This fact . . . has little to do with the question of the guilt of the young man now on trial for his life for having slain him." On that point the paper would refrain from comment. It had merely wished to register how much "the public sense of decency has been shocked by the production of these Walworth letters."

As he rested over the weekend, O'Conor might well have felt he had accomplished the most difficult of tasks: turning the trial of a killer into a trial of the person he had killed.

15

∿∿∿∿∿

The Trial, Second Week: "The Obnoxious Man Has Been Laid to Rest"

F RANK and his mother seemed more relaxed Monday morning, as far as could be judged by those who managed to get a look at them through the crowd of relatives doing their best to shield the pair from view. After a long delay—a juror arrived hours late because of a railroad accident—O'Conor went straight to the matter of Mansfield's attacks on Ellen. She gave a restrained but sufficiently harrowing account of her husband's outbreaks of rage, right down to the evening at her mother's house when he had bitten her fingers to the bone.

Ellen's brothers were called to the stand, Lem chiefly to praise Frank as "the best boy I ever knew," Martin to tell of the attack that Mansfield—"very much excited" and in search of Ellen—had made on him in his hotel room. The prosecution raised no objections to the testimony of the one-armed general, who admitted he had never fully recovered from his war wounds.

The tales of Mansfield's depredations served as prelude for a suite of witnesses describing Frank's erratic behavior in the months before the shooting. Friends and teachers reviewed his outbursts and unaccountable symptoms—the stained pillows and sudden fits of abstraction—and his loss of interest in what had once amused or engaged him. An old friend recalled the time he had been hit on the head playing baseball and was knocked out for half an hour. Dolly (identified for the record as Dorothy Smith) brought up Frank's fall from a railroad car at seven or eight, resulting in a bloody cut on the back of his head. She reeled off a long list of more recent ailments: headaches, convulsions, screams in the night, frothing at the mouth. Winnifred Roach, a housekeeper at Pine Grove, chimed in with similar details: "He'd travel around the room and around the yard as if he was lost entirely and ready to drop away."

Frank's billiards companion Dr. Grant, the day's last witness, testified at length about various episodes of distraction and confusion. It became clear why the medical man had been called when ex-Judge Garvin asked him what these symptoms suggested to him. "To my mind," the doctor answered, "they indicated a condition of epilepsy." Dr. Grant went on to explain that epilepsy could produce unconsciousness and mental irresponsibility." "Under the influence of epileptic mania is there consciousness or will?" "Not when fully under the influence of the mania."

ON Tuesday morning the defense introduced their expert witness. Dr. John Gray was superintendent of the State Lunatic Asylum at Utica, editor of the *American Journal of Insanity*, and one of the best-known psychologists in America. He was hailed by many for his humanitarian efforts to improve the treatment of the insane, although dissenting voices were already beginning to question the reliability of his medical views. For Gray, insanity was a consequence of physical malady, since the mind partook of the same immortality as the human soul: "The mind is not, itself, ever diseased. It is incapable of disease or of its final consequence, death."

O'Conor and Garvin questioned Gray for several hours, eliciting a detailed description of the nature and symptoms of epilepsy. The disease's causes were various, Gray asserted, and its effects were manifested in various ways: in one form spasms, cries, convulsions; in another, memory loss and mental impairment. The onset of the disease might be announced by nearly imperceptible signs: a slight shiver, the eruption of small spots on the face. The seemingly milder form was actually the more dangerous, as it led—through lassitude, hesitation, irritability, confusion, bewilderment, frenzy, raving—finally to dementia, with the strong probability of homicidal mania.

The disease could develop with frightening rapidity. Dr. Gray recalled the case of a lawyer who had come to him for treatment of nervousness and memory loss, and then, as Gray was making some notes in the consulting room, "I happened to look up when I discovered him in the act of attempting to stab me." He was also reminded of Professor Jackson in Poughkeepsie, who not long since had shot his father to death allegedly for wronging his mother: another clear case of epilepsy. O'Conor drew the doctor out on one point that referred back to the earlier rejected questioning about Frank's sleeping habits: "The effect of waking up a person subject to epilepsy two or three hours before his usual hour would be likely to bring on a fit." Gray also noted that even close friends might be unaware that the condition existed.

District Attorney Phelps, on cross-examination, asked Gray directly if he thought Frank had killed Mansfield in an epileptic fit. Gray evaded making such a categorical statement but mentioned other details that struck him as indicative of epilepsy: the convulsions and other physical symptoms, his loss of acuity in his legal studies, his forgetfulness of the German phrases previously mastered. Phelps reminded the witness that Frank had demonstrated no memory loss after the shooting but had recounted the events clearly and concisely. Gray demurred that he did not have sufficient data to determine Frank's condition that morning. He further explained that epileptics were often perfectly capable of conducting ordinary business; indeed, Julius Caesar, Alexander the Great, Muhammad, and Napoleon were all said to have been subject to epileptic fits.

WITH Gray's testimony the defense closed. The prosecution now came back with a series of witnesses designed to rebut the negative—not to say demonic—characterization of Mansfield so far presented. They could scarcely have found a more upbeat witness than the publisher Francis Street of Street & Smith, whose *New York Weekly* had been the primary vehicle for Mansfield's recent writing. Street had spent a good deal of time with the author in the past year—an hour or two at a time several times a month—and was quick to describe him as "affable, pleasant, and agreeable." O'Conor jumped in and objected to the attempt to steer the questioning toward Mansfield's character, good or otherwise, but Judge Davis ruled that if the defense had sought

to prove Mansfield mad, the prosecution was entitled to try to prove
him sane.

Street had nothing but good things to say. He had never seen
Mansfield exhibit the slightest trait of violence or eccentricity; had
never known him to drink or use bad language; and the only time he
had ever alluded to the family was to express pleasure at a complimen-
tary newspaper account of Ellen and the Walworth Academy. On
cross-examination he told O'Conor that Mansfield had enjoyed an
exclusive contract with Street & Smith, and that on the very day he
was shot he had been scheduled to meet at the *Weekly*'s office to agree
on payment for his next, already completed serial. Such was Street's
enthusiasm that he had published an editorial denying the ugly
rumors about Mansfield and had posted placards around the city—
O'Conor called them "inflammatory"—declaring, LET MANSFIELD
TRACY WALWORTH SPEAK FOR HIMSELF!

The character witnesses who followed offered inadvertent testimony to the reduced circumstances of Mansfield's last months. The
owner of a Third Avenue restaurant said he had eaten there every
day—breakfast, lunch, and dinner—for thirty or thirty-five cents, and
had displayed an unfailingly cheerful disposition. Once he had seen
him take a drink at the bar. Henry Ackerman, the German barber who
shared Mansfield's love of choral singing, likewise said that Mansfield
had dropped into the barbershop nearly every day, and that although
he occasionally had a glass of beer he was never visibly intoxicated. A
local grocer and liquor merchant noted how promptly he had paid the
bills—no more than seventeen dollars a month—for the provisions,
including occasionally whiskey and wine, that he bought from him
regularly. Finally the superintendent of the local post office described
him as "a well-bred gentleman" who spoke endearingly of his father.

District Attorney Phelps then attempted to enter *Beverly*, Mansfield's last novel published in book form, as evidence of his sanity.
Judge Davis observed that he had read parts of it and been struck by
how closely, except for the blasphemy and obscenity, it echoed Mansfield's letters to Ellen. But after all, O'Conor objected, the novel held
up as a hero a man who threatened to take his wife's life. "Yes," said
Phelps, "but who did not do it." "No, because he takes up with another
woman. We have letters to show a parallel fact, but I did not think

them exactly proper, and withheld them." With that, any further consideration of Mansfield's fiction was excluded as irrelevant; and any evidence concerning another woman in Mansfield's life was buried.

To conclude, the prosecution called up three experts to contest Dr. Gray's testimony. Each, while not denying the possibility, said there was not sufficient evidence to attribute Frank's behavior to an epileptic fit. Defense counsel Beach, while cross-examining Dr. Parsons of the New York City Lunatic Asylum, brought up what the defense was trying to turn into a crucial point: the fact that Frank, as evidenced by his telegram from the Sturtevant—they had produced the actual telegram so there could be no mistake about it—recalled firing only three of the four shots. But the witness responded that the same might have been true of "any person in an excited state of mind."

The final expert, Dr. Meredith Clymer, told how he had gone to the Tombs two weeks ago to interview Frank and assess his mental condition. When Frank was ushered in by a guard, he greeted the doctor courteously but told him straight off that his lawyers had counseled him to speak to no one. So they had stood for three or four minutes in total silence until Frank said there was no use in his staying any longer, and in any case it was his hour for exercise: "I want you to understand," he said in parting, "that I have no objection myself to having a conversation with you, but I follow the direction of my counsel." With that bit of information, the taking of testimony ended.

Aᴛ three o'clock Charles O'Conor rose to address the jury. It was a star turn in which he seemed bent on displaying the full range of his persuasive art. For the full three hours and thirty-five minutes of his discourse, the courtroom listened with what was described as "the most painful interest and silence."

His summing up was a curious mix of emotional appeal and nearly pedantic insistence on seemingly marginal details of the prosecution's case. O'Conor's chief concern was to cast Frank's action as part of a human drama: "I desire to begin at that stage of this terrible drama which may be pronounced the last act, and which consisted of several scenes." But first he asked the jurors to clear their minds of that action as the prosecution had presented it—as nothing more than "a gross, vulgar, common, everyday, malicious murder"—and, also, paradoxically, as a crime anything but everyday: "the killing of a father, a crime at which humanity revolts." O'Conor agreed that parricide was an unparalleled crime; he only denied that in Frank's case any such crime had been committed.

He would take them back to the Thursday before the shooting, when Frank was apprised of his uncle's invitation to accompany him to Europe. His behavior had not been that of someone contemplating murder, but of someone preparing to go away on just such a long voyage. He had spent a day, "preparatory to parting with his little brother," in innocent amusements calculated to give Tracy pleasure; and had then devoted himself to packing books and clothes as one would expect. Only at that point—"on this very fatal Saturday"—did something else intervene in the form of his father's intercepted letter, "another installment of the horror that had been preying upon him for years." He could not tell his mother, whom he wished to shield from such threats. He had no friend in whom he could confide. Instead it fell on him alone to find a way by which "this terrible evil might be turned aside." It was a wild hope to think that he could somehow persuade his father to cease his persecutions, but wild hope was the province of youth.

He had not acted with the secrecy of someone plotting murder; any secrecy reflected his desire not to cause pain or anxiety to his mother. He had written frankly to Clarence about his plan to meet with his father in New York. He might have concealed his tracks and gone clandestinely to the city, but instead all his movements had been open. He had borrowed only enough money to go to New York for a day and a night, and made evident—in his promise to repay the borrowed money and to play whist with his friend the gunsmith—his intention to be back in Saratoga by Tuesday.

The prosecution claimed Frank had checked into the Sturtevant and then coldly and deliberately lured his father to the hotel room. But there had not been time between the train's arrival at 2:35 and his appearance at Eliza Sims's boardinghouse at 3:00 for him to go to the hotel. No, he had gone first, his clothes still dusty from travel, to his father's address in the hope of meeting with him right away. There was no implication of his having laid a trap; he had left a note for him only at Mrs. Sims's suggestion, and the note asked his father to call on him at his convenience, not at a fixed hour.

Now O'Conor came to the events of that Tuesday morning. "It is an extravagant thought," he ventured, "but it would seem as if a certain doom or fatality followed this man Walworth, and led him to adopt exactly the course that was, under the circumstances, calculated to bring about this unfortunate catastrophe." Mansfield had come home late and thus had only gotten Frank's message when it was too late to call at the hotel. Instead he had gone there early the next morning—at an hour when Frank was accustomed to be asleep in bed. The father thus found him in a confused state, at first too sleepy to come down to meet his visitor, and then dressed unaccountably in hat and overcoat as if preparing to go out.

The shooting itself O'Conor would for the moment skip over. He would focus instead on Frank's actions immediately afterward. Instead of fleeing the consequences of his act, he went immediately to the hotel office to report what he had done and to ask for a policeman: "He seems to have acted with wonderful calmness." Now came the matter of the telegram Frank had sent to Clarence. Mr. Barrett had claimed, and all the newspapers had reported, that the text ran: "Have shot father. Look after mother." But O'Conor had entered in evidence the copy received by Clarence and the original from the telegraph company, and the crucial phrase read "Have shot father three times," proving that Frank had no consciousness of having actually fired four shots.

O'Conor turned now to the question of parricide. Undoubtedly the first announcement that a young man had killed his father struck horror into the community. But to what extent could Frank have regarded Mansfield as his father? Frank had grown up with his parents in the household of Chancellor Walworth, who was more of a father to him than Mansfield had ever been. O'Conor had been barred, he suggested, from presenting evidence that would have cast a harsh light on Mansfield's behavior toward his son even in those early years. In any case the family broke up thereafter, and the mother and her children went to Kentucky to seek the protection of Ellen's family. In the next six years Frank and the other children scarcely saw Mansfield once.

Frank's reunion with his father, in 1869, coincided with his learning of his father's brutal treatment of his mother: "From that time forward he knew his father only as a fierce, bloodthirsty, revengeful, impious, and abominably wicked persecutor of his mother." He had never known Mansfield as a father. Mansfield had addressed no kind or tender word to him from the moment of his birth. He had never taken him to a church or to a place of amusement. If Mansfield had ever behaved like a father, the shock attending the crime of parricide would be in order; but this "shameless monster of impiety and wickedness" had done nothing to engender feelings of tenderness or affection.

Instead such feelings on Frank's part were focused, quite rightly, on his mother. O'Conor could not say enough about the strength and purity of Ellen's character. He knew that some in the audience took an unfavorable view of the "firmness" she had exhibited throughout the trial. But what they took for coldness was strength. As long as she was "pursued by the demons of the law and persecuted by action against her boy," she would have no tears to shed. Even if he were condemned, she would have no tears to shed; only by a verdict of not guilty would the jury see her shed tears. Frank too, O'Conor admitted, had been criticized for his behavior in court: "It has been said that he has acted with a sort of boldness." He asked them to see this rather as calm decisiveness.

The address went on for many more hours, peppered with references to bygone legal doctrine and ancient instances, from Orestes' slaying of his mother to Beatrice Cenci's bloody vengeance on her incestuous father, and leading to the determination that in fact parricide was an offense unknown in modern times. He reviewed the evidence regarding Frank's sanity, and reminded the jury that the prosecution had not been able to refute convincingly Dr. Gray's testimony, and that if they had the least doubt about Frank's soundness of mind they must acquit.

At around seven in the evening he wound up with a kind of last-ditch argument, a plea to the jury not to impose on the "great, happy, and enlightened" United States of America the onus of convicting a man of this unheard of crime: "That shame ought not to be fastened upon him, and it ought not to be fastened upon your country."

WEDNESDAY morning was unusually hot, and the courtroom packed almost to overflowing. District Attorney Phelps launched straight off into his two-and-a-half-hour address, beginning with a compliment to O'Conor. The case was exceptional, he noted, not only because of the nature of the crime and the nature of the defendant—"not brought up in misery and trained to sin and vice"—but because of the exceptional quality of his legal defense: "His case has finally been presented to you by one who has been for many years looked upon as the leader of our profession. He has come here with all the fires of his youth and his intellect to the defense of this young man." Whatever could be done for Frank had been done.

But Phelps could not assent to the implication of O'Conor's defense: that, because of his character and because of his special circumstances, Frank should somehow be exempt from the penalty for murder. Even the vilest of men was entitled to equal treatment at the bar, and that applied to victims as well as perpetrators. The law did not prohibit the murder of a "good and pure and lovely" human being; it prohibited the murder of any human being at all. Nor should the jury give special weight to the fact that it was his father that Frank had killed; murder was murder; the law made no such distinctions among victims. For Frank it was another matter, of course: he ought to carry to his grave the memory of what he had done, and "no hum of human life, no silence of the midnight, should be permitted to remove from his ear the solemn cry of 'murder.'"

At the outset Phelps dismissed out of hand the suggestion that Frank was insane: "They have not got so far even as to prove that he had epilepsy, much less insanity arising therefrom, at the time this act occurred . . . Why, gentlemen, it would be an insult to your common sense if I should longer consider this question." With that ground removed, there remained only the question of Mansfield's behavior and how it had influenced Frank. The letters that had been read in court were unquestionably "outrageous, disgusting, and brutal"; but he would show that they never instilled the slightest fear in their recipients.

He would not defend Mansfield. Mansfield was not on trial. There was not much good that could be said: "He was a weak, proud, vain, passionate man, believing, what probably no one believed who knew him, in his own literary genius and the coming fame that was to crown his efforts." Like too many men, he had vented his "bitterness and spleen" on his wife with undoubted brutality. Yet no man was entirely bad. The jury had heard contrary evidence of Mansfield's amiability and gentleness. And must it not have been so? After all, Ellen had "given her young heart to him."

Ellen and the rest of the family had known his character all too well. Why, then, had they taken no action when he began to send his threatening and abusive letters? Because they knew better than to take them seriously. They had even laughed at some of them just the other day: "The true value which this whole family set upon these threats, disgusting and brutal as they were, is illustrated by the fact that even here in this courtroom they were received with the same derision with which they were received at the outset by this young man. From the moment Ellen had left Mansfield she had broken off all communication with him. The torrent of letters came, and yet not a word of reply was made. No attempt was made to restrain him or reconcile him. If they really believed he intended to slaughter them, wouldn't they have done something about it? Instead many of the letters were unread, even unopened." Here, almost imperceptibly, Phelps began to make the defense of Mansfield he had said he would not make: "His child died and was buried, and not one word was sent to him. I leave you to draw your own conclusions from these facts."

Frank was an ardent and excitable boy who, if he was descended from a great Chancellor and a brave general, as the defense had constantly reiterated, had also perhaps inherited something of his father's wayward disposition. He had been brought up, if not to hate that father, then certainly not to love him. When, on the brink of a European trip he must have anticipated with pleasure, he received yet another menacing letter from his father, his reaction must surely have been: "Why, here is this father who has been the pain of my existence turning up again. He is constantly vexing and annoying me, and I won't submit to it any longer; I will put an end to it." He had made up his mind to murder at once. When he wrote to his uncle Clarence, he already knew what the outcome of his New York trip was likely to be. Perhaps he had not determined altogether to kill his father; but he had certainly strongly considered the possibility.

What did he take with him on his journey? No baggage, not even the ordinary items people take with them on an overnight trip: nothing but a loaded pistol. Had he gone to New York to attempt, as O'Conor had suggested, a peaceful settlement? "There is nothing to indicate . . . that anything like an amicable settlement was intended . . . It was to be compelled, and compelled at the mouth of a pistol." The curt note he left at his father's lodgings bore no trace of friendly intentions. Yet this was the first communication that Mansfield had received from his family, "and I tell you, gentlemen, that there seems to be no justifiable reason to believe that he received it in any other frame of mind than a happy one, looking upon it as a harbinger of peace between himself and his family." When he went to his son's hotel room at six the next morning, he brought nothing with him but Frank's note. He did not have so much as a penny on him. The loaded pistol he was said to habitually carry was left in his room; it was his son who brought a loaded pistol to the encounter.

Here Phelps summoned his rhetorical powers to conjure that moment when Mansfield entered Frank's room, never to leave it alive: "What occurred during that period and in that dreadful interview? We have the statements of one of the actors . . . but there was another party to the scene, and where is his account of it? Shall I say to the crier of this Court: 'Crier, call Mansfield T. Walworth as a witness in this case, that he may tell to the Court his story of that fatal room'? Oh, gentlemen, he may call, and call again, but from that shattered jaw, that pierced heart no answer shall ever come from this side of the grave, and he shall never tell that story until he tells it before that awful bar where no secrets are hid and where no judgment can annul. All, all that we have left of Mansfield Tracy Walworth is this poor note found next his heart, stained with blood that came rushing from the wound that his own oldest boy inflicted upon him."

From the position of Mansfield's body, it was clear that Frank had stood with his back to the door, blocking the only egress as he shot his father four times. Frank had said that his father was closing in on him as the last shot was fired. Phelps maintained, based on the forensic evidence, that Frank had shot Mansfield while the latter was sitting down—Mansfield had risen, striving to get past Frank to the door—and Frank had continued firing. The third shot, piercing Mansfield's chest on the right side, was fired downward, so Frank must by then have been standing over his father. The final shot—the one that left powder burns on Mansfield's shattered jaw—would have been fired when "that irregular, unhappy, broken-hearted father" was sinking to the floor. The question of whether Frank remembered firing three or four shots seemed irrelevant: "He knew that he had left him dead on the floor."

He came at last to Frank's conversation with the coroner at the station house. Asked why he had come to New York, he had replied, "To do this." "To kill your father?" "Well, to settle this family difficulty." The exchange had been rehashed repeatedly in the course of the trial. O'Conor had insisted that Frank's second remark had been misinterpreted as a confession; on the contrary, he meant to clarify that he had come *not* to kill his father but rather to settle the family difficulty. Phelps was not persuaded by such exquisitely fine parsing. "So far as the relations between this husband, father and son were concerned," he told the jury, "he certainly did settle their family differences. There shall be no question hereafter in this community about the division of that property; there shall be no question about the custody of the children . . . The obnoxious man whom his family blame for all the trouble has been laid quietly to rest in his grave, and the grass shall grow over his fame and he shall disturb his family no longer."

THEN it was the judge's turn. Davis proceeded to charge the jury in a discourse of some three hours. It was a speech much admired at the time and subsequently for the scope and precision of its arguments. Davis was obliged to explain at some length the implications of the new murder law, as well as the nuances of the laws regarding self-defense and insanity as justifications for killing. After the emotional appeals of O'Conor and Phelps, he adopted a tone of scrupulously rational analysis.

Davis lingered over the fact that Mansfield's behavior, no matter how atrocious, did not justify his having "his grave raked open . . . for the mere purpose of creating a public sentiment that he was so bad a man that he ought to die." Such "wild justice" had no place in law. He repeated all the points previously made about Frank's statements immediately after the shooting—especially his remark that he had come there to do what he had done—and emphasized that if the jury felt Frank had inwardly assented in advance to the idea of killing his father, even if he had not definitively resolved to do so but had fixed on it only as a last resort, then their verdict must be murder in the first degree.

If they had any doubt about Frank's prior intentions, they could find for murder in the second degree, which allowed for a clear intent to kill but without deliberation or premeditation: "It may be formed upon the instant; it may be the result of that instantaneous action of the mind which oftentimes accompanies the commission of crime, when from some cause arising upon the moment the thought flashes into the mind, 'I will kill,' and the act follows the thought." If Frank—armed, it could be argued, merely to be prepared for any event that might arise—had in the midst of his conversation with his father suddenly determined that the difficulties between them could not be resolved, and had there and then abruptly determined "I will terminate this by his death," it was a matter of murder in the second degree.

The defense's case had been twofold: that Frank was very probably insane, and that in any case he had acted in self-defense. The question of insanity Judge Davis dealt with cursorily. He was willing to accept that Frank was to some degree affected with epilepsy; but the laws of New York did not accept that a disease of the mind causing an irresistible impulse to kill was in itself a justification. The only rule was the ability to judge the nature of one's act and to know whether it was right or wrong.

With regard to self-defense he had a great deal to say. If Mansfield had stormed into Pine Grove and drawn a pistol with apparent intent to shoot down Ellen, Frank would have been justified in killing him on the spot. But to kill him from the fear that at some future time he might carry out his threats was something the law could never allow. In that room alone with Mansfield, Frank's only legitimate motive to kill would be a threat to his own person. They had little evidence to go on to make a determination of what level of threat had existed in the room. The only testimony regarding what had happened there was Frank's.

They should remember as well that Mansfield was in the room at Frank's invitation—doubly, since he had written him the note and then had told the bellman to show him up. When a man invited an enemy to see him, someone he believed to be dangerous to him, his claim to have then killed that enemy in self-defense needed close examination to avoid suspicion of entrapment. Here, unfortunately, reliable evidence was almost nonexistent. Therefore the jury was entitled to turn to Mansfield's threatening letters. Had they, as the defense argued, justified Frank in the idea that his life was in danger from his father?

The judge analyzed the letters that had been presented in evidence, and in doing so repeated some of the prosecution's arguments as well as some points he had himself brought up earlier in the trial. There had been two main waves of letters to Ellen, the first throughout July 1871 and relating to the divorce, the second from July to September 1872 concerning both money matters and visitation rights. Then for over eight months the letters stopped until the one received by Frank on the afternoon of May 31, 1873. He noted that by writing such letters Mansfield had broken the law and could have been arrested, possibly for extortion in the case of those aimed at bullying Ellen into a divorce settlement favorable to him. But the main point was that Mansfield's threats had not been executed.

If the letters had produced such a shocking effect, it was in part because "they come in masses upon us, upon you and me, and upon the community, in an avalanche. They are all read here by the learned counsel in tones of great force and eloquence, and come in a mass of vileness, filth, profanity." But Ellen and the family had gotten them piecemeal over a long period of time, and so their force must eventually have been much diminished, especially since Mansfield had so signally failed to act on his threats. If anything, the letters may have made their author look pathetic rather than frightening: "Some weak-minded men think that they accomplish a purpose by writing brutal and threatening letters. I think I may characterize them (because I have received a great many of that kind of letters) as the offspring of cowards and fools." In any case, writing such letters was not a capital offense. It was not even an offense that could justify a physical assault. They provided no one with a license to kill, and were legitimate evidence only for the effect they might have had on Frank's mental state.

Davis charged the jury to bring in their verdict without regard to the crime's ripple effects on the family of the accused: "It is one of the misfortunes of this world that when a person commits a crime, its consequences are not limited to himself." Frank's guilt or innocence was their only concern. At about 4:30 the jury filed out for their deliberations.

JUDGE Davis went home for dinner, but most of the crowd lingered in the courtroom, despite the stifling heat. After the room was cleared, Frank and Ellen and some family friends stayed on hand in an adjoining chamber. Members of the press remained at their tables, writing up their notes and exchanging views. "The plea of insanity did not appear to find much favor among those who had been present during the trial," the *Times* reported. "The general opinion appeared to be that young Walworth was fully responsible for his acts." Around seven the jury sent word they had reached a verdict, and the spectators filed back in, with spillover crowds filling halls and vestibules. It was another hour and a half before the cry of "Hats off!" announced the judge's return.

Frank took his seat next to his mother. Tracy made his way among the adults and clambered over Frank's knees to sit on his other side. Sarah, Martin, and Clarence were also near at hand. Frank showed signs of nervousness, fanning himself with his hat and running his fingers through his hair, while Ellen appeared simply exhausted. The clerk took the roll call of jurors and was told by the foreman that they had reached a verdict. Frank was directed to stand, and the foreman read the verdict, fumbling the wording: "Guilty in the second degree." "Guilty of what?" the clerk was obliged to ask. "Of murder in the second degree." A fleeting smile was observed to pass over Frank's face. As he sat down he loosened his necktie.

16

~~~~~~~~~~

Sentence and Removal

ELLEN appeared relieved. The rest of the family seemed uncertain if the verdict was cause for celebration. O'Conor approached the judge and urged him to defer sentencing, stating that it would be regrettable and unusual to pass sentence that evening, as the defense wished to prepare a bill of exceptions. After a quiet conference, Davis announced that sentence would be passed on Saturday morning.

A reporter managed to get a word with Frank on his way back to the Tombs. He expressed relief that the judge had not spoken at any greater length: "I am glad I did not have to endure the long lecture I had anticipated." He understood his position, he said, and did not require any additional instructions. All he asked was a few days to get his affairs in order, after which he would "submit myself to my fate with all the equanimity I can command."

O'Conor too spoke to the press after the verdict came down. Asked about the appeal that everyone expected, he admitted that it might not be filed at all, and certainly not right away. He was of course disappointed in the verdict; he had expected an acquittal. Putting Mansfield and Frank in the same room was like putting powder and spark together; one might just as well send the spark to state prison. Anyway, Frank had been half asleep at the time the incident had occurred.

Despite all the evidence presented, O'Conor added, there had been more to the story. "The world does not know what that boy and his family have had to bear. The letters read in court were bad enough, but they are mild as compared with those I could not read. I would not defile my mouth with the blasphemy and indecency that the letters withheld contained . . . The badness of that boy's father was only known to those who knew the father best." He was asked how the family was bearing up. "They're a wonderful family . . . And Mrs. Walworth—she's a wonderful, she's a splendid woman." He had asked for the sentencing delay simply to give Frank time to settle his affairs: "If a man is going to be imprisoned for life it is no good to hurry matters unnecessarily."

The reporter remarked that the public seemed to accept the verdict. O'Conor agreed, but added that "had Frank shot his father in Saratoga Springs, and the trial held there, the jury would have acquitted him. The character of both father and son were well known there, and the putting of the father away would have been regarded as only that which was deserved." He felt that he had been perhaps too emotionally involved in the case to be fully effective. "I knew how noble a boy Frank was, and that his devotion to his mother blinded him to every obligation. It is a noble feeling, sir, and whatever our calmer judgments may indicate there is no man but must admire him for that."

ON Saturday Frank remained apparently as calm as ever, if perhaps a bit paler. "He gazed about the room," the *Times* wrote, "with a half-contemptuous smile upon his lips." At the bidding of the clerk he rose to hear the sentence pronounced. Asked if he had anything to say, he raised his left hand to his face, straightened his posture, then kept his hand on his breast. He said nothing. Judge Davis waited what seemed like a very long half minute before proceeding.

There was no question what the sentence would be. The new murder statute offered only one punishment for murder in the second degree: life at hard labor. As Davis addressed Frank his voice trembled. "Walworth," he opened, "I have never been called upon in my life to perform a more painful duty than the one which devolves upon me now." Frank had been found guilty after a trial in which he had benefited from a defense team unsurpassed in ability and learning. His sentence was a foregone conclusion, but the judge did not think it too severe. The sentence was justified, and indeed the judge had grave doubts whether the proper verdict would not have been murder in the first degree: "I cannot conceive what motive you had in preparing yourself as you did with a pistol loaded, coming to New York, seeking an interview with your father, and almost immediately shooting him down, except upon the idea that you had deliberately determined that his life should be terminated by your hand." He hoped that God would find otherwise.

Davis's task was doubly painful because of Frank's distinguished lineage. One of his grandfathers, the Chancellor, had left an unparalleled record of "purity and integrity and . . . all the private virtues that advance and elevate man"; the other had fallen nobly on the field of battle. It was regrettable that the memory of such forebears had not restrained Frank's impulses. However understandable the shame and indignation Frank had felt at his father's conduct, he had no mandate to be the avenger of his own and his mother's wrongs.

It was finally to Mansfield's fate that Davis reverted, Mansfield who, whatever he had done, had done nothing to merit death at the hands of his son: "When I look back at that moment when you constituted yourself his executioner and slew him in that room with no one present but yourself, I cannot but feel that that death must have been more horrible than a thousand deaths in any other form . . . What thoughts must have rushed upon him at that moment . . . what terrible thoughts must have rushed upon him when he received the leaden messenger of death in his bosom from the hands of his eldest boy! I shudder when I think of it, and I think you ought to devote your whole life to a repentance such as God only can accept for so horrible a crime." The judge seemed on the verge of choking up as he spoke. He concluded, "The sentence of the Court is that you be imprisoned in the State Prison at Sing Sing, at hard labor, for the full term of your natural life."

There was a silence after his last words. Frank remained as motionless and inexpressive at the end as he had at the beginning of the trial. Neither his mother nor anyone else in the family showed any outward emotion. Then, as at the end of a reception, Frank began quietly shaking hands with his friends and relations as they filed out of the courtroom.

FRANK'S departure to Sing Sing was delayed for several days. The papers were full of rumors that O'Conor would launch an immediate appeal, but nothing seemed to come of it. In the meantime much favorable comment had been published on the conduct of the trial. After all the tricky delays and sleazy goings-on in the cases of Stokes, Sharkey, and others, the Walworth case had been disposed of with admirable rigor. Even the *Nation* admitted that "compared with the majority of murder trials in this city," the trial "was on the whole a very gratifying and encouraging affair."

The *Tribune* likewise applauded the way things had been handled: "The rapidity with which the prisoner was arraigned, the alacrity with which his counsel submitted his story to the judgment of a jury, the frankness of the defense, the utter disregard of dilatory motions, of technical pleas, of devices for manufacturing sympathy, and obscuring testimony, took the whole town by astonishment." Public sentiment toward Frank had shifted dramatically in the course of the trial, the *Tribune* noted. The revelations about "the miserable madman whom he called father" led people to hope that the boy might at least be saved from hanging, and the new homicide statute had allowed the jury to do just that: "Frank Walworth has fairly earned his terrible fate."

The *Nation* was less satisfied with the verdict. In its view the fact that Frank was armed with a pistol should have been proof of premeditation, and it proposed a law "simply declaring that a man who goes about armed is a would-be murderer, which in the majority of cases would be true in fact." In any case Frank was unlikely to serve out his sentence: "We may as well say here that the sentence passed on him does not, in our opinion, amount to much. Neither he nor any of his family, we venture to say, look on it as more than a temporary inconvenience." The arguments O'Conor had marshaled for the defense would doubtless figure in a plea for a governor's pardon, "and they are arguments which governors are in the habit of regarding, and which will in the present case be urged with unusual force and backed up by unusual influence."

What most worried the *Nation* was not Frank's particular fate but the example he set. The case had fed "the morbid condition of feeling and imagination out of which murders grow and through which murderers escape justice." If a privileged young man like Frank was seen as justified in ridding his family of a brute like Mansfield, what about all the others out there, the masses of helpless and impoverished women and children subjected to "tyrannical beasts, compared to whom Walworth was harmless and decent and merciful"? Should they be taught that the appropriate response to such domestic torment was taking the law into their own hands?

George Templeton Strong, who had followed the trial closely, was likewise dissatisfied with its outcome. The verdict was "possibly correct under our recent legislation, but then so much the worse for our recent legislators! I suppose he will be pardoned out of prison in a year or two." The whole thrust of O'Conor's defense Strong found morally indefensible. Perhaps, he whimsically surmised, the fact that O'Conor had no children made him indifferent to the social risks of defending such a crime. "His argument in support of the praiseworthiness of parricide whenever a boy thinks his pa objectionable has been read in the newspapers by many hundred thousand people, including, doubtless, no end of ill-conditioned boys who think themselves how aggrieved by their respective 'governors.'"

The *Times*, which had carefully withheld comment during the trial, expressed its qualified approval of the verdict, even if in its view the new homicide law, by making premeditation so much harder to prove, had virtually abolished the death penalty in New York. The trial had shown that Frank was "a morbid boy, who committed an unnatural and inexcusable crime." However provoked he had been, society could not afford to consider those provocations without giving "to everyone the right to avenge his own wrongs, fancied or real . . . An acquittal would have been an invitation to every youth having a dissolute or tyrannical father to slay him." The paper ventured, all the same, to put in a word for the family: "The conviction is indeed another and dreadful blow to an already desolated family for whom there is much sympathy, but the rights of society are paramount."

ON Wednesday morning a group of eleven prisoners emerged from the Tombs under the guard of Deputy Sheriff William Shields, who made the run up to Sing Sing regularly on the Hudson River line. Frank was still in his cell, having a last shave before leaving for prison. He wore the same suit he had worn coming down from Saratoga on the morning of June 2. His mother, grandmother, and younger brother had gathered to see him off; Dolly was there too. At twenty to ten it was time for him to take his place in line. The last farewells were managed, in what was now seen as the Walworth style, with a total absence of demonstrative feeling. Frank maintained the good cheer of someone embarking on a minor excursion.

A place had been reserved for him at the end of the line, between William Jones, a fifteen-year-old burglar who had already escaped from prison once and was now looking at four and a half years in Sing Sing, and Francis Gillen, a machinist of previously unblemished life who in a fit of jealous rage had stabbed his fiancée to death at the corner of Prince and Mulberry streets, and who, like Frank, was to serve a life sentence. In short order Frank was handcuffed and attached to Gillen. He recoiled involuntarily as Shields frisked him.

Ellen walked alongside Frank all the way out. As the line of prisoners approached the outer gate of the prison, a basket of flowers was delivered to him. His mother took charge of it. She had tried to persuade Shields to let her conduct Frank separately to the station, with a guard to keep watch, but the request had been refused. The prisoners, their cuffs clanking, now piled into the waiting van. Frank had stuffed a bunch of cigars in his pocket and handed them out to the rest of the group as the vehicle made its way toward the Forty-second Street depot. "The smoke neutralized the bad odor of the prison van," he told a reporter later. Ellen followed by streetcar, getting there ahead of the van and purchasing a first-class ticket at the rear of the same train. When the prisoners arrived they were led into the smoking car, accompanied by Shields, his deputies, and a bunch of reporters who had come along for the ride.

The prisoners were a fairly gaudy group for journalistic purposes. The consignment included "General" Abe Greenthal, a notorious "green goods" man, or fence, who was on his tenth trip upstate; "Wes" Allen, a burglar who had achieved some notoriety for throwing red pepper in the eyes of the policeman who had caught him in the midst of his crime; and the tall and massively built Gillen, who despite the savagery of his crime had narrowly escaped the gallows, chiefly, it was said, due to his pleasant personality and previously clean record. Some of the papers had contrasted Gillen's sincere acknowledgment of his wrongdoing with Frank's air of disdainful superiority. But today Frank was without question the star attraction. When word got around that he was on the 10:40, passengers from the other cars, and from the platform while the train lingered for a long time in the station, made their way to the smoking section to get a look at him.

To a reporter who had taken a seat behind him, Frank remarked that the crowd's anxiety to see a man who had been victimized was quite something: "You see what it is to be a murderer. These men are all here to see me. I only hope they are satisfied with the show." A man with blue-tinted glasses stopped near Frank and looked at him intently, then moved on. "I will bet that man will come back again to look at the menagerie." He did, and stood again for several minutes gazing at him. "It doesn't seem to annoy you much," the reporter commented. "No. I hope we shall get the car cleared of the crowd soon and get some fresh air." As the train finally took off, cries of "That's Walworth!" could be heard from outside. "We will have a little air now, at all events," said Deputy Sheriff Jarvis.

The moldy dampness of the air in the Tombs had been the hardest thing to bear, Frank said. He didn't know if it had to do with the unhealthiness of the place, but he had lost fourteen pounds since being inside. "I had been accustomed to a great deal of outdoor exercise, boating and similar occupations, and I was in excellent health." Sports had always been important to him. "I was fond of all athletic sports, but baseball is my specialty. I have been banged about and hurt generally in that . . . I think I can manage a sailboat as well as the best of them. I have been brought up to exercise myself in every way possible, and I believe that is the way to bring a man up."

Frank felt like talking, and the reporters encouraged him all the way up the river. Didn't it gall him to be linked to these low-life felons? "Some of the best friends I have ever met," Frank replied, "have been in just such low company as this." He had nothing but good to say about the men he had met in the Tombs. "I found those whom I got very intimate with very decent sort of fellows. I think there is a great deal more good in criminals than people generally suppose." As for his keepers at the Tombs, they had treated him fairly and he had no complaints. "Of course, it was not like being outside. You are a prisoner, and it is just as well to remember that and make up your mind to it."

The receptive audience put him in a mood to make jokes. The handcuffs, he quipped, were the most well-starched cuffs he had ever enjoyed. When the boys came through selling candy—a regular annoyance of train travel—he said that he now realized the advantage of handcuffs; it prevented him from having to be pestered by the candy boys. From time to time the conductor came through and slipped him notes from his mother. She had pleaded with his guards to let him take his handcuffs off, to no avail. The murderer Gillen, to whom he was cuffed, was also complaining loudly about the discomfort of traveling like that. Frank's resolute cheerfulness may have grated on him. In any case the pleasant disposition Gillen had displayed while on trial rapidly eroded. When the repeat offender "General" Greenthal proclaimed loudly that he was going to be a good boy in jug this time and get out in a year, Gillen muttered that he would sooner spend five years in hell than where he was going.

Near Tarrytown there was a refreshing breeze. "This wind is nice," Frank rattled on. "Do you know I like the trees and all things green . . . The only consolation I have, except that of having done my duty, is that I shall have plenty of green things and the dear old Hudson to look at in Sing Sing." Despite what they might think, he was not going to break down when he got to the prison. "I am happy wherever I am—that is, so far as circumstances will permit."

At Sing Sing, as they were escorted off the train, Frank's mood saddened: "And this is my last ride on the Hudson River Railroad." They did not go directly to prison. It was Sheriff Shields's long-standing custom to take new prisoners to Daly's American Hotel, just outside the station, and to buy each of them a last drink before passing within the walls. Gillen knocked back a tumbler of brandy and seemed to grow more melancholy with each moment.

Ellen, who had gone ahead in a carriage, was waiting for Frank at the prison gates. After a long embrace she left, apparently faint. Gillen looked on at the scene with not a trace of fellow-feeling. From that point routine took over. The prisoners filed in, and their names and ages were recorded. They surrendered any valuables. Frank handed over a pair of gold sleeve buttons. They were weighed, and their physical descriptions were entered in a book. Now they were led into the dressing room, where they were to strip and put on prison clothes. Frank got down to his undershirt and asked if he had to take that off too. "Yes," a guard barked at him. The patched and ragged prison clothes that were handed to him looked as if they had been worn by generations of convicts. As he put them on—shuddering despite himself—Frank remarked brightly, "I feel as if I was going to play a game of baseball." For Gillen, still at Frank's side, the attempt at levity visibly fell flat.

The prisoners were lined up in Indian file and marched in lockstep across the yard, the right hand of each on the right shoulder of the man before him.

17

~~~~~~~~~

The Prisoner

FRANK Walworth would never again dominate the news as he had for five weeks in the summer of 1873. But for a while the papers continued to keep track, as best they could, of his life behind bars: at first all the papers, and then, after a time, mostly the local ones. For upstate New Yorkers the story of the Walworths lingered in mind long after the rest of the country had moved on to other shocks and fresher outrages.

Ellen sparked news reports when, dressed in mourning and with young Tracy in tow, she showed up to worship at a Catholic church in Sing Sing. She had been in town since Frank's arrival the previous Wednesday, and was expected to stay for some time. She had already had several conferences with prison officials—a privilege rarely granted to relatives of convicted murderers—and was said to have requested, successfully, that Frank be kept out of public view to deter curiosity seekers.

He had been put to work as a stock clerk in the shoe department, a trust deemed appropriate for someone of his upbringing. He had killed his father, but no one had accused him of any inclination toward personal dishonesty. Nevertheless the arrangement drew some fire. Many editorialists still felt that Frank had essentially gotten away with murder, and were alert to any efforts by his family to procure him special treatment. The *Albany Argus* wondered "whether the mighty influence which has already been directed towards mollifying the asperities of his prison life will prove sufficiently puissant to secure for him a pleasant sojourn (whether permanent or otherwise) in his present quarters." Ellen, following Frank to prison with bouquets of flowers and private messages, pulling strings on his behalf, yet preserving in public a demeanor almost icy, came under attack from the *Brooklyn Eagle*, for whom her "singular conduct from the day he killed his father until now has challenged public astonishment and dissipated its sympathy."

In a diatribe titled "Our Christian Age and Country," the *New York Times* railed against Frank's relatively comfortable prison assignment and made it a symbol of general moral decadence: "He now remains a sort of hero in Sing Sing, and is allowed to work 'where visitors cannot see him, so that his feelings may not be hurt.' If he were poor, and without money or influence, would anybody have cared much for his 'feelings'?" The *Times*'s outburst was echoed by the *Sussex* (New Jersey) *Register*: "The morals of this community are in a very unhealthy condition, if a majority of the New-York Press can be taken as exponents. They make a hero of young Walworth because he is rich, handsome, intelligent, and so engaging in his manners. He did not beat his father to death in the street as a vulgar brute would have done; no, indeed, but quieting any suspicion of harm by pretending to hold out the olive branch of peace, he invited his father to comfortable rooms at the hotel, and shooting him before he had time to dream of treachery, left him to die of his wounds."

Some defense of Frank did make its way into print. A letter to the *Saratogian* from "an intimate friend of Frank Walworth"—he signed himself FRATER—argued that Mansfield had plainly intended to murder his wife, that his crazy letter to his sister Liza had been a deliberate maneuver to prepare an insanity defense, and that Frank had been entirely justified in taking measures to prevent that. A number of Clarence's associates chimed in. James McMaster, a lawyer who had been a fellow student at the seminary, launched a lengthy defense of "that broad-chested, free-breathing youth, Frank Walworth," declaring that Frank had been unjustly convicted "by the force and clamor of newspaper and street influence," and calling for a gubernatorial pardon and the impeachment of Judge Noah Davis. He accused Davis and others of having cast aspersions on Ellen simply because "the heartbroken mother did not and could not howl like a common fish-wife." (The *Albany Law Journal* promptly denounced McMaster's argument as "absurd" and "ignorant.")

Orestes Brownson, the best-known Catholic convert in America, added his voice: "Frank Walworth is really suffering the penalty of imprisonment for life at hard labor for having loved and endeavored to protect his mother from the violence of a madman." The distinguished Catholic physician Henry Hewit, another friend of the Walworths, just before his death in August 1873 wrote a passionate plea on behalf of Frank. The youth, in his view, had committed no crime at all, and could be blamed at worst for going to New York to meet his father without his mother's consent. Hewit expressed a sort of pity for Mansfield—whose character, he suggested, might well reflect "the terrible influence of a Calvinistic religious education, acting upon a sensitive and highly organized nature"—but argued that his death, under the circumstances, had been more or less inevitable: "When a man habitually carries a pistol, is subject to sudden fits of violent rage, and iterates and reiterates the fiercest and most terrible threats, he is virtually an outlaw, and the slightest hostile action towards another person will justify any necessary measure of self-defense."

THE prison Frank had entered was at a turning point in its history. Built in 1825 by convict labor, from stones the convicts themselves had quarried, Sing Sing had early on acquired a fearsome reputation. Alexis de Tocqueville, visiting the prison in 1831, expressed "astonishment and fear" at the utter subjugation of the convicts—fear, that is, of what might ensue if that discipline were ever relaxed. The regime was founded on silence, isolation, forced labor, and the harshest of punishments. The prisoners were crammed in cells less than seven feet high, just over six feet deep, and less than four feet wide—"so small," observed the journalist Richard Harding Davis many decades later, "that if you try to turn or walk in one of them you wipe the damp walls with your body." Freezing in winter, furnace-hot in summer, without running water, the cells were theoretically intended as places for solitary religious reflection.

From time to time over the years the public had been aroused by accounts of the extreme cruelty routinely practiced at Sing Sing. Frank could have read all about it in a book written by, of all people, his father. *Beverly*, the last novel Mansfield published, opened with a purportedly documentary chapter, "The Disgrace of New York State—Sing Sing," which described in detail and in a tone of savage protest the torture of a sick prisoner accused of malingering: "He was to be painfully suspended between the floor and the ceiling . . . The keeper commenced to haul away at the other end of the rope, and the other assistant united his efforts to those of his superior, to raise the convict from the floor *by his thumbs*." Efforts to ban the practice had failed, and thus, according to Mansfield, "to-day, in the Christian year one thousand eight hundred and seventy-two, the thumb-pulley is in full operation, and the number 'pullied' yearly is two hundred and eight."

For once Mansfield did not exaggerate. A report of the New York State Prison Association in 1870 confirmed "the domination of force" and "the infliction of the punishments commonly known as the shower-bath, crucifix, or yoke and buck" at Sing Sing and other New York State prisons. By 1873 some major reforms had taken place—floggings with the cat-o'-nine-tails and near-drownings with the notorious cold water baths had been abolished by legislative act—but the prison was still a place of harsh and humiliating punishments. There is no indication that Frank was ever subjected to such tortures. He was never, at any rate, to make any complaints about his treatment by the staff.

In other respects as well the implacable code of the prison regime had evolved. Absolute silence had proved an unenforceable discipline. The rigors of isolation had given way—for better or worse—to those of overcrowding. Convict labor had become enmeshed in an immense and profitable contract labor system, bringing inevitably in its wake a prevalence of bribes and kickbacks and favoritism. A government inspector in the 1870s was appalled by the spectacle of "inmates lounging, without restraint, about the docks and grounds, conversing freely with the less depraved and younger criminals" and observed that "waste, filth, disorder, and chronic insubordination prevailed on every hand."

On August 17, a little over a month after his arrival at the prison, Frank celebrated his twentieth birthday.

At Sing Sing he wrote a poem about his mother. The prison schedule could not have allowed much time for literary composition—there
was a ten-hour workday, and the favored occupation for leisure
hours was Bible reading—but he did manage to convey his sonnet to
Ellen, who arranged for its publication in a newspaper. It was a strange
sort of valentine to the woman on whose behalf he had taken a life. He
envisioned her as a radiant universal empress, her heart controlled by
her "ruling mind," peering from a "dizzy summit" on those who would
wrong her.

The poem has the air of a school exercise triumphantly completed,
a satisfactorily achieved justification not just for his deed but for his
whole life, as the loyal servant of such an exalted being.

MOTHER

Kings have their Kingdoms and Queens have their Kings.
   And thou of royal caste—O what has thou?
   The star of empire glitters on thy brow.
And thou wast born, methinks, to regal things.
Great boon was thine: Seraphic beauty flings
   Her twilight radiance round thee even now;
   But fate to thee did nobler gifts allow,
For Birth but props, and Beauty hath fleet wings.
A dauntless spirit, heart within control,
   Move in accordance with thy ruling mind;
And from the dizzy summit of thy soul
   Thou peerest on traducers of thy Kind:—
And thou art mine by test, determined but royal
And I, thy son, belied, proud, storm'd, yet loyal.

In the long hours that had opened up after the turmoil of the weeks
following the shooting—the mere six weeks that had ended with
Frank's entry into prison—Ellen was writing poems too. Although she
declared in one, "I am dumb to friend and foe," she could not permit
herself to lapse into inactivity. To surrender to her emotions would
have been the ultimate moral weakness. She marked a passage in a
novel she was reading by the Irish writer Justin McCarthy: "She knew
that there is a sensualism of grief which the heart with a high purpose

can no more indulge than the sensualism of joy. She arose and went about her daily tasks, taking no pleasure in them, but still striving to give pleasure to others. The household was, indeed, sadly changed. A cloud seemed to hang always over it." Ellen had more than household duties to keep her occupied. Her energies would focus above all on righting the wrong done to her son,

> bound in chains
> That blinded justice will not break.

She did not lack for sympathy. Many in Saratoga and elsewhere shared her view that Frank had been justified. Even if they did not, they admired her fortitude. Mary Todd Lincoln, herself in a spiral of grief and depression following the death of her son Tad in 1871, had written to Ellen's mother after the shooting: "Only those who have passed through deep affliction can really understand others who are similarly tried . . . My prayers often ascend for your lovely daughter and the son who loves her just as my worshipping one did me." Yet the Walworth Academy would resume its fall schedule as if nothing had happened, and Ellen would fill any remaining spare time with a growing number of additional projects, chief among them the preparations for the approaching centenary of the Battle of Saratoga in 1878.

There were of course the children. Clara was home for the summer from the Kenwood convent school, Tracy would remain in Saratoga before going off to study in Georgetown in the fall, and Ruby was still young enough to have passed apparently unscathed through the recent tribulations. Nelly, the eldest girl, who like Clara had scarcely been seen at Frank's trial—it may well have been felt that they should be shielded from the more shocking bits of testimony—was far away. Taking Frank's place, she had gone off with her uncle Clarence on what was now a trip around the world, the traversing of Europe followed by stops in Egypt and Japan. They sailed right after the verdict and by late July were exploring the highlands of Scotland. Nelly's long letters home provided Ellen with something else to pass the time with, as she carefully edited them and sent them off for publication in the *Albany Sunday Press*.

The letters, published in book form a few years later as *An Old*

World Seen Through Young Eyes, offered no trace of what Nelly and the family had undergone, unless a reader were to look between the lines of her standard voyager's descriptions: "O, the feeling of desolation that comes over one as the last point of *terra firma* disappears below the horizon! Country, kindred, all, are sinking, vanishing into the sea with the fading shore—away from one's grasp, out of one's sight." With her uncle to instruct her at every turn, Nelly could lose herself in the details of the scenes she had grown up imagining: the settings of Walter Scott's novels and poems, the birthplace of Shakespeare, the executioner's block at the Tower of London (where an old raven struck her as "the embodied spirit of all the dark deeds that were hissing through our memories"), the castles of the Rhine (including that tower where the cruel bishop of Bingen was devoured by rats and mice), and the castle of Chillon in Switzerland, where she could hardly have failed to remember the prisoner of Byron's poem, "consign'd / To fetters and the damp vault's dayless gloom."

On November 3, in the Alps, she felt a sudden despondency and recalled that it was her fifteenth birthday—and wondered if anyone at home remembered.

A request for a pardon had already been filed, but—unsurprisingly, in view of the controversy that made any intervention politically delicate—there was no sign that Governor Dix would acquiesce. (John Dix was well acquainted with the Walworth family. He had argued cases before the Chancellor in Saratoga, and in 1862, as a Union general in charge of the treatment of prisoners of state, had overseen Mansfield's interrogation and eventual parole.) But for better or worse, Frank's situation was about to change. In late November an order went out that, as one of a consignment of fifty convicts, he should be transferred to Auburn Prison, far to the west in Cayuga County, an action intended to relieve overcrowding at Sing Sing.

At first his removal was delayed for health reasons. Frank's mood was said to have grown steadily more depressed since his incarceration, and although he showed no resistance in submitting to prison discipline he appeared, according to a *Times* reporter, "overwhelmed with sorrow and remorse." (The reporter might have modified his account if he had seen Frank's poetic self-description as "belied" and "proud.")

Frank spoke in quiet tones, seemed unnaturally pale, and had "the appearance of an old man." After collapsing at a Sunday chapel service he was taken to the hospital, where his lungs were found to be infected with pleurisy.

In a few weeks he was judged sufficiently recovered to make the move, and on December 5 he was released from the hospital and taken, with a second batch of prisoners, to board the train for Auburn. Ellen had been belatedly informed of the transfer and departed instantly for Sing Sing, arriving at the prison in a hired carriage just after the prisoners had left: "Is my son going to Auburn?" she asked the warden. "He has gone," was the reply. She was just able to get to the station in time to board the same train as Frank. With her was five-year-old Ruby, who was heard to ask, "Where momma going to-night?" Mother and daughter kept out of the way of the band of convicts who, two by two in handcuffs and leg irons, were being marched through the station. But Ellen did manage to catch a glimpse of Frank, and waved her white handkerchief to him as she boarded the train with Ruby.

While Frank was cuffed to a common criminal named Anderson, a "tough customer" in the estimation of the press, his fellow prisoners also included two newly convicted associates of Mayor Tweed. James Ingersoll and John Farrington had been convicted just a few weeks earlier and seemed crushed by what had happened to them. Ingersoll—who had only been at Sing Sing for a few days—had tried until the last moment to avoid being moved to Auburn, pleading illness. On the train, handcuffed to a wiry watch-thief, he sat with his flannel prisoner's cap pulled low, covering his face with his hand. Reporters who went along for the ride found the millionaire contractor a spectacle of abject misery, as he wept and poured out his troubles: "This is awful—awful . . . I did try hard to keep up my nerve, but I've weakened now. And I've got a family—think of that."

Frank, despite his illness—he acknowledged, clutching his side, feeling "under the weather"—seemed determined to project a mood of stoic endurance, puffing on a cigar and enlarging on his state of mind for the benefit of the newspapermen: "I've been well treated at Sing Sing—I can't complain. About going to Auburn, well, you know I've got to like it and there's no good in grumbling. My friends tell me to keep my courage up. I try to. Sometimes I hope there is daylight ahead. Perhaps I shall see it before the gray hairs get thick, but perhaps—oh, if Governor Dix would only make a little allowance!" He asked about Ellen: "You say you have talked with my mother? Well, you are right. I've got a good mother—yes, sir, a good mother." And here, as if on cue, a train porter entered with a cold supper that his mother had ordered for him at Poughkeepsie: "Why, here she's sent that waiter with some chicken and lunch for me." He asked the reporters to greet his mother for him and tell her to keep her courage up. "But if Judge Davis and General Dix knew what I do, and if it only could have been shown at the right time."

Ellen was also giving an interview to the press as the train headed for Auburn. She had only seen Frank two or three times since his imprisonment, she told them, and had learned of his transfer by sheer accident. She was worried about his health and hoped for the day when he would be restored to his family. (When she got back to Saratoga she would write to Dolly: "He had a great deal to suffer in this last removal, it would make your heart ache if I had time to tell you all as it really was, but he still maintains the same cheerful patience through all.") As for Frank's keepers from Sing Sing, also on the journey, they said they were sorry to lose him. His behavior had been excellent, and they could see him only as "a romantic youth who had no conception of the enormity of his crime."

A large crowd had gathered at the Auburn station. After the train pulled in they followed the prisoners all the way to the prison's imposing gates. Once inside, Frank and the rest were marched through the basement to the mess-room, where one by one their shackles were removed by two thick-bodied blacksmiths armed with sledge hammers and chisels. The din of clanking iron echoed against the stone walls. Then the convicts were permitted to wash their hands and faces in the yard before having their breakfast dished out.

At the end of a row, in the farthest corner, Frank seemed to hold himself apart from the rest. He looked, according to an onlooker, as if it all had nothing to do with him.

THE prison authorities assigned Frank a job as a packer in the cigar-making shop, but it didn't last long. His health—mental as well as physical—continued to worsen, and he was unable to work. He never referred to his father or to the events at the Sturtevant, and some suggested that he had lost all awareness of what had happened. By early February, on the advice of Dr. John Ordronaux, the state commissioner of lunacy, he had been transferred to a post in the prison hospital. It was suggested that he would be able to nurse ailing inmates, even though a reporter from the *New York World* who was allowed to visit him in the hospital noted that "he shrinks from the gaze of strangers with something not unlike physical pain." Indeed, when a reporter attempted to interview him he fled abruptly into an adjoining bathroom.

Dr. Ordronaux and his colleagues implied that the fundamental reason for putting Frank to work in the hospital was to keep a better eye on him. Frank's epilepsy, in the doctors' view, had become aggravated by imprisonment, and he was in danger of a complete mental breakdown. A team of psychiatric professionals had taken an interest in Frank's case, most significantly the much-respected Dr. John Gray. Gray, who had testified on his behalf at the trial, had now become a powerful influence behind the scenes in the campaign to alleviate Frank's incarceration.

Ellen had been in close communication with Gray ever since the trial. She could not have chosen someone better positioned to help her son. Her hope was to get Frank separated from the common prisoners on grounds of mental illness—as a first step toward getting him freed altogether. Little documentation remains of her sustained efforts except for a letter to Dolly in which she asked for help in building a case for hereditary madness: "I want you . . . to write down for me anything and everything you can remember that you did not tell on the trial, to prove that the Walworth family have a crazy streak through them."

Dolly was not to tell anyone that Ellen had asked her for this information, nor was she to mention Dr. Gray's involvement: "Try to think of all you told Dr. Gray but don't mention his name or anything about this except to one you can trust . . . You know there is a good deal about the Chancellor's last weeks, Mrs. Jenkins, Mrs. Platt & others."

No further details have survived about Chancellor Walworth's final days, or of what other hints of the "crazy streak" might have been discernible in the behavior of his oldest daughter Mary Elizabeth Jenkins—who had largely assumed the task of looking after Mansfield following their mother's death—or of the Chancellor's sister Anna Eliza Platt, whose husband was a young midshipman who after surviving West Indian pirates and yellow fever lived out his days horribly maimed and disfigured as a result of an explosion at the Brooklyn Navy Yard, to be survived by his widow for another twenty-three years. The secret history of Walworth madness was written in whispers and rumors, hovering between the lines of the official record.

Iᴛ may have been Dr. Gray who encouraged Frank to continue writing poetry, both as a distraction and as a therapeutic tool. Gray had demonstrated his interest in such methods, having previously established a literary magazine for inmates of the Utica Lunatic Asylum. In June 1874, at any event, Frank began to fill a red-covered notebook with an assortment of lyrics and fragments, translations from Heine, and bad puns excoriating the New York press.

Frank's interests up to this point appear to have been more athletic than literary. But writing poems was not a stretch for him. In his world almost everyone did it, with varying degrees of skill. His maternal grandfather John J. Hardin had wooed Sarah with homely heartfelt verses; his uncle Clarence applied a scholar's care to poems that ranged over theology, American Indian folklore, and the landscape of upstate New York; and his mother could turn out a conventional verse for any occasion, although Frank had probably not seen the poems that Ellen worked on in secret, the outpourings in which she mourned the death of her most intimate hopes.

Frank's poems were certainly an odd mix. He was an amateur, but an amateur with a sophisticated toolbox in hand. The English poets from Spenser and Herrick to Byron and Shelley were kicking around in his head, lending him fragments of form and attitude and phraseology. He took to verse-writing with real enthusiasm, judging from the length of some of his effusions, although of course there was not much else for him in the way of respite from his confinement. His red notebook seems tantalizingly close to disclosing, at last, a real picture of the young man who was now beginning his second year of incarceration. Here, if anywhere, ought to be some trace of the person he imagined himself to be.

That person is hard to find, though, amid the play of quickly changing masks. Writing in isolation, Frank seemed to be performing for an imaginary audience, striking poses of languid sensuality, self-sacrificing love, bitter recrimination at those who had condemned him, cackling caricatural humor at the expense of prudish women or exploitative editors, or morbid gothic terror. If any note predominated, it was of an underlying pride, pride that he could do this, muster these words into stanzaic forms echoing perfectly the anthology pieces he had learned to imitate. He flaunted a sense of self-mastery in the midst of impossible circumstances.

> *Know I am dealt with by no gentle hand:*
> *In bondage, gloomy and alone I stand.*

Many of his poems were addressed to women, responding to gifts and messages from outside. A gaudy sonnet on receiving a bouquet of flowers permitted him to evoke, within prison walls, a compensating sense of suffocating aromatic profusion:

> *The halcyon gift of memory full oft*
>   *Wraps me in bonds musk-sweet with dense perfumes,*
>   *Blown from living censers censed with balmy blooms,*
> *Tuberous lilies of the vale: how soft*
>   *Are clasp'd the downy fetters!*

A romantic rumor had circulated, in the early days of Frank's imprisonment, that the bouquet delivered to him as he was leaving the Tombs came from a young woman from a distinguished southern family who had met Frank in Saratoga. In view of her extreme youth, her parents were said to have taken her on a tour of Europe to discourage the intimacy; she had returned to America just as the news of the murder hit the newspapers, and "has never recovered since, and is to-day a sad, listless, broken-hearted woman." She was said to keep his cell at Sing Sing scented with regular gifts of flowers.

The story was not necessarily unfounded. Frank certainly knew and may very well have formed a close attachment to Governor Bramlette's daughter Corinne—whether during his Kentucky sojourn or on her visits to Saratoga with her family. Corinne could certainly have been the anonymous addressee of most of the poems, and the secret subject of Frank's amorous and sometimes erotic effusions. It may well have been she who wrote the message he transcribed in his notebook: "By the time my ship comes in Frank will be pardoned, when I shall immediately build him a gala castle with a boudoir of pearls and diamonds."

At Saratoga, alone in the middle of the night at Pine Grove, Ellen was sending out her own poetic cry, in a long wail destined for no eyes but her own.

> *O cease! Thou cruel night wind, cease!*
> *The fearful silences within my life*
> *Intenser grow and vaster mid thy strife*
> *That whirls about their stillness; or release*
> *My captive spirit.*

Her sense of isolation grew deeper when in mid-July, after years of slow decline amid the family upheavals, her mother, Sarah, died at Pine Grove. Sarah had just arrived in Saratoga after a visit with Frank at Auburn, and at least one newspaper implied that the visit and its "terrible associations" had been partly responsible for her death.

Ellen's attempts to help Frank proved fruitful, at least to the extent of taking him out of the prison. At the beginning of August, after he had been subjected to a two-hour examination by a team of physicians, it was announced that he would be transferred to Auburn's Asylum for Insane Convicts. The move came after what the medical staff at Auburn described as a precipitous decline in Frank's condition, a revival of epileptic symptoms that might foreshadow much worse to come. His stint as a nurse at the hospital, intended to benefit him, had ended up having the reverse effect; the "sight of sickness and suffering," the *New York Times* reported, had apparently induced "a demented state of melancholia." The *Times* anticipated that this transfer would be followed by further efforts to have Frank moved to a private institution, if he were not to be pardoned altogether.

His change of status did not go unobserved. The *Brooklyn Eagle* decried "the tricky maneuvering of the Walworth family to carry out their boast and effect the release of that remorseless parricide, Frank

Walworth." Some defenders of Frank had argued that he was now utterly harmless and need no longer be confined, but the *World* shot back that if he ever became well enough to be released from the asylum, he should be returned to prison to complete his sentence: "It is altogether too early to begin to talk about a pardon for Frank Walworth. He has not yet been confined half so long as many a poor devil who is sentenced to State prison for appropriating a few dollars' worth of goods from the bounty of a wealthy merchant or banker." Much to the *World*'s indignation, Frank seemed to be comfortably installed at the asylum, "strutting about the yard with a kind of martial cloak around his shoulders."

FRANK had also, according to the papers, been receiving a considerable number of visitors. Ellen came to see him in late August along with Governor Bramlette of Kentucky. The governor was accompanied by his wife and son but not, apparently, by his daughter Corinne. Her absence might be accounted for by a poem Frank had just entered in his notebook, a farewell to an unnamed lover in which he formally broke off all ties: "The last link is broken, / The last tear is shed." The rift was depicted as being sought by him, not her, in acknowledgment of the hopelessness of his situation. He could not count on any end to his confinement, even if (as he made clear) he was far from as mentally incapable as the newspapers had described him.

> Poor wretches surround me,
>   Insane to be free;
> Their voices all round me
>   In sorrow and glee—
> My mind were it failing,
>   Less tortured would be;
> My heart it is ailing,
> Thus severed from thee.

He was not a prisoner for any crime he had committed—he continued to firmly assert his "innocence" and "merit"—but because of the unjust actions of the contemptible democratic hordes: "The herd hath enslaved me, / The pack hath assail'd." He was "belied and degraded," his name "soil'd." It would be better for her to perish than to share his accursed reputation. But it was a long good-bye, going on for many stanzas before the final exhortation: "Farewell, and be brave!"

When his birthday rolled around again on August 17, he observed that in fact he was still nineteen going on twenty, since all the time he had been confined he had been legally dead. He added an abrasive little rhyme—

> *An ode on my birthday the* devil *can't write—*
> *No birthday is mine—I was born in the* night!

—to which he appended, "Which is significant!" Such manic interjections seem at once to mock and to indulge the idea of himself as madman. At this point his odd and mordant sense of humor—apt to bite any target including Frank himself—may have provided a sliver of personal identity to cling to, a sarcasm all his own, like the private smile he had cultivated in the midst of the crowded courtroom.

A letter he wrote to Dolly in September—she seems to have been the only one who took the trouble to preserve one of his prison or asylum letters—was laced with such jests, seemingly meant as much for Frank's amusement as Dolly's: "I take my pen handle between finger and thumb to give you the scribbled information that I am not well and hope that you are not enjoying the same blessing. I received a letter from you some months ago and if you never received an answer to it, it was probably because I never wrote one." He assured Dolly that his health had improved since the move to the Asylum, and the doctors were making favorable noises about his chances for recovery. The letter consisted mostly of messages for his mother: Dolly was asked to tell Ellen "I have seated myself clean through my breeches and that they are barely as thick as a silk handkerchief in any other spot," and to request that she send, by way of reading matter, "any of the standard poets I can get." In a final dark joke, he apologized for the illegibility of his handwriting: "I seldom take pains nowadays—I get enough without an effort."

18

The Maniac's Dream

I F Frank took pains with anything it was with his poetry. The pages of the red notebook filled for a time with increasingly ambitious compositions, culminating in "The Maniac's Dream," whose forty stanzas, judging by the variations in handwriting, evidently took up a good deal of his time. In this poem—"wherein," the subtitle promised, "is an allegory"—Frank secreted as much of his inner life as he ever managed to express, couched in the language of those standard poets whose works he had requested, but struggling against the boundaries of decorum. The allegorical import remained dark, but right from the start a muffled violence reverberated, an aspiration to Byronic magnificence.

> I love all nature, but her night and play
> Of Storms are loveliest her gifts among;
> They are congenial to my humor; they
> Fathom my soul's abyss, where life is strong
> With deep Aeolian chords, o'er which are flung
> Wild melancholy melodies . . .

He reveled in "the war and havoc of the hurricane," in which nature's parts, flung violently against each other like human passions in war, were brought to a destruction that nothing could avert: and of these elements, these "atoms" of the storm, "the first, the last, the deadliest / Are imaged in the secret caverns of my breast."

Yet the storm was "ambrosial nutriment," "grandeur unconfined," an enormous blast of vigor and fresh air for a dying soul. The destructiveness of lightning embodied the energy of life itself, and for a moment Frank's line came alive in a cluster of fraught monosyllables that must have given him surprise and pleasure, a sense of poetic power triumphing over darkness and confinement.

> Forth from the clouds dart fatal tongues that lap
> From the split tree's rent heart the gushing sap.

But this day of storm, described at inordinate length, was but prelude to the night of cursed dreams that followed, as "phantom-forms conversed / In whispers ominous around my bed . . . The dead were living and the living dead." And from the midst of images of shrouds and coffins, skeletons and worms, emerged a vision of erotic promise,

> the matchless figure of a maid
> Of beauty marvelous, and not unknown,
> Sweet to my sense of sight her charms display'd,
> Until ecstatic phrenzies did pervade
> My being to that pitch intense that mars
> All calm.

He knew the girl; she had been the companion of his "blasted youth"; innocent as Eve before the fall, she had soothed and caressed and "taught me bliss." Here Frank allowed himself stanzas of barely restrained sexual anticipation before he was interrupted, or rather interrupted himself, in the very moment of embracing his love, by the grip of an immense rattlesnake crushing his life out.

Still the maiden rushed toward him, oblivious to the snake—he warned her to stand back—until the snake sunk its fangs into her breast: "Lifeless, yet fresh and beautiful she lay, / Death's victim, shrouded in her golden hair—/ Love's martyr unavenged." The dreamer, in despair, wished only that her form might be preserved petrified and immortal, a Bride of Stone.

He woke to find the "nude form" of his beloved not dead but sleeping—"I watched her dream-thoughts play"—and relished keeping vigil over his unprotected love, perfect in sleep as no one could ever be in waking life. Yet to think of the "hallow'd bliss" of sleep was to be reminded of the horror of death—"Sleep's beautiful, Death's hideously foul." On she slept; and, impatient, he thought lecherously of enjoying "the boons voluptuously seen"—and, leaning forward to kiss and embrace her, found that she was indeed "rigid—stark—and cold."

Here again he woke from yet another dream within his dream: he had fallen asleep on a gravestone. He found himself in a moonlit cemetery where he "heard crisp bones / By subterraneous vipers crunch'd." The shock of waking there recalled the memory of her death, the emptiness it brought, the "sleepless awful nights through which I raved and toss'd." He had wandered half sleepwalking ("benumb'd or phrensied") from his bed to the graveyard. It was not in some ethereal heavenly sphere that he wished to join her. He wanted to be with her in the flesh—"preferring for my love / A tangible existence."

At his expression of this wish she rose up, "the same nude form shrouded in golden hair," draped in shadows until the full moon shone on the hideousness of a form eaten by snails and maggots and leeches, tangled in vipers, half-eaten by worms: "And from her eyes, whose luster long had pall'd, / In lieu of pearly tears, two slimy grub-worms crawl'd." It was all a lesson to cure him of lust, to "leave the heart as hollow as the skull." The body crumbled into dust. The dust was a mound in which ants crawled frantically.

And then, at last, he woke once more, this time into the reality of "the maniac's low wailing cry," which swelled to "a hellish yell" and then died out. Moonlight made checkerboard lines on his cell wall and revealed the images hanging there "of her who haunts my dreams." He looked out beyond the asylum walls toward a landscape hidden by darkness, and ended his poem with a hymn of praise to the night in which he was born and to whose worship he was pledged: "Beneath thy ebon sceptre's sway I bow . . . Voluptuous Night, thou art my mistress now!"

It may indeed have been when he lost himself filling the pages of his notebook that Frank felt most grounded. It was not much to be grounded in, those states of half sleep and half waking, scenes of frustrated desire recollected in isolation, moments of silence constantly interrupted by the screams of lunatics. He could only reiterate the drama of the love he had voluntarily cut himself off from, the lover he had renounced when "a righteous mob's erroneous deed / Dishonor'd me most falsely." He longed "to crush / My passions pale on thy lithe form," but was content to know that he had done the right thing by saving her from a hopeless love. Apart from that there was nothing for him to do but to register the simple passage of time, the blank hours to which his life had been reduced. In that blankness he could only testify to a sense of inexorable deterioration.

> *Like an uprooted weed,*
> *My nerves are lapsing—Love and rage are breeding*
> *Disease.*

Gᴏᴠᴇʀɴᴏʀ Dix of New York, approaching the end of his term and in the midst of a reelection campaign, made something of a triumphal tour of the state, inspecting National Guard units and a variety of public institutions. Arriving at Auburn on October 9, he was greeted by an enormous crowd and a twenty-one-gun salute, and after entering the prison grounds—"the portals," a reporter elaborated, "were hung with bunting, and the ponderous gate swung back slowly, as if reluctant to let the pardoning power within them"—he made a full tour of the prison, where at every turn he was approached by prisoners seeking pardons or commutations of their sentences.

Moving on to the asylum, he was introduced to the most celebrated inmates, each of whom, in a manner that recalled some feudal ritual, was permitted a brief conference with the governor. Henrietta Robinson, known as "the Veiled Murderess," was a woman of great beauty and mysterious but evidently respectable origins who, after a scandalous career as a rich man's kept woman in Troy, had been arrested twenty years ago for murder. The crime was unusual—she had been convicted of murdering a saloon keeper, for no apparent motive, by poisoning his beer—and the veil she insisted on wearing at her trial

earned her the evocative nickname which kept her fame alive for decades afterward. After years in Sing Sing Mrs. Robinson was acknowledged to be incurably insane and transferred to the asylum at Auburn,
where she seemed to have settled into a sort of quiescence. She had no
request for the governor, only best wishes for his reelection.

Kate Stoddard, another notorious inmate, was a recent arrival. In
March 1873, in the apartment on DeGraw Street in Brooklyn they
had shared for several years, she killed her lover, Charles Goodrich.
He wanted to break off with her; she shot him three times with one of
his own revolvers and then made herself scarce. "I killed him for love,"
she told the police when they finally caught up with her after three
months on the run, "I couldn't part with him." Kate's capture, with the
help of a wily female detective, had been the next great criminal sensation after the conclusion of Frank's trial. That she might be insane had
been suggested by the way she had washed her lover's body after the
murder, dressed it in clean clothes, and laid it out neatly before leaving
the apartment. When arrested she was found to be wearing a locket
containing dried blood. She ingested it before the police could stop
her, saying it was Charlie's. Eventually investigators located her family
and old acquaintances in Boston—Kate Stoddard was not, it turned
out, her real name—and discovered that her behavior had been decidedly eccentric since puberty. "She seemed to be all imagination," her
mother testified. The reporters who accompanied Governor Dix to
Auburn found that she retained "all the sad beauty which wrought her
misfortune." Shaking the governor's hand, she told him she was as
contented as the circumstances would permit but that time hung heavily on her.

Minnie Davis, another relative newcomer to the women's ward, was
less resigned. Her troubles had started in 1868 with a failed insurance
fraud—she had insured for two thousand dollars a trunk containing
nothing but worthless rags, and then set it on fire—and grown more
acute when she attempted suicide at police headquarters by hanging
herself from a doorknob with a torn towel. Classified as a lunatic, she
had spent the last several years at Auburn, even though she assured
Dix she was not so ill as she had been. Seizing hold of the governor's
hands and transfixing him with her gaze, she pleaded to be released to
care for her aging parents: "Will you let me, sir?" She thanked him

effusively as Dix muttered that he would see what he could do. (When she was let go a few years later, a newspaper described her as "one of the cleverest of New York's clever thieves," and warned citizens to be on the alert.)

Moving on to the men's ward, Dix met briefly with Frank. He had been informed that the prisoner's condition had improved markedly since his admission to the asylum, and Frank agreed that—physically at least—he was much better than he had been. Any hope that the governor's visit might be the prelude to a pardon was quickly dashed. Even though he lost the election in November, Dix did not take advantage of his lame-duck status to make the potentially unpopular decision. To Ellen he communicated privately, in a letter which has not been preserved, the motives for his refusal. "I should be very glad," the governor added in a follow-up letter in early December, "if I could come to a conclusion different from that which I communicated to you: but my duty seemed too clear to leave me in any doubt." He did reassure her, however, that no official action had been taken and that therefore no unfavorable precedent had been established; the new governor, Samuel Tilden, could make a fresh start in considering Frank's case.

About six months after his visit to Frank at Auburn, Governor Bramlette of Kentucky died suddenly in Louisville. His funeral was marred by a disorderly episode that made its way into the newspapers and that cast an embarrassing light on the family's private history.

After the death of Corinne's mother, it appeared, the governor had maintained a mistress, Laura Bell, so flagrantly that at last local outrage had made the situation politically untenable. He was said to have paid her off with ten thousand dollars, money that she put to use by opening a brothel in Cincinnati. Not long thereafter Bramlette had remarried. Evidently the relationship with Bell did not end there, since after the governor's death his widow hired detectives and gave them strict orders not to let her appear at the funeral. Despite their efforts she managed to make her way to the graveside and place a wreath on the coffin to the scandal of onlookers.

It would not be long before Corinne and her stepmother would move out of Kentucky, to renew their old ties with the Hardin and Walworth families in Saratoga Springs.

"Frank Walworth grows stupid." Such, in its entirety, was the notice provided by the *Auburn Daily Bulletin* in March of 1875. The *Watertown Daily Times* echoed the report, describing Frank as "a fat boy, fast losing what mind he may have possessed . . . His prospect now is to die an idiot in an asylum." Some suggested a state verging on catatonic immobility and muteness. Others spoke of violent outbursts. Learning that a sketch artist from the *New York Graphic* had visited Auburn to make some sketches inside the asylum, Frank was said to have become agitated and threatened to make trouble if anyone attempted to draw his portrait.

Ellen continued her campaign, privately circulating the evidence she had amassed to prove Frank innocent by reason of insanity. She found a powerful supporter in William Cullen Bryant, who combined the prestige of a great poet—"Thanatopsis," his ode on reconcilement to death (written when he was a teenager), was a cornerstone of the American canon memorized by schoolchildren across the land—with the immense influence that accrued to him as publisher of the *New York Evening Post*. Now in his eighties, Bryant was one of the gray eminences of the Republican Party, famous for introducing Abraham Lincoln at Cooper Union in 1860, and in a tainted era had managed to stay free from any hint of corruption.

Bryant told Ellen that he fully sympathized with her attempts not only to free Frank but to remove the stigma of criminality from his name, and that he had sent Governor Tilden a letter to the same effect. Bryant wrote to Tilden: "If a jury were now to pass upon the evidence in the case, I think they would acquit the accused . . . He was not accountable for his acts, is therefore not a proper subject for criminal punishment, and was not such at the time of his conviction." Tilden, however, was not disposed to give way. He let it be known that he found the argument for a pardon based on Frank's deteriorating condition unconvincing; the life sentence Frank had received meant just that. The law intended him to die in confinement.

Tilden, riding high after his public triumph over the Tweed ring, was already contemplating a run for the presidency, and doubtless did not relish the prospect of being saddled with the charge of setting free a parricide. Most of the New York papers continued to present the story as one of a privileged family using any means to rescue their scion from the consequences of an unspeakable deed. Some depicted Ellen as nearly maniacal in her relentlessness: "A lady of powerful magnetic attraction, and versed in all the accomplishments of society, she has found no difficulty in drawing to her side the sympathies of all with whom she has come in contact . . . From the meanest attachee of the asylum or prison, to the highest functionary of either—and even to the most powerful minds in the State government—all seem to surrender their convictions and become enlisted on the side of the suffering woman."

Seen in that light, Ellen might have passed for one of the heroines of the wildly popular sensation novels, a Lady Audley or Lydia Gwilt, possessed of mesmeric powers and bent on subverting society to her own purposes. Her campaign seemed sinister because it was directed not to the public—she showed little interest in persuading mass opinion that Frank had suffered an injustice—but to the inner precincts of power. The campaign was in fact working, as she won over an ever longer list of well-placed allies in the legal and medical fields. The medical testimony—emanating chiefly from Dr. John Gray—was beginning to influence the opinions expressed in newspapers: "That the boy was epileptic from childhood is plain. That he shot his father . . . in a sudden access of fear, seems probable." In July 1876 Tilden appointed Gray and Judge William Bacon to visit Frank at Auburn and perform tests to determine his mental state. Each examined him separately, and submitted a confidential report to the governor.

No action was forthcoming. "The victim of mental malady," complained the *Albany Evening Times*, "still suffers like a felon in the hard clutch of inexorable law . . . While the iron which has entered the soul of Frank Walworth is killing him, so too, slowly and surely, the vitality of others that cannot avoid the blighting influence of his most unrighteous sentence is growing exhausted." Dr. Gray complained repeatedly in private that Frank should never have been sent to prison and that his defense had been bungled by O'Conor. As Tilden accepted the Democratic presidential nomination, he was content to hand over responsibility of the case to his successor.

DELIVERING Frank from bondage may have been at the heart of Ellen's concerns, but it was far from consuming all her time. In fact she had never been caught up in so many different enterprises. She was transforming herself into a public personage, constantly finding new causes to promote and new organizations to head up. She had taken over her mother's role in the Mount Vernon association, making her first public speech on behalf of the association's plans for the American centennial celebrations of 1876. The speech became a stirring evocation of the family as the spiritual center from which American life radiated. In view of her own domestic history, it was an optimistic leap: "To no people on earth is home more essential and more sacred than to the American people ... The principles, the habits and the tastes that are acquired and confirmed there, around the breakfast table, in the parlor, sitting-room or kitchen, where the evening hours are spent; the unpremeditated actions and talk of the every-day life, direct and establish the energy, the soul, the heart, of this republic." In the home, she added, woman enjoyed a domain in which she could dominate: "Here we are Presidents, legislators and judges, and as we administer, so will our kingdom flourish."

She had a flair for organizing, and by all accounts a will to lead, that found an outlet in a growing number of clubs and associations, most of which she founded: the Women's Centennial Banner Movement, the Society for Decorative Arts, the Art and Science Field Club of Saratoga Springs, the Cooking Club, the Shakespeare Club. The list of her memberships and honorary titles was beginning to rival the late Chancellor's. Nelly and Clarence had come back from their trip around the world, and Ellen involved herself in the editing and marketing of the travel book created out of Nelly's letters home. Ellen's multiple commitments often kept her away from home—Washington and New York City drew her with their promise of a wider field of action—and in June 1877 her daughter Clara, home for the summer from the convent school at Kenwood, wrote to her plaintively: "When are you coming home? This year?"

In addition to everything else, Ellen had a book of her own in hand as well, a monograph on Burgoyne's defeat at Saratoga in September 1777, accompanied by a visitors' guide to the hotels and pastimes of Saratoga Springs, an outgrowth of her long involvement in the preservation of the battlefield and the campaign to erect a monument there. This business of the Battle of Saratoga was no sideshow or pastime for Ellen but a central concern. She had been engaged with the theme for years and would continue to be for years more. To some degree it was a matter of filial piety, enabling her to pay tribute to her great-grandfather for his heroic service at Saratoga under the command of General Gates, and to recall in passing her father's death in the Mexican War; it was also an opportunity to establish herself as a historian, an administrator, and a woman who had managed to achieve eminence among an otherwise all-male set of political worthies.

In the details of the battle she could happily lose herself. It was a serenely untainted victory, in which even the enemy commander, General Burgoyne, was endowed with "honor" and "calmness" and "quiet dignity." To re-create the actions of the battle was to savor the working-out of a happy destiny, in which suffering and stoic endurance were rewarded by tremendous breakthroughs, evoked by Ellen in the language of Scott's and Cooper's historical romances.

> As the great Hudson, when suddenly loosened from his winter chains of ice, rushes with resistless force over all obstructions, so from their restraining earthworks the impetuous Americans poured furiously upon their adversaries in the front.

And in Benedict Arnold, the hero of the day, Ellen might almost have found an analogue of her late husband, a disgraced figure remembered for the fire and inspiration he had once radiated.

> The genius of war thrilled Arnold's soul, as epic metres stir the poet, as rugged landscapes, shadowed under sunset lights, influence the artist's brain. Genius ever lives and conquers! It may be desecrated and destroyed, as Arnold buried his in ignominy; but while it lives and inspires its own peculiar work, it rules and is supreme.

The epic of American history represented a reality superior to the painful present. It was a parallel world where one could dwell eternally in the reenactment of admirable acts ideally executed.

ELLEN'S *Saratoga* was published in the summer of 1877 to the expected local acclaim ("worthy ... authoritative"), more or less in tandem with Nelly's *An Old World Seen Through New Eyes*, which likewise drew praise for its "charm" and "freshness" and earned Nelly a description in a national newspaper as "an impressionable and singularly brilliant girl of fourteen." The family's celebration of these forays into authorship was prelude to happier news. At the beginning of August the new governor, Lucius Robinson—an old Democratic Party hand who as a lawyer in chancery had served before the Chancellor for a number of years—announced an unconditional pardon for Frank.

The lengthy statement in which Robinson justified his action took as its sonorous text this proposition: "The law is majestic in that it is never revengeful and always just." Frank's conviction had been legally proper but morally unjust. Condemned by the letter of the law, he had yet been wronged, an intolerable contradiction. Only by the power of executive pardon could that imbalance be righted and the community absolved from guilt for his persecution.

The governor rehearsed Frank's story much as his lawyers had: he had been "a quiet, well-behaved child, marked mainly, then as now, by an affectionate devotion to his mother." The citizens of Saratoga "testify with enthusiasm to the blameless purity of his entire life up to the very day of the fatal encounter with his father." The epilepsy from which he had suffered since childhood predisposed him toward mental paroxysms, and thus, on becoming aware of the brutal actions of Mansfield toward Ellen, he "from that moment shared with her the insane hatred of the father." Robinson implied, as had a number of newspapers, that Mansfield had done and threatened far worse even than had been reported at the trial, leaving no doubt as to "the sincerity of his deadly intent." By the time father and son were alone together at the Sturtevant—Frank suffering from a morbid mental condition and not even having had a proper night's sleep, and his father greeting him (as the governor presumed on the basis of past actions) with "looks or words of hatred" and, quite possibly, a real intent to do harm—the outcome was inevitable.

In fact Mansfield was the author of his own murder. Frank's enfeebled and terror-stricken mental and physical state had been altogether shaped by his father's behavior: "The act was as thoroughly the result of Mansfield Walworth's own passionate conduct as if he had himself discharged the fatal shot." As to the final significance of what had happened, Robinson gave the last word to William Cullen Bryant: "The meeting between the father and the son would be regarded as an encounter between two insane persons, in which one of them was slain."

In any case, between epilepsy and imprisonment, Frank had been sufficiently punished. His condition had grown steadily worse. Anything further would be mere vengeance on society's part. Further detention—medical authorities assured the governor—would result in "complete idiocy," while there remained an outside chance that "immediate change of scene and air" might bring some improvement. Newspapers speculated that Frank would be whisked off to Europe and never heard from again.

The governor's action occasioned a few parting shots. "The public, as a whole," remarked the *Brooklyn Eagle*, "will acquiesce in rather than approve of the pardon." The *Eagle* predicted that the supposedly deteriorated Frank could now be expected to make a rapid recovery: "It is the rule in such cases." The *Auburn Morning News* speculated that if Frank had been stricken with a terrible malady it was as punishment for what he had done. The *Rochester Union* detected the pressure of "influential friends," while continuing to argue that "this slayer of his father should be allowed to end his days, and the sooner the better, shut out from the eyes of the world."

ON August 1 Ellen and Tracy arrived in Auburn on the evening train and took a hack to the asylum. There they picked up a silent Frank— his long hair falling over his shoulders, his face pale and haggard—and headed for the depot. It took them three separate trains and an all-night journey to get home. Clarence and other family members and friends—including Governor Bramlette's widow and her stepdaughter Corinne—had gathered at Pine Grove to greet them. Flowers and congratulatory notes poured in. A sympathetic reporter in Saratoga wrote glowingly of the reunion: "The keen joy the household have known since the happy return, words are inadequate to describe. They tell me that yesterday they all were fairly delirious with delight, the servants sympathized and the very dog shared in the prevalent excitement . . . Here, where she came a stranger and where her husband's family had always lived, and where the true history of her married life is most fully known, Mrs. Ellen Hardin Walworth is appreciated in all the beauty of her womanly purity and maternal devotion . . . A higher courage than that which animated her father on battle-fields has sustained her through the cruel trials of near a quarter of a century. Looking at her still handsome face, through all its gentle expression, one sees the strength which comes only through patient suffering."

TEN weeks later the cornerstone of the Saratoga Monument was laid. A procession two miles long—"the most splendid civic, Masonic and military pageant ever witnessed in Northern New York"—wound from the village to the battlefield. Speeches, songs, and poems were presented, along with a letter written by Ellen for the occasion. A copy of her *Visitor's Guide* was deposited within the cornerstone. That night, after a grand banquet, a "brilliant military spectacle" reenacted the surrender of Burgoyne.

THE newspapers had almost done with Frank, but for a while they looked in occasionally. In January 1878, some five months after his release, it was reported that he was living quietly at home at Pine Grove. He had put on some weight and seemed more cheerful. He spent most of his time playing billiards.

19

~~~~~~~~

Ellen's Book

FRANK came home. But who, after what he had done and where he had been, was Frank? It was hard indeed not to wonder who he had ever been.

Who, for that matter, was Ellen? Years later she still asked herself the question. On a melancholy day nearly on the brink of the next century, she would be sitting at Pine Grove making a list of years, arranged out of order, trying to make sense of the story her life had become. Among the entries was this: "1877: The year in which hope once more arose on the return of my son." She did not write down how long the hope persisted.

Frank went in search of what he could retrieve from his past. Within a couple of weeks of his homecoming he undertook a trip to New York City as a free man. He went on to Swampscott, Massachusetts, to stay with his old Saratoga friend Wally Barbour, now married, the same Wally Barbour who had testified at the trial about Frank's troubled sleep and about the curious incident in which for no apparent reason he had knocked down their mutual friend Charles Pond.

During the Massachusetts trip Frank consorted with various Walworth cousins and made a tour of the Cambridge area, looking in at the Agassiz Museum and the Longfellow homestead—"a very fine old spacious mansion"—and sent word that he was enjoying himself. He was worrying about some letters he had sent—presumably from the Auburn asylum—to a family friend, but to the wrong address: "I suppose they have gone to the Dead Letter Office. If they have, I hope they have been utterly annihilated." He wrote his mother that he would be back the next Saturday, but also told her: "You need not be uneasy if I fail to arrive. My movements are sometimes uncertain." He did return, however, and thereafter Pine Grove would remain his base.

AT a Mardi Gras celebration at the Walworth Academy the following spring, Frank read a poem (now lost) called "The Angel of Sorrow," and gave a talk (its text also lost) about how it came to be written. One of his sisters played Gottschalk's piano piece "A Last Hope." He had returned to his legal studies, and within the year obtained his license.

The next summer a Saratoga correspondent from the *Boston Globe* gave the paper's readers an update on Frank's condition: "He has not a single feature or trait of character that would indicate that he was a parricide. His health is poor . . . He is tall, fair and manly in bearing; but he has an inexpressibly sad, preoccupied expression. He is, of course, isolated from society. On his exit from prison his former friends cut him, and his proud spirit felt it keenly." The reporter added that Frank's mother "has been very busy with her literary work on art and science . . . She is a beautiful woman on the brink of fifty; but, despite her sorrows, she looks ten years younger." The talk was that she would soon sell Pine Grove and take Frank and her other children off to some corner of Europe that carried no reminders of past unhappiness.

Ellen was indeed busy with her work, with her school, her science club, her cooking club, her Shakespeare club. She was worried about Frank and what was to become of him. She worried about all her children, as she nursed Nelly, Tracy, and Ruby through one illness after another. A new fear emerged about the dark and serious Clara: now nineteen, the girl was becoming preoccupied with religion. "Must be watchful," Ellen wrote to herself, "the hereditary streak of fanaticism may do mischief."

She was already unhappy about the close bond that Clara's older sister Nelly had formed with her uncle Clarence during their trip around the world. Since their return it had become clear that Nelly regarded him with a nearly filial obedience; she would remain attached to him thereafter as unofficial secretary and research assistant. Now Ellen watched as Clara too gravitated toward Clarence's influence. It was to Clarence that Clara poured out her intimations that God had chosen her for a religious vocation.

Eʟʟᴇɴ did not sell the house, and she did not take the children to Europe. Instead she put her Saratoga life, and the life of her family, in a state of suspension; leaving the household in the care of Dolly and the servants, she went off on an extended journey into the country of her past. She had decided to write a biography of her father. An extraordinary awakening had taken place in her since Frank's return. What she had experienced until now had been prelude: "I have dreamed, I have felt, I have suffered all these years of my life—now I must begin to think and to act."

To mark the divide she wrote her own epitaph: "Here lies one who found Happiness through suffering."

Within herself she rehearsed the realities of this new life. Only now could she write how incredibly difficult it was to struggle on with barely enough money, to respond to constant demands made on her by children and others, to digest endless failure and humiliation and still continue. The worst was to think that life would always be like this. The burden would never lift. Not that she wanted to shut herself off from her family. The door was always open. If they needed her, they only had to knock.

But really she would rather be alone, reading, immersing herself in the books with which she surrounded herself but never had time to read. She wanted to make progress toward a goal she could barely describe: "a supreme object rises now repeatedly, though vaguely, before me." It had to do with creating order out of what had been the chaos of her life. She was like a child who had to begin with the most rudimentary steps. She could do this if she did not let her feelings—the feelings connected with what had happened in the past—get the better of her. She must control herself, her thoughts, her fancies. She made lists of what she needed: organization, discipline, dignity, accuracy, balance. The modern world called for tolerance and freedom; despite herself she began to acknowledge the need for authority and enforceable standards.

She fought inwardly. She must not be too lenient to herself. Only facts could save her, and conscientious application to details. The struggle was constant. "I have been suffering sharply from the old pain." "The way looks dark and perplexing before me." No one would ever understand the strain and anxiety it cost just to keep things running smoothly around her.

But she felt that she was breaking free. She sat in her room at Pine Grove, "crowded full of terrible memories but now quiet and peaceful as the dead who once filled it." All of life until this moment had been the anticipation of a freedom always just out of reach. She had always been on the verge of permitting herself to shut out petty anxieties and become detached from everything except the high place she called the intellectual life. Arriving in Chicago, she exulted, "Oh! for freedom, freedom!" Life was beginning. "My spirit trembles yet with its unuttered throes . . . I say goodnight to my own restless spirit that thrills and throbs with reawakened life."

CLARA accompanied her for the first part of the trip, a short stay with her brother Martin in Chicago. Then, heading south, Ellen revisited her childhood home in Jacksonville, looked up what was left of the Hardin clan in Illinois and Kentucky, and spent time with her dearest of old friends, Mary Duncan, now married and living in Iowa. But as the journey went on she felt less fulfilled. She wondered why she felt so separated from everyone she met, not superior to them but merely different in some fundamental way: "It is a fact that I must learn to admit and act upon without allowing it to render me supercilious or cold."

She found herself chiefly appreciating silence and solitude and "entering into the existence of nature and becoming identified with her." But such moments were hard to attain. She felt tired, numb, torpid. The old events returned unbidden: "Memory only is awake, telling her story over and over, repeating the hours, rehearsing the words, reviewing the sensations of the past." She wondered why, tender and caring as she was, people found her cold and indifferent. Even her children could not grasp her love for them. "Let me only strive with a calm and free spirit and all will be well." As for the planned biography, she decided after spending time with her relatives that it would "be wise to let the life of the Hardins rest until some of the family are gone to rest."

She did not get back to Saratoga until May. Within a week she was caught up in organizing the floral exhibition for Decoration Day. By June—as the anniversary of Mansfield's death and Frank's arrest came round—she was plunging into depression: "The shadows approach." "Raining & headache." "Tired—memories." "Tired—soul & body."

FRANK now enjoyed regularly the company of Corinne Bramlette. He took up archery—founding a local society, the Saratoga Bowmen— and in a remarkably short time distinguished himself as a champion. "It is doubtful," wrote the sporting publication *Forest and Stream*, "if his equal can be found in America. This is admirable work." At the national archery tournament in the summer of 1881, in Brooklyn's Prospect Park, he took first prize. Privileged to select his own award, he chose—in addition to an expensive set of bow and arrows—a silk top hat.

The dark poetic rhapsodies of the asylum were now replaced by technical observations on the art of archery: "*The aim should be perfected at a full draw . . .* the pile should be distinctly seen and noted— shifted if need be—in its relative position to the gold and the axis of the aiming eye by the indirect vision." Success in archery, he opined— like success at chess or whist or billiards—came not so much to those who practiced constantly or were naturally gifted but to "him who cares to bring his intelligence to bear upon his pastimes." He had taken up the new pastime of bicycling as well, becoming a charter member of Saratoga's bicycle club and contributing articles to the journals *Bicycling World* and *American Wheelman*.

All in all, it looked as if he was becoming the sort of person he might have been if his life had not been interrupted. Perhaps—it was just possible—he had never stopped being that person. When Frank was admitted to the New York bar in May of the same year, the *National Police Gazette* took the opportunity to run a story about a gardener at Auburn asylum, a frequent companion of Frank during his confinement there, who would reply only with a smile and wink when asked about how crazy the famous parricide had really been.

In an undated photograph in which he posed with Tracy at Pine Grove, he looked gaunt and haunted, a stranger in his own surroundings.

To her diary Ellen continued to confide her need for "freedom for books, freedom for writing, freedom from the self-sacrifice, the constant denial of the literature that I need and desire." She was trapped by the rounds of housekeeping and school administration, the physical and mental troubles of the children, the social rituals that were meaningless to her but from which she could not extricate herself. At the same time she kept adding to those demands. She traveled to Boston to address the American Association for the Advancement of Science on the importance of amateur fieldwork. She allowed herself to be persuaded to run, along with two other women, for Saratoga's board of education—the first women to make such a challenge. When their ticket was elected in October 1880, it caused "quite a ripple of excitement," a harbinger of further ripples to come.

Secretly she was bent on one primary object: the novel she had been drafting since the summer, *Judith Holingsworth*. It was to be a book in which she could create an idealized version of her own experience: "the life of a noble woman who makes the best of the vicissitudes that encompass her." Her protagonist would be a woman "of fine natural powers . . . yet a delicate organism, or rather sensitive—impulsive, passionate, yet self contained because reserved . . . She is adrift; her husband is insane, she can do nothing for him."

There was another man in the novel, someone with whom she had frequent conversations on general topics. Harry was noble-minded and intellectually vigorous. But here it became unclear to her where the story line should go: "She finds she is abandoning her own will, drifting into principles of action that she does not approve . . . Here is a mental struggle. Shall this be an unlawful love which she resists." Apparently not. Harry would find his "relief and satisfaction" in work alone, as would Ellen's heroine, Judith. It was the only place in all her private papers that Ellen would allude even to the possibility of another man in her life.

Through the autumn months she kept a record of her daily work on the manuscript, despite the demands of the school board and of her children; no sooner had Tracy recovered from a bout of illness than little Ruby became desperately sick. In her few private hours Ellen worried about style and structure. Looking for a literary model, she read George Eliot's new novel *Daniel Deronda*. Just before Christmas she finished her book and sent off the manuscript to a publisher. She had given it a new title, a description of her own life: *Self-Made*. She gave it a dedication, too, but then suppressed it: "*This work is a wreath of autumn leaves laid on the grave of one whose love knew no consummation.*" Two months later the manuscript was returned as unpublishable. She did not preserve it among her papers but expressed no regrets: "It is a satisfaction to have written the novel though it has proved a failure."

She was reviewing her life, marking in her journal the crucial years: "1851—a new life began, a revolution in the transition . . . from Illinois to New York—followed closely by the change from girlhood to matron. 1861—Another transition. A revolution in the change from New York to Kentucky, from the dependent wife and daughter to the isolated woman with her little children. 1871—After ten years of peace, of struggles, of agonies, of experiments, a change and a revolution in the return to the New York Homestead and the determination to remain at all hazards as a proper refuge for the children." Another crisis was approaching, she felt: "There must be a change."

Some things, she felt, had already changed. She had made progress in achieving a more tranquil and intellectually focused life for herself. In the process she had left behind her earlier religious beliefs, Catholic or otherwise: "Gradually and finally effectually and for years I have discarded all those beliefs of the past, and have been safer and happier and more peaceful ever since." She would have gone public with this loss of faith except for the children: "I had enlisted my little army under a religious flag . . . therefore, I would not endeavor to strip my children of this belief to which I had subjected them."

ELLEN'S public life had become stormy. There had been controversy from the moment she assumed her position on the school board. With her two female associates—viewed as little more than her lieutenants— she brought a critical approach to public education in Saratoga Springs. She wanted the curriculum broadened and modernized, and made no secret of her contempt for the backwardness and cronyism of the town's educational establishment. Angry letters protested the female board members' "constant attempts at revolutionary measures, in the introduction of new and wholly experimental methods, new laws and regulations, new textbooks, new organizations . . . These female novices have seemed to ignore all wisdom superior to their own . . . They have assumed to dictate, manage and control as their own sweet wills have prompted them." When Ellen made an effort to get the sensational novels of Wilkie Collins (notorious for their themes of adultery and illegitimacy) removed from the public library, the *Saratoga Eagle* remarked caustically that perhaps they ought to be replaced by the works of Mansfield Tracy Walworth.

She worried about what Frank would do with himself. "Would it be well for him to drift along in this slow community?" Perhaps he should move away from Saratoga to find some more active and energetic career. Her other children's prospects seemed equally uncertain. It was hard to imagine them standing up for themselves in the world. They were prey to sickness and nervousness. Tracy had gone off to Union College but had repeatedly shown signs of the kind of mental troubles with which Ellen was too familiar. Through Ellen's efforts he had been enrolled in the Georgetown Medical School, and she could only hope that the work would have a therapeutic effect. Nelly and Ruby had both been persistently unwell. Ellen herself succumbed in the autumn of 1881 to a severe bout of typhoid fever. Lying in bed, she contemplated her status as "head of a house without means—a scepter without power."

While she recuperated, Frank read her the newspaper accounts of President James Garfield's shooting by an apparently deranged office seeker. The president would linger on for months in terrible pain before dying. At the trial of his assassin, Charles Guiteau, a familiar figure came to the fore: Dr. John Gray, who had played so influential a role in getting Frank out of prison and ultimately pardoned, would testify for the government on the prisoner's mental condition. The assassination shocked Ellen profoundly, but, she cautioned herself, "I must not allow myself to drift, and must hold command of the circumstances of my own life." Remarkably, considering all that had occurred previously, the year 1881 had been for her "perhaps, the most trying year of my life."

IN late November, following a stay with Clarence in Albany, Clara left home without any warning, declaring her intention to become a nun. "She had a theory," her mother commented, "she would practice it." For Ellen, Clara's defection was as bad as anything that had come before—"there is no language to express supreme agony"—and the memory of her old troubles swept over her again as she went in search of her daughter. She was able to bring Clara back home—in fact she was too young to take the veil without her mother's consent—but it was like bringing back a captured fugitive. "She is here bodily—her spirit wanders, her heart is astray, her conscience perverted."

Ellen had lashed out at what she saw as Clara's ingratitude, but as she studied her daughter's behavior she decided that her intention— "inspired apparently by the noblest motives"—sprang rather from mental imbalance and suggestibility. It was Clarence and the sisters of the Sacred Heart at Kenwood that Ellen now perceived as the forces conspiring to lure Clara into "intellectual slavery." In her journal Ellen reviewed the history of her own conversion: "I see the follies of my own youth not only repeated but multiplied a thousand fold . . . It is too horrible to contemplate."

As winter came on, Ellen's state of mind darkened. She had sacrificed everything for her children, had built up a life in the Saratoga community to protect them and give them an identity. It was not from any worldly vanity that she had created for herself the prominence and unimpeachable respectability that she enjoyed in Saratoga. None of that meant anything—least of all Saratoga itself, to whose narrow parochialism and petty fashionableness she had never really warmed. The purpose was to defend her family, to shore up a social position from which they could not easily be dislodged.

But, whether disdainful or ashamed or simply incapable of mixing in, the children kept themselves apart from that world. They began to seem like voluntary outcasts, a family of strangers pent up in their antique dwelling. Perhaps they sensed that on the outside—in the ever more touristy and modernized place that Saratoga was becoming— they would always be exhibits to be whispered about, characters in an unforgettably grotesque public drama. Ellen had given her children freedom—"as long as they kept within certain large boundaries"—to develop as they wished, only to find they lacked the spirit of enterprise.

To herself she scarcely bothered to disguise her disappointment in them: "When we labor for others we cannot tell what the harvest may be." She determined therefore that she would cease trying to govern the household. She would resign herself to being her children's agent and (if they required) friend, but the older ones would now be permitted to direct their own lives. "How will it be with them when all the barriers are down? For me it can make little difference because the anxiety and solitude continue and must follow me always."

She undertook to purchase herself a plot in Greenridge Cemetery. She found the thought comforting. Death was a matter of indifference to her, but she had always liked the idea of having a place of her own: "I think the desire to have a fixed place of burial arises from the strong home sentiment which pervades my being."

ONE night in early January Frank disappeared. Ellen knew nothing of where he had gone, and walked out into a winter storm trying to learn his whereabouts—"the mental anguish annihilated the physical discomfort." He showed up in the middle of the next day, apparently none the worse for wear; he had gone to Albany without telling anyone. She was shocked at how much she had allowed herself to suffer during his absence. She had deluded herself that she had "reached a stage of self control or of harness," only to find the horrors of the past always lurking. She sifted through the Walworth family papers, "stirring up the old miseries which have been dead for years. It is well. They must be over-hauled some time."

In her journal she wrote little about Frank beyond the most superficial notations of his comings and goings. She worried but did not quite spell out her worries: whether he would "throw his interest, his energy, his talent into good and useful channels—this is still an open and anxious question. I hope for the best but am on the rack."

She ventured not a hint about what either might have felt about the other. He had killed for her. Did he harbor the belief that she had sent him, however tacitly, on his mission of death? Might she have done so, if only by a gesture or a glance or a tone of voice? Did he think she ought to show some gratitude for the sacrifice he had made to free her from an intolerable situation? Did she feel, or could she acknowledge, such gratitude?

Or were there moments when she feared the young man she lived with, who had so decisively demonstrated his capacity for sudden violence? Did she even recognize him fully, after what prison and asylum had done to him? Not just the physical effects—although his lungs had never been the same—but the unspeakable knowledge he had acquired? How much of all that he had seen and heard about and undergone did he ever relate to her? Did she ask?

The world of pain and madness that Frank had inhabited was erased from speech and recollection. Likewise no more was heard about epilepsy. The trances, the midnight screams, the fits of pallor and paralysis—if any of those symptoms, of which so much had been made, persisted, not a trace found its way into Ellen's private jottings.

CLARA remained reluctantly at home. Her mother studied her, disturbed to find her behavior transformed in every way—corroded, cramped, paralyzed—by the action of fanatic religiosity. Ellen herself, in her twenties, had used one religion as a form of leverage to escape from another, and thereby assert her independence, but now she blamed herself for leading her children along the same path. If religions were pernicious, Catholicism seemed the worst of all. "What is this religion that turns right into wrong?"

As Ellen looked back on Clara's ancestry, considering once again the characters of Sarah Hardin and Maria Walworth and of Maria's sons Clarence and Mansfield, she detected a fatal predisposition now being realized in the third generation. "The Puritanism of one grandmother, the Calvinism of another; the crazy enthusiasm of an uncle—the mad capers of a father—all these things boiled down, in a slim, sensitive, morbidly conscientious girl. Alas! What could have prepared more effectually for a medieval nun in the last half of the nineteenth century?"

The certainties of religious believers—"the superstitions and the slaveries of the past with its myths and its mysticism"—were like the certainties of children and the unlettered. Ellen no longer needed such pieties: "Sharp sorrow and practical trouble taught me their worthlessness." She respected scientific knowledge and political power. She wanted a world of clarity and sanity, a rational order from which her children seemed determined to retreat.

Clara told her mother that at a certain moment, three years ago, she had received a direct message from God. She was to live a life of perfection. Was this to atone for Frank's sin? Or in recompense for his liberation, fulfilling some vow she had made at the time of his trial? Stories to that effect worked their way slowly into accounts of the family.

For Ellen, it was Clarence who now clearly emerged as the force manipulating her daughter. Clara was his tool, his victim. Her mind had been "clouded and twisted" by "a man who has known no law but his own wishes." How deliberately he had set about sequestering her from family and friends—even from other priests who might counsel her differently—and had fostered her belief in her divine call, which for Ellen amounted to no more than "unconsciously concealed self-love . . . What madness! What delusion!" Clara was physically weak, high-strung, overimaginative, afflicted by terrors of conscience, and Clarence had played expertly on her "rapt and nervous state."

He had so successfully isolated her that even now, restored for the time being to her family, she was utterly alone; yet not alone at all, for it was Clarence's will, Clarence's thoughts that guided her at every instant. Invisible, the priest was everywhere. Had he not always been the underlying controlling power within the Walworth family, overseeing their destinies with almost demonic energy cloaked by a mask of benevolence? "He will dare to say that he did not advise this! Yet he told her over and over again that to doubt was to have no vocation." Her daughter was to be condemned to a life of meaningless drudgery, sweeping cells or making puddings for the glory of God; and this by the same man who had with such spiderlike patience brought all the rest of them—Ellen, Mansfield, Sarah, Martin, Lemuel, Dolly—into the church.

Clarence's tactics were psychologically acute and quite merciless. Before Clara had run away to Kenwood last fall, he had kept her in his house for a week: ostensibly a guest, but subjected to a subtle campaign of influence. He had poisoned her mind with criticisms of her family— of her mother—as trivial and materialistic, all so as to encourage her not to listen to anyone's advice. He had pushed her to the edge and helped her make her escape, "running from home like a vagabond." Ellen felt that finally she saw Clarence plain. "He is known," she acknowledged, "to be at times of unsound mind."

Clara proposed a compromise. She would stay at home for at least three months. She would for the time being give up her plan of entering the convent. She would submit herself to the care of a physician. She would also, however, attend Mass every morning.

Dr. John Gray had been much in the newspapers during the trial of Charles Guiteau. He had argued confidently and at length that Guiteau was indeed sane, sane enough to try to pass himself off as insane, even as the defendant shouted out from the sidelines: "You are talking about cranks! Talk about Abraham and the thirty-eight cases in the Bible where God Almighty directed people to kill!" The trial ended in March; although many in the audience were unconvinced by Gray's arguments, Guiteau was sentenced to death.

When Gray got back to his home in Washington, he was confronted in his study by a tall intruder armed with a revolver, who without hesitation shot him in the face. Gray survived the attack, although with aftereffects that were ruinous and would lead to his death within a few years. His would-be assassin turned himself in to the police later in the day, surrendering to them a pistol, a revolver, a dagger, a bottle of chloroform, and thirty bundles of cartridges. He turned out to be the swimming instructor of Dr. Gray's children. A Civil War veteran who was currently working in the Turkish bath of a Washington hotel, he had for the past eighteen months entertained the idea that "he was an ambassador from heaven to shoot Dr. Gray." He expressed "insane joy" at having succeeded in his mission.

In the Walworth household there were more long months of illness, first Clara and then Ellen. Nelly was off on an extended trip with Clarence, touring the Onondaga reservation upstate to assist her uncle with his researches into the religious history of seventeenth-century Mohawk converts.

In the fall Ellen stepped down from her position on the school board, delivering a farewell speech to her students in which she spoke of how much she had enjoyed her work, "notwithstanding the days and months when I have been misunderstood and misinterpreted, when I have been regarded as a quarrelsome old lady." She described sleepless nights when she had wept and prayed on their behalf.

Frank announced that he and Corinne Bramlette would marry. On December 20, 1883—dragging herself out of bed after nearly a month of illness—Ellen went off to the wedding. Returning to Pine Grove, she prepared the house for a reception in two days' time, after bride and groom got back from a two-day sojourn in Albany. Tracy and Ruby presided at the reception table, cutting the wedding cake late in the evening under "a splendid oil portrait" of Governor Bramlette, and flanked by a silver tea set donated by the citizens of Frankfort, Kentucky. Frank and Corinne departed for New York City, where they intended to take up residence and where Frank proposed to practice law.

A few days later Clara left home for good, heading up to Kenwood to become a novitiate of the Order of the Sacred Heart. Months passed before Ellen saw her again. Finally in early March—forcing herself again from a sickbed—she left for Kenwood in the middle of a winter storm to make a final plea to "this deluded child." It was a dreary day: "I am used to suffering but I can count on the fingers of one hand the days that have contained such hours of pain." After climbing the slippery hill to the convent, she sent word to Clara by the female gatekeeper. Clara seemed contented, Ellen was forced to admit, even if thinner. But Ellen found herself scolding her like a child: "I set before her as forcibly as I could some of the consequences of the step she is taking, nor did I disguise from her something of the suffering she inflicts upon me . . . Yet she remained immoveable."

They stayed in the room together until dark. After a time the mother superior—"the typical Jesuit, adroit, amiable, clever and agreeable"—took Ellen aside for a confidential conversation, saying that she would be happy to order Clara to go home and defer her vows until she was older if only Ellen would agree to drop her opposition. Ellen remained silent. She wanted more time. In the end Clara stayed at Kenwood.

Ellen told herself that finally it did not matter. "My own course is simple enough under all circumstances, work and endure, to the best of my ability and strength, and whatever the result may be the work and patience are a gain in self-discipline at least." There was plenty of work. Ruby—a promising student, keen on poetry and art—was at Vassar now, while Tracy came back from medical school in the spring having earned high honors. Plans were afoot to expand Pine Grove dramatically. Ellen had decided to transform it into a boarding school on a grander scale, in keeping with the aggressive opulence of the new Saratoga Springs, where castlelike Gothic mansions sprouted fantasias of ornament.

Tracy set about the preliminary labor, and when Frank and Corinne came back to Pine Grove to stay, Frank having abandoned any idea of practicing law, life became an endless round of construction work. In the midst of the building, the business of running the school had somehow to be carried on. The Walworth Academy was a more ambitious institution than ever. In a revised brochure, Ellen promised parents of prospective pupils that she would oversee "a personal and careful supervision of the mental and physical condition of each one" and would be "unremitting in an effort to stimulate the weaker points of mind or character, and to repress or guide the dominant ones."

AROUND this time it was reported in the newspapers that Lewis Leland, the owner of Sturtevant House, who had been on the premises the day Frank shot Mansfield—most of his energy on that occasion had gone into seeing that his guests were minimally disturbed and the corpse removed from the premises as quickly as possible—was himself under treatment at a private asylum. The *Oswego Times and Express* reported that "overwork and worry over business affairs are said to be the cause of disease. It is said he recently tried to cut his throat." In view of the recent highly publicized suicide of the celebrated hotelier Charles Delmonico, the paper titled its story "Another Hotel Proprietor Insane."

FOR some time Dolly's health had been in decline. By the fall of 1884 her condition was desperate. And in December—as Ellen noted laconically in her journal—"Tracy became helpless." Her youngest son had undergone a breakdown that made any return to school unlikely. In the new year he remained at home, looked after by Ellen while carpenters and plasterers came and went. Frank pored over the writings of Poe and quarreled with his mother about money matters.

Dolly died on January 25 in an Albany hospital. Clarence conducted a requiem mass for her at St. Peter's in Saratoga Springs, and a local paper, describing her as a "colored cook," paid tribute: "'Dolly' was a faithful and devoted servant and was treated with that care and respect by Mrs. Walworth and family, which her attachment deserved." (She was to be buried with the rest of the Walworths in Greenridge Cemetery, her grave—at the foot of Sarah's—marked by a small stone with the bare inscription DOLLY SMITH.) Ellen, however, was not present at St. Peter's. Although an attempt was made to get word to her of Dolly's death, she had already left with Tracy for New York City. From there they were to set sail for Florida.

It was meant to be a healing journey, but Tracy's state of mind shifted constantly and unnervingly. Ellen kept notes on every alteration of mood: "out alone, came in distressed . . . gloomy . . . several hours distress . . . very nervous, depressed . . . sat in room alone . . . nervous still." In Saint Augustine they went shopping and visited the fort. Ellen watched for signs of improvement. "T. all right. Is it a dream?"

Somehow Ellen kept everything going, even if Tracy never fully regained the cheerful disposition that had once made him a well-liked boy. Pine Grove was in turmoil all the time now, with students during the school year and boarders in the summer, and an army of workmen erecting a sprawling Queen Anne structure around the house's original core, adding a second story and dozens of new rooms. Once the basic construction was done, it became a question of carpets and furnishings, cleaning and sewing and provisioning. Even with Corinne helping her, Ellen was constantly exhausted: "Work, work, work and endure. No rest day or night."

Frank seemed unwell. The mood at home was not harmonious. Ellen noted in her journal: "Frank and I do not work well together." And again, cryptically: "Then the night anxieties about Frank." Nelly had taken Tracy to Europe—another journey of recuperation—looking after him while she pursued her researches, spurred by Clarence's interests, into the life of the Mohawk convert Kateri Tekakwitha.

Ruby had interrupted her studies at Vassar and was now teaching at the Walworth Academy. At Christmas she enlisted the students in a production of a fantasy play she had written for the occasion: *Where Was Elsie, or The Saratoga Fairies.* Of all her children, only Ruby seemed to be developing as Ellen might have wished. In her mother's eyes she was kindly and affectionate, a lover of artistic beauty, with an aptitude for teaching and a capacity for hard work. For the modesty and reserve of her character Ellen took to calling her "my little Puritan," but she discerned not a trace in her of any fanatical religious impulse.

The mass of details involved in the remodeling of Pine Grove kept everyone busy, and the fatigue at each day's end ensured that there were few moments for dwelling on unspoken worries or regrets. The past was buried in rounds of programmed activity. Now there was actually the promise of a future: Corinne was pregnant. Early on the morning of March 11, 1886, Clara Grant Walworth made her appearance in the world. Beyond the mere fact of her birth, no one preserved any thoughts or emotions prompted by the occasion.

THE school carried on its business, with Ellen and Ruby and Frank teaching. Ellen took time for long conversations with Frank about philosophy and theology and real estate. At Kenwood, Clara took her final vows as a nun.

In the autumn Frank began to feel decidedly unwell. The lung trouble he had contracted in prison was again severe. He wrote a letter, addressed to the youth of future generations, to be entrusted to his daughter when she was old enough to understand. He attempted to explain how he had gone astray by allowing his love for his mother to sweep aside laws and scriptural commandment. "No matter how great your own suffering and sorrow," he wrote, "or how great must be the suffering and sorrow of one you love above all else, there is still before you God's law—thou shalt not kill. Could youth driven by emotions and tempestuous temper, but remember God's great commandment so much sorrow and suffering could be averted, in the world of your day as it could have in mine. As time goes on if youths of the generation that reads this letter is inclined to lawlessness and crime—God forbid—let them ponder over what I say here."

He lingered for ten days, as a doctor desperately administered whiskey and chloral hydrate. On October 29 Ellen wrote in her journal: "My dear Frank died today—at six o'clock a.m. it was evident that he was dying—he was unconscious—about 8 or 9 his restlessness ceased and the last quiet effort of life continued until 12 o'clock noon."

The death was ascribed to acute bronchitis. Ellen was almost too sick to attend the funeral. She left flowers on the grave and then stayed in bed for a week, unable to carry on the work of the school.

The *Saratoga Journal* respectfully summarized Frank's career by saying, "He was a lawyer by profession, but had not been actively engaged in practice for a couple of years." Other newspapers revisited once more the drama of his crime, but already the elements of the story were losing their currency. The brief life of an American sensation was being consigned to American oblivion. The last of the chancellors? The hero of Buena Vista? The author of *Warwick*, "which," readers needed to be reminded, "had such a sensational sale on its publication"? The country had fresher sensations to think about: the labor unrest that had culminated in the Haymarket Riot in Chicago, the explosion of violence against black freedmen in Mississippi and Chinese immigrants in Seattle, the final surrender of Geronimo to General Nelson Miles. In New York the Statue of Liberty was dedicated, and the saloon keeper Steve Brodie convinced some that he had jumped off the Brooklyn Bridge. A new drink called Coca-Cola went on the market. The texture and pace of things was slipping into a different gear. It was just about to become a world of induction coils and electromagnetic waves and gasoline-driven automobiles.

AFTER Frank died, what was left of the family broke up rapidly. Nelly moved to Albany to be near her uncle. Her life was entirely caught up in his projects: his campaign for the beatification of Kateri Tekakwitha, the "Lily of the Mohawks," about whom Nelly would write a book; his memoirs of his religious career; his projected volume of collected poems. A year later Corinne joined her. Tracy too had grown closer to Clarence, helping him manage the research for an undertaking on which, following in the Chancellor's path, he had been engaged for years: a comprehensive genealogy of the Walworths of America.

It was now that Ellen, "infected with solitude"—having buried a daughter and a son in Greenridge Cemetery, buried her husband, then buried the son who had killed her husband; having become alienated from two of her three surviving daughters and having watched her youngest son succumb to mental impairment—once again set about starting a life of her own.

She closed the school, continuing to give private lessons for only as long as it took her to organize her plans to quit Pine Grove altogether. During that interim period she published poems and for the *Troy Press* wrote reports on anything that came to hand: a blizzard, a naval disaster in Samoa, the government's Indian policy. Then, having procured a position as a clerk in the census office, she leased the homestead to a hotel manager who continued to advertise it as the Walworth Mansion, and relocated to Washington. After Ruby finally got her B.A. at Vassar, she joined her mother in the capital.

Ellen joined with two other women in her Washington set to establish a new organization. It was designed "to perpetuate the memory and spirit of the women and men of the Revolutionary period, to collect and preserve historical and biographical records, documents, and relics, and to obtain portraits of eminent American women." They called it the Daughters of the American Revolution.

Tʜᴇ historic founding took place in Washington on August 8, 1890. In short order the group's goals were reformulated in somewhat grander terms: "To cherish, maintain and extend the institutions of American freedom, to foster true patriotism and love of country, and to aid in securing for mankind all the blessings of liberty." The DAR, in Ellen's words, would rescue American patriotism from the "bombast and folly" of traditional Fourth of July braggadocio—all that noise and nonsense that had emanated, although she did not say so, from men—to restore to love of country a sense of sober earnestness and civic responsibility. The group was not to be a hodgepodge of local clubs, a mere hobby for unoccupied women. "The esprit de corps," she wrote, "is to be national, as it is in the army and navy."

She discovered in herself a gift for political organizing and bureaucratic procedure. She was writing rules and regulations, keeping the society's internal management to a rigorous standard. She discovered a gift for rhetoric as well, a public language of power: "As woman is supreme in the home, so in the development of national life, she is destined to become a factor if not a guide in the affairs of a nation. This is inevitable . . . That duty is to unite us as Americans, to stem the torrent of socialism and anarchy that threatens us from foreign countries and to stimulate the best men of the country to hold fast to the early principles of our government." The organization initiated, for example, a campaign to instill respect for the national anthem by encouraging anyone hearing it to stand and by requesting that it be sung at least once a week in all public schools.

For Ellen it was the organization's early emphasis on preserving the historical record that continued to matter most. Under the DAR's aegis she became founding editor of *American Monthly*, in whose pages she would publish her lengthy account of her father's death at Buena Vista. At the Chicago World's Fair, addressing the American Historical Association, she issued a call, which proved influential, for the establishment of a national archive of historic documents. She promulgated an initiative to match the presidential portraits in the White House with portraits of their wives, and soon a portrait of her friend Mrs. Benjamin Harrison was unveiled. Although now she was based mostly in Washington and New York City, she still found time for her former residence, inaugurating in 1894 the Saratoga Springs chapter of the Daughters of the American Revolution.

IN 1897 Clarence published *The Walworths of America*, a work of exacting research which permitted its author to cast his eye over the expanse of the past as if it were one of those novels by Scott or Cooper to which he continued to return in old age, as Nelly or Clara read to him through an ear trumpet. He wanted, he said, to put some life into the ancestors, to offer the reader "a Walworth standing in his own doorway, the children smiling through the window-panes, or chasing the dog in the orchard . . . I love men, women and children with the flesh on them." In its pages he also managed, where appropriate, to obscure as much as he revealed.

His brother Mansfield's life became a bare listing of published novels, pointedly leaving out *Married in Mask* with its scurrilous caricature of Ellen, and the date of his brother's death was noted with no further detail. Ellen received a fine encomium: "Mrs. Mansfield Walworth, a lady of much literary talent and acquirement, has interested herself especially in educational matters and American history . . . The public are especially indebted to her judgment, zeal and energy for the many memorial tablets with which the battle-ground from Bemis Heights to Schuylerville has been illustrated and enriched."

He lavished praise on Nelly's biography of Kateri Tekakwitha, and publicly thanked Tracy—whose "feeble constitution" had forced him to abandon a medical career—for his assistance in compiling the genealogy. Of Clara's later life he preserved a single emblematic anecdote: resident at the Manhattanville Convent in Massachusetts, weak from a severe attack of fever, she remained quiet in her room as she had been advised by her superior when a tremendous fire broke out. While "wild excitement" prevailed among others, Clara—who survived the fire—"sat still in her chair, tranquil and without moving, notwithstanding the bustle and confusion."

Concerning his nephew Frank's life, beyond the facts of birth, baptism, education, marriage, fatherhood, and death, Clarence observed only: "Though licensed in 1878 as a lawyer, his inclination leaned more to literature, and especially to poetry. Some lyric poems of his have appeared at times in periodicals, but numerous others of singular beauty exist in manuscript, sufficient to fill a volume. He was an excellent sportsman and an adept at almost all athletic exercises, notably in horsemanship. In the National Tournament at Brooklyn in 1882 he received first prize in archery, securing the national championship."

Of Ruby, Clarence left a final picture of her conducting outdoor sketching classes in Saratoga during summer vacations. Most surviving traces of her had to do with painting and poetry and theatricals, starting with her little Christmas play about the fairies of Saratoga. She studied for years at the Art Students League in New York. A poem she published in 1896 enlarged for a number of stanzas on "the palace of my dream," a wondrous sylvan place abounding in childish bliss and furnished with lyrical hand-me-downs from Byron and Keats. In the end—and it was the closest she came to a last testament—the cherished abode was chillingly transformed.

> *Now the flowers have died away,*
> *For a frost has come to kill;*
> *Now my feet no more can stray*
> *Where wood robins loved to trill,*

Where the blue birds used to bill,
Hall and tower now I deem
    But a haunt for owlets shrill
In the palace of my dream.

Ruby was Ellen's constant companion, the only one of her children on whom she could rely as her life became progressively busier. Ellen contended with political infighting at the DAR that led to a sort of palace coup unseating the original governing body, Ellen included. For years she would engage in a combative campaign to preserve her status as one of the organization's three founders. She studied law at New York University—not in order to practice law, something from which women were still barred, but simply to master the principles—and taught a course on parliamentary procedure. With her name on the masthead alongside Julia Ward Howe, Thomas Wentworth Higginson, Lew Wallace, and other distinguished literary figures, she served as treasurer of the recently established Authors' Guild. She found time to give a lecture on "Art and Science in Summer Clubs" at the convention of the State Federation of Women's Clubs and Societies. She returned to Pine Grove—which Corinne had for several years been running as a hotel—and relying on Ruby's aesthetic counsel restored it to a livable summer residence. But in her journal she wrote obscurely about "breaking rage" and aspired to "a certain repose of spirit."

The stature Ellen had achieved was confirmed when, at the outbreak of the Spanish-American War, she was appointed director of the Women's National War Relief Association. Ruby promptly gave up her job teaching art and took a course in nursing. Mother and daughter went to Fort Monroe in Virginia, and when it seemed to Ruby that her work there was done she went on alone to Camp Wikoff, the center that had been established at Montauk Point, Long Island, for sick soldiers shipped back from Cuba. She tended diphtheria, measles, and yellow fever patients, and was later described as notably unsqueamish for someone of her background.

She fell ill and was taken to Ellen's home on West Eighty-eighth Street in New York. As her condition grew worse she was moved to New York Presbyterian, where her illness was diagnosed as typhoid fever. For weeks she lingered in a delirium—"she babbled continually of the blue sea and swaying boats she had seen from her hospital quarters, she talked French and German by turns"—and for a time there was hope. On October 18, 1898, she died. It was two days before Ellen's sixty-sixth birthday.

Ruby was buried with full military honors. Her death attracted a good deal of attention from the newspapers. She was praised as a model of self-sacrifice and as an example of what women could contribute to the war effort. Poems and editorials were written. Eventually an obelisk was dedicated to her memory. Ellen wore black for the rest of her life.

NOW, in the pages of her journal, Ellen looked at what was left of her life and prospects. The pages were often scarcely legible. The handwriting appeared to disintegrate under the pressure of grief. "Can I live! Shall I live! Why! Why! Why! So hard before—years & years ago—but still hope with this beloved one to live for—to struggle for! Now why? Why? Why? . . . she was killed! killed! martyred—and who cares!" She attempted to concentrate on books and papers and magazines. She dedicated herself to honoring Ruby's memory: "only holding torture at bay—only trying to forget the 'might have been' . . . Death my own death is nothing when compared with this might have been."

Months later it was still "all a dream, a horrible waking dream . . . I have worked, have traveled . . . have seemed to take rest . . . yet always it is this strange unnatural dream . . . I cannot really, I cannot get back to that other life that I left on October 18, 1898." She wrote prayerlike passages in praise of her lost daughter. With her she had lost all. Everything else was long since gone.

> *What is all else that is gone!*
> *Fortune—happiness, husband*
> *children—father, mother*
> *ambition—hope—all lost*
> *My darling—my one precious jewel beyond price—Yes*
> *live in her presence if at all.*

Once again she reviewed the past, and it revealed horrible patterns. As she pieced together her life, it was a story of successive abandonments. "1883 Dec—My son married. 1883 Dec—Clara deserted me. 1884 Dec—Tracy became helpless. 1887—Nelly left me for her uncle. 1888—Corinne began living with Nelly." She thought about her other children, even those still living: "All are dead—they died long ago—those other children—all—and I did not quite see & understand." Since Ruby's death she had measured the extent of her distance from Nelly and Clara. "I beheld the corpse of that happy loving family life that I created & cherished . . . Is it through failure of duty or judgment or affection on my part? That this further strange thing has befallen me? Did I forget? Was I negligent, was I cold—No! no! no!"

The explanation lay elsewhere. She saw now clearly that it had been Clarence casting a blight on her all along: "An enemy has been in the camp—in the centre of the family life—an enemy clothed with the shape & the dignity of religion—but cruel, hard & revengeful as an octopus. His ways and his will was not regarded—his spiritual pride and his worldly pride was hurt—therefore the heel must be placed upon the neck of the woman—if she did not submit then she must lose all that she has left in the world, for he had the power—authority of a certain kind, money—& persuasiveness—and abuse & misrepresentation of me—with no chance for explanation or defense—until at last the weeds have taken root, the poison is absorbed & my own children are polluted—alienated—without one shadow of reason—it is all religion—oh! the mockery of saintliness! the wickedness of holiness."

A few lines further on she wrote, "Shall I have strength to arise and go forward to help others & to lift my own soul above desperation?"

CLARENCE by now was sightless and paralyzed. "There is news," Ellen noted, "of disaster to my poor helpless enemy, God help him." His passing in 1900 was accompanied by an outpouring of tributes to the depth of his faith and the eloquence of his preaching. Nelly set about writing his biography, published in 1907 as *Life Sketches of Father Walworth*. The frail man in his skullcap and cassock, blind and deaf at the end, had left extensive records of himself—accounts of his early friendships at the seminary and his years as a Redemptorist missionary, sermons addressing spiritual and political questions, theological arguments crafted to keep modern materialism at bay, poems evoking Mohawk war cries and upstate landscapes—but not a word that addressed the inner history of his family. Mansfield, Ellen, Frank, Clara: their stories were to be part of the domain of silence.

To his translation of the old Latin hymn "Dies Irae" (Day of Wrath), with its phrases that might have been aimed squarely at Mansfield's wrongdoings—

> *Lo! the Book of Doom! Each action,*
> *Secret sin, or bold transgression,*
> *Idle word, foul thought, is noted.*

—he added lines that could have served as a discreet act of mourning for his brother.

> *Peace to thee, departed brother,*
> *Tenant once of this cold clay!*
> *Jesus! give him rest alway.*

But Clarence, on the evidence of his own verse, was far removed from all of them. It was from a great distance that he looked on earthly things.

> *Vain are all creatures, and unstable,*
> *False, insufficient, and unable*
> *To satisfy a heart like mine.*
> *They were made for me, not I for them.*
> *I was created for things divine—*
> *For God . . .*

ELLEN resumed her public activities and showed no slackening as years and honors accumulated. Her life became, even more than before, a record of monuments and dedications and honorary memberships. She was now seen as a pioneer of what was beginning to be called "the woman movement," and was frequently asked to comment on the role of women in national and private life. Her maxims were widely circulated by newspapers: "Women attain the higher path in the line of moral energy, and spiritual life which embraces the principle of self-sacrifice." "The education of a mother comes in the education of her child." "Your child will not be a good workman, a good citizen, a good soldier if he is not trained to obey." "The mother of the family is the main spring of all good order, and the home is like a clock . . . Contentment means a life of activity, progress, joy and repose. An ugly, querulous, discontented person is worse than the darkest clouds of a dark day. Cheerfulness is not easy, and is attainable only through hard discipline."

In her journals she struck other notes: "Our griefs are all from within." "My soul is dead, my heart is broken." "I cannot work. I cannot think—there is only the intense desire to get through with what is necessary—and to lie down and die." But a few months later she would exhort herself to "try, try, try!" And again: "Work, still work until the final rest comes, and is welcomed." She remembered that even as a child she had felt as if her spirit wanted to break out of its bounds. There had been something she wanted to say, something that demanded expression.

Her activities on so many fronts did not permit her to complete any of the books she had envisioned, neither the novel nor the biography of her father nor the history of the Mexican War. Late in life she wrote some fragmentary recollections of childhood. In the early moment when she stood, unnoticed, in the corner of the room where her father was having his ruined eye removed without anesthesia—observing how he did not cry out and vowing to do likewise—she might have seen the emblem of what her life was to be: a confrontation between catastrophe and endurance. Any cry of pain was to be inward, private, swallowed back.

Alone of her family, her memory was to survive by means of plaques and monuments and sculpted heads. In October 1912, the Saratoga Battle Monument, envisioned since the time when Frank was in Sing Sing, was finally completed. Ellen was present at the dedication.

She died, following a series of strokes, on June 23, 1915. In her obituaries no mention was made of Mansfield's death or Frank's imprisonment.

20

~~~~~~~

The Hermit

A FTER his mother died Tracy went to live in the woods.
In a forested region of Glen Carlyn, Virginia, he built himself a
hut. He had learned a great deal about building during the transformation of Pine Grove into a fifty-five-room mansion. As the years went by
he began to graft additional rooms on to his one-room dwelling. In its
final form his home was said to have resembled "a woodland fortress."

He was apparently much concerned with religious questions.

On the morning of December 2, 1928, he appeared at a neighbor's
house with a two-inch gash on the left side of his throat. He had, he
said, "walked into a knife" by accident. A doctor was summoned, and
the wound was stitched and bandaged. Tracy then sat down and had
breakfast with his neighbors. When the family left him alone for a few
minutes, he disappeared.

Later in the day someone thought it advisable to check on him. They
found him lying in bed, still alive, with a deep gash on the other side of
his throat. By the time a doctor got there he was dead. A hunting knife
was found lying near his body.

People in the vicinity recalled that he had become mentally unbal-
anced a few years earlier. He had crashed his bicycle into the post
office in Glen Carlyn and had been hospitalized for several weeks.

Locals believed that he came from a prominent family in Washington, D.C., and that his mother had been a founder of, some thought, the Daughters of the Confederacy. He had sought a life of seclusion because of tragic events in his early life. It was said that his brother had shot and killed their father because of his ill treatment of their mother.

He was fifty-seven at the time of his death. His sister Nelly took the train down to oversee the shipping of his body for burial in Greenridge Cemetery with the rest of the family.

Epilogue

AFTER the rest of them died—Tracy in 1928, his sisters Nelly in 1931 and Clara in 1934—Corinne, after a long absence, came back to the Walworth Mansion with her daughter Clara. She had determined that they would restore the place to its old splendor and settle there for the rest of their lives. For a brief interval the old home began to live again. Outsiders came to admire it on festive occasions; articles were published about its historical treasures. But only a few years after their return, in 1937, Clara's mother died. Thereafter Clara lived on alone, less and less inclined to step outside.

The history of her later years was a matter of moving in and out of those rooms, endlessly retracing the steps of earlier inhabitants, physically as long as she had the mobility, eventually in mind alone. The care and preservation of Pine Grove's artifacts and records became her chief concern. She listed each item: the brass clock and the candlesticks with crystal prisms and blue enameled trimming from her mother's wedding, the portrait of her father as a child with his little brother Johnny who had died so young during the war, the sheaf of tributes published when her great-uncle Father Clarence died, the old-fashioned child's chair in the corner that (she wrote in trembling hand on her notepad) "was mine as a girl, that was given to me by Mrs. Colonel Balch, a very old lady who had also sat in that chair as a child." There was a comfort in knowing that every space you could move through, every place you could sit, had been moved through or sat in before by someone to whom you were closely connected. So little of all this originated with herself. So little of anything originated with her; it had all come down from the ancestors.

She remembered floats and brass bands going by on North Broadway to honor the soldiers departing for the Spanish-American War, when she was thirteen. It was still painful to think of her aunt Ruby, who died of the disease the soldiers brought back from the tropics.

There were happier things to think of. How pleasant it had been when the members of the New York State Historical Association came to visit the house after the annual meeting in 1912. Clara was twenty-six then. The historians and antiquarians had trooped up in the rain from the casino, where a paper on the Battle of Saratoga had been presented, and her grandmother Ellen had "thrown open" the whole house to the inspection of the guests, laying out room after room of relics. Some rooms were lit only by candles to give the authentic feel of colonial times. Mother and two of her cronies from the Daughters of the American Revolution poured tea, and young Miss Bosworth did duty at the punch bowl.

Time itself had been suspended—they might have been in another century—until the hour came for the visitors to make their departure amid the odor of ashes and damp wood. Then the treasures were one by one laid in their boxes, tied up with ribbons, deposited each in the appropriate cupboard or closet, amid the murmur of the women as they discussed the appearance and conversations of the guests—it was so rare to have something new to talk about. As they talked they wove in recollections of the guests' forebears and family lines, a tale that stretched back into the original darkness where everything had been harmoniously bound together.

Occasionally in her later years Clara had houseguests, but the occasions grew infrequent. Looking after guests had always been difficult for Clara, and after her mother died she gave it up. Her mother had possessed a gift for being with people. Corinne had kept up the traditions of the old South against all odds; everyone said she could bring life to a room. Good manners weren't enough. You had to make it seem as if you were really enjoying yourself.

Clara was incapable of cutting such a figure in the world. When a young cousin from Kentucky came to visit, it took Clara months to get a bedroom ready for her. The placement and condition of every object—sheets and washcloths, glasses and plates and napkins, the mementos too long undusted or too fragile to leave lying casually about—had to be considered afresh in the light of this extraordinary event, the arrival of an outsider. It was just as hard to get herself ready for her visitor. Receiving company was an obligation involving an infinity of delicate choices.

In the end, after all the labor of preparation, her cousin stayed only one night. Their much-anticipated conversation had amounted to little, inquiries about the old and ailing, scattered reminiscences about the dead. Her guest took leave with strained politeness. She was unable to disguise how uncomfortable she had felt staying there. It was as if the house itself had driven her out.

Clara was afraid of intruders. Awake in the middle of the night, she listened for the sound of robbers creeping in. The sound would have been difficult to detect amid the squeaks and drafts and nameless thuds that murmured in the vast house.

At her death in 1952—paralyzed by a stroke and cared for by nurses in constant attendance—she still hoped that the mansion would be preserved as a historical museum.

By then the homestead at Pine Grove was in too derelict a condition for that purpose. Its confusion of contents—dresses, tables, candlesticks, lockets, scrapbooks, diaries, daguerrotypes, the chancellor's intricate genealogical notes, Mansfield's novels, Mansfield's shell collection, Ellen's historical articles and her youthful letters to Mary Duncan, Frank's archery scores and his poetry manuscript from Auburn Asylum—were transferred to the Walworth Memorial Museum on the premises of the Historical Society of Saratoga Springs, housed in the 1870 casino.

THE Walworth Mansion stood deserted for a few more years, a disintegrating hulk. At that time a movie theater stood next door on

Broadway. After dark, children walking back home—their nerves perhaps already on edge from *Godzilla* or *The Creature from the Black
Lagoon*—crept cautiously past the mansion because of the ghosts said
to dwell in it. It was demolished in 1955. A gas station occupies the
site today.

Notes

1. A HAUNTED HOUSE

5 **"stirring up the old miseries"** Ellen Hardwin Walworth, journal, January 9, 1882, Walworth Memorial Museum Archives.

6 **October 19, 1886** Evelyn Barrett Britten, "Tragedy Haunted Frank Walworth to Early Grave," *Saratogian*, May 10, 1956. No copy of Frank's letter is known to survive, and Mrs. Britten's transcription contains some wording that appears inauthentic. I am operating on the assumption that for journalistic or other reasons Mrs. Britten—a close friend of Clara Grant Walworth and the author of many articles on the history of the family—embroidered an existing letter, and have restricted myself to quoting what seems most plausible.

2. ROOM 267

8 **"just about intellectual enough . . ."** *Brooklyn Eagle*, June 24, 1873.

9 **"I am of the opinion . . ."** *The Walworth Parricide in New York* (Philadelphia: Old Franklin Publishing House, 1873), p. 44.

10 **"Prepare yourself for the inevitable . . ."** Ibid., pp. 44–45.

10–11 **Frank and Mrs. Eliza Sims** Ibid., pp. 14–17.

13 **"I have made myself the unhappy hero . . ."** Cited in Evelyn Barrett Britten, "The Walworth Tragedy: Speedy Trial Resulted in Conviction," *Saratogian*, May 24, 1956.

13 **"the patient toiler, the indefatigable man of will . . ."** Mansfield Tracy Walworth, *Beverly; or, The White Mask* (New York: G. W. Carleton, 1872), p. 129.

13 **"He looked very weary and care-worn . . ."** Ibid., pp. 100–101.

13 **"Quiet, rest for his brain . . ."** Ibid., p. 129.

14 "selected from among the dregs of the populace . . ." *New York Times*, May 8, 1858.

14 "a rollicking Irishman . . ." *New York Times*, August 9, 1858.

15 "When I heard of his death I was struck dumb . . ." "A Yellow-Covered Murder," *Chicago Daily Tribune*, June 16, 1873.

15 Mansfield and Michael Tuomey on the evening of June 2nd "His Last Night on Earth," in *The Walworth Parricide* (New York: Thomas O'Kane, 1873).

16 "There was no excitement about him"; "I knew who he was by his card" *The Walworth Parricide in New York*, p. 21.

17 "just like a telegraph operator sending a message" Ibid., p. 18.

20 Frank's conversation with Barrett *New York Times*, June 7, 1873.

20 "Not the slightest paleness whitened his cheek . . ." *The Walworth Parricide in New York*, p. 4.

20–21 "go quick as lightning" Ibid., p. 22.

3. ANOTHER SENTIMENTAL MURDER

22 "A most uncommonly shocking murder this morning . . ." Allan Nevins, ed., *The Diary of George Templeton Strong*, vol. 4 (New York: Macmillan, 1952), p. 483.

23 "another sentimental murder" *Brooklyn Eagle*, June 4, 1873.

23 "he has the prettiest mouth . . ." *Rochester Democrat*, quoted in *Daily Saratogian*, June 13, 1874.

24 "The coolness and deliberation displayed . . ." Quoted in *Daily Saratogian*, June 4, 1873.

24 "modern society has produced a monster . . ." *New York Evening Post*, June 4, 1873.

24 "The Thug in India . . ." *New York Sun*, June 9, 1873.

24 Nelly Walworth on the train *Albany Journal*, June 6, 1873.

25 "he went to the station house himself" *Daily Saratogian*, June 4, 1873.

25 Frank at the station house *The Walworth Parricide* (New York: Thomas O'Kane, 1873); *The Walworth Parricide in New York* (Philadelphia: Old Franklin Publishing House, 1873), pp. 5–6; *New York Times*, "A Terrible Parricide," June 4, 1873.

27 "I have seen a great many murderers . . ." *New York Herald*, quoted in *The Walworth Parricide*.

27 "There was no excitement about him . . ." *New York Herald*, quoted in *Daily Saratogian*, June 4, 1873.

29 "As Frank came into the room his mother sprang toward him . . ." *Daily Saratogian*, June 5, 1873.

29 Frank weeping in his mother's arms "The Walworth Parricide: The Prisoner's Mother Visits Him in the Tombs," *New York Times*, June 5, 1873.

29 "Oh Frank! what have you done! what have you done! . . ." *The Walworth Parricide in New York* (Philadelphia: Old Franklin Publishing House, 1873), title page.

29 "If Frank Walworth goes from his prison cell to the ignominy of the gal-

lows . . ." "A Yellow-Covered Murder," *Chicago Daily Tribune*, June 16, 1873.

30 **"laughing and in very excellent spirits"** Reported in the *Brooklyn Eagle*, June 10, 1873.

31 **"seem to be retained in advance"** *Brooklyn Eagle*, June 6, 1873.

31 **"imperial faculties"** James C. Carter in *In Memory of Charles O'Conor: Report of a Meeting of the Bar of the Courts of the State of New York and of the United States . . . May 23rd, 1884*. New York Public Library.

31–32 **"he began his career as a low Irishman . . ."** Allan Nevins, ed., *The Diary of George Templeton Strong*, vol. 4, p. 487.

32 **Edwin Forrest divorce suit** See Thomas N. Baker, *Sentiment and Celebrity: Nathaniel Parker Willis and the Trials of Literary Fame* (New York: Oxford University Press, 1999), pp. 146–47.

32 **"It is not injustice . . ."** James F. Richardson, *The New York Police: Colonial Times to 1901* (New York: Oxford University Press, 1970), p. 131.

32 **"O'Conor's face is much shriveled . . ."** *Rochester Democrat*, quoted in the *Daily Saratogian*, June 13, 1873.

32 **"aversion to, and distrust of, the new political authorities . . ."** William C. Evarts, in *In Memory of Charles O'Conor*.

32–33 **O'Conor's interview** *New York Herald*, reprinted in the *Daily Saratogian*, June 6, 1873.

33–34 **"the sacred name of mother is lugged in . . ."; "His son and murderer parrots a pretty tale . . ."** "Another Sentimental Murder," *Brooklyn Eagle*, June 4, 1873.

34 **"He is said to have been spurred to it . . ."** "The Walworth Parricide in Solution," *Brooklyn Eagle*, June 5, 1873.

34 **"A son avenges the wrongs of an injured mother . . ."** Quoted in the *Daily Saratogian*, June 4, 1873.

34 **"any of the attempts at whitewashing . . ."** *Nation*, June 12, 1873.

34 **"secret means are at work . . ."** Letter from George Forshew, *Brooklyn Eagle*, June 9, 1873.

34 **"Will the young man be hung? . . ."** Quoted in "The Walworth Case," *Daily Saratogian*, June 6, 1873.

34 **"The general conviction here . . ."** "The Walworth Tragedy," *Daily Saratogian*, June 4, 1873.

34–35 **"As usual, when a tragedy . . ."; "It is our belief that young Walworth . . ."** "The Walworth Case," *Daily Saratogian*, June 6, 1873.

35 **"manly form and gentleness of manner . . ."** *Albany Times*, quoted in the *Daily Saratogian*, June 4, 1873.

35 **"The writers who thus describe Mansfield Tracy Walworth . . ."** "The Walworth Case," *Daily Saratogian*, June 6, 1873.

36 **"a careless, jaunty walk"** *The Walworth Parricide in New York*, p. 13.

36 **A reporter moving through the crowd** *The Walworth Parricide in New York*, pp. 13–14.

36 **The coroner's inquest** See report of coroner's inquest, June 6, 1873, New York City Archives; also *The Walworth Parricide in New York*, pp. 12–27.

4. EARLY LIFE OF A CHANCELLOR

40 **"His face, though somewhat disfigured . . ."** *The Walworth Parricide.*

41 **"the tone of the funeral was distant . . ."** Ibid.

43 **"three springs whose water is very cold . . ."** Elizabeth Cometti, ed., *Seeing America and Its Great Men: The Journal and Letters of Count Francesco dal Verme, 1783–1784* (Charlottesville: University Press of Virginia, 1969); cited in Field Horne, *The Saratoga Reader: Writing About an American Village, 1749–1900* (Saratoga Springs: Kiskaton, 2004), p. 9.

44 **"a water, in some neglected valley . . ."** Quoted in Thomas A. Chambers, *Drinking the Waters: Creating an American Leisure Class at Nineteenth-Century Mineral Springs* (Washington, D.C.: Smithsonian Institution Press, 2002), pp. 54–55.

44 **an appropriately atmospheric myth of origin** Later historians have determined that the spring visited by Johnson in 1767 was located elsewhere, and that he did not visit Saratoga Springs until a number of years later. See Chambers, pp. 54–55.

44 **"amid a wild and strange chant . . ."** William L. Stone, *Reminiscences of Saratoga and Ballston* (New York: Virtue and Yarston, 1875).

44 **Congress Spring** See Theodore Corbett, *The Making of American Resorts: Saratoga Springs, Ballston Spa, Lake George* (New Brunswick, N.J.: Rutgers University Press, 2001), pp. 76–78.

45 **"Got up early this morning . . ."** From the diary of Alexander Coventry (1766–1831), cited in Horne, *The Saratoga Reader*, p. 55.

45 **twelve hundred bottles a day** See George Waller, *Saratoga: Saga of an Impious Era* (Upper Saddle River, N.J.: Prentice-Hall, 1966), p. 67.

45 **career of Reuben Hyde Walworth** See Constance J. Carroll, "Reuben Hyde Walworth, 1788–1867: New York's Last Chancellor," unpublished BA thesis, Middlebury College, 1974.

45 **father's farm in Bozrah** A window from his father's house in Bozrah, Connecticut, was placed by the Chancellor in Pine Grove; it is installed at the Walworth Memorial Museum at the Saratoga Springs History Museum.

46–47 **family origins** For this and other details of ancestral history, see Clarence A. Walworth, *The Walworths of America* (Albany: Weed-Parsons, 1897).

47 **"the wounded were thrown into carts . . ."** Henry B. Stanton, *Random Recollections* (New York: Harper and Brothers, 1887), p. 6.

47 **That was what you did** See Paul E. Johnson and Sean Wilentz, *The Kingdom of Matthias* (New York: Oxford University Press, 1994), p. 14.

47 **"Mrs. Walworth was a lady . . ."** Unidentified newspaper clipping in a Walworth family scrapbook, Walworth Memorial Museum Archives.

48 **"Friendship then, like the Mentor of Tellemachus . . ."** Reuben Hyde Walworth to Elizabeth DeLord, December 1, 1810, Walworth Memorial Museum Archives.

49 **"This day is the twenty second anniversary . . ."** Reuben Hyde Walworth to Samuel Gardener, October 25, 1810, Walworth Memorial Museum Archives.

49 **"I had rather be called anything . . ."** Reuben Hyde Walworth to Elizabeth DeLord, December 22, 1810, Walworth Memorial Museum Archives.

49 **trial of an English spy** *Biographical Sketches of Eminent American Lawyers*, June 1852.

50 **"Marcy, Walworth, Dickinson, and others of the Albany Regency . . ."** Quoted in *Hudson River Chronicle*, September 4, 1849.

51 **"Your dear wife is all alive . . ."; "Take courage from her example . . ."; "the times are about to change . . ."** Samuel W. Whelpley to Reuben Hyde Walworth, February 15, 1822, Walworth Memorial Museum Archives.

52 **"burned-over district"** See Whitney R. Cross, *The Burned-Over District: The Social and Intellectual History of Enthusiastic Religion in Western New York, 1800–1850* (Ithaca, N.Y.: Cornell University Press, 1950).

53 **"struck under deep conviction"** Samuel W. Whelpley to Reuben Hyde Walworth, February 15, 1822, Walworth Memorial Museum Archives.

53 **"Our Sunday evening conferences . . ."** Ibid.

54 **"the morals of the people soon became corrupted . . ."** Reuben Hyde Walworth, address to National Sabbath Convention, November 1844.

54 **"It is . . . my wish that no part of this trifling sum . . ."** Reuben Hyde Walworth to Cadwallader Colden, October 30, 1819, Walworth Memorial Museum Archives.

55 **"rioting, drunkenness, and every species . . ."** 1826 pamphlet, quoted in Louis P. Masur, *Rites of Execution: Capital Punishment and the Transformation of American Culture, 1776–1865* (New York: Oxford University Press, 1989).

55 **"Three brothers bent on crimes . . ."** Quoted in Negley K. Teeters and Jack H. Hedblom, *Hanged by the Neck* (Springfield, Ill.: Charles C. Thomas, 1967), p. 276.

56 **"When each brother had been placed by the sheriff . . ."** "The Mark Hodge Papers," in *Recalling Pioneer Days*, ed. Frank H. Severance (Buffalo: Buffalo Historical Society, 1922); quoted in Mark Goldman, *High Hopes: The Rise and Decline of Buffalo* (New York: SUNY Press, 1983), pp. 26–27.

57 **"some of the language used . . ."** L. B. Proctor, *Lawyer and Client; Or, The Trials and Triumphs of the Bar* (New York: S. S. Peloubet, 1883), p. 294.

57 **"To be compelled at one and the same time . . ."; "You stole upon him unperceived . . ."** *The Life, Trial, Condemnation and Dying Address of the Three Thayers . . . Executed for the Murder of John Love at Buffalo, New York, June 17, 1825* (Buffalo, printed for the publisher, 1825).

58 **"Then the Judge pronounced . . ."** "A Buffalo Classic," *Scribner's Monthly*, May 1875.

58 **Peggy Facto** For an account of the Facto case, see Penelope D. Clute, "Peggy Facto—Murderess or Victim?" *Historical Society of the Courts of the State of New York*, 1, 2 (Spring/Summer 2005). I am indebted to Judge Clute's researches for all the information on this case.

58 **"Wretched and deluded woman! . . ."** *Plattsburgh Republican*, January 29, 1825; cited by Clute, op. cit.

59 "a catch-penny pamphlet . . ." *Plattsburgh Republican*, April 23, 1825; cited by Clute, op. cit.

59 "the woman was perfectly abandoned . . ." De Witt Clinton to Peter Sailly, February 28, 1825; cited by Clute, op. cit.

59 "If terror loses its influence . . ." De Witt Clinton to Peter Sailly, February 28, 1825; cited by Clute, op. cit.

60 "females of various ages . . ." *Plattsburgh Intelligencer*, reprinted in *Malone Telegraph*, March 31, 1825; cited by Clute, op. cit.

60 "Brought up a farmer . . ." Irving Browne, "Reuben Hyde Walworth," *The Green Bag*, June 1895.

61 "Here am I, at thirty-eight . . ." "Questions Answered," *Brooklyn Eagle*, January 16, 1887.

5. SPA AND COURTROOM: THE CHANCELLOR IN HIS WORLD

62 leisure . . . more than merely lazing about See Janice Zita Grover, "Luxury and Leisure in Early Nineteenth-Century America: Saratoga Springs and the Rise of the Resort," Ph.D. dissertation, University of California at Davis, 1969.

63 "To this spot, perhaps more than any other . . ." G. M. Davison, *The Fashionable Tour*, 4th ed. (Saratoga Springs, 1830).

63 "The pale emaciated and lame . . ." Field Horne, *The Saratoga Reader: Writing About an American Village, 1749–1900* (Saratoga Springs: Kiskaton, 2004), p. 66.

63 "champagne, and ice-cream, and blancmange"; "antiquated belles of a by-gone generation . . ." *The Diary of Philip Hone, 1828–1851*, vol. 2, ed. Bayard Tuckerman (New York: Dodd, Mead, 1889), July 19–July 24, 1835.

63 "hosts of cheerful pretty faces . . ." Charles Joseph Latrobe, *The Rambler in North America*, cited in Horne, *The Saratoga Reader*, p. 93.

63 "the oddest and most ill-matched" Cited in Horne, *The Saratoga Reader*, pp. 74–75.

64 "a mean little country town . . ." Cited in Theodore Corbett, *The Making of American Resorts: Saratoga Springs, Ballston Spa, Lake George* (New Brunswick, N.J.: Rutgers University Press, 2001), p. 86.

64 "humbuggers and humbugged" Philip Hone, diary, August 12, 1839, cited in Horne, *The Saratoga Reader*, p. 133.

64 "a game at billiards or a chance fraternization . . ." Nathaniel Parker Willis, "Manners at Watering Places," *Hurry-Graphs* (London: Henry G. Bohn, 1855).

64 "fellows who possess a pretty good gift of gab . . ." *Microscope* (Albany), August 3, 1839.

65 "Life at the Springs . . ." *New-York Mirror*, August 3, 1839.

65 "There is nothing in the whole compass of yawns . . ." Caroline Gilman, *The Poetry of Travelling in the United States* (1838), cited in Horne, *The Saratoga Reader*, p. 111.

65 "We stroll down the street to Congress Hall . . ." George William Curtis, "Saratoga," in *Lotus-Eating: A Summer Book* (New York: Harper and Brothers, 1852).

66 **"And then . . . he liked to saunter in parlors . . ."** James Gerard, remarks to New York City Bar Association, 1868.

68 **"Through the activity of his mind . . ."** Charles O'Conor, eulogy for Reuben Hyde Walworth, New York City Bar Association, 1868.

68 **"this habit of his seems to be almost involuntary"** *Daily Plebeian*, November 18, 1843.

69 **"his habiliments not remarkably neat . . ."** Bayard Tuckerman, ed., *The Diary of Philip Hone*, vol. 2, pp. 36–38.

69 **"guardian of the interests of infants . . ."** *Hudson River Chronicle*, March 6, 1838.

70 **"little susceptibility to poetry"** L. B. Proctor, *Lawyer and Client; Or, The Trials and Triumphs of the Bar* (New York: S. S. Peloubet, 1883), p. 301.

6. THE TWO BROTHERS

72 **"Strive to be first in your class . . ."** Ellen Hardin Walworth [Jr.], *Life Sketches of Father Walworth* (Albany: J. B. Lyon, 1907), pp. 10–13.

72 **"Why I could dance to such time as that!"** Clarence Walworth, convocation address at Albany, cited in ibid., p. 23.

73 **Elder Jacob Knapp in Schenectady:** George Rogers Howell and John H. Munsell, *History of the County of Schenectady, New York, from 1662 to 1886* (New York: W. W. Munsell, 1886), p. 107.

74 **"He is a great man in his way . . ."** Edmund Huling, diary, September 23, 1840; Saratoga Springs, archives of the city historian.

74 **"real, substantial, and lasting"; "upon those sacred privacies . . ."** Clarence Walworth, in *The Doctrine of Hell, Ventilated in a Discussion Between the Rev. C. A. Walworth and Wm. Henry Burr, Esq.* (New York: Catholic Publication Society, 1873), p. 16.

74 **"like a lawyer arguing a case . . ."** Henry B. Stanton, *Random Recollections* (New York: Harper and Brothers, 1887), pp. 40–41.

74 **"You dirty dog! You blackhearted rascal! . . ."** Walworth, *Life Sketches of Father Walworth*, p. 50.

75 **"that peculiar atmosphere . . ."** Clarence A. Walworth, *The Oxford Movement in America* (New York: Catholic Book Exchange, 1895), p. 8.

75 **"I remained for a long time sleepless . . ."** Ibid., p. 9.

76 **"was low and sweet, and had a quietness . . ."** Ibid., p. 11.

76 **"I do not look upon myself . . ."** Walworth, *Life Sketches of Father Walworth*, p. 63.

76 **"a religious and political agitator . . ."** Walworth, *The Oxford Movement in America*, p. 19.

76 **"I never heard such bitterness . . ."** Ibid., p. 15.

76 **ordination of Arthur Carey** See Clarence A. Walworth, *Early Ritualism in America* (New York, 1893), p. 17.

77 **"I sat down on the centre of the sofa . . ."** *The Proceedings of the Court Convened under the Third Canon of 1844 . . . for the Trial of the Right Rev. Benjamin T. Onderdonk, Bishop of New York* (New York: D. Appleton, 1845), p. 129.

77 **"maudlin familiarities indulged in . . ."** Walworth, *The Oxford Movement in America*, p. 131.

78 **"brought up in the barrenness of Protestantism"** Walworth, *Early Ritualism in America*, pp. 30–31.

78 **"In a few minutes I shall be gone . . ."; "Everything was new and poor . . ."** Walworth, *The Oxford Movement in America*, p. 144.

78 **one last improbable effort to keep Clarence in the family fold** See Walworth, *Life Sketches of Father Walworth*, pp. 85–86.

80 **A fugitive glimpse of Mansfield at twelve** L. B. Proctor, *Lawyer and Client; Or, the Trials and Triumphs of the Bar* (New York: S. S. Peloubet, 1883), pp. 295–98 and p. 309.

81 **"corporal punishment, as a means of moral discipline . . ."** Cited in Lyman Cobb, *The Evil Tendencies of Corporal Punishment as a Means of Moral Discipline in Families* (New York: Mark H. Newman, 1847), p. 222.

81 **"He was not only ready for the spasm of profanity . . ."** *Utica Morning Herald,* July 7, 1873.

81 **"ruled his household with a rod of iron . . ."; "The boy who when at home . . ."** "Sketch of M. T. Walworth," in *The Walworth Parricide* (New York: Thomas O'Kane, 1873).

82 **Senate Whigs resisted** See "Richelieu's Reminiscences," *Brooklyn Eagle,* September 26, 1880.

82 **"He is recommended by many distinguished Members . . ."** "Reuben Hyde Walworth," *Dictionary of National Biography* (New York: Scribner's, 1936).

83 **a letter from Clarence** Walworth, *Life Sketches of Father Walworth,* p. 80.

83 **an earlier wave of judicial reconfiguration** Sean Wilentz, *The Rise of American Democracy* (New York: W. W. Norton, 2005), p. 192.

83 **Anti-Rent Wars** See Charles W. McCurdy, *The Anti-Rent Era in New York Law and Politics, 1839–1865* (Chapel Hill: University of North Carolina Press, 2001), p. 206.

84 **"pro-nigger, anti-gallows, eternal peace . . ."** James Fenimore Cooper, *The Ways of the Hour* (Boston: Dana Estes & Co., 1850), p. 207.

84 **"made his rules of practice so tedious . . ."** "Legislature of New-York—A Bad Day's Work," *New York Tribune,* March 26, 1847.

85 **"Mark the Chancellor's logic . . ."** E. S. Abdy, *Journal of a Residence and Tour in the United States of North America, From April 1833 to October 1834,* vol. 1 (London: John Murray, 1835), p. 347.

85 **"that *unconstitutional* and dangerous emancipation . . ."** See *The Baptist Magazine for 1836,* p. 142.

86 **"You cannot legalize robbery and murder . . ."** Gerrit Smith to Reuben Hyde Walworth, August 25, 1849 (Syracuse University Library).

86 **"That precious band of politicians . . ."** *Hudson Chronicle,* September 4, 1848.

87 **"the breaking of that alabaster box . . ."** *Brooklyn Eagle,* June 16, 1873.

87 **"Many of us knew . . ."** Cited in Albert Tracy Chester, *A Sermon Occasioned by the Death of Maria Ketchum Walworth . . . April 24, 1847, in the 52nd Year of Her Age* (Saratoga Springs: G. M. Davison, 1847).

87 **funeral sermon in Saratoga** Albert Tracy Chester, ibid.

87 **"In a dim and silent chamber . . ."** Mansfield Tracy Walworth, *Hotspur: A Tale of the Old Dutch Manor* (New York: G. W. Carleton, 1864), pp. 150–51.

7. HARDINS AND WALWORTHS

90 **"I feel highly flattered . . ."** Sarah Hardin to Reuben Hyde Walworth, December 2, 1850, Walworth Memorial Museum Archives.

91 **"The requisites I desire in her . . ."** Reuben Hyde Walworth to Sarah Hardin, December 1850, Walworth Memorial Museum Archives.

92 **"a new world, socially embryonic . . ."** Truman August Post, *Truman Marcellus Post, D.D.: A Biography, Personal and Literary* (Boston and Chicago: Congregational Sunday School and Publishing Society, 1891), p. 51.

92 **on the verge of fighting a duel** Mary Todd Lincoln to Francis Bicknell Carpenter, December 8, 1865; in Justin G. Turner and Linda Levitt Turner, ed., *Mary Todd Lincoln: Her Life and Letters* (New York: Knopf, 1972).

92 **"We all recollect . . . the great display . . ."** Unidentified newspaper clipping, Walworth Memorial Museum Archives.

93 **"I remember when boyant with health and with joy . . ."** Hardin Family Papers, Chicago History Museum.

93 **"My heart dies within me . . ."** Sarah Hardin to Myra Hardin, n.d., Chicago History Museum.

93 **"Life is too short to be wasted . . ."** Sarah Hardin to John J. Hardin, December 15, 1848, Chicago History Museum.

93 **"a good & fearless rider"** Martin D. Hardin, "Reminiscences," undated manuscript, Chicago History Museum.

93 **Ellen remained in a corner** Ellen Hardin Walworth, "Earliest Recollections," typescript, n.d., Walworth Memorial Museum Archives. See also Richard Lawrence Miller, *Lincoln and His World: The Early Years, Birth to Illinois Legislature* (Mechanicsburg, Pa.: Stackpole Books, 2006), p. 190.

94 **his daughter would describe the scene** Ellen Hardin Walworth, "The Battle of Buena Vista," *American Monthly Magazine*, January 1894.

94 **"like a long continued fairy story . . ."** *Christian Herald*, January 25, 1905.

94 **"I have never met anyone . . ."** Ellen Hardin Walworth, "Earliest Recollections," typescript, Walworth Memorial Museum Archives.

94 **Martin . . . recalled simpler pursuits** Martin D. Hardin, "Reminiscences," Chicago History Museum.

95 **"I sometimes think I must be one of fortune's favorites . . ."** Ellen Hardin to Sarah Hardin, March 21, 1851, Walworth Memorial Museum Archives.

95 **she had been acquired as an infant** See Miller, *Lincoln and His World*, pp. 196–98.

95 **"great friend"** Martin D. Hardin, "Reminiscences," Chicago History Museum.

95 **"a bond of mutual interest . . ."** Ellen Hardin Walworth, undated typescript 34-4-47, Walworth Memorial Museum Archives.

96 **"It is rather strange . . ."; "Would you know me . . ."** Sarah Hardin to Reuben Hyde Walworth, March 9, 1852, Walworth Memorial Museum Archives.

96 "plain, low, old fashioned frame manse" Ellen Hardin to Mary Duncan, April 30, 1853, Walworth Memorial Museum Archives.

96 "When the tall and swaying pines . . ." Ellen Hardin Walworth, untitled typescript, n.d., Walworth Memorial Museum Archives.

96 "A cold climate and a free state . . ." Sarah Hardin to Reuben Hyde Walworth, January 4, 1851, Walworth Memorial Museum Archives.

96 "decidedly the last place to raise children . . ." Sarah Hardin to John J. Hardin, December 15, 1848, Chicago History Museum.

97 "educated to despise the Yankees" Martin D. Hardin, "Reminiscences," Chicago History Museum.

97 "so outrageously conceited and selfish . . ." Ellen Hardin to Mary Duncan, July 27, 51, Walworth Memorial Museum Archives.

97 "the ravings of a fanatic . . ." Ellen Hardin to Mary Duncan, October 23, 1851, Walworth Memorial Museum Archives.

97 "I was so deeply hurt by this . . ." Martin D. Hardin, "Reminiscences," Chicago History Museum.

97 "the most brilliant I have ever seen . . ." Ellen Hardin Walworth, "Reuben Hyde Walworth, The Last of the New York Chancellors," *New York Genealogical and Biographical Record*, July 1895.

98 stabbing incident "Latest News Items," *San Francisco Evening Bulletin*, June 27, 1873.

99 "a strange boy as ever lived" Ellen Hardin to Mary Duncan, May 11, 1851, Walworth Memorial Museum Archives.

99 "I wrote so much of brother Manse . . ." Ellen Hardin to Mary Duncan, June 26, 1851, Walworth Memorial Museum Archives.

100 "It is always dangerous . . ." Mansfield Tracy Walworth, *Warwick, or The Lost Nationalities of America* (New York: G. W. Carleton, 1969), p. 219.

100–101 "He was dramatic without being theatrical . . ." Reverend Walter Elliott, C.S.P., quoted in Ellen Hardin Walworth [Jr.], *Life Sketches of Father Walworth* (Albany: J. B. Lyon, 1907), p. 133.

101 "I received a letter from mother . . ." Martin D. Hardin to Ellen Hardin, February 13, 1852, Walworth Memorial Museum Archives.

101–2 "I believe the whole affair is gotten up by him . . ." Sarah Hardin Walworth to Ellen Hardin, n.d., Walworth Memorial Museum Archives.

102 "nothing is gained by his continuing here in idleness . . ." Reuben Hyde Walworth to Clarence Walworth, February 16, 1852, Walworth Memorial Museum Archives.

102 "Your conversion to Romanism . . ." Sarah Hardin Walworth to Ellen Hardin, February 22, 1852, Walworth Memorial Museum Archives.

103 "I think he will make a smart and honorable man . . ." Martin D. Hardin to Ellen Hardin, March 23, 1852, Walworth Memorial Museum Archives.

103 grandmother signaled her unhappiness Ellen Hardin Walworth to her grandmother, August 3, 1852, Chicago History Museum.

103 "so deathly sick . . ." Ellen Hardin Walworth to Mary Duncan, July 22, 1852, Walworth Memorial Museum Archives.

103 "the fashion and beauty of Saratoga . . ." *New York Herald*, August 1, 1852.

103 "mental faculties refreshed . . ." Washington Irving to Catharine Irving, July 28, 1852, in Washington Irving, *Letters*, vol. 4, 1846–1859 (Boston: Twayne, 1982).

8. SORROWS AND JOYS OF MARRIED LIFE

104 "The Chancellor . . . made an idol of the little fellow" Ellen Hardin Walworth to her grandmother, October 25, 1852, Chicago History Museum.

105 "I do not go out of the house or yard . . ." Ellen Hardin Walworth to Mary Duncan, June 1853, Walworth Memorial Museum Archives.

106 "We are here again . . ." Frederick W. Seward, *Seward at Washington . . . A Memoir of His Life, With Selections from His Letters, 1846–1861* (New York: Derby and Miller, 1891), p. 238.

106 "I wish you would explain . . ." Ibid., p. 236.

106 "a series of interminable delays . . ." Henry B. Stanton, *Random Recollections* (New York: Harper and Brothers, 1887), p. 142.

107 new mineral springs "Boring for More Springs at Saratoga," *Auburn Weekly Journal*, October 24, 1855.

107 "I am glad he has seen the country . . ." Ellen Hardin Walworth to Reuben Hyde Walworth, n.d., Walworth Memorial Museum Archives.

107–8 a missionary priest in eighteenth-century New York The historical John Ury was by his own account a dissenting Anglican, one of the many innocents sent to their death in the panic over an alleged Negro Plot that had swept Manhattan in 1741. See Jill Lepore, *New York Burning: Liberty, Slavery, and Conspiracy in Eighteenth-Century Manhattan* (New York: Alfred A. Knopf, 2009), pp. 195–96.

108 "The silver lamps of heaven . . ." Mansfield Tracy Walworth, *The Mission of Death* (New York: D. and J. Sadler, 1853), p. 123.

108 "And may not the Almighty Creator . . ." Ibid., pp. 63–64.

108 "Harry had offered her his hand . . ." Ibid., p. 123.

109 "the sweet heaven of our love . . ." Ellen Hardin Walworth, poetry typescript, n.d., Walworth Memorial Museum Archives.

109–10 "I know that in commencing life with one so young . . ." Ellen Hardin Walworth to Mary Duncan, July 1, 1852, Walworth Memorial Museum Archives.

110 "Married life . . . has its own peculiar sorrows . . ." Ellen Hardin Walworth to Mary Duncan, December 16, 1854, Walworth Memorial Museum Archives.

110 "noble, beautiful boy"; "it seemed so like tearing myself from him . . ." Ellen Hardin Walworth to Mary Duncan, July 6, 1854, Walworth Memorial Museum Archives.

110 "It was *maternity* . . ." Ellen Hardin Walworth to Mary Duncan, March 21, 1855, Walworth Memorial Museum Archives.

111 "I must tell you what a fond father . . ." Ellen Hardin Walworth, letter to Mary Duncan, January 9, 1856, Walworth Memorial Museum Archives.

112 "I cannot find in my present life . . ." Clarence A. Walworth to the Paulist Fathers, December 15, 1850; cited in Joseph McSorley, *Father Hecker and His Friends: Studies and Reminiscences* (St. Louis, Mo.: B. Herder, 1952), p. 115.

112 "when the hand of Black Republicanism . . ." Horace Greeley, *The American Conflict*, vol. 1 (Hartford: O. D. Case, 1865), p. 392.

113 "It would be as brutal, in my opinion . . ." Greeley, ibid., p. 393; "Civil War Deprecated," *New York Observer and Chronicle*, February 7, 1861.

113 **Jefferson Davis would remember** See Jefferson Davis, *Rise and Fall of the Confederacy* (New York: D. Appleton, 1881), p. 255.

113 "Of what was happening on the other side . . ." Martin D. Hardin to Sarah Hardin Walworth, January 4, 1861, Walworth Memorial Museum Archives.

9. CIVIL WARS

114 "There is great rejoicing here . . ." Reuben Hyde Walworth to Sarah Hardin Walworth, March 13, 1861, Walworth Memorial Museum Archives.

116 **Bird's Nest** See Samuel W. Thomas et al., *Crescent Hill Revisited* (Louisville: George Rogers Clark Press, 1987).

116 "I can scarcely realize the strange situation . . ." Sarah Hardin Walworth to Ellen Hardin Walworth, April 22, 1861, Walworth Memorial Museum Archives.

117 "It was midnight . . ." Sarah Hardin Walworth to Ellen Hardin Walworth, n.d., Walworth Memorial Museum Archives.

117 **A hint of his talk turned up** *Official Records of the Union and Confederate Armies*, series 1, vol. 6, chap. 16 (Washington, D.C.: Government Printing Office, 1882).

117–18 **Mansfield's activities in Washington** See Mary E. Dougal, *An American Victorian Family: The Walworths of Saratoga*, master's thesis, State University of New York College, Oneonta, Cooperstown Graduate Program, 1980.

119 **Old Capitol prison** See Ann Blackman, *Wild Rose: The True Story of a Civil War Spy* (New York: Random House, 2005), pp. 205–8.

119–20 **Mansfield wrote to Ellen in Kentucky** Mansfield Tracy Walworth to Ellen Hardin Walworth, February 10, 1862, Walworth Memorial Museum Archives.

120 "All is sickness and sorrow . . ." Mansfield Tracy Walworth to Eliza Backus, March 11, 1862, Walworth Memorial Museum Archives.

120 "a sort of—*nothing* . . ."; "not knowing who I am . . ." Quoted in *Syracuse Daily Courier*, February 19, 1862.

121 "impossible for the Secretary of War Stanton . . ." Reuben Hyde Walworth to Ellen Hardin Walworth, February 21, 1862, Walworth Memorial Museum Archives.

121 "I am broken down and desperate . . ." Reuben Hyde Walworth to Sarah Hardin Walworth, March 31, 1862, Walworth Memorial Museum Archives.

122 "there is strong suspicion . . ." *Savannah Daily Morning News*, April 18, 1862.

122 **Jesse Wharton** See Ernest B. Furgurson, *Freedom Rising: Washington in the Civil War* (New York: Knopf, 2004), pp. 185–86.

123 "a revolution in the change . . ." Ellen Hardin Walworth, diary, March 1, 1881, Walworth Memorial Museum Archives.

124 "could only have been happy in contemplating nature . . ." Sarah Hardin Walworth to Ellen Hardin Walworth, n.d., Walworth Memorial Museum Archives.

124 "this unnatural and horrible civil war . . ." Reuben Hyde Walworth to Sarah Hardin Walworth, June 22, 1863, Walworth Memorial Museum Archives.

124 **"General Graham who was the particular friend . . ."** Reuben Hyde Walworth to Mansfield Tracy Walworth, March 17, 1865, Walworth Memorial Museum Archives.

126 **"a gay, talented youth of nineteen . . ."** Mansfield Tracy Walworth, *Lulu: A Tale of the National Hotel Poisoning* (New York: G. W. Carleton, 1861), p. 82.

126 **"Like the far-reaching sea . . ."** Ibid., p. 83.

126 **"Our hero possessed a ready flow of eloquence . . ."** Ibid., p. 214.

126 **"His eye had detected every point of beauty . . ."** Ibid., p. 211.

126 **"In the top basket was an almost finished gaiter . . ."** Ibid., p. 219.

127 **"fine linen, brocade silks . . ."; "calico, plain black silks . . ."** Ibid., p. 88.

127 **"at home or in distant lands"; "He regarded the poor-house system . . ."** Ibid., p. 80.

128 **"her lovely soul eyes . . ."** Ibid., p. 305.

128 **"the meeting of two bright intellects . . ."** Ibid., p. 221.

128 **"And she, the earnest loving woman that she was . . ."** Ibid., p. 306.

128 **"That wild, eager, impulsive heart . . ."** Ibid., p. 365.

129 *tableaux vivants* . . . ; A local retailer: *Daily Saratogian*, July 15, 1863.

129 **John Morrissey** See George Waller, *Saratoga: Saga of an Impious Era* (Englewood Cliffs, N.J.: Prentice-Hall, 1966), pp. 119–27, and Thomas A. Chambers, *Drinking the Waters: Creating an American Leisure Class at Nineteenth-Century Mineral Springs* (Washington, D.C.: Smithsonian Institution Press, 2002), pp. 189–92.

130 **"wide-spread & bloody riot . . ."** See Barnet Schechter, *The Devil's Own Work: The Civil War Draft Riots and the Fight to Reconstruct America* (New York: Walker, 2005), pp. 1–2.

130 **"Is Mob Violence to Rule?"** *Daily Saratogian*, July 15, 1863.

130 **fate of Colonel H. T. O'Brien:** See Schechter, *The Devil's Own Work*, p. 189.

130 **"When one suddenly feels the earth rising . . ."** Ellen Hardin Walworth [Jr.], *Life Sketches of Father Walworth* (Albany: J. B. Lyon, 1907), p. 162.

131 **"Tell Manse Nellie has had some views taken . . ."; "The guerrillas have been . . ."; "It takes more to travel with . . ."** Sarah Walworth to Reuben Hyde Walworth, June 16, 1863, Walworth Memorial Museum Archives.

131 **December 13, 1863** See Martin D. Hardin, "Chapter 12. Bristae Station . . . Oct. 14/63," manuscript, Chicago History Museum.

131 **"they disappeared . . ."** Sarah Walworth to Reuben Hyde Walworth, December 13, 1863, Walworth Memorial Museum Archives.

132 **"he keeps going to forget his misfortune . . ."** Sarah Walworth to Reuben Hyde Walworth, February 13, 1864, Walworth Memorial Museum Archives.

132 **"I have succeeded in the object . . ."** Sarah Walworth to Reuben Hyde Walworth, July 4, 1864, Walworth Memorial Museum Archives.

133 **"I may never have another opportunity . . ."; "There are forty thousand sick here . . ."** Sarah Walworth to Reuben Hyde Walworth, July 4, 1864, Walworth Memorial Museum Archives.

134 **"There was an indescribable aspect . . ."** Mansfield Tracy Walworth, *Hotspur: A Tale of the Old Dutch Manor* (New York: G. W. Carleton, 1864), p. 151.

10. THE DISINHERITED

135 **"For myself I scarcely know . . ."** Joseph McSorley, *Father Hecker and His Friends: Studies and Reminiscences* (St. Louis, Mo.: B. Herder, 1952), p. 117.

136 **"in the still hours of the night . . ."** Mansfield Tracy Walworth, *Stormcliff: A Tale of the Hudson* (New York: G. W. Carleton, 1865), p. 27.

137 **"He was fastidious and proud . . ."** "Sketch of M. T. Walworth," in *The Walworth Parricide* (New York: Thomas O'Kane, 1873).

137 **"five feet and eleven inches in height . . ."** Walworth, *Hotspur: A Tale of the Old Dutch Manor* (New York: G. W. Carleton, 1864), p. 40.

137 **"as attractive a picture of neat and muscular . . ."** Walworth, *Stormcliff*, p. 8.

138 **"I will show you how you will leave me . . .";** **"with great violence";** **"he had been in the habit of acting . . ."** Court testimony of Ellen Hardin Walworth in *The Walworth Parricide* (New York: Thomas O'Kane, 1873).

138 **"women, especially cultivated women . . ."** Sarah Hardin Walworth to Ellen Hardin Walworth, October 30, 1865, Walworth Memorial Museum Archives.

138 **"the dentist . . ."** Sarah Hardin Walworth to Reuben Hyde Walworth, July 26, 1866, Walworth Memorial Museum Archives.

139 **"The whitening of the head . . ."** Henry McGuier, *A Concise History of High Rock Spring* (Saratoga Springs: G. M. Davison, 1867), p. 27.

139 **"boldness and freedom from conventional laws . . ."** *Home Journal*, September 1866.

139 **"Manse . . . writes me that he is very sick . . ."** Ellen Hardin Walworth to Sarah Hardin Walworth, February 11, 1867, Walworth Memorial Museum Archives.

140 **"I do not know any way you can spend your time . . ."** Sarah Hardin Walworth to Reuben Hyde Walworth, July 2, 1867, Walworth Memorial Museum Archives.

140 **"We opened the little white gate . . ."** James W. Gerard, eulogy for Reuben Hyde Walworth, New York Bar Association, 1868.

141 **"the *genealogy* of many families . . ."** Ibid.

141 **"I never had an idea . . ."** Ibid.

141 **"His memory . . . reached beyond the personal knowledge . . ."** William L. Stone, *Reminiscences of Saratoga and Ballston* (New York: Virtue and Yarston, 1875), p. 354.

142 **"glorious, happy, and eminently useful . . ."** Charles O'Conor, eulogy for Reuben Hyde Walworth, New York Bar Association, 1868.

143 **his sorrel Araby** See Stone, *Reminiscences of Saratoga and Ballston*, p. 351.

143 **"Died at Saratoga, his residence . . ."** Allan Nevins, ed., *The Diary of George Templeton Strong*, vol. 4 (New York: Macmillan, 1952), November 29, 1867.

144 **"We all regretted very much . . ."** Ellen Hardin Walworth to Dolly Smith, December 4, 1867, Walworth Memorial Museum Archives.

145 **"prepare or cause to be prepared . . ."** Reuben Hyde Walworth, last will and testament, July 18, 1867, Walworth Memorial Museum Archives.

145 **Mansfield had conspired** *Saratogian*, June 12, 1873.

146 **would later detail for an upstate newspaper** "The Walworth Murder: The Story of a Member of the Bereaved Family," *San Francisco Daily Evening Bulletin*, June 18, 1873.

146 **"In the morning glad I see . . ."** William Blake, "A Poison Tree," in *William Blake: The Complete Poems*, ed. Alicia Ostriker (Harmondsworth: Penguin Books, 1977).

147 **"mahogany cabinets of shells & minerals . . ."** Mansfield T. Walworth and Jennings Brothers, legal agreement, January 7, 1868, Walworth Memorial Museum Archives.

11. THE LOOK OF A WILD BEAST

148 **"She is adrift . . ."** Ellen Hardin Walworth, journals, October 30, 1880, Walworth Memorial Museum Archives.

149 **"He took her heart . . ."** Ellen Hardin Walworth, "Retrospection," n.d., Walworth Memorial Museum Archives.

149 **"O lordly head . . ."** Ellen Hardin Walworth, typescript, Walworth Memorial Museum Archives.

149 **"1867—The year in which my heart was broken"** Ellen Hardin Walworth, journal, February 28, 1899, Walworth Memorial Museum Archives.

150 **"universally liked, as a boy . . ."** *Georgetown College Journal*, October 1886.

150 **An assistant librarian who aided him** See *New York Sun*, reprinted in *Daily Saratogian*, June 6, 1873, for an account of this interview.

151 **"the long-lipped bear of the Terai . . ."** Mansfield Tracy Walworth, *Warwick; or, The Lost Nationalities of America*, p. 172.

152 **"the paradise of a *littérateur* . . ."** Ibid., p. 360.

152 **"the harbinger of a new literary millennium"** Ibid., p. 251.

152 **"at the junction of the brain and spinal cord . . ."** Ibid., p. 76.

152 **"her seat beside the great white throne . . ."** Ibid., p. 19.

152 **"There is a mental night . . ."** Ibid., p. 250.

152 **"Why struggle? . . ."** Ibid., p. 219.

152 **"resolute and earnest pen marked down . . ."** Ibid., pp. 73–74.

153 **"delicate finish to every limb"; "symmetrical rounding . . ."; "slender, effeminate hands . . ."; "perfect as those . . ."; "perfection of elegance . . ."; "had sprung from a pure . . ."** Ibid., pp. 16–17.

153 **"Beautiful as Picus!":** The reference is to Ovid's *Metamorphoses*, book 14.

153 **"soft and lustrous . . ."** Walworth, *Warwick*, p. 17.

153 **"magnetic in their influence"** Ibid., p. 112.

153 **"Christ scourged at the pillar"** Ibid., p. 47.

153 **"exciting the imagination . . ."** Ibid., p. 273.

153 **"The woman who had once gazed . . .":** Ibid., p. 273.

153 **"The personal beauty of Constant Earle . . ."** Ibid., p. 265.

154 **"alternate exaltations and depressions"** Ibid., p. 265.

154 **A journalist who met Mansfield** "Sketch of M. T. Walworth" in *The Walworth Parricide* (New York: Thomas O'Kane, 1873).

155 **"He was always extremely pale . . ."** Quoted in *The Walworth Parricide in New York* (Philadelphia: Old Franklin Publishing House, 1873), pp. 30–32.

156 **he began to scream at her** Ellen Hardin Walworth, divorce complaint, January 27, 1871, Walworth Memorial Museum Archives.

156 **Daniel McFarland** See George Cooper, *Lost Love: A True Story of Passion, Murder, and Justice in Old New York* (New York: Pantheon, 1994).

157 **"He would lock himself in the room with me . . ."** Barbara Goldsmith, *Other Powers: The Age of Suffrage, Spiritualism, and the Scandalous Victoria Woodhull* (New York: Knopf, 1998), p. 203.

157 **"Hardin shall not rob me . . ."** *The Walworth Parricide.*

158 **"a pinched look on his features . . ."**; **"This must not be"** Ibid.

158 **"still suffering from the effects . . ."**; **"I'll show you damned Hardin . . ."**; **"to her great terror"**; **"I'll blow your damned brains out!"** Ibid.

159 **"wildly and rapidly up and down"** Ibid.

159 **"Be quiet, father"** Ibid.

12. FRANK IS SICK

161 **"After ten years of peace, of struggles . . ."** Ellen Hardin Walworth, journal, March 1, 1881, Walworth Memorial Museum Archives.

162 **"very unfortunate in my domestic relations . . ."** Ellen Hardin Walworth to Gerrit Smith, September 30, 1871.

162 **"endeavoring to inculcate . . ."** Flyer, Walworth Academy, Walworth Memorial Museum Archives.

162 **"ladylike manner and urbane ways"** *Daily Saratogian*, January 6, 1872.

162 **"God took her in her innocence . . ."** Clarence Walworth to Dolly Smith, January 17, 1872, Walworth Memorial Museum Archives.

163 **"You must not think that I have forgotten you . . ."** Dolly Smith to Reubena Hyde Walworth, October 26, 1871, Walworth Memorial Museum Archives.

163 **"They is no little children in this house . . ."** Dolly Smith to Reubena Hyde Walworth, November 18, 1871, Walworth Memorial Museum Archives.

163 **Phillips would relate** All quotes from Phillips's interview in the *New York Sun*, reprinted in *Daily Saratogian*, June 6, 1873.

164 **Eli Perkins . . . received regular visits** *Buffalo Evening Courier and Republic*, June 9, 1873.

164 **A female journalist who met him** *Daily Saratogian*, June 6, 1873. On Mansfield's rejection of Catholicism, see *Daily Saratogian*, March 11, 1871, and *Methodist Quarterly Review*, December 2, 1871.

166 **"Why do you not sign . . ."** "Walworth's Defense," *New York Tribune*, June 25, 1873.

166 **"Great God, woman, let me go to my work . . ."** Ibid.

166 **"That same pleading, ever-present . . ."** *The Walworth Parricide in New York* (Philadelphia: Old Franklin Publishing House, 1873), p. 52.

166–67 **"I cannot hold out any longer . . ."** "Walworth's Defense," *New York Tribune*, June 25, 1873.

167 **"Murder for $950, you ask? . . ."** Ibid.

167 **"I went to Judge Barbour's to kill you . . ."** Ibid.

167 **"You damned dishonorable bitch! . . ."** *The Walworth Parricide in New York*, p. 53.

167 **"You are delaying . . ."** Ibid., p. 54.

167 **"You have miscalculated . . ."** Ibid., p. 54.

167–68 **"I am a hungry demon . . ."** Ibid., p. 54.

168 **"You robbed me of my children . . ."** Ibid., p. 54.

169 **"Now sign this paper . . ."** Ibid., p. 55.

171–72 **Others began to notice the changes:** The testimony of von Below, Hill, and Grant can be found in *The Walworth Parricide* and *The Walworth Parricide in New York*.

13. THE LAST WARNING

173 **"Listen to these terrible words . . ."** *The Walworth Parricide in New York* (Philadelphia: Old Franklin Publishing House, 1873), p. 46.

175 **"hush your God damned woman's rights . . ."** "Walworth's Defense," *New York Tribune*, June 25, 1873.

175 **he told her he would kill her on sight** *New York Times*, June 29, 1873.

176 **"My Dear Sister: I have conceived . . ."** *The Walworth Parricide* (New York: Thomas O'Kane, 1873).

176 **Judge Barbour . . . recalled** "The Walworth Shooting Case," *Saratogian*, June 12, 1873.

177 **"a man of varied gifts, an orator . . ."** Mansfield Tracy Walworth, *Beverly, or The White Mask* (New York: G. W. Carleton, 1872).

177 **"sarcasms and complaints"; "he retaliated upon her in words"; "withdrew into his sanctum . . ."** Ibid., p. 16.

177 **"He never failed in his mental predictions . . ."** Ibid., p. 14.

177 **"to escort her to boating excursions . . ."** Ibid., p. 16.

177 **"the demon-heart of the mother . . ."** Ibid., p. 141.

177 **"The cruelty of the mother . . ."** Ibid., p. 142.

178 **"Day after day he struggled . . ."** Ibid., p. 237.

178 **"terrible as the old chieftains of the Highlands"; "without stint . . ."** Ibid., p. 372.

178 **He had forgiven the woman** See Hendrik Hartog, *Man and Wife in America: A History* (Cambridge: Harvard University Press, 2000), pp. 239–41.

178 **"Limbed and formed . . ."** Walworth, *Beverly*, p. 132.

178 **"Larger and more luminous . . ."** Ibid., p. 132.

178 **"his entire family"; "talking her to sleep . . ."** Ibid., p. 295.

178 **"For a moment he thought . . ."; "I thought you were turning . . ."** Ibid., p. 271.

179 **"the little elf"** Ibid., p. 263.

179 **"the communication she gave him . . ."; "physical contact of the most intimate . . ."** Ibid., p. 277.

179 **A professor at the College of New Jersey** John S. Hart to Mansfield Tracy Walworth, May 6, 1872, Walworth Memorial Museum Archives.

180 "very affable, agreeable . . ." *The Walworth Parricide.*

181 "From the most trivial circumstances . . .": *Buffalo Evening Courier and Republic,* June 9, 1873.

181 "His eyes were faded . . ." Francis Gerry Fairfield, *Ten Years with Spiritual Mediums: An Inquiry Concerning the Etiology of Certain Phenomena Called Spiritual* (New York: D. Appleton, 1875), pp. 97–98.

181 "There are bounds . . ." See *The Walworth Parricide.*

182–83 "Prepare yourself for the inevitable . . ."; "I know that you have no personal fear . . ."; "I shall die with a feeling of luxury . . ." *The Walworth Parricide in New York,* pp. 44–45.

14. THE TRIAL, FIRST WEEK: "IDIOCY AS A PROFESSION"

185 she "would allow no one to speak ill . . ." "The Walworth Murder: The Story of a Member of the Bereaved Family," *San Francisco Daily Evening Bulletin,* June 18, 1873.

185 "a somewhat noted outlaw" *The Farmers' Cabinet,* June 11, 1873.

186 Stokes was visited at the Tombs "Walworth and Stokes," *San Francisco Evening Bulletin,* June 26, 1873.

187 "Young Walworth is very quiet . . ." "Our New York Letter: The Lions of the Tombs," *Jefferson County Journal,* June 19, 1873.

187 "Killing No Murder . . ." "Killing No Murder," *New York Times,* November 25, 1872.

187 "For months and months . . ." "New-York Murders," *New York Times,* November 20, 1872.

187 juries were understandably reluctant "Law Reforms," letter to the editor by Henry L. Clinton, *New York Times,* December 28, 1872.

189 "startle the entire community" *Oswego Palladium,* June 1873.

189 A restless crowd had gathered "Young Walworth's Trial To-Day," *New York Daily Tribune,* June 24, 1873.

190 "His hair was carelessly brushed back . . ." *The Walworth Parricide in New York* (Philadelphia: Old Franklin Publishing House, 1873), p. 33.

191 "A disdainful, haughty look . . ." "Walworth: Looking for Jurors to Try the Emotional Murderer of His Father," *Brooklyn Eagle,* June 24, 1873.

192 "had no penalty for parricide . . ." *The Walworth Parricide* (New York: Thomas O'Kane, 1873).

192 "every act and expression of the prisoner . . ." "The Walworth Murder: Continuation of the Trial of Young Walworth," *New York Times,* June 27, 1873; "The Walworth Trial: A Jury Easily Obtained," *New York Daily Tribune,* June 25, 1873.

192 Rollins's address *The Walworth Parricide in New York,* p. 34.

192 "He looked . . . as one listening . . ." "The Walworth Trial: A Good Day's Work," *New York Daily Tribune,* June 26, 1873.

193 "He did not look as cross . . ." *The Walworth Parricide.*

193 "the usual and proper warning"; "a most dangerous innovation"; "Well then, I suppose . . ." Ibid.

194 "his counsel will find it . . ." Allan Nevins, ed., *The Diary of George Templeton Strong,* vol. 4 (New York: Macmillan, 1952), June 26, 1873.

194–95 **Beach's address** *The Walworth Parricide in New York,* pp. 35–36; "The Walworth Murder: Trial of Frank H. Walworth . . . Address of Mr. Beach," *New York Times,* June 27, 1873.

195 **dropped his face into his hands** "The Walworth Trial: A Good Day's Work," *New York Daily Tribune,* June 26, 1873.

195 **"old stagers in the murder trial line . . ."** *The Walworth Parricide.*

196 **"Generally he has been noticeable . . ."** "The Walworth Trial: A Story of Unhappiness," *New York Daily Tribune,* June 27, 1873.

196 **"Most of these witnesses testified that he had no vices . . ."** *The Walworth Parricide.*

196 **"His character is as near perfect . . ."** Ibid.

197 **"In the summer of 1861 . . .";** "we discussed the question . . .";** "Mr. Walworth addressed me very frequently . . ."** Ibid.

197 **"Though she had been so brutally treated . . ."** Ibid.

198 **"He invariably had a loaded pistol . . ."** "The Walworth Trial: A Story of Unhappiness," *New York Daily Tribune,* June 27, 1873.

199 **the judge delivered his decision** Ibid.

200 **"with heads craned forward . . ."** "Walworth's Defense: The Plea of Insanity," *New York Daily Tribune,* June 28, 1873.

200 **"The importance of this victory . . ."** "Walworth's Defense: The Plea of Insanity," *New York Daily Tribune,* June 28, 1873.

200 **"the sentiment of the crowded Court . . ."** *The Walworth Parricide.*

201 **"When you lived together . . ."** Ibid.

201–2 **"We don't wish to detail . . ."** The exchange between O'Conor and Davis is quoted from "Walworth's Defense: The Plea of Insanity," *New York Daily Tribune,* June 28, 1873.

202 **"imagined that the action . . ."** Ibid.

203 **"At times he was prostrated . . ."** Ibid.

203 **"a vein of insanity . . ."** Ibid.

204 **nervous laughter** "The Walworth Murder: Third Day of the Trial of Young Walworth," *New York Times,* June 29, 1873.

204 **"entirely too filthy . . .";** "Imagine the blasphemies . . ."** Ibid.

204 **"On Friday . . ."** "A Look at the Courts," *Utica Morning Herald,* July 1, 1873.

205 **"I can stand up . . ."** *The Walworth Parricide in New York,* p. 56.

205 **"sensational to the last degree"** "Walworth's Defense: The Plea of Insanity," *New York Daily Tribune,* June 28, 1873.

205 **"have unquestionably done a good deal . . ."** "The Walworth Murder," *Nation,* July 10, 1873.

205 **"Could the letters be published . . .";** "It seemed as if the imaginative talent . . ."** "Walworth's Defense: The Plea of Insanity," *New York Daily Tribune,* June 28, 1873.

206 **"Idiocy as a Profession"** "Idiocy as a Profession," *New York Times,* June 30, 1873.

15. THE TRIAL, SECOND WEEK: "THE OBNOXIOUS MAN HAS BEEN LAID TO REST"

208 **"the best boy I ever knew"; "very much excited"** *The Walworth Parricide in New York* (Philadelphia: Old Franklin Publishing House, 1873), p. 65.

209 **"He'd travel around the room . . ."** Ibid., p. 67.

209 **"To my mind . . ."; "Under the influence . . ."; "Not when fully . . ."** "The Walworth Trial: Supporting the Plea of Insanity," *New York Daily Tribune*, June 29, 1873.

209 **"The mind is not, itself, ever diseased . . ."** Cited in *Final Report of the Joint Commission on Mental Illness and Health* (New York: Basic Books, 1961).

209–10 **Dr. John Gray's testimony** "Walworth's Fate: Dr. Gray's Analysis of Epilepsy," *New York Daily Tribune*, June 30, 1873.

212 **"I want you to understand . . . that I have no objection . . ."** "Walworth's Fate," *New York Daily Tribune*, July 2, 1873.

212–15 **O'Conor's address** "Walworth's Fate: Mr. O'Conor's Plea for Acquittal," *New York Daily Tribune*, July 2, 1873; "The Walworth Murder: Mr. O'Conor's Address for the Defense," *New York Times*, July 2, 1873.

215–16 **Phelps launched straight off** "Walworth Convicted: Murder in the Second Degree," *New York Daily Tribune*, July 3, 1873; "Walworth Found Guilty: Murder in the Second Degree," *New York Times*, July 3, 1873.

219 **a discourse of some three hours** The full text of Davis's address is in "Oyer and Terminer—New York County. July 1, 1873. People *v.* Walworth," *New York Criminal Reports*.

222 **"The plea of insanity did not appear . . ."** "Walworth Found Guilty," *New York Times*, July 3, 1873.

222 **the foreman read the verdict, fumbling** "Walworth Convicted: Murder in the Second Degree."

16. SENTENCE AND REMOVAL

223 **managed to get a word with Frank** "The Walworth Case: Judge Davis' Remarks on Pronouncing Sentence," *Utica Morning Herald*, July 6, 1873.

223 **O'Conor too spoke to the press** "What Charles O'Conor Says of the Walworths and the Verdict," *Georgia Weekly Telegraph*, July 15, 1873.

224 **"He gazed about the room . . ."** "The Walworth Tragedy: Sentence of the Murderer," *New York Times*, July 6, 1873.

224 **Davis addressed Frank** "The Walworth Tragedy: Sentence of the Murderer," *New York Times*, July 6, 1873.

226 **"compared with the majority of murder trials . . ."** "The Walworth Murder," *Nation*, July 10, 1873.

226 **"The rapidity with which the prisoner . . ."** "The Walworth Case," *New York Daily Tribune*, July 8, 1873.

226–27 **"simply declaring a man . . ."; "We may as well say . . ."; "the morbid condition of feeling . . ."** "The Walworth Murder," *Nation*, July 10, 1873.

227 **"possibly correct under our recent legislation . . ."** Allan Nevins, ed., *The Diary of George Templeton Strong*, vol. 4 (New York: Macmillan, 1952), July 3, 1873, p. 487.

227 **"a morbid boy, who committed . . ."** "The Walworth Verdict," *New York Times*, July 3, 1873.

228 **"The smoke neutralized . . ."** "On the Road to Sing Sing," in *The Walworth Parricide* (New York: Thomas O'Kane, 1873).

229 **"You see what it is to be a murderer . . ."** "News Summary," *Brooklyn Eagle*, July 10, 1873.

229 **"I will bet that man . . ."** "On the Road to Sing Sing."

229 **"That's Walworth!"** Ibid.

229 **"I had been accustomed . . ."; "I was fond . . ."** Ibid.

229 **"Some of the best friends . . ."** "News Summary," *Brooklyn Eagle*, July 10, 1873.

229 **"I found those whom I got . . ."** "On the Road to Sing Sing."

230 **"Of course, it was not . . ."** Ibid.

230 **"This wind is nice . . ."; "I am happy . . ."** Ibid.

230 **"And this is my last ride . . ."** "Caught: Extraordinary Career of a New York Murderer," *Brooklyn Eagle*, July 7, 1882.

231 **"I feel as if I was going to play . . ."** Ibid.

231 **Frank's journey to Sing Sing** "On the Road to Sing Sing," *The Walworth Parricide*; "Caught: Extraordinary Career of a New York Murderer," *Brooklyn Eagle*, July 7, 1882; *The Farmers' Cabinet*, July 16, 1873.

17. THE PRISONER

232 **Sing Sing** To avoid association with the prison, the town's name was later changed to Ossining.

232 **was said to have requested, successfully** "News Summary," *Brooklyn Eagle*, July 10, 1873.

233 **"whether the mighty influence . . ."** "Sing Sing Surprised," *Albany Argus*, reprinted in *Auburn Daily Bulletin*, August 4, 1873.

233 **"singular conduct from the day he killed his father . . ."** "Personal: Walworth," *Brooklyn Eagle*, July 14, 1873.

233 **"He now remains a sort of hero . . ."** "Our Christian Age and Country," *New York Times*, July 15, 1873.

233 **"The morals of this community . . ."** Reprinted in *New York Times*, July 18, 1873.

233 **A letter to the *Saratogian*** *Saratogian*, July 1873.

233 **"that broad-chested, free-breathing youth . . ."** *Freeman's Journal and Catholic Register*, New York, September 13, 1873.

234 **denounced McMaster's argument** "James A. McMaster on the Bench, Bar, Press and Medical Faculty of New York," *Albany Law Journal*, October 18, 1873.

234 **"Frank Walworth is really suffering . . ."** Orestes A. Brownson, letter to the *Tablet*, reprinted in *Brooklyn Eagle*, August 28, 1873.

234 **"the terrible influence of a Calvinistic religious education . . ."** Colonel H. S. Hewit, M.D., "The Walworth Calamity," *Brownson's Quarterly Review*, vol. 1, no. 4, October 1873.

234 **"so small . . . that if you try to turn or walk . . ."** Richard Harding Davis, "The New Idea at Sing Sing," *New York Times*, July 18, 1915.

235 "The Disgrace of New York State . . ." Mansfield Tracy Walworth, *Beverly; or, The White Mask* (New York: G. W. Carleton, 1872), pp. 7–12.

235 "the domination of force"; "the infliction of the punishments . . ." Frank Marshall White, "Sing Sing: An Evolution," *Atlantic Monthly*, September 1916.

235 **Sing Sing punishments and reforms:** See Ted Conover, *Newjack: Guarding Sing Sing* (New York: Random House, 2000), pp. 171–85.

235 "inmates lounging, without restraint . . ." *First Annual Report of the Bureau of Labor Statistics of the State of New York* (Albany: Weed, Parsons, 1883), p. 74.

236 MOTHER Unidentified newspaper clipping, Walworth Memorial Museum Archives.

236–37 "She knew that there is a sensualism of grief . . ." Justin McCarthy, *Lady Judith: A Tale of Two Continents* (New York: Sheldon, 1871), p. 119.

237 "bound in chains . . ." Ellen Hardin Walworth, "Flowers for Another," typescript, Walworth Memorial Museum Archives.

237 "Only those who have passed through deep affliction . . ." Mary Todd Lincoln to Sarah Hardin Walworth, June 1873, Walworth Memorial Museum Archives.

238 "O, the feeling of desolation . . ." Ellen H. Walworth [Jr.], *An Old World Seen Through Young Eyes: Travels Around the World* (New York: D. and J. Sadler, 1877), p. 5.

238 "consign'd / To fetters . . .": Lord Byron, "The Prisoner of Chillon," *Lord Byron, Selected Poems* (London: Penguin, 1996).

238 "overwhelmed with sorrow and remorse" "Stokes and Walworth," *New York Times*, November 20, 1873.

239 "Is my son going to Auburn?" "Ingersoll and Walworth," *New York Times*, December 6, 1873.

239 **Frank's journey to Auburn** "Frank Walworth. His Transfer with Other Prisoners to Auburn," *Saratogian*, December 18, 1873.

240 "He had a great deal to suffer . . ." Ellen Hardin Walworth to Dolly Smith, December 18, 1873, Walworth Memorial Museum Archives.

240 **Frank seemed to hold himself apart** "Sing Sing Transfers," *Auburn Daily Bulletin*, December 6, 1873.

241 "he shrinks from the gaze of strangers . . ." *New York World*, reprinted in "Walworth and Ingersoll in Auburn Prison," *Syracuse Daily Courier*, March 2, 1874.

241 **he fled abruptly** "Insane Criminals," *Chicago Daily Tribune*, May 21, 1875.

241 "I want you . . . to write down for me . . ."; "Try to think of all you told . . ." Ellen Hardin Walworth to Dolly Smith, December 18, 1878, Walworth Memorial Museum Archives.

242 **Anna Eliza Platt** Clarence A. Walworth, *The Walworths of America* (Albany: Weed-Parsons, 1897), pp. 126–28.

242 **Frank's poems** Frank Walworth, poetry notebook, Walworth Memorial Museum Archives.

243 **A romantic rumor** "Walworth's Betrothed," *San Francisco Evening Bulletin*, August 2, 1873.

244 "O cease! Thou cruel night wind . . ." Ellen Hardin Walworth, untitled poem, March 1874, Walworth Memorial Museum Archives.

244 **"terrible associations"** "Death of Mrs. Walworth," *Auburn Daily Bulletin*, July 16, 1874.

244 **"sight of sickness and suffering . . ."** "Frank Walworth Insane," *New York Times*, August 2, 1874.

244 **"the tricky maneuvering of the Walworth family . . ."** "The Insanity Dodge," *Brooklyn Eagle*, September 7, 1874.

245 **"It is altogether too early . . ."** *New York World*, reprinted in "Frank Walworth," *Auburn Daily Bulletin*, September 7, 1874.

245 **"The last link is broken . . ."** Frank Walworth, "The Reply (To the Same)," poetry notebook, Walworth Memorial Museum Archives.

246 **"An ode on my birthday . . ."** Frank Walworth, poetry notebook.

246 **"I take my pen handle . . ."** Frank Walworth to Dolly Smith, September 25, 1874, Walworth Memorial Museum Archives.

18. THE MANIAC'S DREAM

247 **"The Maniac's Dream"** Frank Walworth, poetry notebook, Walworth Memorial Museum Archives.

250 **Governor Dix at Auburn** "Gov. Dix at Auburn," *New York Times*, October 10, 1874.

250 **Henrietta Robinson** "The 'Veiled Murderess,'" *New York Times*, July 31, 1855.

251 **Kate Stoddard** "The Goodrich Murder," *New York Times*, July 11, 1873; "The Goodrich Murderer Discovered and Arrested," *Utica Morning Herald*, July 11, 1873; "Two Insane Women," *New York Times*, July 11, 1873; "The Goodrich Murderess," *New York Times*, July 15, 1873.

251 **Minnie Davis** "Attempted Suicide," *New York Times*, December 29, 1870; "Trial of Minnie Davis for Burning Her Trunk to Recover $2,000 Insurance Money," *New York Times*, January 24, 1871.

252 **"one of the cleverest of New York's clever thieves"** *Syracuse Morning Standard*, April 1, 1881.

252 **"I should be very glad . . ."** Governor John Dix to Ellen Hardin Walworth, December 4, 1874, Walworth Memorial Museum Archives.

252 **a disorderly episode** "A Sensation at Governor Bramlette's Funeral," *Cincinnati Gazette and Courier*, February 1, 1875.

253 **"Frank Walworth grows stupid"** *Auburn Daily Bulletin*, March 13, 1875.

253 **"a fat boy, fast losing what mind . . ."** *Watertown Daily Times*, n.d., 1875.

253 **Frank was said to have become agitated** "Insane Criminals," *Chicago Daily Tribune*, May 21, 1875.

253 **Bryant told Ellen that he fully sympathized** William Cullen Bryant to Ellen Hardin Walworth, March 16, 1875, Walworth Memorial Museum Archives.

253 **"If a jury were now to pass . . ."** "F. H. Walworth Pardoned," *New York Times*, August 2, 1877.

253 **Tilden . . . let it be known** "Walworth," *Syracuse Daily Standard*, November 8, 1875.

254 **"A lady of powerful magnetic attraction . . ."** "Frank Walworth. The Commission to Investigate His Case," *Auburn Morning News*, August 3, 1876.

254 **"That the boy was epileptic . . ."** *Syracuse Daily Standard*, December 9, 1875.

254 **"The victim of mental malady . . ."** "Frank Walworth," *Albany Evening Times*, reprinted in *Oswego Daily Times*, January 15, 1877.

255 **"To no people on earth is home more essential . . ."** "An Appeal for funds to repair and furnish the residence at Mount Vernon preparatory to the Centennial Celebration at Philadelphia 1876," Walworth Memorial Museum Archives.

255 **wrote to her plaintively** Clara Walworth to Ellen Hardin Walworth, June 15, 1877, Walworth Memorial Museum Archives.

256 **"As the great Hudson . . ."** Ellen Hardin Walworth, *Battles of Saratoga, 1777*, 2nd ed. (Albany: Joel Munsell's Sons, 1891).

257–58 **"The law is majestic in that . . ."; "The act was as thoroughly . . ."; "The meeting between the father . . ."** Gov. Lucius Robinson, Statement of Executive Pardon, August 1, 1877.

258 **"The public, as a whole . . ."** *Brooklyn Eagle*, August 2, 1877.

258 *Auburn Morning News* **speculated** "Walworth at Large," *Auburn Morning News*, August 2, 1877.

258 **"influential friends . . . this slayer of his father . . ."** "Pardon of a Parricide," *Rochester Union*, August 3, 1877.

258 **family members and friends** "Frank Walworth at Home," *New York Times*, August 6, 1877.

258 **"The keen joy the household have known . . ."** Undated transcription, The Saratoga Room, Saratoga Public Library.

259 **it was reported that he was living quietly** *Auburn News and Democrat*, January 31, 1878.

19. ELLEN'S BOOK

260 **"1877: The year in which hope . . ."** Ellen Hardin Walworth, journal, February 28, 1899. Walworth Memorial Museum Archives.

260–61 **Frank . . . sent word** Frank Hardin Walworth to Ellen Hardin Walworth, August 22, 1877, Walworth Memorial Museum Archives.

261 **"He has not a single feature or trait . . ."** "The Boy Who Killed His Father," *Washington Post*, August 27, 1879; "The Walworths," *Watertown Daily Times*, July 25, 1879.

261 **"Must be watchful . . ."** Ellen Hardin Walworth, journal, August 23, 1879.

262 **"I have dreamed, I have felt . . ."** Ibid., July 9, 1879.

262 **"Here lies one . . ."** Ibid., August 12, 1879.

262 **"a supreme object rises now . . ."** Ibid., August 12, 1879.

263 **"I have been suffering sharply . . ."** Ibid., September 7, 1879.

263 **"Oh! for freedom, freedom!"** Ibid., December 11, 1879.

263 **"My spirit trembles yet . . ."** Ibid., December 20, 1879.

263 **"It is a fact that I must learn to admit . . ."** Ibid., March 27, 1880.

263 **"entering into the existence of nature . . ."** Ibid., March 28, 1880.

263 **"Memory only is awake . . ."** Ibid., April 11, 1880.

263 **"Let me only strive . . ."** Ibid., April 12, 1880.

264 **"be wise to let the life of the Hardins rest . . ."** Ibid., April 13, 1880.

264 **"The shadows approach . . ."** Ellen Hardin Walworth, diary entries, June 5–10, 1880. Walworth Memorial Museum Archives.

264 **"It is doubtful . . . if his equal can be found . . ."** "Archery: Private Practice Club," *Forest and Stream*, November 4, 1880.

264 **he took first prize** "End of the Tournament," *New York Times*, July 15, 1881.

264 **"The aim should be perfected at a full draw . . ."** Frank Walworth, "Notes of a Novice," *Bicycling World and Archery Field*, December 17, 1880.

264 **a story about a gardener** "Frank's Progress," *National Police Gazette*, May 28, 1881.

265 **"freedom for books, freedom for writing . . ."** Ellen Hardin Walworth, journal, October 30, 1880.

265 **"quite a ripple of excitement"** "Autumn Days in Saratoga," *Waterville Times*, November 25, 1880.

265 **"the life of a noble woman . . ."; "of fine natural powers . . ."** Ellen Hardin Walworth, journal, October 30, 1880.

265 **"She finds she is abandoning . . ."; "relief and satisfaction"** Ibid., November 15, 1880.

266 *Daniel Deronda* Ellen Hardin Walworth, diary entry, November 15, 1880.

266 **"It is a satisfaction to have written . . ."** Ellen Hardin Walworth, journal, June 13, 1881.

266 **"1851—A new life began . . ."; "There must be a change":** Ibid., March 31, 1881.

266 **"Gradually and finally . . ."** Ibid.

267 **"constant attempts at revolutionary measures . . ."** Letter, *Saratoga Eagle*, June 11, 1881.

267 **"Would it be well for him to drift . . ."** Ellen Hardin Walworth, journal, December 26, 1881.

267 **"head of a house without means . . ."** Ibid., September 19, 1881.

267 **"I must not allow myself to drift . . ."** Ibid., September 24, 1881.

268 **"She had a theory . . ."; "She is here bodily . . ."; "inspired apparently . . ."; "I see the follies . . ."** Ibid., December 26, 1881.

269 **"as long as they kept . . ."; "When we labor for others . . ."; "How will it be . . ."; "I think the desire to have a fixed place of burial . . ."** Ibid., December 30, 1881.

269 **"the mental anguish annihilated . . ."; "reached a stage of self control . . ."** Ibid., January 4, 1882.

269 **"stirring up the old miseries . . ."** Ibid., January 9, 1882.

269 **"throw his interest, his energy, his talent . . ."** Ibid., January 31, 1882.

270 **"What is this religion . . ."; "The Puritanism of one grandmother . . ."; "the superstitions and the slaveries . . ."; "Sharp sorrow . . ."** Ibid., January 9, 1882.

271–72 **"clouded and twisted . . ."; "unconsciously concealed self-love . . ."; "He will dare to say . . ."; "He is known . . . to be at times of unsound mind"** Ibid., January 16, 1882.

272 **"You are talking about cranks! . . ."** Charles E. Rosenberg, *The Trial of the Assassin Guiteau* (Chicago: University of Chicago Press, 1968), p. 194.

272 **confronted in his study by a tall intruder** "Trying to Kill Dr. John Gray," *New York Times*, March 17, 1882; "Death of Dr. John P. Gray," *New York Times*, November 30, 1886.

273 **"notwithstanding the days and months . . ."** *Daily Saratogian*, October 20, 1883.

273 **a reception** "Frank Walworth and His Bride," *New York Times*, December 27, 1883.

273 **Ellen visits Clara at Kenwood** Ellen Hardin Walworth, journal, March 9, 1884.

274 **"a personal and careful supervision . . ."** Walworth Academy brochure, 1884, Walworth Memorial Museum Archives.

274 **Lewis Leland** "Another Hotel Proprietor Insane," *Oswego Times and Express*, March 8, 1884.

274 **"Tracy became helpless"** Ellen Hardin Walworth, journal, May 19, 1899.

275 **Dolly died** "Death of a Faithful Servitor," *Albany Evening Journal*, January 26, 1885.

275 **"out alone, came in distressed . . ."; "T. all right . . ."** Ellen Hardin Walworth, journal, January 28–February 4, 1885.

275 **"Work, work, work . . ."** Ibid., January 1886. The passage is retrospective.

275 **"Frank and I do not work well together"; "Then the night anxieties . . ."** Ibid.

276 **He wrote a letter:** Evelyn Barrett Britten, "Tragedy Haunted Frank Walworth to Early Grave," *Saratogian*, May 10, 1956. See end note for chapter 1: "A Haunted House."

276 **"My dear Frank died today . . ."** Ellen Hardin Walworth, journal, October 19–November 3, 1886.

277 **"He was a lawyer by profession . . ."** *Saratoga Journal*, quoted in "Frank H. Walworth's Death," *New York Times*, October 31, 1886.

278 **"bombast and folly"; "The esprit de corps . . ."** Ellen Hardin Walworth, statement on Daughters of the American Revolution, 1892.

278 **"As woman is supreme in the home . . ."** Ellen Hardin Walworth, address at United States Hotel, Saratoga Springs, September 1894.

279 **read to him through an ear trumpet** Ellen Hardin Walworth [Jr.], *Life Sketches of Father Walworth* (Albany: J. B. Lyon, 1907), pp. 321–22.

279 *The Walworths of America* Clarence A. Walworth, *The Walworths of America* (Albany: Weed-Parsons, 1897). This is the source for all information and quotes on pages 279–80.

280 **"Now the flowers have died away . . ."** Reubena Hyde Walworth, "Ballade," *Vassar Literary Magazine*, 1896.

282 **"she babbled continually . . ."** "A Nurse Dies of Typhoid," unidentified newspaper clipping, Saratoga Springs Public Library.

282 **"Can I live! Shall I live! . . ."** Ellen Hardin Walworth, journal, March 5, 1899.

282 **"all a dream, a horrible waking dream . . ."** Ibid., May 19, 1899.

283 **"There is news . . . of disaster . . ."** Ibid., February 1, 1900.

284 **"Lo! the Book of Doom! . . ."** Clarence A. Walworth, *Andiatorocté, or The Eve of Lady Day on Lake George, and Other Poems, Hymns, and Meditations in Verse* (New York: G. P. Putnam's Sons, 1888), p. 117.

284 **"Vain are all creatures . . ."** Ibid., p. 136.

285 **"Our griefs are all from within . . ."** Ellen Hardin Walworth, journals, 1900–1902.

20. THE HERMIT

286 **December 2, 1928** "Hermit Is Suicide in Virginia Hut," *Washington Evening Star*, December 3, 1928; "Glen Carlyn Hermit Slashes Throat in Two Places; Dies," *Washington Daily News*, December 3, 1928; "Hermit Found Dead in Hut," unidentified newspaper clipping, n.d.

EPILOGUE

291 **a young cousin from Kentucky came to visit** "Notes on recorded conversation with Mrs. Maude Bramlette Spivey, age 89, and her daughter, Mrs. Emily Lewis (mid-50s?) with Mary Dougal, Museum Director on September 10, 1975," typescript, Walworth Memorial Museum Archives.

Acknowledgments

It was in 2001, while at Yaddo to work on another book, that I walked into Congress Park in Saratoga Springs, New York, and came upon the exhibit that provided the starting point for the present work. At the Walworth Memorial Museum—housed under the same roof as the Historical Society of Saratoga Springs—I caught a rough overview of the story recounted in these pages. As tends to happen with such undertakings, it has taken a good deal longer than originally anticipated to get that story told. Along the way I have been helped by many individuals and institutions.

Without the collection of the Walworth Memorial Museum, no such book would have been possible. The existence of this extraordinary archive of the Walworth family made it possible to study the lives of these individuals from many angles and at times with great intimacy—even if the family did not always choose to preserve documents relating to some of the principal events with which this book is concerned. Doris Lamont, archivist, was unfailingly helpful in guiding me through the archive's holdings over what turned out to be more than a few years of research, and I am deeply grateful to her and her colleagues Jamie Parillo, John Conners, and Rebecca Codner.

In going through the archives, I became aware of work previously done by others which made my path much easier. These earlier researchers included Constance Carroll, Mary Dougal (whose thesis on the Walworths was immensely valuable in bringing the story into focus), and Yvonne Divak. In Saratoga I also received valuable information from Minnie Bolster, who shared her wide acquaintance with the history of Saratoga Springs, and Mary Ann Fitzgerald, Saratoga Springs city historian. The Saratoga Room of the Saratoga Springs Public Library was an endless source of enlightenment on local history, and I owe much to the library's staff past and present, including Ellen de Lalla, Teri Blasko, and, especially, Victoria Garlanda. I am also indebted to the Honorable Penelope Clute of the Plattsburgh City Court for sharing her research on the early judicial career of Reuben Hyde Walworth. I would also like to thank the staffs of the Chicago History Museum, the New-York Historical Society, the New York Public Library, the Elmer Holmes Bobst Library at New York University, the Library of Congress, the Union College Library (Special Collections), the Filson Historical Society in Louisville, Kentucky, and the New York City Municipal Archives. Richard N. Pope provided expert help in filling out the genealogy of the Walworths.

Conversations with many individuals played a part in the making of this book. In particular I would like to thank Robert Polito, Luc Sante, and Dr. Kent L. Robertshaw for their illumination on a range of matters. My dear friend Robert Fagan died just before the completion of this book; it would not have been the same without the benefit of years of wide-ranging discussions with him.

All my colleagues at The Library of America have contributed, over the years, to deepening my sense of the American past, and I would like to thank, among others, Cheryl Hurley, Max Rudin, and the late Richard Poirier. Derick Schilling and Brian McCarthy have on numerous occasions during the writing of this book given me the benefit of their wide historical knowledge. David Cloyce Smith offered expert advice on the illustrative material. Matthew Parr and James Gibbons helped me find my way in the labyrinth of archival research and, more importantly, made penetrating commentaries on many aspects of the book and its period as it evolved; James Gibbons and Brian McCarthy also very helpfully read the completed manuscript.

My agent, Zoë Pagnamenta, not only encouraged me from the start of this project but worked closely in shaping a proposal that played a great part in finding the book's ultimate form. My editor, Jack Macrae, has been tremendously supportive of this work as it evolved, and especially in helping me cut through the morass of an earlier draft.

My daughter, Heather O'Brien, read each chapter as it was drafted and helped immensely with the care, candor, and acuteness of her responses. Harold Schechter generously assisted at every stage of this project with his knowledge of legal and criminal matters in the period in question—not to mention his immense savoir-faire in the matter of storytelling—and made valuable comments on the manuscript as it progressed. Albert Mobilio likewise provided insightful response to the manuscript for which I am extremely grateful. Brenda Wineapple read an earlier draft of the manuscript and made abundant suggestions that proved of great value in arriving at a final version. Constance Carroll shared her knowledge of the Walworth family and of Saratoga Springs history and helped me in clearing up a variety of errors in the manuscript.

Flaminia Ocampo, to whom this book is dedicated, brought her empathy, her intellect, and her perceptive readings of archival evidence to bear on the characters and situations in this narrative in ways that constantly made me see them afresh. She not only helped in the researching of the book but contributed immeasurably to its structure and approach.

Index

About the author

GEOFFREY O'BRIEN's books include *Hardboiled America* (1981), *Dream Time: Chapters from the Sixties* (1988), *The Phantom Empire* (1993), *The Times Square Story* (1998), *The Browser's Ecstasy* (2000), *Castaways of the Image Planet* (2002), and *Sonata for Jukebox* (2004). He has published six collections of poetry including *A View of Buildings and Water* (2002), *Red Sky Café* (2005), and *Early Autumn* (2010). He is editor in chief of The Library of America and lives in New York City.